AF594010

Rain and Snow: The Umbrella in Japanese Art

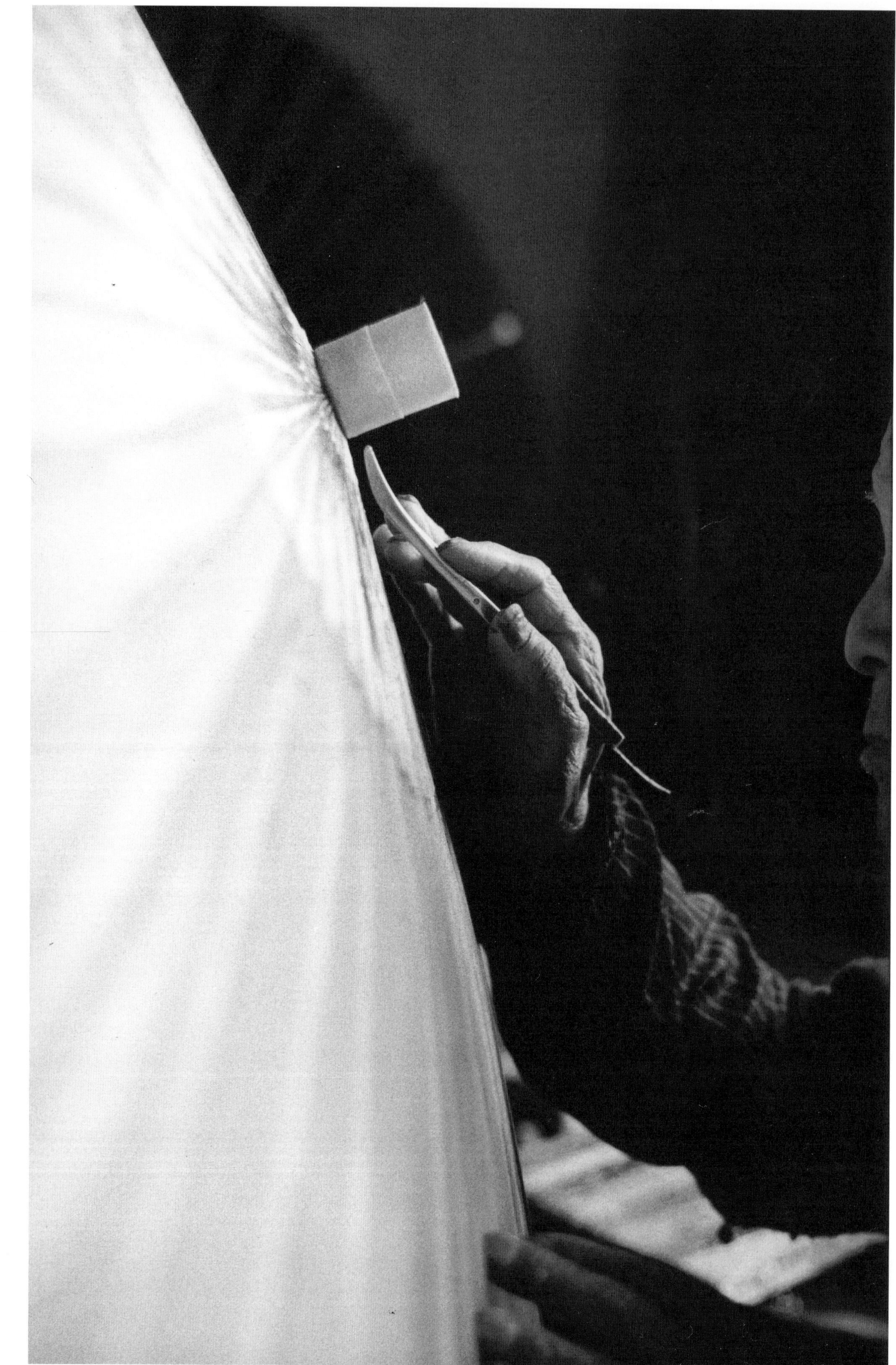

Rain and Snow: The Umbrella in Japanese Art

Julia Meech

with essays by

Hiroshi Yabushita

Stephan Köhler

Japan Society, Inc., New York, 1993

This catalogue is published in conjunction with the exhibition *Rain and Snow: The Umbrella in Japanese Art*, shown at the Japan Society Gallery, New York, from April 28 to June 27, 1993.

The exhibition was organized by the Japan Society, New York, with the cooperation of the Gifu City Museum of History, Japan. It was made possible with funds from the Lila Acheson Wallace/Japan Society Fund, established at Community Funds, Inc. by the co-founder of Reader's Digest; The Japan Foundation; The Tokai Bank Foundation; Marubeni America Corporation; and the Friends of Japan Society Gallery. In-kind support was provided by the Law Offices of C. Steven Horn.

Editors:
Essay by Julia Meech and catalogue entries: M.E.D. Laing
Essays by Stephan Köhler and Hiroshi Yabushita: Erica Hamilton Weeder
Translator: Hiroaki Sato for Hiroshi Yabushita's essay
Designer: Stefanie Krieg-Elliott

Set in Rotis Serif
Text paper: Diadem spezial gestrichen Offset elementar chlorfrei
Printed and bound in Germany by the Benedict Press, Münsterschwarzach, in an edition of 1,500

Library of Congress Catalogue Card Number: 92-83864
ISBN: 0-913304-36-0

Frontispiece: Hayashi Giichi smooths paper over umbrella ribs, fig. 9, p. 15

Exhibition design:
Art Clark and Gunhild Avitabile
Installation: Jeffrey Nemeth

Note to the Reader:
Japanese names are printed in the Japanese order, surname first, except in the case of individuals who have chosen to adopt the Western system. In discussion, Japanese artists are referred to in the form most commonly cited, usually by the given name. In this catalogue, a circumflex is used instead of a macron.

In dimensions listed, height or length precedes width. Unless otherwise indicated, print sizes are those of the sheet, not the image.

Diagrams appear on pp. 33-35. A glossary of terms not defined in catalogue entries appears on p. 65.

Contents

Foreword

When I was about eight years old, a small red silk parasol, which is still in my possession, provided my delightful first contact with Japan. I found it intriguing to visualize the far-away land from which it had come. The Japan I envisioned was a gracious fairytale place with ladies in fanciful kimonos, who held parasols above their heads to protect their delicate complexions from the sun. I had admired similar scenes on wall paintings in the elegant salons of the Baroque castle in the city where I was living.

Later, when my interest in Japan became more serious, I discovered that many Japanese artists shared my love for this charming accessory of daily life. I became aware that the different shapes an umbrella could assume made it an important element in pictorial composition. This exhibition, with catalogue, is an exploration of the traditional umbrella's history, production, and use as a motif in art. We read in this catalogue that the craft of making *wagasa* is in danger of becoming extinct. We hope that this exhibition will help keep it alive.

This project was first presented many years ago to the Japan Society Gallery by Yoshinobu Tokugawa, executive director of the Tokugawa Art Museum in Nagoya. It was his idea not only to display traditional umbrellas, but also to include a performance by the famous Kyôgen player, Motohide Izumi, as a way of showing the actual use of the *wagasa* within a classical context. My special thanks go to this concerned mentor who initiated the collaboration between the Gifu City Museum of History and the Japan Society.

The Gifu City Museum of History with its director, Hiroichi Ogawa, has permitted us to show some of its most splendid umbrellas and has provided much assistance. In particular, Hiroshi Yabushita, one of the museum's curators and an expert on *wagasa*, has generously shared his professional knowledge. With great patience, he has answered numerous requests for all types of information. His essay enables us to understand the complicated process of creating a traditional *janome* umbrella.

On the Western side, I want first to thank Julia Meech, the show's curator. She has assembled a stunning collection of objects by both Japanese and Western artists principally from the United States and Europe. Her scholarly essay and entries, with their poetic spirit, reveal her outstanding ability to explicate an unusual field of culture and art.

Stephan Köhler, a German artist who has lived for several years in Hachiman, Mugegawa-chô, Gifu prefecture, has provided a vivid insight into the world of traditional umbrella makers. He undertook a real pilgrimage for the Japan Society in order to find those craftspeople in Japan who are still making these umbrellas. Mr. Köhler may be the only Western artist whose creation of Japanese-style umbrellas is his art form.

I want to express my deepest gratitude and respect to Mary Laing, whose patience and long experience as an editor have helped to shape this publication. Hiroaki Sato has translated Hiroshi Yabushita's essay with great skill. The many lenders, listed separately, receive my warmest thanks. Without their generosity and enthusiasm, this exhibition would not have been possible.

This project has been generously supported by: the Lila Acheson Wallace/Japan Society Fund, established at Community Funds, Inc. by the co-founder of Reader's Digest; The Japan Foundation; The Tokai Bank Foundation; Marubeni America Corporation; and the Friends of Japan Society Gallery. In-kind support was provided by the Law Offices of C. Steven Horn.

Last, but not least, I want to thank Stefanie Krieg-Elliott for designing this attractive catalogue; Art Clark for expert advice about the design of the installation; and Jeffrey Nemeth who helped me install the show. My staff has completed a difficult task in making this exhibition a reality. I extend my gratitude to them: Elizabeth Rogers, assistant director; Erica Weeder, curator of education; Yoko Inoue, administrative assistant; Dana Dince, part-time registrar; and Chie Hayashi, our intern during part of the planning process. A special thank-you goes to my former assistant, Chinami Kondo, who has returned to Japan, and to Robert Aguilla, systems administrator at the Japan Society.

Dr. Gunhild Avitabile
Director, Japan Society Gallery

Foreword

Wagasa, the traditional Japanese umbrella made of bamboo and paper, developed as an item of daily necessity long ago and was once widely and routinely used. Many Japanese artists, inspired by the elegant simplicity of *wagasa* design, have utilized it as a motif on different types of artwork, including ukiyo-e prints, folding-screen paintings and *inrô*.

Although *wagasa* were formerly widely produced throughout Japan, the number of districts in which they are made has rapidly diminished; now only a few remain. Initially this decrease was due to the rapid influx of Western culture during the latter half of the 20th century—an influx that led to drastic changes in the lifestyle of the Japanese people, including the widespread growth in popularity of the Western-style umbrella made of fabric and having metal ribs. Nowadays *wagasa* survive only to be used in the special worlds of Kabuki performances and traditional Japanese dance forms, as well as during certain festivals.

While there are still a few *wagasa*-producing districts remaining in Tokyo and Kyoto, Gifu City has become the center of Japan's *wagasa* industry and of efforts to preserve values long associated with this craft. Although we face many obstacles—including an aging and declining population of *wagasa* makers—the Gifu City Museum of History has undertaken a campaign to educate the public about the importance of preserving and carrying on traditional cultural values. As part of this effort, the museum has been presenting special exhibitions devoted to *wagasa*, and now offers courses or workshops on the art of making these umbrellas. I strongly support all such attempts to preserve *wagasa* traditions.

This exhibition hopefully will make it possible for people in the United States to gain a deeper understanding of Japanese culture. This includes being able to feel, firsthand, the respect the Japanese have traditionally held for fine craftsmanship, and their belief that such skill should be applied to even the most common, everyday objects.

I extend best wishes for the success of this exhibition and express my heartfelt gratitude to Dr. Gunhild Avitabile, director of the Japan Society Gallery, and to her staff, who organized this special event. My gratitude extends to Mr. Yoshinobu Tokugawa, director of The Tokugawa Art Museum, who acted as an intermediary in making it possible, as well as to Dr. Julia Meech, guest curator. I also thank The Tokai Bank Foundation and the Association for the Promotion of the Wagasa Industry of Gifu for their support. Finally, I am exceedingly grateful to those who have loaned their precious objects.

Hiroichi Ogawa
Director, Gifu City Museum of History

Acknowledgements

I wish to acknowledge the many contributions I received from friends and colleagues in the preparation of this catalogue. I am especially indebted to Gunhild Avitabile and the staff of the Japan Society Gallery, as well as to the Kajima Art Foundation, Tokyo. Hiroshi Yabushita, Kakehi Mariko and Shiromizu Tadashi of the Gifu City Museum of History generously shared their expertise, as did the umbrella makers of Gifu and Tokyo: Hayashi Giichi and Kazue, Ban Seikichi, Fujisawa Ken'ichi, Tsuji Anzô and Yabuta Takeshi. Lisa and Ken Normand, ages 14 and 11, were kind enough to lend a comic book from their collection (no. 94). I am very grateful to my editor, Mary Laing, and to those who took the time to read and comment on portions of my manuscript: Maggie Bickford, Brown University; John Carpenter, a graduate student at Columbia University; Sebastian Izzard, Christie's, New York; Joan B. Mirviss, New York; Mark Oshima, a graduate student at Harvard University; David B. Waterhouse, University of Toronto; and Lucie Weinstein, Hamden, Connecticut. I take full responsibility, of course, for the opinions expressed here and for any errors.

The following individuals have also given invaluable assistance with this complex project and deserve heartfelt thanks:
Ann B. Abid, Head Librarian, The Cleveland Museum of Art
The Art Institute of Chicago: James T. Ulak, Mary Albert and Jamyn Flynn
The Brooklyn Museum: Amy G. Poster and Elizabeth P. Weiland
Elizabeth Childs-Johnson, Hamilton College
Christie's, New York: Yoshinori Munemura and Jeanne Sloane
Jeanne-Claude Christo and the artist Christo, New York
Michael Cooper, S.J., Sophia University, Tokyo
Cooper-Hewitt National Museum of Design, Smithsonian Institution, New York: Megan Smith and Joanne Warner
Louise Cort, Freer Gallery of Art and Arthur M. Sackler Gallery, Smithsonian Institution, Washington, D.C.
William J. Dane, The Newark Public Library
Neil Davey, Sotheby's, London
Jeremy W. Farrell, Museum of Costume and Textiles, Nottingham
Matthi Forrer, Rijksmuseum voor Volkenkunde, Leiden
Robert E. Haynes, Seattle
William Hosley, Wadsworth Atheneum, Hartford, Connecticut
Miki Izzard, New York
Kobayashi Tadashi, Gakushuin University, Tokyo
Eloy F. Koldeweij, University of Leiden
Los Angeles County Museum of Art: Robert Singer and Hollis Goodall-Cristante
The Metropolitan Museum of Art, New York: Caroline Goldthorpe, Martin Fleischer, Colta Ives, Marica Vilcek, Stuart Pyhrr, Donald Larocca, Ann Willard, Morihiro Ogawa, Claire Le Corbeiller, Oscar Muscarella, and Suzanne G. Valenstein
Museum of Fine Arts, Springfield, Massachusetts: Emil G. Schorr and Stephen S. Fisher
Niikura-Matsumura Eri, The National Museum of Modern Art, Tokyo
Nishida Hiroko, Nezu Museum of Art, Tokyo
Barbra Teri Okada, New York
Ronald Y. Otsuka, Denver Art Museum
Andrew Maske, Oxford University
Gratia Williams Nakahashi, Curator, The Mary and Jackson Burke Collection, New York
Jürgen Uwe Ohlau, Kulturstiftung des Freistaates Sachsen, Dresden
Robert Ravicz
J. Thomas Rimer, University of Pittsburgh
Mari Saegusa, Greenwich, Connecticut
Takako Sato, New York
Joseph Seubert, Geibundô, Kawasaki City
Shimizu Isao, Narashino City
Andrew Stevens, Elvehjem Museum of Art, University of Wisconsin, Madison
Sumi Fusako, Gifu City
Tokyo National Research Institute of Cultural Properties: Yonekura Michio, Satô Dôshin and Kamakura Keiko
Tsao Hsingyuan, Stanford University
University of Tokyo: Tsuji Nobuo and Kôno Motoaki
Michael Verne, The Mitzie Verne Collection, Inc., Shaker Heights
Roberta Waddell, The New York Public Library
Irwin Weinberg, Chicago
Johannes Wieninger, Österreichisches Museum für Angewandte Kunst, Vienna
Yamaguchi Keizaburô, Risshô University, Tokyo
Martie W. Young, Herbert F. Johnson Museum of Art, Cornell University

Julia Meech
Guest Curator

Lenders to the Exhibition

Ayako Abe
The Art Institute of Chicago
The Brooklyn Museum
Christer von der Burg and Chris Uhlenbeck Collection
Mary Griggs Burke and The Mary and Jackson Burke Foundation
Raymond and Frances Bushell
The Cleveland Museum of Art
Cooper-Hewitt National Museum of Design, Smithsonian Institution, New York
Jeanne-Claude Christo
Denver Art Museum
Elvehjem Museum of Art, University of Wisconsin, Madison
Mr. and Mrs. Joel H. Frankel
Gifu City Museum of History, Japan
William Green
Haneda Hisatsugu
Michael and Claire Higgins
Honolulu Academy of Arts
Horesh Collection, London
Ken Jacobson
Jitsugetsukan, Tokyo
Herbert F. Johnson Museum of Art, Cornell University, Ithaca, New York
Andrew Terry Keats
Stephan Köhler
Kupferstich-Kabinett, Staatliche Kunstsammlungen Dresden, Germany
H. Kwan Lau Collection, New York
Donna Levis
Mr. and Mrs. Leighton R. Longhi
Penelope Mason
The Metropolitan Museum of Art, New York
Robert O. Muller
Musées Royaux d'Art et d'Histoire, Brussels, Belgium
Museum of Fine Arts, Springfield, Massachusetts
The Newark Public Library
The New York Public Library
Lisa and Ken Normand, Sugamo, Tokyo
Geoffrey Oliver
Orientations Gallery, New York
Philadelphia Museum of Art
Porzellansammlung, Staatliche Kunstsammlungen Dresden, Germany
John and Kimiko Powers
Private Collection, New York
Ravicz Collection
Rijksmuseum voor Volkenkunde, Leiden, The Netherlands
Patricia Salmon
Charles Schwartz Early Photography, New York
Seattle Art Museum, Christensen Fund Collection of Japanese Textiles
Floyd Segel
Mutsumi and Misako Suzuki, Kyoto
Yabuta Takeshi, Tokyo
Ukiyo-e Books, Leiden, The Netherlands
Vancouver Museum, Canada
Griffith and Patricia Way
Lawrence and Bessie Weinberg Collection, Chicago
The Weston Collection
The Jane Voorhees Zimmerli Art Museum, Rutgers, The State University of New Jersey, New Brunswick

Stephan Köhler

Parents of Private Skies

No academic ambitions such as writing a thesis for a degree made me come to Japan, nor was I sent on an illustrious grant or fellowship. While following my invisible trail around the globe, I had gone to art schools in New York and Vienna to paint, draw, photograph and write. In Japan I got caught longer than expected, staying only to spend some time with a few great people of a kind we might never meet again—craftspeople in the winter of their lives—a species about to become extinct. Therefore my contribution to this catalogue will consist of a collage—bits and pieces gleaned from my experiences while apprenticing with masters of umbrella making.

A strongly built man with large eyes, slanted steeply at uneven angles, came up to me one evening in 1987 after I had given a talk at the German-Japanese Society of Gifu City. The man introduced himself and began to talk about his work. I was intrigued when he said that he produced paper and bamboo umbrellas with craftspeople in his neighborhood, using techniques which had been passed down for centuries. Having grown up in the middle of Hamburg, Germany, I had had, ever since childhood, a longing to meet "real" people similar to the old shoe-repair man whose cluttered workshop closed when I was about six and was replaced by a spotless Mr. Minit chain store. My new friend immediately invited me to spend a morning with him at work, so that I could see how these archaic umbrellas were being made. He warned me though, saying that the craftspeople were shy and reluctant to receive visitors in their workshops.

I rang the bell of his house and waited outside. A diesel pick-up car was parked in front, a layer of dust muting its chalky whiteness. The compact car looked too small for work and I wondered whether it was actually his. The rear seats were folded down to provide space for a long paper bag. My friend came out with a roll of red paper under his arm, sliding his modern building's heavy iron and glass door closed with one hand. "*Guten Morgen.* Shall we go?" A minimal nod, which did not need to be big since it reflected a deeper one within, emphasized his greeting.

"Our umbrellas are made in the homes of a number of craftspeople, who each specialize in a different step of the production," he said. "None of them makes a whole umbrella by him- or herself. It is a product of cooperation. I drive around and take supplies to the masters, then sell the finished product. There are still twelve people in Gifu, including myself, who continue this work. We are called *kasa tonya-san* (wholesalers of traditional umbrellas)." We cruised smoothly along a busy main street lined with gaudy *pachinko* pinball parlors, gas stations, fast-food stands and twenty-four-hour convenience stores. My friend surprised me with a sharp left turn. We dove into another world—a small bumpy alley, sudden silence, a jungle of old wooden houses whose ceramic-tiled roofs

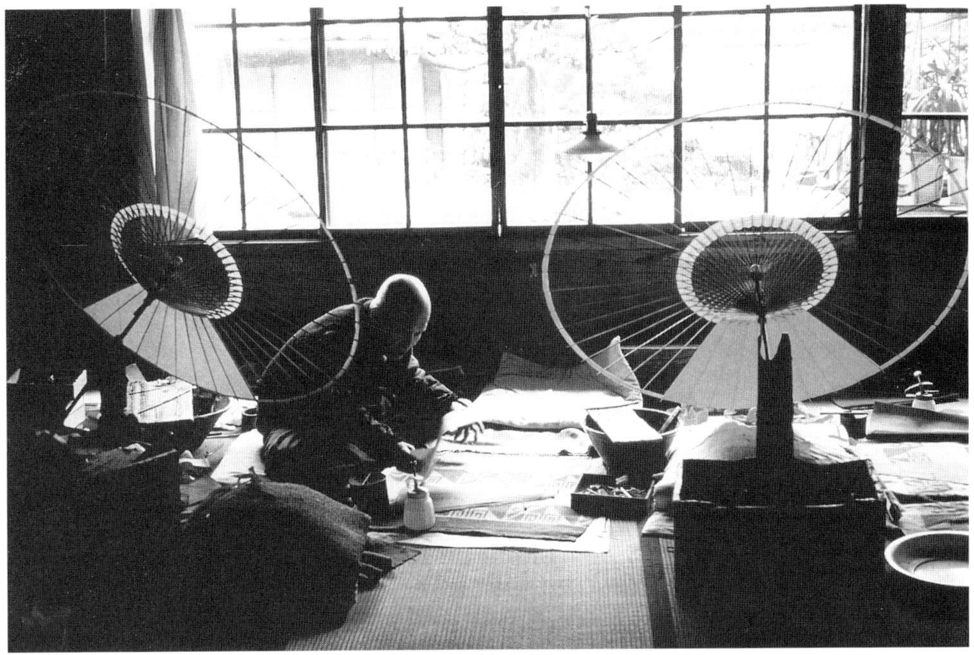

Fig. 1. In their workshop in Gifu City, umbrella makers Hayashi Giichi (b. 1905) and his wife Kazue (1906-1993) work side by side pasting paper covers onto bamboo skeletons, 1988. Gifu craftsmen use box-type umbrella stands rather than the tripod version traditionally found in Tokyo (see no. 3). Hayashi Giichi is seen here moistening paper for umbrella covers.

seemed an unbearable burden for the beams below. Treetops peeked over old flaking mud walls, as if curious to see who was driving by. "Come on, have a look!" he invited me.

Hardly keeping up with his rapid strides, I followed my friend toward a house of dark wood, which appeared generations removed from the world of convenience stores nearby. The glass panes held in the shaky frames of the two old sliding doors gave off a resonant chord—a naturally built-in chime—as my friend pulled them apart. He called out to announce his presence, then proceeded to take off his shoes. By the time I had untied my laces, he was already halfway up a precarious-looking staircase without a railing. The polished wood was slippery and I wished I were barefoot. I found myself emerging into a spacious attic. Numerous dovetailed beams, their joints providing homes to many spiders, looked as if they were bearing the tiles quite patiently and were willing to continue their job for a while.

Below the beams, I was able to see the backlit outlines of two small figures seated on pillows by a window (fig. 1). They had large wheels partly webbed by red and pink paper in front of them. A shaft of sunlight had found a weak spot in the cloud cover, slowly fighting its way through to illuminate the couple. The ray made the suspended paper glow like stained glass and I smiled to myself as a virtual fire cast the rest of the room into cold darkness.

"Ah, *konichiwa*," the man greeted us in a voice gently ripened by age, partly overlapped by a similar greeting from the woman next to him. I nodded and bowed a little, not knowing quite what to answer. As they talked with my friend, the couple continued working, pasting paper to spokes of a wheel as if adding pieces to a pie (fig. 7). The man's wrinkled hands had thick dark fingernails and a spotted Band-Aid covered his right thumb. Her hands were white and slender, fragile like thin porcelain. Quickly and lightly, she manipulated her tools over the paper she was working on. My friend put the bundle of bamboo onto the floor and began to count a batch of umbrellas that resembled red tubes. His hands made a practiced dance, each finger softly touching, one by one, the tops of the umbrellas. He recorded the count in a worn notebook with rounded corners.

"How old are those two?" I asked, back in the car. "He is eighty-eight and she is a year or two younger." "Why are they still working at this age?" "They have

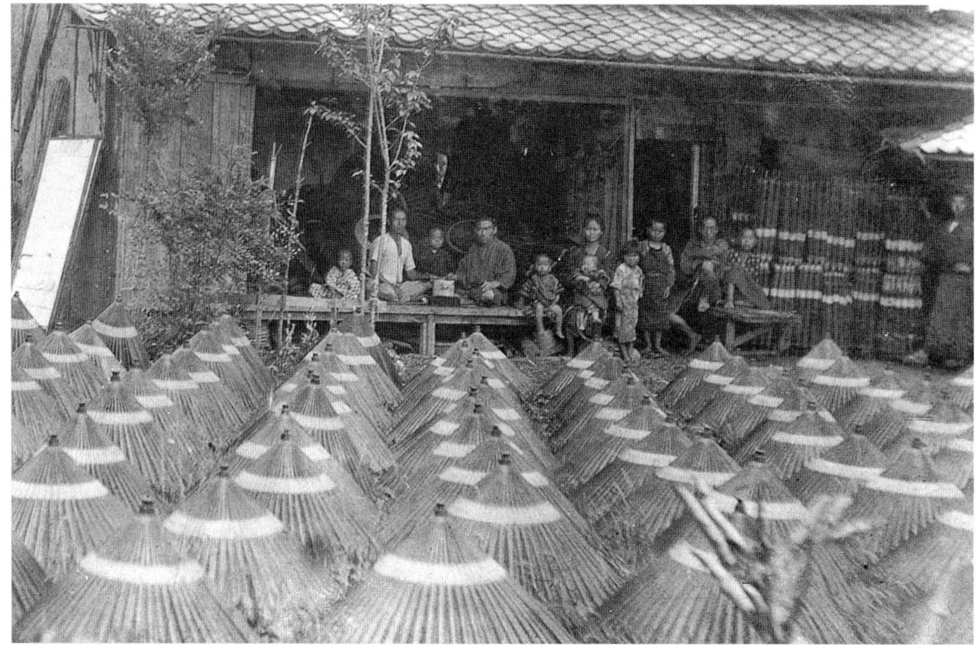

Fig. 2. A family of umbrella makers in Gifu. Late Meiji period, early 20th century. Oiled umbrellas are set out to dry on the lawn (see no. 2). Closed umbrellas that have not yet been oiled are stacked against the house at the upper right. Courtesy of Matsui Ichi, Gifu City

Fig. 3. Hayashi Kyôkichi connects ribs and top notch with silk threads, 1992 (see fig. 17).

Fig. 4. Hayashi Kyôkichi connects the stretchers with the ribs, 1992 (see diag. 1).

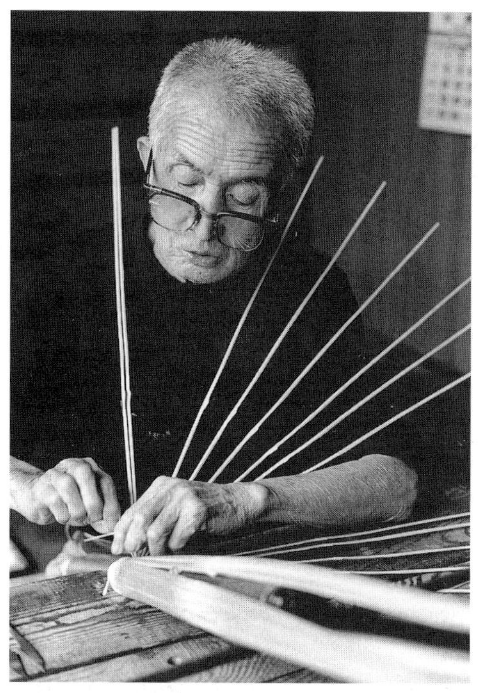

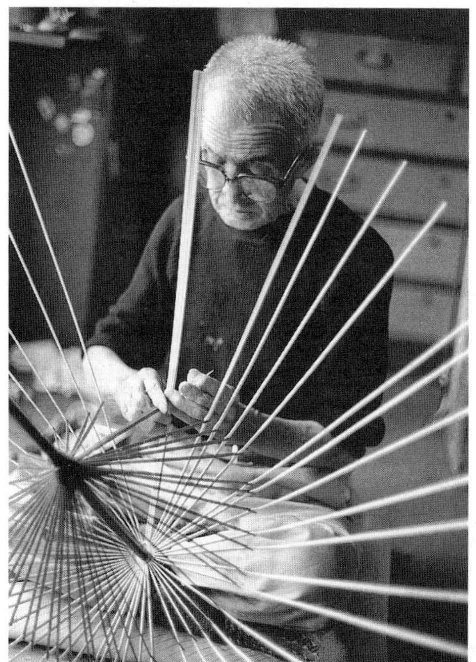

made umbrellas for over seventy years. Working everyday keeps their bodies and minds young. They will do it until the end." "And in winter, isn't it cold up there?" "Sure, your breath makes a cloud. I never saw them using a stove."

We drove for a while along main streets. Both having dry mouths, we silently agreed to go to a coffee shop. My friend placed my order; the waitress brought his serving without having to ask what he wanted.

"How come you speak English and even some German?" I asked. "Have you always been working with umbrellas, or did you do something else before?" "I went to a university and studied chemistry," answered my friend, remembering a path he had chosen a long time ago. "I had planned to be a pharmacist, but in my third year my father, who was an umbrella producer, got sick and could not continue to work by himself. Then I stopped studying and moved back to Gifu." "Would he have resented it, if you had not come home?" "His sudden illness made me realize that I had the chance to make a choice of lifestyles, of worlds: to become an employee of a major company and live in a big city, or to work with a small group of craftspeople and make something basic–like an umbrella. I do not regret my decision."

Back in the car, I thought about my friend's relationship with his "family" of craftspeople. Like a dog with its nose to the ground, I felt on the right track, close to the people and world I was searching for. I began to understand that one person could not make an umbrella alone, any more than a violinist could play a symphony all by him- or herself. The harmony of the group makes the quality of the sound. The hidden community of umbrella makers was still making beautiful music from long ago. Even though their umbrellas had been replaced by cheaper and sturdier ones, there must be a reason why the craftspeople were still around.

Being so few in number and without apprentices, the craftspeople themselves are likely to be more important than the product they make. My friend kept driving silently, respecting the cloud of thoughts in my head: these people keep alive the warm and natural qualities of being human; if they go, a lot goes with them. Few are aware of what we might be losing. Perhaps, among millions of subway commuters, someone will feel a twinge in his heart, wondering what is wrong, realizing that something is missing, but not quite remembering what. And not only in Japan.

My friend drove back to his house in the rain. The morning's tour was finished. I asked whether I could buy an umbrella from him. He gave me a bargain and we parted, having agreed to meet again. I carefully opened my new umbrella. When it was finally fully extended, I found myself surrounded by smells of oil, bamboo and lacquer, the whispering of raindrops amplified a hundred times. Red light tinted my hand and probably my face. It was like being inside a room with red windows. The umbrella felt warm and kind, as if I could feel the care and serenity of the people who had made it. Below the umbrella, I was with all the members of the orchestra at one time, enjoying the fruits of their melody.

Near the train station, the streets were crowded with people carrying umbrellas. Only I had a Japanese one. A thousand shades of nylon surrounded me—blue, black, flowers, stripes—but none of the manufactured umbrellas was round. They looked like frozen wings of bats (see p. 54). Many of the eyes underneath stared at me. All glances seemed to say: "A foreigner with a traditional umbrella! I used one when I was a kid. But now we have something cheaper and more practical. Those times arc over. Those foreigners are romantic. I would feel awkward to be seen with such a thing. No one uses them anymore."

After a while I felt lonely, exposed as if nude, and helpless against the glances and unspoken remarks. Instead of looking at the crowd, I looked above me into the red roof suspended by myriad filigree bamboo ribs (*oyahone*) radiating from the stick (*e*), reaching out for infinite points in the universe, yet all united by a yellow cotton star. I felt safe and protected again. The umbrella in my hand had become my companion. Both of us were foreigners. It was a shield not only for the rain. It guarded my world, defined my space. It was my private sky.

A couple of days later, Matsui Ichi, a barber, self-taught historian, and one-man publisher in central Gifu City, told me about the background of the umbrella makers while cutting my hair. "Raise your head a little, thank you. The families were rather poor before the war. Most children had to work as soon as they returned from school. Assembling bamboo frames, cutting paper and attaching decorations were the most common tasks delegated to children. They did not do this as a part-time job to increase their pocket money to buy records, go to movies or get some candy. It was all part of ensuring the survival of their family. Many adults grew up in those circumstances and, to tell the truth, everyone wants to forget the poor times. Young kids, now growing up in affluence, don't even know that such a world existed. No one tells them." Matsui parked his coffee cup among some magazines on a side table and picked up his comb and scissors. "It's not such a popular topic, the local history of a place like the Kanô quarter—mostly about umbrella makers. The public wants to read about heroes, kings and samurai, something dramatic. Or about modern stuff, Star Wars

*Fig. 5. Hayashi Kazue pastes on the central reinforcing strip of paper (*nakaokigami*; see diag. 1), 1990.*

Fig. 6. Hayashi Giichi cuts pie-shape wedges of paper for umbrella covers on his sixty-year-old cutting board, 1990.

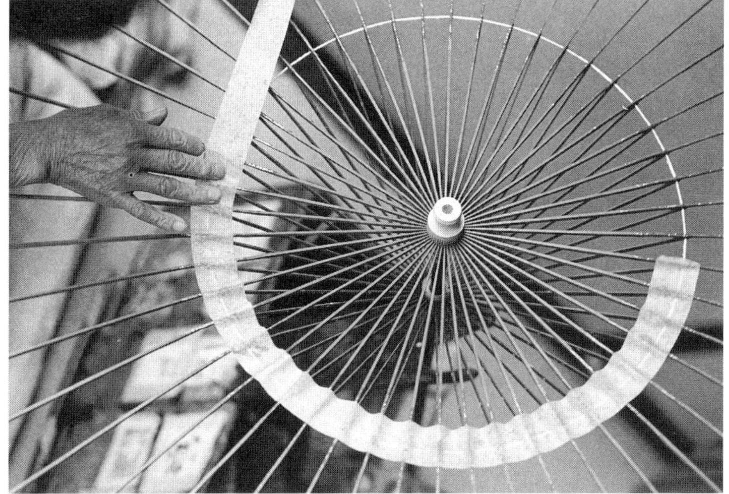

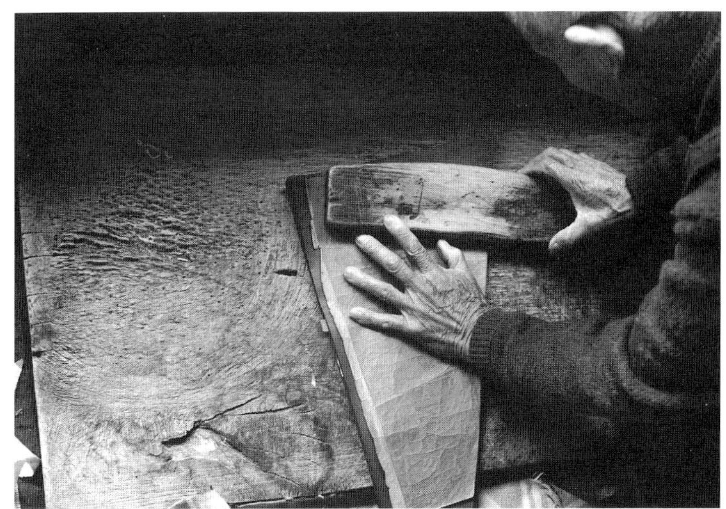

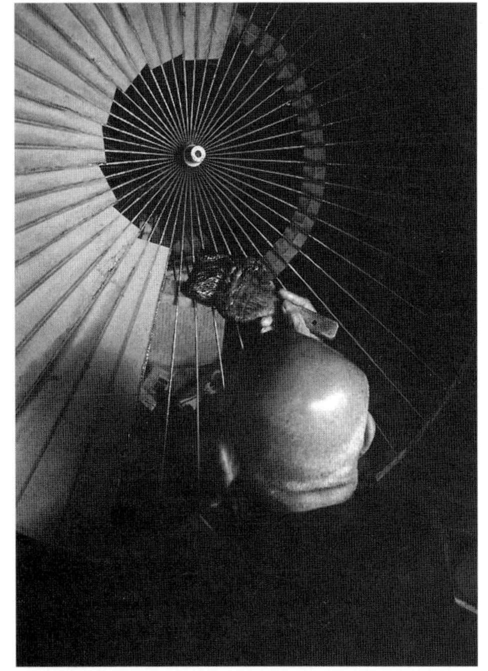

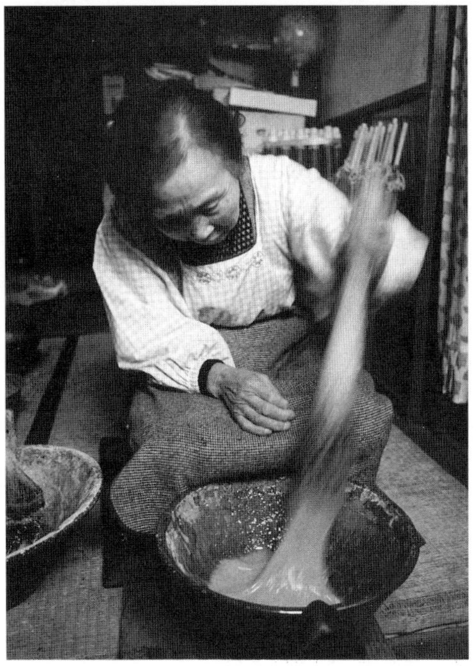

Fig. 7. Hayashi Giichi brushes the bamboo ribs with paste before applying the paper cover, 1990.

Fig. 8. Hayashi Kazue prepares paste with mortar and pestle, 1990.

comics with lots of sex. There used to be thousands of craftsmen and -women here. Everyone made their living on paper and bamboo umbrellas, until a couple of years after the Second World War. Then the nylon umbrella won."

"There is no history of the umbrella. Umbrellas are not Raku or Kiyomizu temple teacups which people collect because they last long and increase in value. There are not even any old umbrellas left! Bamboo and oiled paper are the most perishable materials one could think of. How do you want your sideburns trimmed, straight or diagonal?" "Straight, please. Perhaps umbrellas are like flowers. They blossom, get spots and holes from the weather, then wither and return to earth. I mean, teapots will also eventually turn to dust, it's all just a question of time. Compared to the ages of mountains, it becomes a tiny difference."

Later, over a cup of bitter green tea, we sat among the dryers, shampoo bottles, tables with scissors and combs, and enjoyed the absence of further customers. "Here, this picture shows an umbrella-making family about seventy years ago." The faded print showed a large family posing on the porch of a dilapidated wooden house. In front of them umbrellas are drying on the lawn (fig. 2). "It looks like a grove of umbrellas. Did they make a profitable living with a turnover like that?"

"They didn't. Umbrellas were cheap and they could not sell them themselves. Their producers and dealers would, and collected most of the profit. See their shabby clothes and the small size of their home? The people gathering here are not neighbors and friends coming for a birthday party. This is one family and they share this tiny place, which also houses their workshop." Matsui patiently explained to me how umbrella production blossomed around 1825, as the Lord of Kanô Castle realized that making money by producing and selling umbrellas would keep his head above water and even enable him to finally have the leaking roof of his residence repaired. . . . Then the next customer came into the barber shop.

Later, my friend the umbrella wholesaler took me once more to the home of the Hayashis, the fragile couple he had introduced me to on our first tour. . . . The brush resembled a fish with a bushy tail (fig. 7). It fit snugly in the eighty-eight-year old hand of Hayashi Giichi. Its handle, once a square piece of wood, had become an organic curve, aligning perfectly with the slope of Giichi's right thumb. The old man dipped the brush in cassava-starch paste (i.e., *tapioka nori*, see p. 26), which had coated his hands so many times that his fingernails resembled old amber. With sure strokes, he coated a group of three or four adjacent bamboo ribs in order to attach a section of the umbrella's paper covering. Wet paste momentarily let the ribs appear as if they were shiny railroad tracks, before they disappeared under a paper blanket.

"This brush is fairly new," Giichi said. "We've used it for only sixteen years. The one we had before was better. We used it for two decades. But then one cold winter night, a rat came into our attic workshop and devoured the bristles." "A new brush is not always the best," added his wife, Kazue. "It is far too heavy in the beginning, with too much hair. After you use it for a couple years, it gets just the right shape and weight." I thought this was odd. "Couldn't you trim it a little after you bought it?" I asked. Kazue, who at age eighty-seven radiated a quiet beauty, ignored my question, preferring to let me ponder the process of organic maturation.

Intermittently, Giichi and Kazue shook excess paste from their tools by hitting the edge of the bowl, making it ring like an old bell. The umbrella sticks rested horizontally in wooden brackets. When either Hayashi let go of an umbrella, it

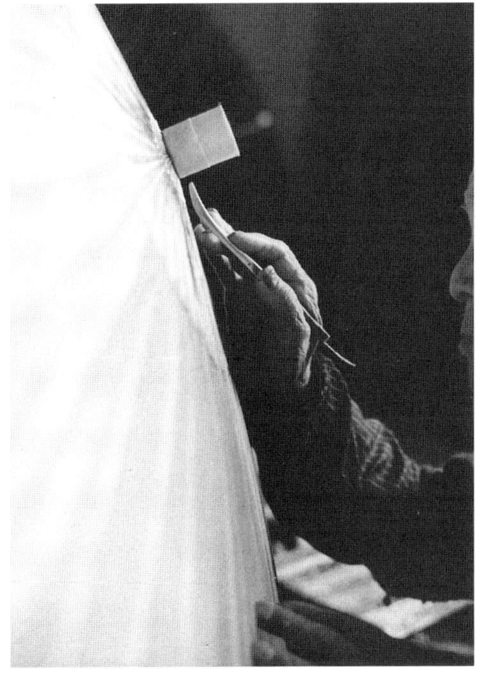

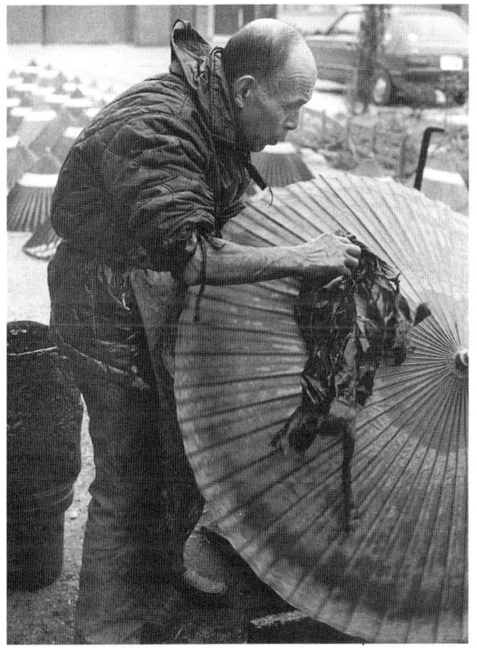

Fig. 9. Hayashi Giichi smooths paper over the bamboo ribs below the top notch of the umbrella cover, 1990.

Fig. 10. The Gifu umbrella oiler Sakaida Kikuichi, age seventy-five, in 1988. In the background are umbrellas that have been sunk in holes in Sakaida's lawn to dry for a few days.

squeaked as it turned toward its center of gravity, coming to rest with covered ribs down, bare ribs pointing up. Initially the toolmaker had cut only a half circle in the bracket to hold the stick. A giant termite seemed to have eaten a narrow path downwards, distorting the shape of the crescent. Could it be that countless turns of umbrellas had left these traces?

"When your tools are worn out, where do you get new ones?" I asked. "We made these workbenches ourselves from apple boxes and some scrap wood," said Giichi, looking up from his umbrella. "I carved the bamboo tools–the pincers, the compass, the stick to attach the covering–myself (figs. 6, 9). Only these, the brass pincers, were made by a specialist. He died ten years ago without a successor. We remaining umbrella makers just have to take good care of the tools that he made for us." The shiny metal was worn out and I wondered who in the end would win the race, Giichi or his last pair of pincers.

At around noon we went downstairs. I was invited for lunch and sat with Giichi at a low table while his wife went to the kitchen. "I began as an apprentice when I was fifteen. We did not go to high school or evening cram schools to pass exams, as most children must now. I lived at my master's house and we worked from 8:00 a.m. to 9:00 p.m. Then we all went to the *sentô* (bath house) because at that time few homes had their own tub. The master was a musician. At night, he played shamisen and danced as well. We apprentices got about fifteen sen a month–just enough to buy a bottle of sake."

After lunch, watching TV seemed to offer a good opportunity for the Hayashis to take naps unnoticed. I took the chance to observe their bodies. Her arms were thin and fragile. Tiny wrinkles, like ripples caused by a breeze on a lake, gave a fine coat of age to her appearance. Her movements, while serving lunch and pasting paper strips, had been so royally graceful that I wanted to nickname her the "Queen Mother of Umbrellas." She and her husband ranked far down the ladder of Japan's social hierarchy. But her gentle presence, combined with Giichi's equanimity and sovereignty over his work, made them members of a secret, unacknowledged aristocracy in my eyes. They had a fine modest air, in contrast to respected businessmen and lawyers whom I had met. It hit me that, unlike anyone else I had met so far in Japan, the Hayashis had never offered me a calling card. They did not need one. They were who they were.

I calculated the hours they had spent and thought they should get a couple of thousand yen for each umbrella. Later, though, I found out that they received one-twentieth of the final retail price. How come? Perhaps money had no relevance in this realm of patience and loyalty to an old brush. I wondered what kept them in their attic–hot in summer, cold in winter–working at this age. Maybe the umbrellas demanded that they keep working as long as they lived because so few people could do this work. Or did they receive some benefits besides pay, which could not be understood unless one did the same work oneself? Certainly they had a serenity and youthfulness that I could not imagine being gained by sitting around all day eating cakes and watching TV.

Weeks later I sat on the porch in front of my room and was at loss. How do I make this fragile strip of paper adhere to the bamboo and cotton strings rather than to my fingers? When I told my friend the wholesaler that I would like to learn how to make umbrellas, he thought for a moment, seated in his armchair by his cluttered desk, then got up and disappeared into one of the storage rooms. He came back with a naked frame of bamboo ribs, a slim pile of paper and a set of carefully folded strips of various widths. "Here you go, take this with you and just do it. This strip goes up here, this one down here, this piece of paper goes all along the rim. With the rest you close the hole remaining in the middle. Got it?"

"Ye . . .Yes, mmh. Yes, of course . . . got it." I stumbled and lied. I had not understood anything of what he had said, but was afraid he might not give me the materials if I asked questions because he might think I could not do it. Off I went, back to my hosts' house. The people in the bus stared at me, wondering how I had gotten hold not only of a traditional umbrella, but also of a not-yet-assembled one.

My friend introduced me to a curator from the area who had recently set up an exhibition of umbrellas made in Gifu in his museum, and who knew many masters in that field. "He has been to many more workshops than I have," my friend told me on the way to the museum. "Why is that?" I wondered. "The other umbrella wholesalers tell him which craftsmen work for them, but they will not tell me. There are so few masters of umbrella making left that we wholesalers keep their names and addresses secret from each other. It did actually happen—a master craftsman was stolen!" These words sounded awkward to me. Were humans things or gold mines which could be owned or kept secret?

"Can't they choose whom they will work for? Aren't they free people?" "Yes and no. It's hard to explain. Maybe the curator can tell you." The curator took me to a workshop just off the old Tôkaidô road linking Tokyo and Kyoto, which also cut through Gifu. In a little courtyard a white-haired, skinny man sat on a wooden floor, looking somewhat like a spider at work. Again and again he pulled a needle through the middle joints of the bare, paperless ribs, connecting them all together (fig. 4).

"Do you enjoy your work?" I knew I had asked a trivial question. "Enjoy? Well, sometimes I do. Also, the wholesaler begs me, because there are so few people who can do this work. I get sixty yen (about fifty cents) a piece—6,000 yen (about fifty dollars) to assemble a hundred frames. It takes me three to four days to get this done. Any kid selling hamburgers would get more than that, maybe twice as much in a single day." "Has it ever occurred to you to ask for a raise?" "No, we craftspeople wouldn't do such a thing. It would be impolite towards the wholesalers. Our wages haven't gone up for maybe fifteen, or twenty years. Instead of gymnastics I do this more as an exercise, just to keep moving—also because I am used to doing it."

Well, why should the producers be altruistic saints? I asked myself, in order not to escape into a distressing moral debate about how the situation should be—full of justice and harmony to fit my initial image. Besides, isn't there always some satisfaction when the victims are strong and rich enough to survive and prosper in spite of any injustice done to them? Craftspeople know that they should get more pay, but they seem not to care that they receive the same salary as twenty years ago. They appear to pity their bosses for not being generous enough in their hearts to pay them more voluntarily. With this attitude, the masters of umbrella making are rich; they are the winners, even though they are probably the last of their kind.

"Will there be a springlike renewal of umbrella making?" I asked the curator while we watched an old man bending into the depths of his radial construction. He shrugged his shoulders. "I doubt it; the seeds are lost. We have no young umbrella makers in Gifu and the wholesalers are paralyzed. There are no support or scholarship programs from the government either. Officials say that so far the guild of producers has made no proposal good enough to be worth allocating funds for. Probably they are right. Wholesalers fighting for the last remaining craftspeople have a hard time agreeing on even one strategy to save this craft. With two or three exceptions, most of them shortsightedly think only of their own company."

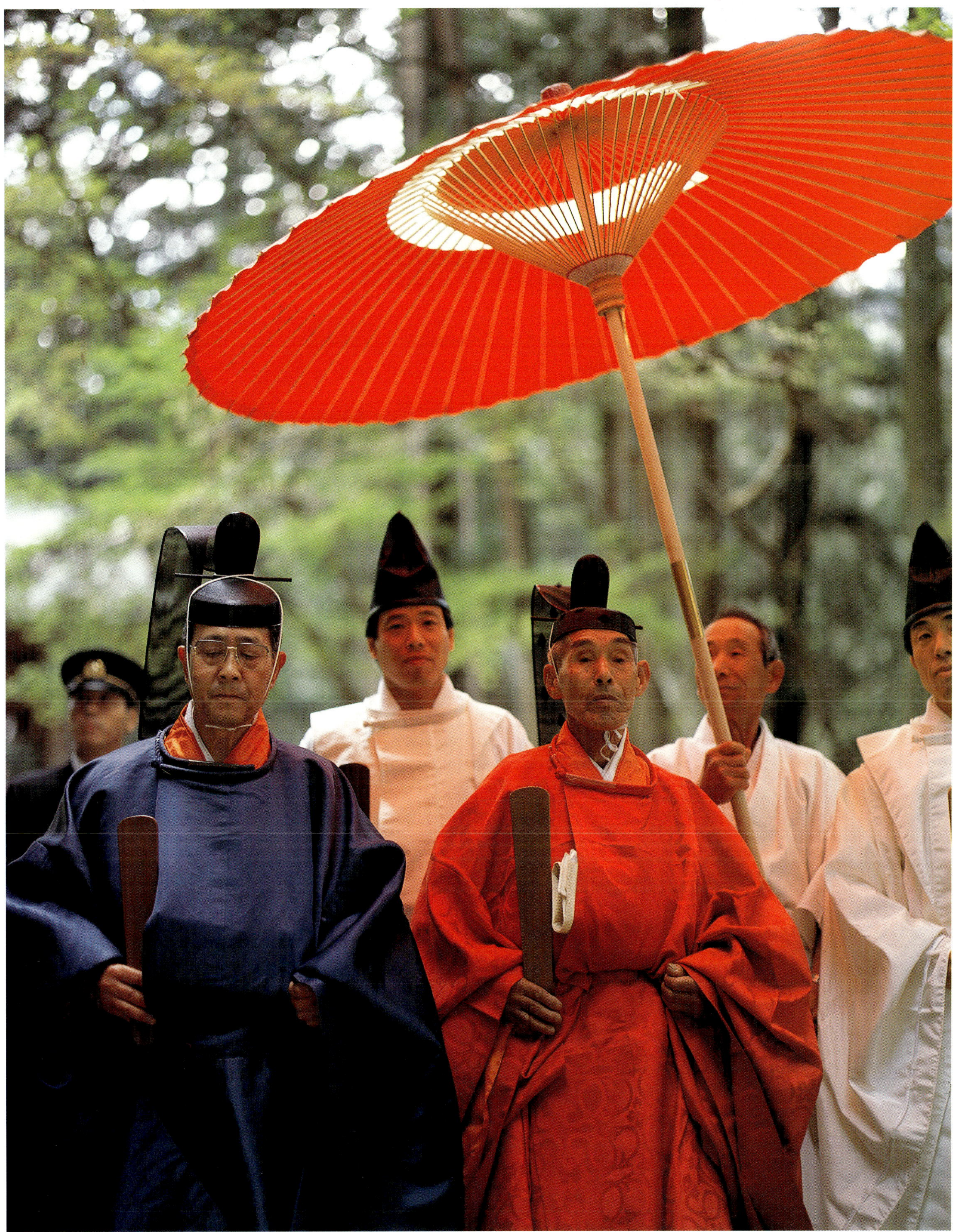

No. 56. Stephan Köhler, *Daisai Festival at the Hachiman Shrine, Hachiman*, 1990

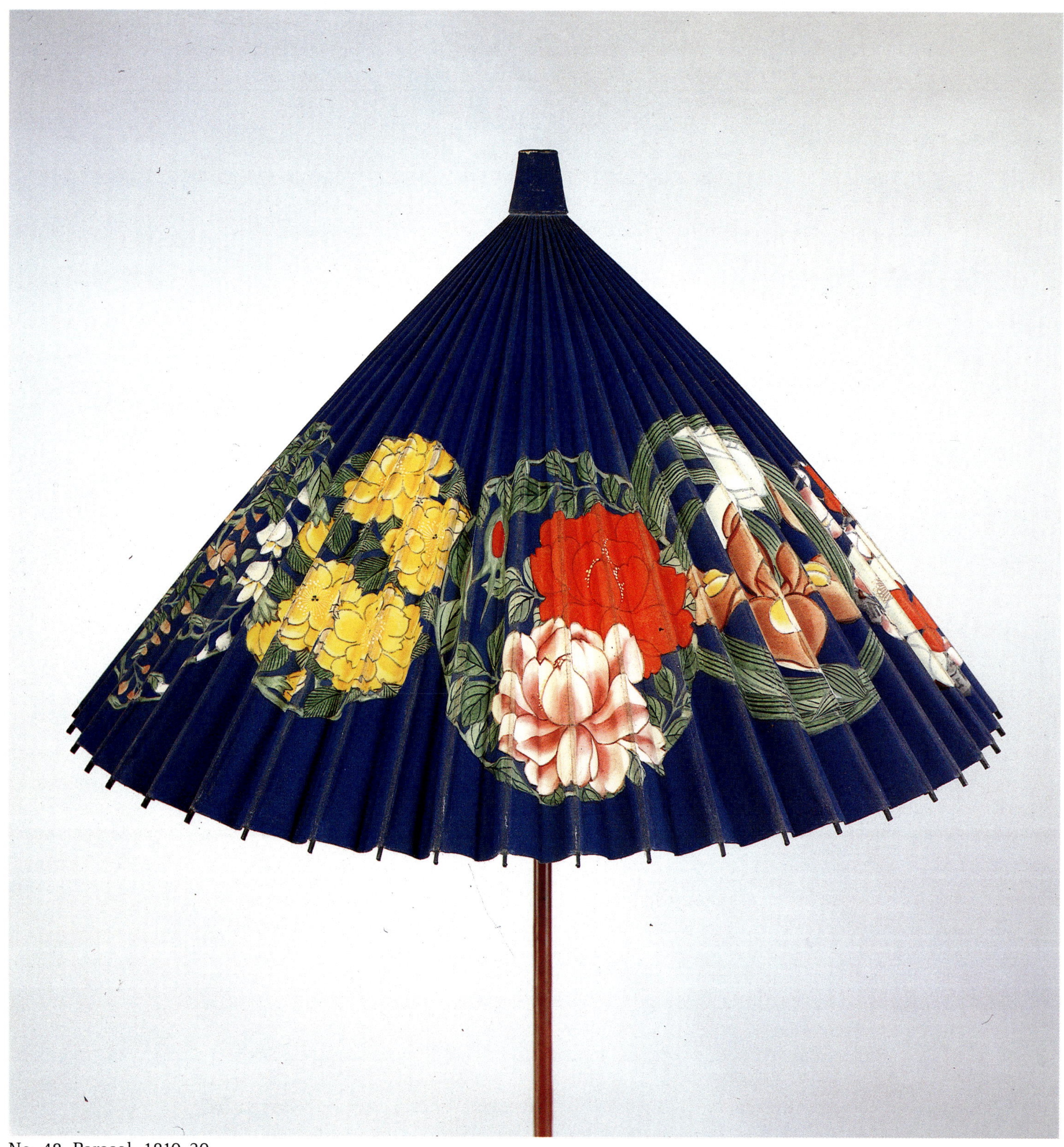

No. 48. Parasol, 1810-30

"I told them," the curator continued, with a slight trace of impatience in his mostly restrained speech, "that they should raise salaries and produce only the most refined, valuable umbrellas from natural materials because nowadays people would buy such umbrellas as art objects, not as tools for coping with rain. Wholesalers should sell fewer umbrellas at double or triple the current price and pass the increase on to those who do the actual work." Probably those words would sound revolutionary to the ears of the producers. I felt sad that a centuries-old process, capable of transforming hands into glowing amber, of creating highly attuned bodies and alert, serene minds, might well vanish from the earth—just because of mismanagement and a lack of innovative ideas.

In the meantime I have been in Gifu almost five years, spending fascinating hours with the "parents of private skies." I hope I have enough of the qualities of a sponge to soak up the treasures they have to offer, treasures which presently are running into the gutter. I have begun to realize that the situation of craftspeople is quite similar to the conditions indigenous people of various countries find themselves in. Both are outsiders, even though each is the originator of a culture. Their kind of person is not needed any more in modern society. The values the craftspeople stand for no longer count—to work according to one's own rhythm; to work with organic materials; to work without machines, training one's body to be the utmost tool; to be alert and sensitive; to stay at home, working primarily with members of one's family; to be peaceful, quiet and centered. It is not only the umbrellas, but also the skills related to their creation—papermaking, carving, restoring old art treasures, carpentry—that have no economic momentum in an ambitious industrial society. Japanese education is geared to make out of free children wheels and parts for the "big machine." For this reason it is unlikely that it would ever enter a high-school graduate's mind to assume a traditional profession. When economic growth is the only factor that counts in a country, craftspeople are useless. Unfortunately, their time has passed.

Nevertheless, if there are factors besides economic growth—to put it roughly, aspects of the "soul" of a country—then it might be worth thinking about the values of these masters before they are gone. I don't need to make any judgments. It's up to the Japanese to find out what they want. All I feel the need to do is document and learn from what I experience and remind people once in a while that they could never have made Walkmen and cameras without the accumulated genes of centuries of craftsmanship and patience. I suggest, at the least, a dignified farewell instead of an unnoticed sliding away.

I found an old house in the countryside and discovered for myself umbrellas as a form of sculpture, while designing and covering them. Some of my old friends have left already and I know that if the feeling of loneliness goes beyond what I can bear, it will be time to move on. However, twenty or thirty years from now, if I am still alive, no matter whether I am painting, making sculpture or doing photography, something might remain with me of the essence of a master's ability to use materials as well as one's body, mind and senses to their maximum.

Hiroshi Yabushita

History and Production of the Japanese Umbrella

In Japan before the 1950s, umbrellas used on rainy or snowy days were mostly traditional paper umbrellas (called *wagasa*). On rainy days, everybody—adult or child, young or old—used to walk about with a great variety of such *wagasa*. These traditional umbrellas were made throughout Japan, but during the first half of this century Gifu, Fukuoka, Wakayama, Kagawa and Mie prefectures were particularly known for their production. Of these, Gifu, with its umbrella manufacturing centered in Gifu City, about eighteen miles north of Nagoya, accounted for nearly one quarter of Japan's total output. According to 1925 statistics, this prefecture produced 25 percent of all traditional umbrellas, valued at 5.2 million yen out of a national total of 21 million yen.

Umbrella production in Gifu peaked again for a few years shortly after World War II—to be exact, during the 1948-50 period—when the prefecture's annual production reached 15 million units. In the five years that followed, however, the situation changed dramatically. Mass production of steel and cloth Western-style umbrellas, called *kômori-gasa* ("bat" umbrellas), began (see nos. 119-121). This, coupled with the wholesale adoption of Western lifestyles by the Japanese, quickly forced the traditional umbrella, which required a complicated manufacturing process, out of the market. Today Gifu City, where production of traditional paper umbrellas is focused, makes only about 70 thousand units a year, with a nationwide total of less than 100 thousand. Thus, the paper umbrella is now nearly forgotten as an item in Japanese life.

As I write this, Japan is entering its rainy season. But even in Tokyo on this rainy day, it would be difficult to find anyone with a paper umbrella among the crowds busily going back and forth with wave after wave of colorful Western-style umbrellas. If you happen to see one, I can assure you that it will be held by someone connected with a traditional Japanese business or profession, not by an average person.

Who uses paper umbrellas today? Among those who use them for professional reasons are *maiko* (dancing girls) in Kyoto, geisha, and kimono dealers; in other words, those who must wear kimono as a requirement of their jobs (fig. 11). Similarly, some Kabuki plays (see pp. 101-113), as well as traditional Japanese dance (*buyô*), require the use of *wagasa* (no. 76). In particular, the type of umbrella called *maigasa* (dance umbrella) is almost indispensable to traditional dance. Because of the sizable population taking dance lessons, a considerable number are produced for this purpose. Depending upon the dictates of the repertoire, these umbrellas use silk or paper covers with a cherry-blossom or peony design (fig. 12). The type of umbrella with a transparent silk cover, used almost exclusively in traditional dances, allows the audience to see the dancer even when he or she is behind it.

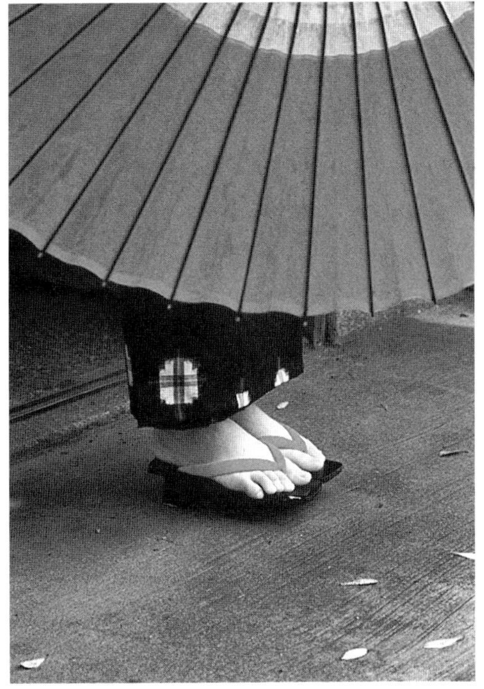

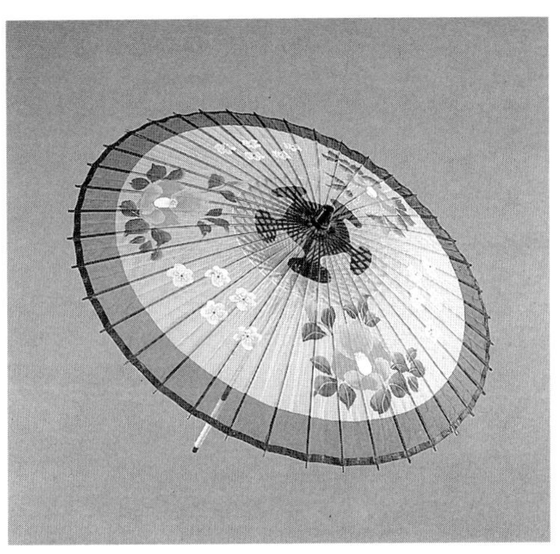

Fig. 11. Traditional apparel and umbrella

Fig. 12. Dance umbrella, Gifu City Museum of History

A variety of shrine and temple festivals (*matsuri*) also use umbrellas, for example, the *Kodomo* Kabuki (children's Kabuki) festival in Tarui City, Gifu prefecture (fig. 13), and the *Okuri-Daishi* (sending off [Kôbô] Daishi) festival in Shônan City, Chiba prefecture. During the latter, a procession goes to the temple and prays (*tera e o-kigan ni iku*; fig. 14). Among these festivals, the *Shanshan-kasa* (*shanshan* umbrella) festival, held during the summer in Tottori City, includes a parade of about two thousand people dancing with umbrellas decorated with gold or silver poem cards and bells (fig. 15). The name of this festival derives from *shanshan*, the sound that bells make as dancers gracefully move, shaking their umbrellas against the night sky. This is probably the largest festival requiring the use of umbrellas.

Another notable festival is the *kasa-yaki* (umbrella burning) *matsuri*, held on the last day of May in Odawara City, Kanagawa prefecture (figs. 16a,b). Also called *Soga-no-kasa-yaki matsuri* (festival of the Soga [brothers'] burning of the umbrellas), this rustic festival, in which old, used umbrellas are brought together and burned, traces its origins to the famous vendetta carried out by the Soga brothers, Jûrô and Gorô, toward the end of the 12th century. As legend has it, the two brothers used their umbrellas as pine torches (*taimatsu*) when they were about to kill their enemy in the darkness.

Temples and shrines also use umbrellas. These large white and red umbrellas held over a priest or monk by an assistant standing behind him are called *sashikake-gasa* ("hold-over" umbrellas, no. 56). Similar large umbrellas, *nodate-gasa*, which are primarily red, are used in outdoor tea ceremonies. Some traditional inns and restaurants also use these tea-ceremony umbrellas as indoor accessories. One of the largest modern umbrellas has a diameter of 4.58 meters (about 15 feet), with ribs 2.41 meters (about 8 feet) long.

Some inns and restaurants also carry inexpensive, simply made umbrellas called *bangasa* (nos. 17-20) to be used by their customers. There are several theories about the origins of this name. Some say the umbrellas are called *bangasa* because the owner of an inn or restaurant used to "*ban*" (number) them; others believe that the wholesalers of such umbrellas used to "*han*" (stamp) on their logos before shipping them out.

All in all, the use of paper umbrellas today is limited to special professions and occasions and is no longer a part of ordinary daily life in Japan.

Where did the kind of umbrella we now recognize as the traditional Japanese paper umbrella originate? Several scholars during the Edo period (1615-1868) asserted that the umbrella (*karakasa*) came to Japan toward the end of the 16th century. The source of these assertions seems to be a passage in the 1712 *Wakan sansai zue* (Japanese-Chinese illustrated assemblage of the three components of the universe), compiled by Terashima Ryôan, which says that when the Sakai merchant Naya Sukezaemon returned from Luzon, the main island of the Philippines, in 1594 (Bunroku 3), he presented the ruler of Japan (Toyotomi Hideyoshi [1536-1598]) with gifts of a thousand candles and a thousand umbrellas which could be freely opened and closed. Structurally the same as those of the mid-Edo period, these were the first such umbrellas in Japan.

This description has traditionally been interpreted to mean that Japan did not have the kind of umbrella that could be easily opened and shut until Naya Sukezaemon brought it into Japan toward the end of the 16th century, and that therefore this particular type had not existed in Japan before that time. I disagree with this view and believe that umbrellas used in Japan as early as the 13th century were the kind that could be freely opened and shut. An illustrated

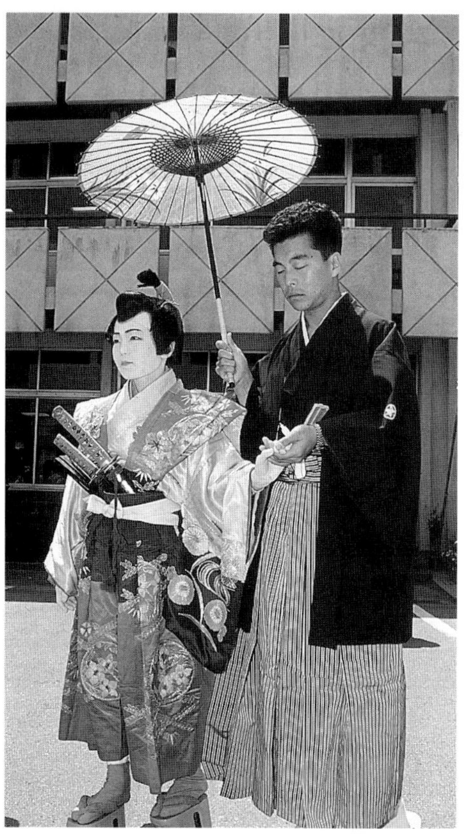

Fig. 13. Children's Kabuki festival, Tarui City, Gifu prefecture

handscroll depicting the life of the itinerant holy monk Ippen (1239-1289), made not long after his death, shows a scene where Ippen (fig. 54) and his followers use black umbrellas as they run through the rain; umbrellas are also shown folded in the same scene.

Structurally, the mechanism that makes it possible to open and close an umbrella freely is the runner or slide (*temoto rokuro*, fig. 25). Among items found at the Asakura Mansion site in Fukui are runners that are the same as those used today. Items excavated at this mansion, established by Asakura Takakage (also named Toshikage, 1428-1481), are thought to date from the first half of the 16th century—many decades before Naya Sukezaemon brought back foreign umbrellas. Ribs (*oyahone*) and stretchers (*shôhone*) are known to have existed earlier (see diag. 1, p. 33). Since it is difficult to imagine an umbrella being used without a runner, we must infer that runners were used long before the Asakura Mansion came into being. This was also noted by a few other Edo-period authors.

Why was Terashima's assertion accepted so widely? Was there anything special about the umbrellas Naya Sukezaemon brought back from the Philippines? The answer is almost certainly that those umbrellas came with springs (*hajiki*, fig. 26), the mechanism that makes it easy to keep the umbrella open or to close it. This conjecture can readily be confirmed by looking at images from earlier periods, such as the Ippen scroll, and comparing them with illustrations from later periods, such as ukiyo-e prints. In earlier images, the device to keep an umbrella open is a pin or small stick inserted horizontally into a hole made at the spot where the runner is supposed to stop. In later representations you seldom see this; instead, you see a spring.

Making the Traditional Japanese Paper Umbrella

The materials, manufacturing process and tools of the traditional umbrella have not changed much over the ages, nor are there many regional differences. What is described below is the manufacturing process for an ordinary *janome* (snake's-eye) umbrella (diag. 1), as used in Gifu City, once called the "Kingdom of *Wagasa*."

What characterizes traditional umbrella manufacture in Gifu City is mass production, which requires a complex division of labor. As a result of this process, the manufacture of a single umbrella requires more than thirty days and the cumulative involvement of fifteen to sixteen people. In this it differs from the single-person manufacture of the Edo-style umbrella, which still survives in present-day Tokyo.

First Stage: Cover Paper Preparations

1-1: Making paper (fig. 18)
Paper used for the umbrella cover is made by hand in Mino City, near Gifu, using mulberry fiber. For this use, uniformity in thickness, as well as horizontal/vertical (woof/warp) toughness, is required.

1-2: Dyeing paper (fig. 19)
Today, dyeing is done mostly during the paper-manufacturing stage. But sometimes designs are painted on white (undyed) paper, using mineral pigments, as was done in the past in traditional Japanese-style painting.

1-3: Making *habutae* (double-feather) covers (fig. 20)
Although a *janome* is usually made with plain paper, sometimes a high-quality, expensive, thin silk cloth, the same color as the paper base, is pasted onto the paper. A layer of silk cloth pasted to a layer of paper is called *habutae*. Layering paper and silk originated in the 1930s as a result of the quest for beauty and strength. The development of slender umbrellas necessitated the use of thin paper, and this double-layering technique protects fragile paper from damage.

1-4: Paper selection (fig. 21)
The initial size of the paper for the umbrella cover (including *habutae*) is about two by three feet (about 60 by 90 cm.); formerly this was cut equally into six smaller sheets, but nowadays it is cut into four (see 4-2: step 3). Each quarter sheet makes two conical sections of the cover. Paper is inspected by holding each sheet up to the sunlight to check for smudges, holes and such things; in this way, only good paper is used. This selection process is called *kamiyori*.

1-5: Cutting out designs (fig. 22)
Sometimes the umbrella design uses family crests, floral motifs and/or geometric patterns. Shapes are first cut from the cover paper, then those parts of the cover with cut-out shapes removed are lined with white, red or indigo silk. These colorful stencil-like cut-outs create a "transparency effect" against the sun—but this manufacturing process is complicated and not often used.

Second Stage: Preparing the Stick (*e*)

2-1: Making the stick (figs. 23, 24)
There are two kinds of stick: one is made from bamboo, the other from wood. Bamboo is more commonly used, but wood sticks are also used for *janome* and dance umbrellas. The preferred bamboo is *madake* (bot. *Phyllostachys bambusoides*), a species indigenous to Japan, which is harvested from autumn to winter in Yamaguchi and Kyûshû. During the Edo period (1615-1868), *madake*, which grew in the area around Gifu City, was used. However, large-scale production of umbrellas from the Meiji period (1868-1912) onward led to a shortage of *madake* around Gifu. Moreover, the development of railroad networks made it possible to import large quantities of bamboo from remote regions. For these reasons, umbrella craftsmen finally turned to Kyûshû to obtain stronger and more flexible bamboo. Bamboo from Kyûshû is still used today, but the choice of type lies with the individual craftsperson. *Madake* is first cut (fig. 23), then heated to correct whatever warp it may have and to remove any oil (fig. 24).

Fig. 14. Okuri-Daishi *festival, Shônan City, Chiba prefecture*

Fig. 15. Shanshan *umbrella festival, Tottori City*

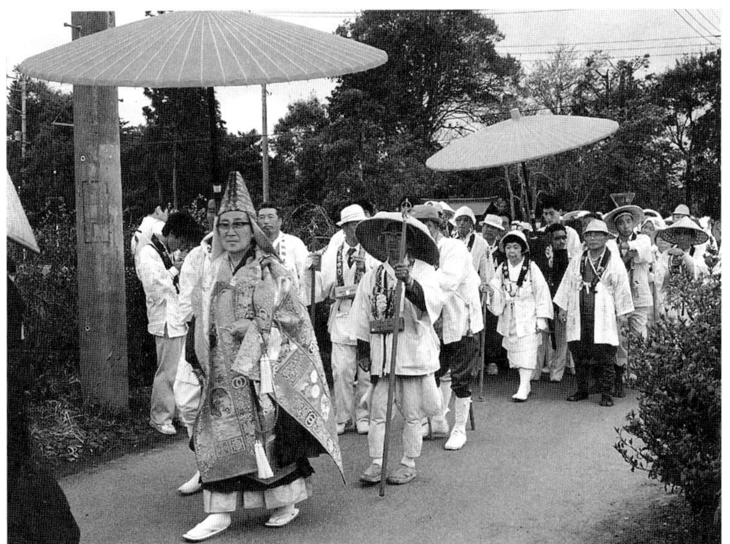

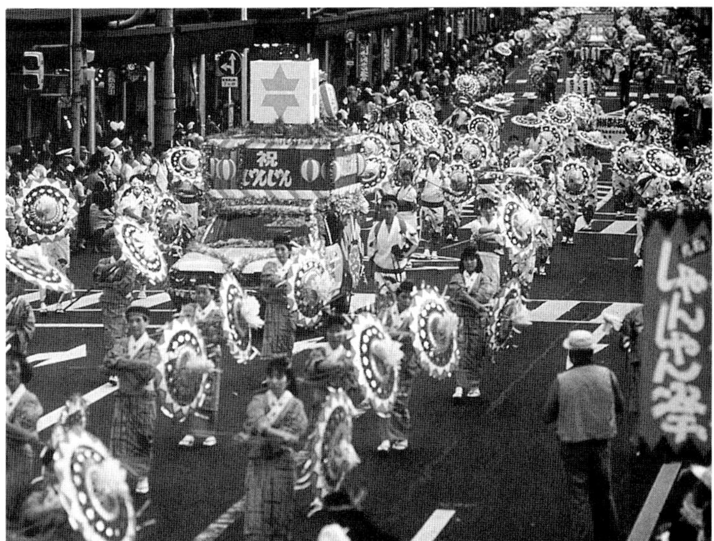

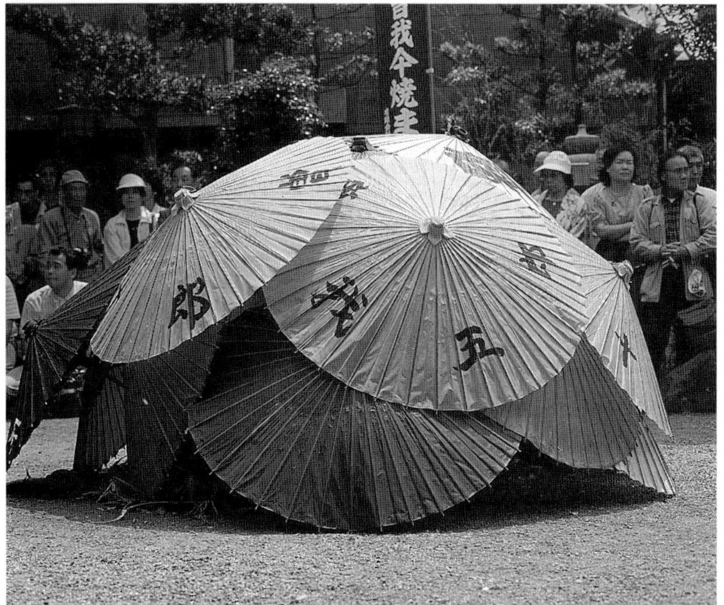

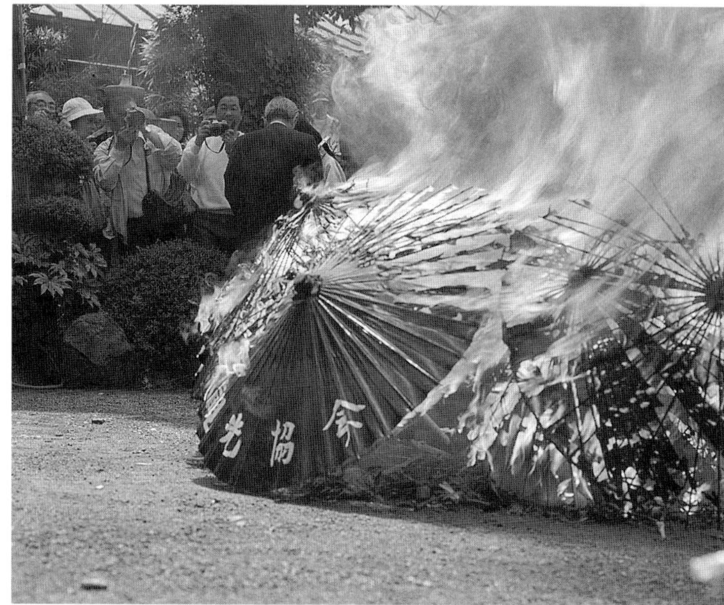

Figs. 16 a,b. Umbrella-burning festival, Odawara City, Kanagawa prefecture

2-2: Making the top notch (*atama rokuro*) and runner or slide (*temoto rokuro*)
(1) The top notch and runner—one fixed at the top, the other movable along the stick—enable one to open and shut an umbrella. The top notch (into which ribs are inserted) and the runner (into which stretchers are inserted) are made as a pair. The process of creating them is the most mechanized in the entire process of umbrella manufacture.

(2) The top notch and runner are made from an ordinary tree called *chisha* (bot. *P. Ehretia ovalifolia Hassk*), a tall, deciduous species growing in the tropics or subtropics. A piece of the tree is cut and hollowed out. Then, the hollowed, tube-like piece, called *marume*, is placed over a shaver to round the exterior (fig. 25). After this process, holes for thread are made in teeth on the top notch and runner; grooves are also made in which to insert ribs and stretchers (fig. 17).

2-3: Attaching the top notch and runner to the stick
Slender vertical holes are made on the upper part of the stick in which to install top and lower springs, called *hajiki* (fig. 26), made from iron or wood. (In the Edo period there was only a single spring at the top.) Then the top notch is fixed at the top of the stick (fig. 27) and the runner is attached further down. This process, called *kurikomi*, nowadays done by umbrella wholesalers, was formerly done by specialists.

Third Stage: Preparing Ribs

3-1: Making ribs (*hone*, figs. 28-31)
(1) There are two types of ribs: external longer ones, here simply called ribs (*oyahone*; literally, "parent bones"), and internal shorter ones, here called stretchers (*shôhone*; literally, "small bones"). Ribs are stuck into the grooves made in the top notch and are then affixed with silk thread (figs. 3, 17). Stretchers are similarly attached to the runner. The outer ends of the stretchers are joined to the ribs at the middle joint (*nakabushi*), one-third of the way down the rib from the top notch (fig. 4, diag. 1*h*). Because of its cone-shape structure, the connected section of stretchers and runner can support the ribs. This structure is very resilient against the power of wind and rain.

(2) Ribs, as well as the stick, are usually made from *madake* (see 2-1, figs. 23, 24). Sometimes, however, a thicker species of bamboo called *môsôchiku* (bot. *Phyllostacys heterocycla*, var. *pubescens Ohwi*) is used.

(3) The manufacture of ribs is only partially mechanized. Bamboo cut to a specified size is immersed in water for several days to soften the skin and kill any bugs and worms that may be living in it. The skin is then scraped off with a knife (fig. 28). An ideal umbrella is one in which all ribs line up neatly in a circle when closed. Each piece of bamboo is marked with a knife or black ink (today with a magic marker) at four points before being split vertically into two pieces. This marking enables the craftsman to reassemble the pieces in their proper order.

(4) The nodes of bamboo, which has already been split vertically into two pieces, become the middle joints (*nakabushi*; see diag. 1*h*), where ribs and stretchers are connected. Then, with a small hatchet (*nata*), the pieces are split again into the number of ribs required (fig. 29). A normal *janome* requires forty-two, forty-four, fifty or fifty-four ribs. The insides of the ribs are shaved thin and round. Also, the sides of the ribs are shaved in a wedge shape (*kusabi-gata*). All ribs are shaved in this manner. In addition, ribs for an umbrella should be made from one piece of bamboo. When a particular piece of bamboo is thick, ribs for more than one umbrella can be produced.

(5) Three holes for thread are drilled in each rib (fig. 30): the first is to attach the rib to the top notch (figs. 3, 17); the second to connect it to a stretcher (figs. 4, 34); and the third to insert thread at the rib tip (fig. 35, diag. 1*i*). In olden times, craftsmen employed a drill called *maikiri* (dancing drill) to make one hole at a time (fig. 31). Today, all three holes are made at once by machine.

3-2: Making stretchers (*shôhone*, fig. 32)
Stretchers are made from what remains of a piece of bamboo after the ribs are taken from it. Small holes are drilled at each end of the stretcher. Then the tip of the stretcher, where it will join a rib, is split about two centimeters deep to enable it to hold the rib. The modern Chinese umbrella is different from the Japanese; in the Chinese, the stretcher is inserted into a slit in the rib. Sometimes the stretchers of *janome*, dance, and large tea-ceremony umbrellas are adorned with decorative thread. If this is the case, several holes are made in each stretcher.

3-3: Dyeing ribs (fig. 33)
Ribs and stretchers of *janome*, parasols and dance umbrellas are dyed black or red-brown. The procedure is a simple one of boiling them in a vat with dyestuff, but the timing is crucial—when boiled too long, bamboo loses its natural oil and will weaken.

Fourth Stage: Preparing the Umbrella Skeleton and Pasting Paper

4-1: Connecting the ribs to the stick
The stick, ribs and stretchers are all connected with silk thread in a process known as *tsunagi*.

(1) First, the top notch is connected to the ribs (figs. 3, 17).
(a) Silk thread is put into a hole in a tooth or prong in the top notch (fig. 17a).
(b) The thread is passed through the hole in a rib and then through the hole in the next tooth (fig. 17b).
(c) When the thread is pulled down, the rib sits between two teeth (fig. 17c). This procedure, in which the top notch is held upside down, is then repeated until all the ribs are connected.

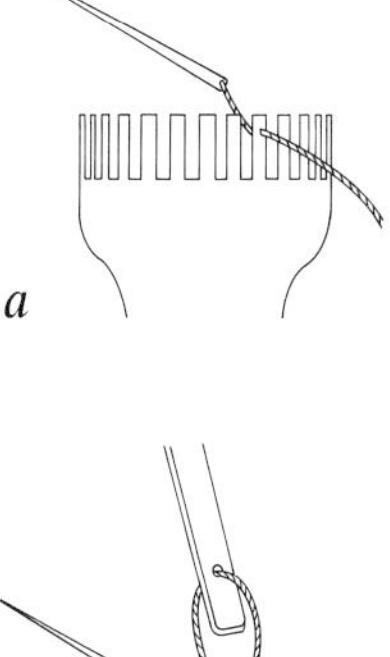

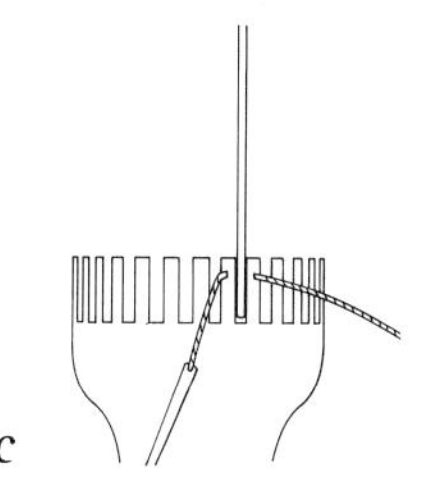

Fig. 17. Connecting top notch to ribs

(2) Thread is then used to connect the runner to the stretchers, and the outer tip of the stretcher to the middle joint (*nakabushi*) of a rib (figs. 4, 34). Finally, the ribs are linked together at their tips (*nokizume*) with a thread (fig. 35). This is a simple procedure performed primarily by women and old people. But it is an important step because the tension of the threads connecting the ribs to the top notch and the stretchers to the runner or slide determines the ease of opening and closing the umbrella.

With this, the final stage of making the skeleton of the umbrella is completed. Many craftsmen have been involved and much time has gone into making the skeleton up to this point. The present appearance of the umbrella will determine its final shape.

4-2: Pasting the paper
There are two ways of pasting paper onto the umbrella skeleton: traditional and new. An explanation of the traditional way follows.

(1) The two kinds of skeleton holder are: Edo (present-day Tokyo) and Kamigata (the Kyoto and Osaka area). The Edo holder is a sort of tripod saddle made of bamboo (no. 3); the Kamigata holder, used in Gifu, is essentially a box (fig. 1). First the skeleton is gently warmed over a charcoal fire to straighten its warped ribs. After this is done, it is spread and placed on the holder.

(2) In order to make the spaces between the ribs even and reinforce the rib tips, tip paper (*nokigami*, fig. 36) is pasted over the thread linking the ribs at their tips. The color of this paper may be indigo, red or pink, depending on the cover paper to be used. There was a practice of stringing additional threads beside the thread at the tip (*nokiito*). These threads are often depicted in woodblock prints and are called "spider's threads" (*kumoito*; no. 30).

(3) Cassava-starch paste, called *tapioka nori* by Japanese craftsmen, contains the prepared flour of the cassava or manioc plant (bot. *Manihot utilissima*). It is brushed on the ribs (fig. 37) before fan-shaped sheets of paper are placed on them (figs. 1, 7, 38). These large sheets, called *hiragami* (flat paper), are pasted onto the lower section of the umbrella cover. The method devised during the Edo period required cutting the sheet to a size equal to three rib spaces (see fig. 6). This is still done by those craftsmen and -women who want to make a higher quality umbrella with less wasted paper. Nowadays, however, often only four sheets—at times even two—are used for the entire umbrella, resulting in a quicker production process. Alignment with the tip paper must be very carefully made.

(4) The movement at the middle joints, where ribs and stretchers are connected, tends to damage the paper, so the craftsman adds reinforcing strips called *nakaokigami* (literally, "paper put in the center") on the interior of the frame (fig. 5).

(5) With the aid of a thread compass centered on the top notch, irregular portions at the top of the *hiragami* are trimmed with a knife. Next, the smaller center band of paper is pasted on. This is the *nakabarigami* ("paper spread in the middle section"); it overlaps a little with the edge of the *hiragami* section of the cover (diag. 1). The paper in the center is also called *kanwa*, referring to the shape of a ring. The *nakabari* paper is usually, but not always, omitted when making *bangasa* (nos. 18, 18a).

(6) The *tenjôgami* (literally, "paper at the upper part," diag. 1*d*) is applied so that it overlaps a little at the edge of the center paper. This *tenjôgami* is pasted up to the top notch in a process called *tenjôbari* (literally, "spreading the upper section").

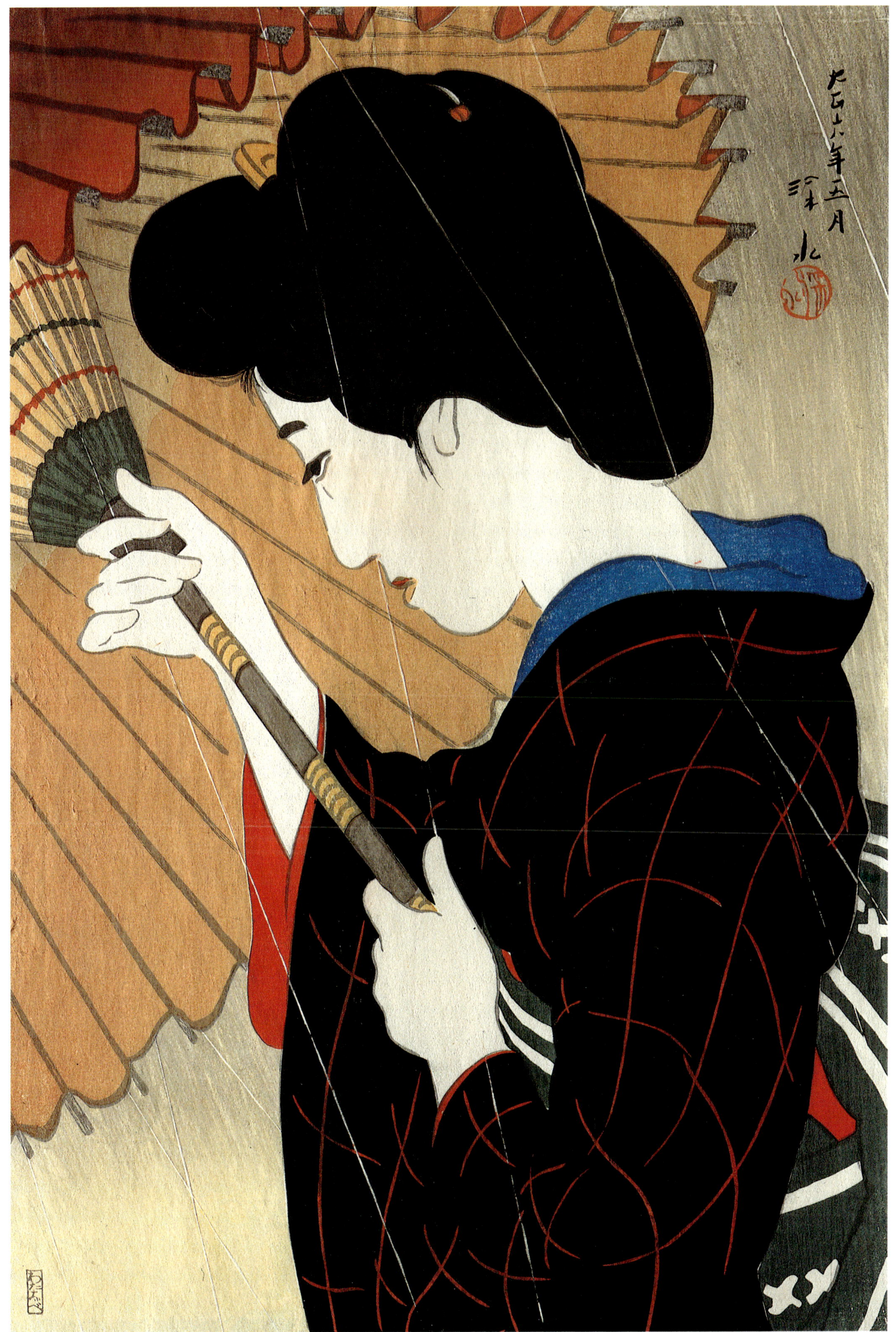

No. 27. Itô Shinsui, *Passing Rain*, 1917

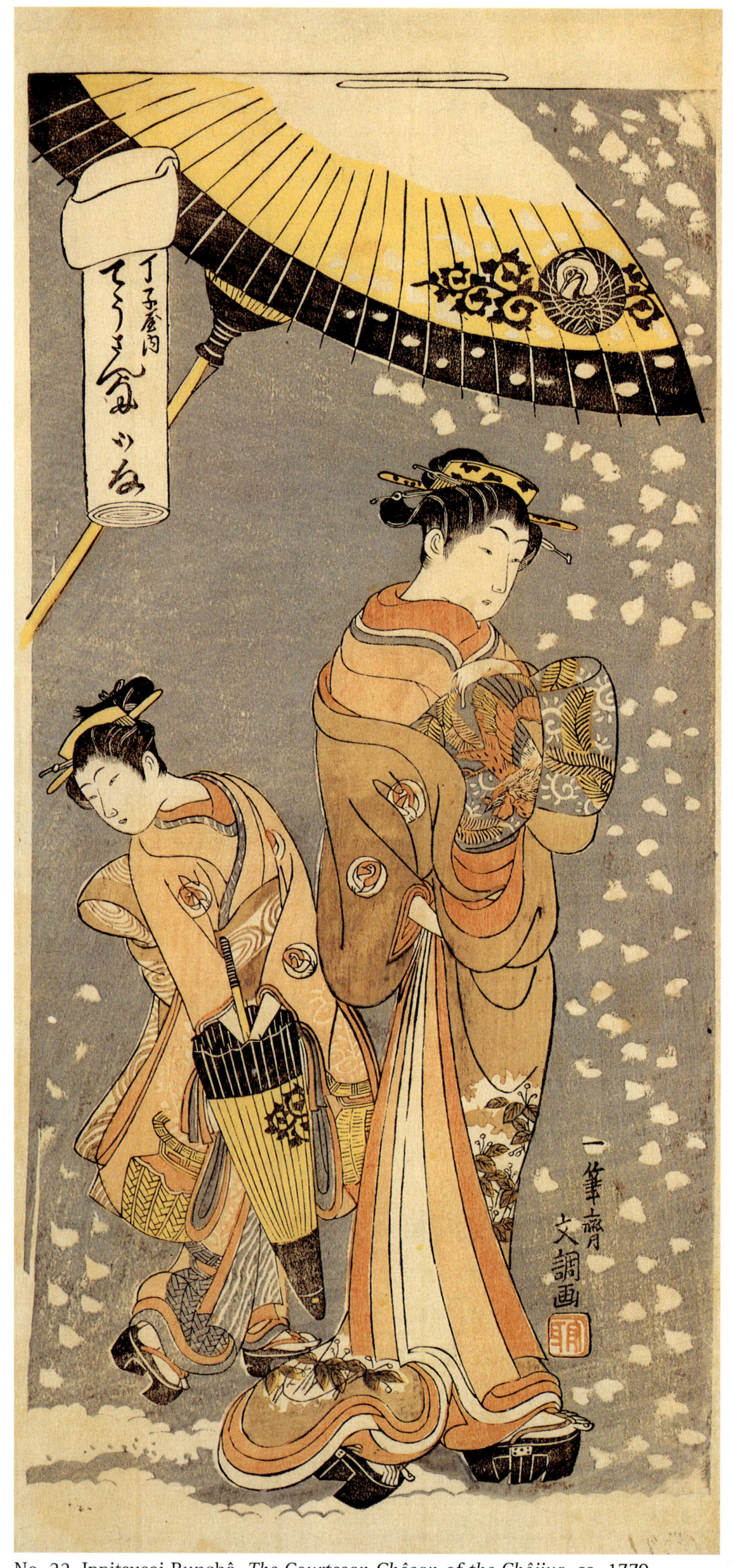

No. 32. Ippitsusai Bunchô, *The Courtesan Chôsan of the Chôjiya*, ca. 1770

(7) The most difficult stage is attaching paper to the top notch. Refined technique is required here. First, the top notch is wrapped with paste-free paper; this is known as the *nakamaki* (middle wrap). Paste is not applied to this paper, in order to facilitate a smooth and flexible movement of the ribs as the umbrella opens and shuts. A few pieces of paper with paste on them are wrapped from the lower part of the *nakamaki* to cover just the upper part of the *tenjôgami* below the top notch. This paper must be stuffed in between the ribs (fig. 39). (The tool used in this process has a small curved blade at one end of the handle and a split, tweezerlike blade on the other.) Then, two layers of rectangular-shaped, ribbonlike paper are pasted around the top notch (fig. 40). These are called the *uwamaki* (top wrap). The curved wooden top notch has now taken the form of a sturdy little cylinder.

(8) Paper is pasted around the base of the stretchers just above the runner. This *temotogami* (literally, "next-to-the-hand paper") strengthens and adds beauty to the umbrella (fig. 41, diag. 2a.c).

(9) After all papers have been applied to an umbrella, it must be placed in the shade for several hours to allow the paste to dry. Then, the umbrella cover is pleated from the top notch down toward the rib tips with a spatulalike tool. After all folds have been correctly adjusted (fig. 42), the umbrella is closed and the pleated cover tightened with a ring made from bamboo, metal or plastic. Any paper sticking out is pushed neatly inside with a spatula.

(10) The top notch, which is already wrapped with more than four layers of paper, is dipped into hot water. The paper is then firmly squeezed to fit the exact shape of the top notch. The dipping should last for only a second.

Fifth Stage: Finishing Touches

5-1: Painting

Paper cut-outs (fig. 22) or printed designs are used for *janome*. For parasols and dance umbrellas, designs are also painted by hand (fig. 43). Designs tend to be based on traditional Japanese floral motifs, such as cherry and plum blossoms. For parasols and dance umbrellas, the cherry-blossom motif is still common today.

5-2: Oiling (fig. 10)

Oiling waterproofs the umbrella, but oil has the disadvantage of acidifying after some years, thereby damaging the paper. Oil in a container, such as a can, should be warmed over charcoal until the temperature reaches about forty-five degrees centigrade. After dipping a rag or thread waste into oil, the artisan spreads it over the cover. If one applies too much oil, it requires an extensive time to dry and can rip the paper. When cold, the oil will harden. After paulownia oil (*kiri-abura*) is added to a base of perilla oil (*e-abura*), the resulting combination becomes smooth. Incidentally, only paulownia or mineral oils are used in China for umbrella making. Perilla oil is a light, yellow, drying oil from the seeds of the perilla plant (especially bot. *Perilla ocomoides*, fam. *Labiatae*). Paulownia oil, sometimes called "wood oil," is made from the seeds of the paulownia tree (bot. *Paulownia imperialis*).

5-3: Lacquering (fig. 44)

The outer surfaces of the ribs are lacquered after the oil has been wiped off with fermented persimmon vinegar. Lacquering must be done with the umbrella tightly folded to prevent any lacquer from getting into the spaces between the ribs. Today, the lacquer used is mostly synthetic; until recently it was natural

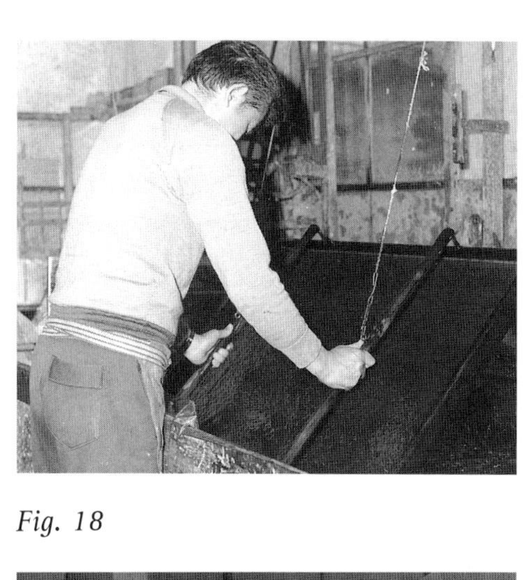

Fig. 18

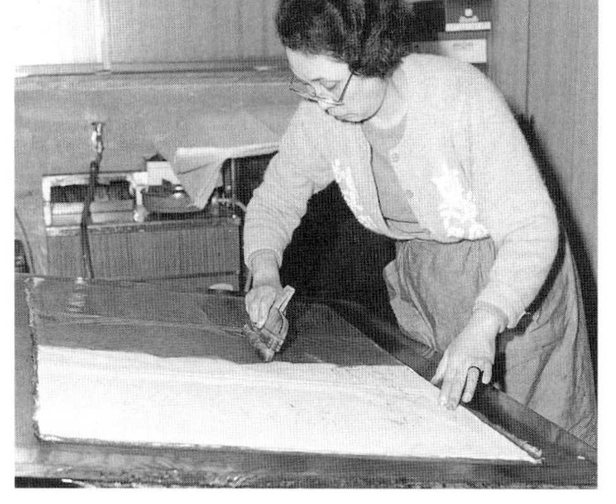

Fig. 19

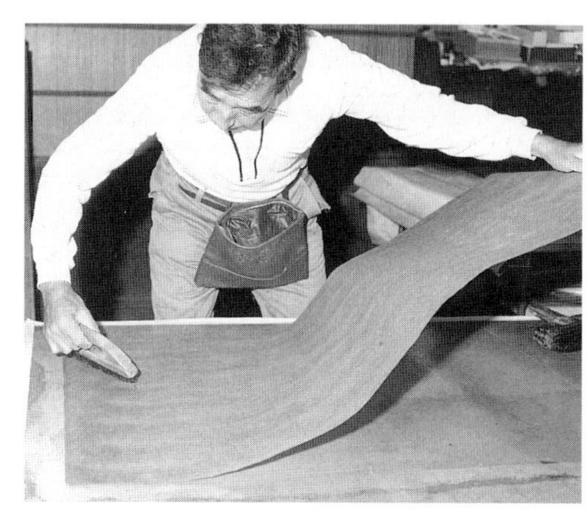

Fig. 20

Fig. 21

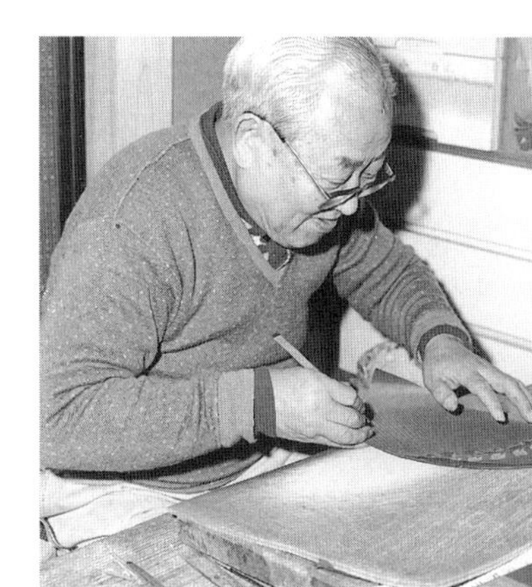

Fig. 22

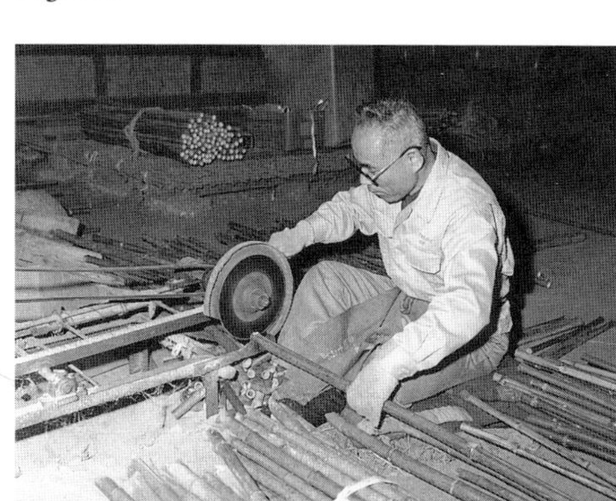

Fig. 23

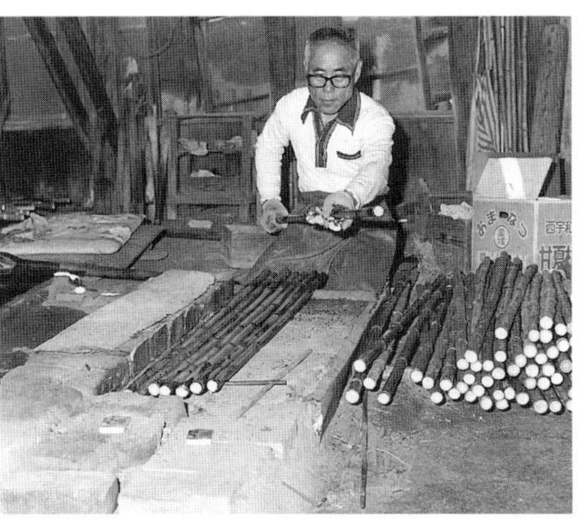

Fig. 24

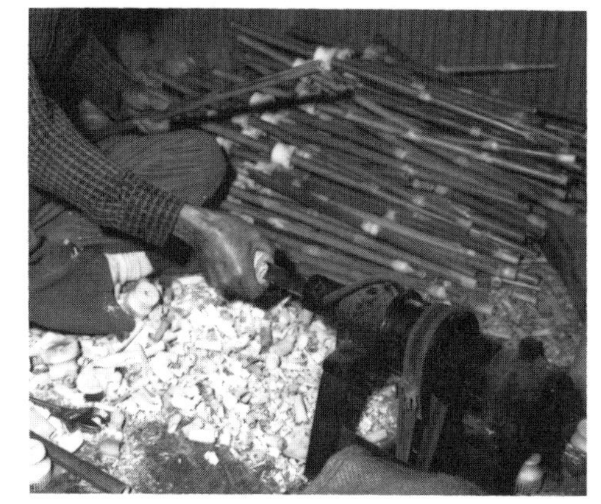

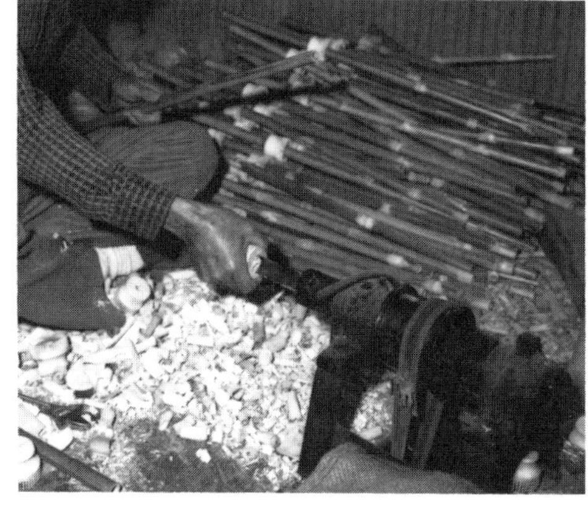

Fig. 25

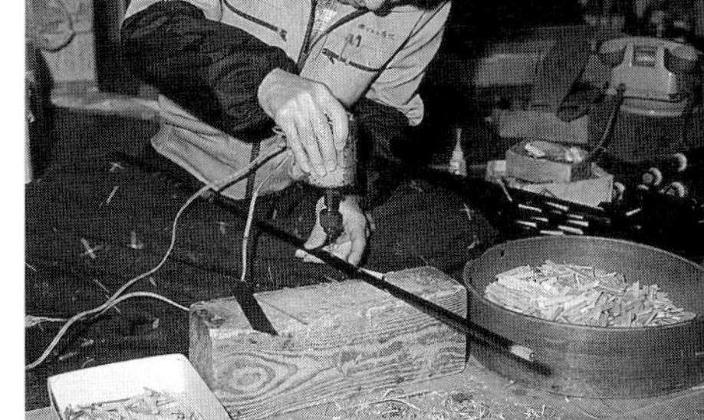

Fig. 26

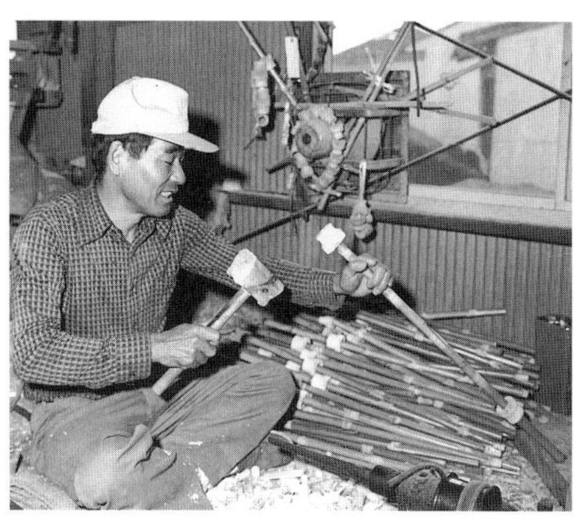

Fig. 27

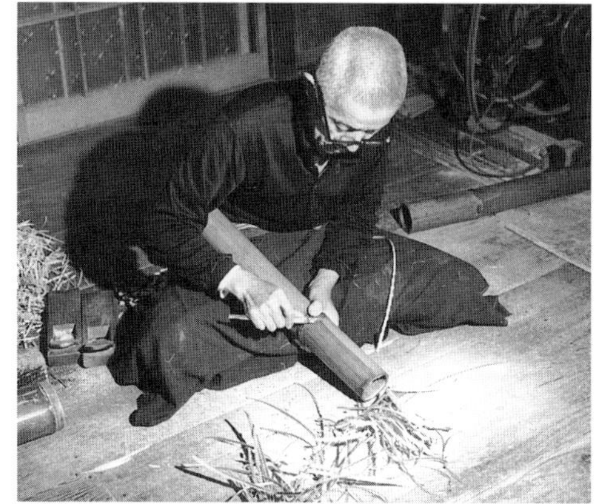

Fig. 28

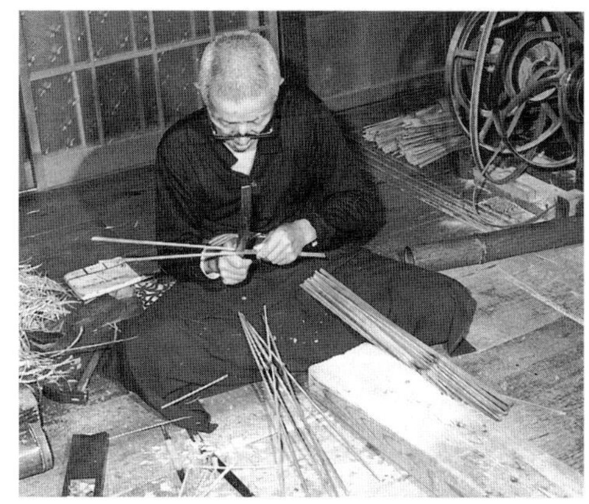

Fig. 29

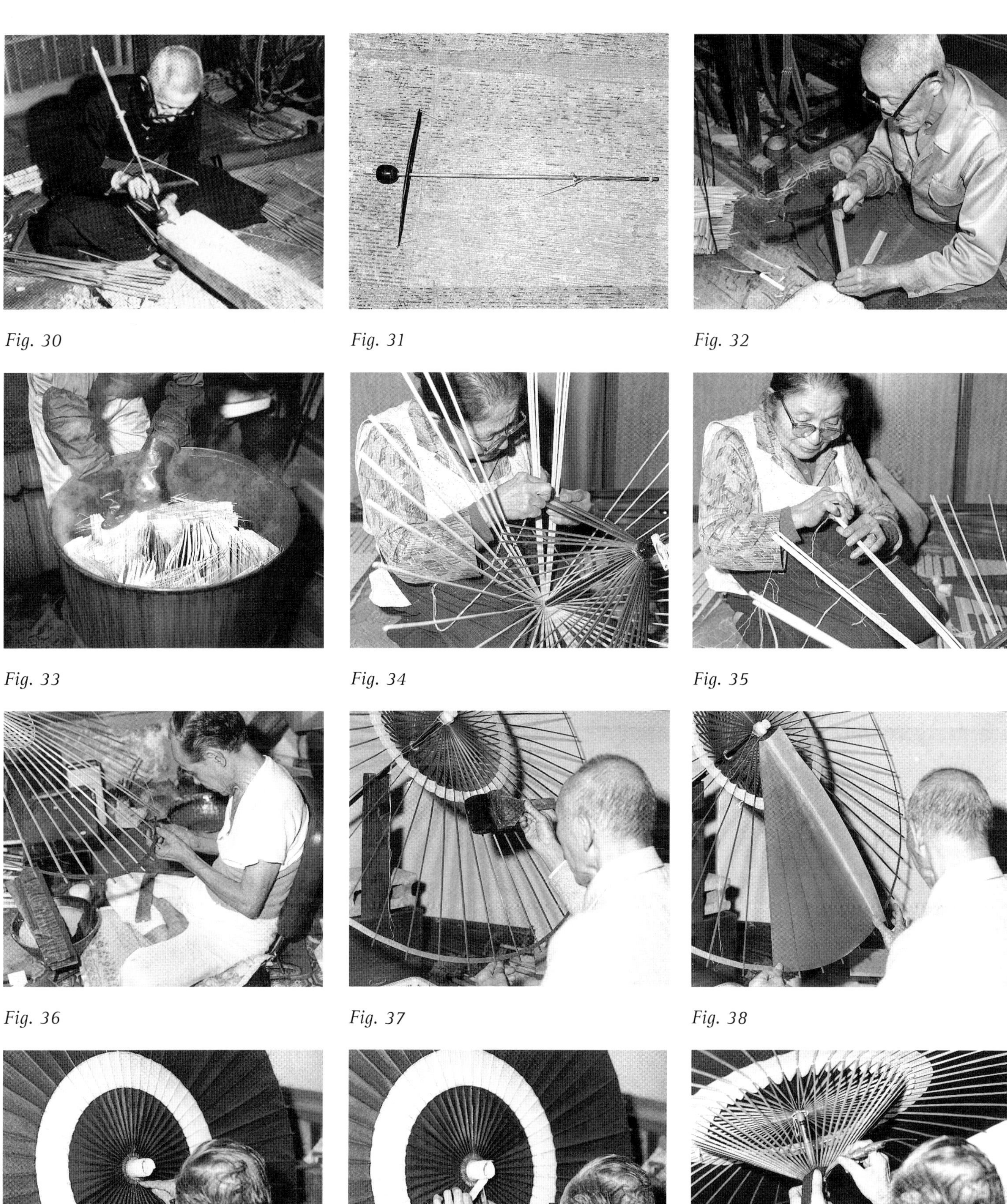

Fig. 30

Fig. 31

Fig. 32

Fig. 33

Fig. 34

Fig. 35

Fig. 36

Fig. 37

Fig. 38

Fig. 39

Fig. 40

Fig. 41

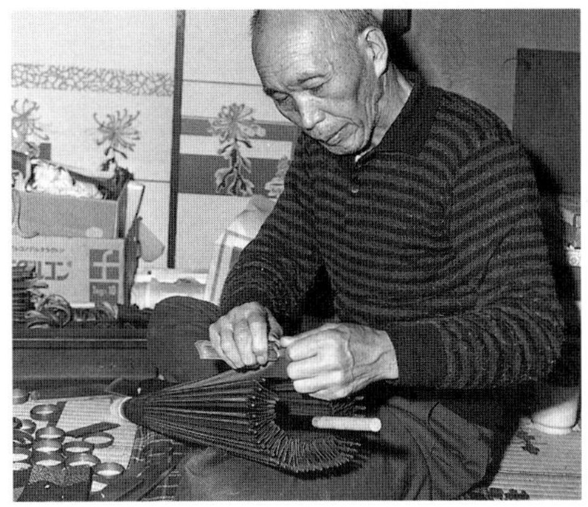

Fig. 42

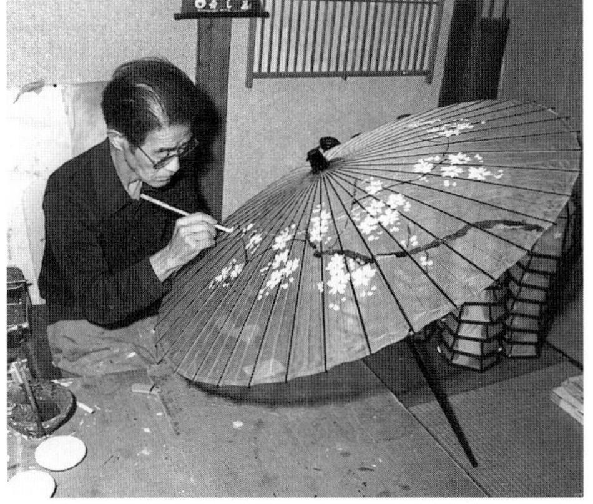

Fig. 43

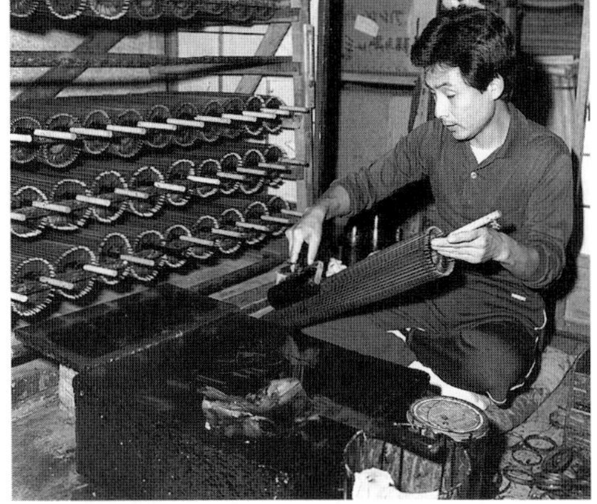

Fig. 44

lacquer, made from the sap of a deciduous tree (bot. *Rhus vernicifera*) of the sumac family (bot. *Anacardiaceae*).

5-4: Adding decorative threads

For *janome*, dance (*maigasa*) and tea-ceremony umbrellas (*nôdate-gasa*), stretchers are decorated with thread embroidery (no. 16a). This decoration is called *kagari* (cross-stitching). There is a variety of decorative thread patterns (diag. 3), including a single thin line called "stick" decoration (*bô kazari*); "single rope" or "mist" (*hitotsu nawa* or *kasumi*); "double rope" (*futatsu nawa*); "triple rope" (*mitsu nawa*); "Chinese bellflower" (*kikyô*), and so on. Decorating is done with red, yellow, blue and green threads. These threads used to be cotton but are now acrylic. Today, the single thin line (*bô kazari*) is the most common pattern since it is not technically complicated. Designs are decided upon by wholesalers. Although thread color combinations may be different depending on the type of umbrella, the designs are almost identical. This decorative work is usually done by women.

5-5: Final attachments and inspection

The umbrella near completion is opened for inspection. Holes and other damages are repaired and smudges removed. Then a strip of rattan (today, usually vinyl) is tightly wound around the handle. The lower tip of the rattan strip is enclosed with a metal cap called *ishizuki*. It is not certain that these metal caps existed during the Edo period. The top notch is covered with protective paper (today, usually vinyl) called *kappa* or *zugami*. This paper used to be fortified by immersing it in persimmon juice, then oiling it. The *kappa* is tightened with silk thread at the indentation in the neck of the top notch and where the tops of all the ribs have been joined together. After the final inspection has been completed, the umbrella is placed in a paper or cloth bag for shipment.

Each stage in the process of manufacturing an umbrella in the Gifu area, as described above, is regarded as an independent profession or craft. Thus the process involves much division of labor by specialized craftsmen. The finished product is stored and sold through wholesalers called *kasa tonya*, who receive orders from shops all over Japan. Wholesalers place orders with umbrella craftsmen involved in each stage of production. The relationship between wholesalers and craftsmen is not one of equal employment, but rather a submissive relationship based on individual contracts. Many umbrellas can be produced with little expense.

The biggest problem facing the umbrella industry in Japan, including that in Gifu, is that few people wish to inherit any stage of the manufacturing process because of the low salaries. Surveys in Gifu show that the number of umbrella wholesalers alone is expected to be halved in the near future. Today, there are only a few umbrella wholesalers in Gifu City. Over half do not have anyone to take over their businesses eventually, and most of these wholesalers are quite old. For these reasons, it is expected that after they are gone, the profession unfortunately will disappear.

When it comes to individual craftsmen, the situation is so precarious that when someone retires or dies, the particular profession in which he or she worked is in danger of becoming extinct. When we consider that the average age of paper-pasting professionals is over seventy, we must be prepared for the likelihood that one of our traditional crafts will soon fade away.

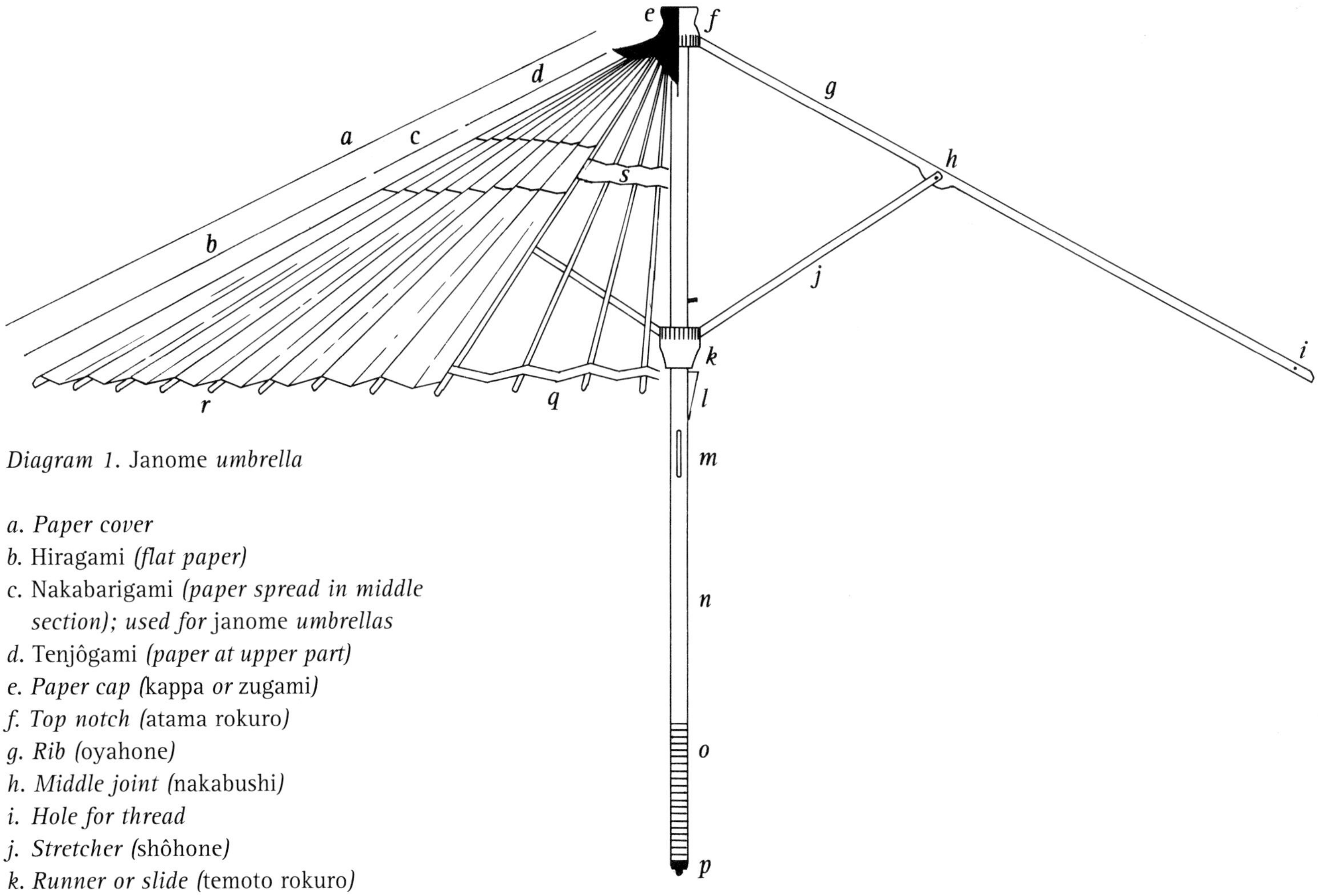

Diagram 1. Janome *umbrella*

a. Paper cover
b. Hiragami *(flat paper)*
c. Nakabarigami *(paper spread in middle section); used for* janome *umbrellas*
d. Tenjôgami *(paper at upper part)*
*e. Paper cap (*kappa *or* zugami*)*
*f. Top notch (*atama rokuro*)*
*g. Rib (*oyahone*)*
*h. Middle joint (*nakabushi*)*
i. Hole for thread
*j. Stretcher (*shôhone*)*
*k. Runner or slide (*temoto rokuro*)*
*l. Top spring (*ue-hajiki*)*
*m. Lower spring (*shita-hajiki*)*
*n. Stick (*e*)*
*o. Rattan-wrapped handle (*tômaki-e*)*
*p. Metal cap (*ishizuki*)*
*q. Tip paper (*nokigami*)*
*r. Rib tip (*nokizume*)*
s. Nakaokigami (*"center-placed" paper*)

Diagram 2. Umbrella open and closed

Diagram 2a

*a. Top notch (*atama rokuro*)*
*b. Cross-stitched decorative thread (*kagari ito*)*
*c. Reinforcing paper above runner (*temotogami*)*
*d. Runner or slide (*temoto rokuro*)*
*e. Top spring (*ue-hajiki*)*
*f. Lower spring (*shita-hajiki*)*

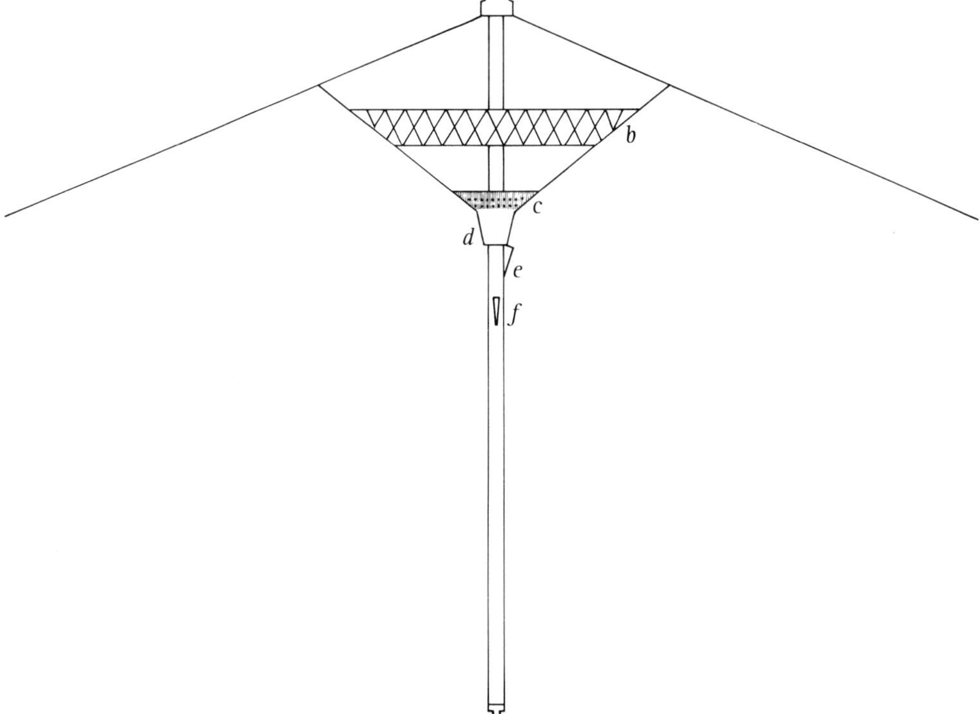

For diagrams 2b and 2c, see overleaf.

Diagram 2 (cont.). Umbrella open and closed

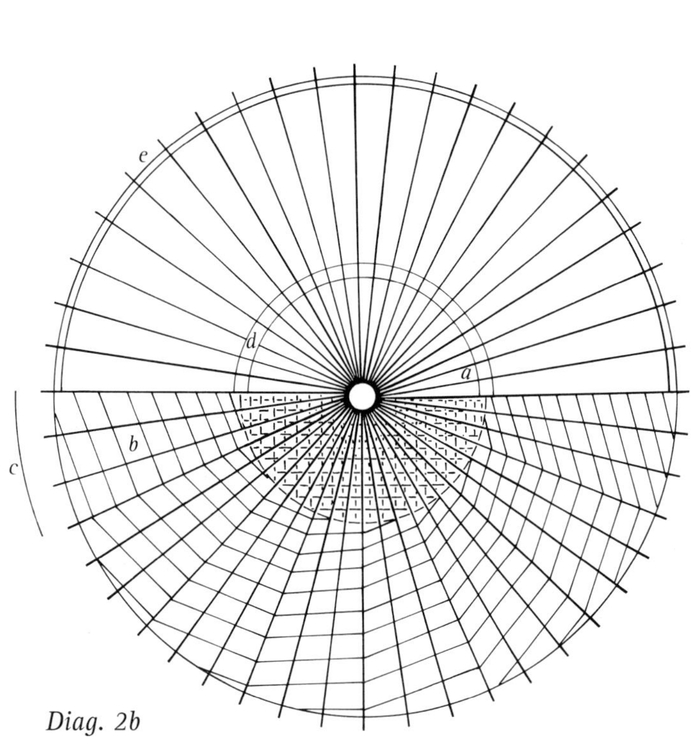

Diag. 2b

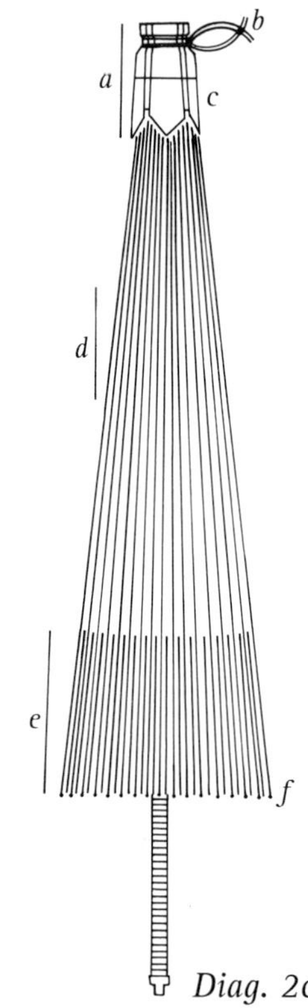

Diag. 2c

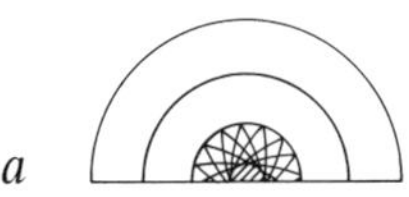

a

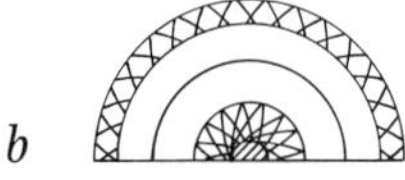

b

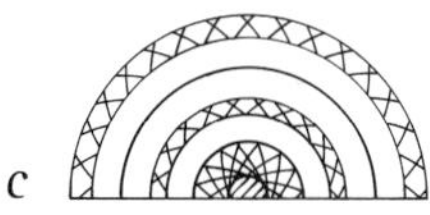

c

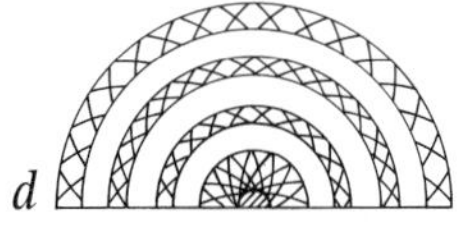

d

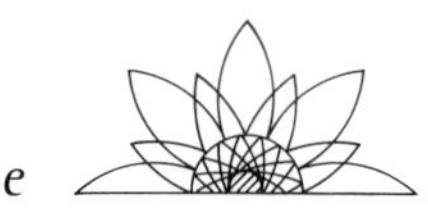

e

Diag. 3

Diagram 2b

a. Tenjôgami *(paper at the upper part of the cover)*
b. Hiragami *(flat paper): the main body of the cover*
c. The paper is cut to cover a three-rib section.
d. Nakaokigami *("center-placed" paper): paper strip reinforcing joints of stretchers and ribs*
e. Nokigami *(tip paper)*

Diagram 2c

*a. Head (*atama*)*
*b. Head thread (*atama himo*)*
*c. Paper cap (*kappa or zugami*)*
*d. Body (*dô*)*
*e. "Eaves" (*noki*)*
*f. Rib tips (*nokizume*)*

Diagram 3. Decorative thread patterns on stretchers

*a. Stick or thin line (*bô*)*
*b. Single rope (*hitotsu nawa*) or mist (*kasumi*)*
*c. Double rope (*futatsu nawa*)*
*d. Triple rope (*mitsu nawa*)*
*e. Chinese bellflower (*kikyô*)*

Diagram 4 (opposite page)

*a. Maple-leaf umbrella (*momijigasa*)*
*b. Priest or doctor's umbrella (*sôigasa*);* janome*-type umbrella used by Confucian scholars, priests and doctors*
*c. Top notch: 1) with indentation for tying on a protective paper cap (*kappa*), and 2) lacquered black, without indentation*
*d. "Clipped-fingernail" umbrella (*tsumaoregasa*)*
*e. Festival or dance umbrella (*furyûgasa*)*
*f. Ceremonial umbrella in storage bag (*fukuroiregasa*)*
*g. Child's parasol (*kogasa*), here decorated with pictures of Kabuki actors*
h. "Spear-bearer" janome *umbrella (*yakko janomegasa*)*
*i. Snake's-eye umbrella (*janomegasa*)*
j. Bangasa, *here inscribed with the character* wa, *meaning "harmony" or "peace"*

Diagram 4. Some 19th-century umbrella types

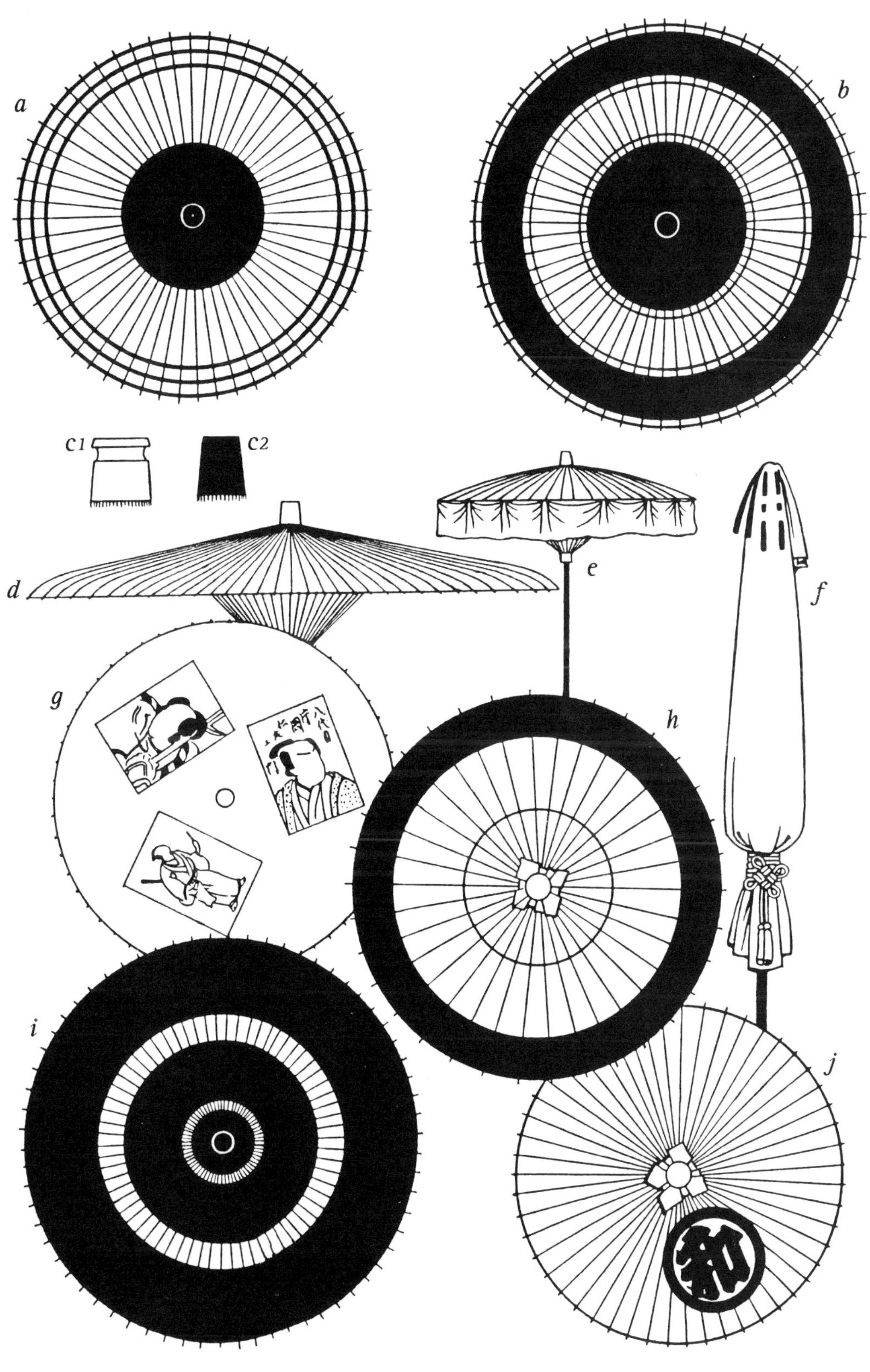

Rain and Snow: The Umbrella in Japanese Art

Harusame ya	The spring rain–
monogatari yuku	telling stories to each other they pass by:
mino to kasa	raincoat and umbrella.
	–Yosa Buson (1716-1783)[1]

The paper umbrella, like the kimono and the fan, is intimately linked in everyone's mind with the image of old Japan. Almost no early umbrellas survive, however. Unlike the round or folding fan, a fashion acccssory that has always attracted both artists and calligraphers as a medium, the cover of the umbrella was rarely thought of as a surface on which to paint. At most, it was decorated with designs of birds and flowers. As a result, umbrellas were not considered works of art and were not collected as such. Most umbrellas, however beautifully crafted, are strictly utilitarian objects for everyday use. Made of bamboo and paper, the Japanese umbrella is fragile, easily damaged, and soon discarded.

It is difficult now to find umbrellas in Japan that predate World War II. One reason so few survive is that the oil used for waterproofing has the inevitable and unfortunate side effect of darkening and weakening the paper. An oiled umbrella has a lifespan of only about three years before it begins to stick together and tear when opened. There used to be itinerant traders in Kyoto and Edo (present-day Tokyo) who roamed the streets calling out "Any old ribs?" (*Furuhone gozai?*) They purchased old umbrellas so that the ribs could be stripped clean and sold to an umbrella maker for repapering.[2] Umbrella covers were also recycled; it seems that the oiled paper was used by butchers to wrap fatty cuts of meat (fig. 45).

Today, with the craft of making traditional umbrellas in decline, an old, worn-out model is more likely to be offered up at the annual umbrella-burning festival in Odawara City and in Kagoshima (see figs. 16a,b).[3] The festival, as Hiroshi Yabushita has mentioned earlier, celebrates the deeds of two 12th-century samurai, the Soga brothers, who are said to have used burning umbrellas to light up a battlefield at night. The very existence of such a festival is a reminder of the special role that the umbrella has played in Japanese life, a role commemorated in literature and also in art.

Origins of the Umbrella

The umbrella, now universal, seems to have originated in hot climates (Mesopotamia, Egypt, India) as a form of protection against the sun. A large shade-giving leaf was perhaps the initial inspiration. Broad leaves or woven reeds were used first to shade and honor the elite–royalty and priests. A parasol is carried over Sargon I in an Akkadian relief from Mesopotamia dating from

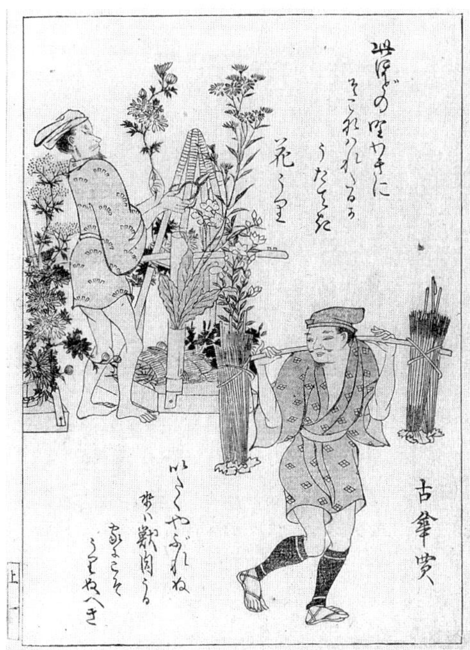

Fig. 45. Keisai Masayoshi (1764-1824), Flower Seller and Used-Umbrella Man. *From* Imayô shokunin-zukushi uta-awase *(Present-day artisans compared in verses), 1825. Color woodblock-printed illustrated book. The British Museum, London*

Flower seller:
Kono hodo no
nowaki ni
sokonawaretaru ka
utateki

Will these autumn gusts
lay my flowers to waste?
Oh my, what a worry!

Used-umbrella man:
Itaku yaburenu
kasa wa jûniku
uru ie ni koso
urinu-beki

Rotten beat-up umbrellas—
I should be able to sell them,
if only to the butcher!
(Translations by John Carpenter)

the third millenium B.C.[4] The parasol reappears as part of the ceremonial regalia of kingship in Assyrian reliefs of the 9th century B.C. (fig. 46). The small cover supported on a long stick is often fringed; stretchers, top notch and what appears to be a runner are clearly visible in most examples. At least one Assyrian parasol is shown with a small pin or stick inserted horizontally just below the runner as though holding it in place. This would suggest that the Assyrians manufactured the first collapsible umbrella. As far as one can tell from representations in Assyrian art, the parasol was a royal prerogative. The earliest remains of an actual umbrella also come from this part of the world: a wooden top notch with eight socket fittings for ribs and fragments of the ribs themselves were found in an 8th-century Phrygian tomb at the ancient city of Gordion in Turkey.[5]

In Egypt the umbrella was associated with the vault of heaven—the source of both sun and rain. Nut, the mother goddess of ancient Egypt, who represents the sky, evoked a gigantic parasol, her body arching over the whole earth. The Egyptian hieroglyph in the shape of an umbrella sometimes signified royalty. It also connoted the shadow in which a person's reproductive powers were thought to be found. T. S. Crawford suggests that "the carrying of the early umbrella could, therefore, have had some sexual significance."[6] Sometime before the 8th century B.C. the Greeks used sunshades in fertility rites connected with Demeter, goddess of the harvest, and her daughter Persephone, goddess of spring. Later the umbrella was a symbol of productivity at festivals in honor of Dionysus. About the 3rd century B.C. the sunshade spread from Greece to Rome, where it became an expensive costume accessory first for women, and by the 6th century A.D. at the latest, for the occasional male as well. The umbrella developed further in a liturgical context as part of ecclesiastical regalia during the Middle Ages. We know that by the late 16th century in Italy leather sunshades were used by horsemen, but the parasol did not come into common use in France until about 1620 and in England not until well after 1700. Umbrellas of oiled cloth (silk, linen or cotton) are known from the 17th century.[7] European parasols by the 17th century had richly embroidered or painted silk or leather covers; and the runners were apparently held up by a pin through the stick.[8]

The Umbrella in India and China

Indian rulers, beginning with Emperor Aśoka (272-232 B.C.), received a white umbrella, symbolizing sovereign power over the world, at their coronation ceremonies.[9] Honorific parasols, often multitiered and gorgeously bejeweled, have retained their importance in parts of India, Southeast Asia, and Africa. When the Laotian king was cremated in 1961, for example, his gilded funeral pyre was surrounded by a dozen seven-tiered umbrellas.[10] The parasol became a sign of respect in Buddhist imagery in India, as well. In the aniconic phase of Indian Buddhist art, umbrella discs were the crowning element of the domed stupa, or relic shrine, the earliest type of Buddhist monument, and relief carvings on stupas from the 1st century B.C. onward also show the umbrella, with a small mushroom-shaped cover and thin ribs, being worshiped as a surrogate for the Buddha or being held over something symbolic of him (fig. 47).[11] A stone umbrella measuring 10 feet in diameter was excavated at Sârnâth, near Benares, with a colossal statue of the standing Buddha Shakyamuni (Sârnâth Archaeological Museum). Dedicated by the priest Bala in the 2nd century A.D., the figure is one of the earliest-known statues of the Buddha.[12]

Long before the arrival of Buddhism, a circular canopy with cosmic decoration was associated with heaven in China. The umbrella had special significance for the Chinese as early as the Zhou dynasty (1045-255 B.C.). The *Zhou li* (Rites of

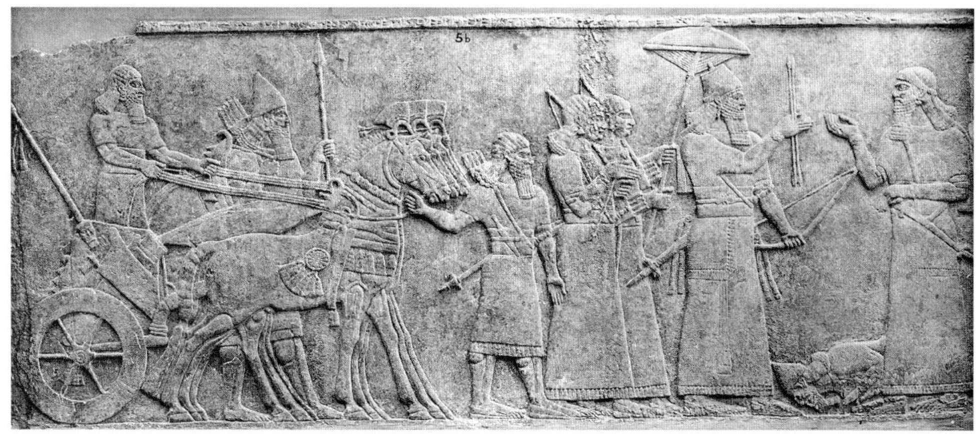

Fig. 46. Royal Procession, *from the Northwest Palace of King Assurnasirapli II, Neo-Assyrian, 883-859 B.C. Alabaster relief. The British Museum, London*

Zhou) identified the twenty-eight ribs of a chariot parasol as representing stars; the central stick symbolized the cosmic pillar, axis of the universe, and the square chariot was the earth.[13] Carried over Zhou kings, the umbrella signified omnipotence. High officials who served the king were also permitted umbrellas. A commentary on the *Zhou li* notes that umbrellas functioned as status symbols, and also served the practical needs of protection from rain and sun.[14]

The earliest image of an umbrella in China is on a silk funerary painting found covering a wooden coffin chamber in a tomb dating from the 4th century B.C. Discovered in 1972 in Zidanku, Changsha, in Hunan province, the painting shows an aristocratic male figure riding on the back of a dragon; over the man's head is a large round parasol.[15] On Han-dynasty tomb reliefs (206 B.C.-A.D. 220) carved on stone or impressed on clay tiles, aristocrats ride in horse-drawn chariots under umbrella-shaped canopies of different sizes and colors (both blue and white are specifically cited in Han records) with clearly defined ribs; tassels are attached to the rims of some of the grander examples.[16] All the evidence suggests that the umbrella was a bureaucratic and Confucian class signifier. In recent years archaeologists have excavated the skeletons of a number of spectacular Han metal frames for chariot canopies. Joseph Needham, in his authoritative *Science and Civilization in China*, identifies the first collapsible parasol as the very large one that the usurper Wang Mang, who ruled from 8 B.C. to A.D. 21, had made as a magic baldachin for a ceremonial four-wheeled chariot.[17]

When Buddhism arrived in China from India during the Han dynasty, it came equipped with religious paraphernalia such as silk banners and canopies or umbrellas. The earliest-known Chinese Buddhist image beneath an umbrella is a small, late-4th- or early-5th-century gilt-bronze seated Buddha.[18] Parasols used in secular life in China were often squared, with tassels at the corners, as seen in early figure paintings (fig. 48) and in images of high-ranking donors in Buddhist caves and on carved stele of the 5th and 6th centuries.[19]

In Chinese paintings umbrellas are in evidence as part of everyday life by the 12th century, and they were no doubt in use much earlier. Large umbrellas of paper or sedge (some are torn) cover the open-air food stalls lining the streets in a marvelous handscroll by Zhang Zeduan datable to between 1111 and 1126 (Palace Museum, Beijing). The scroll documents with impressive detail scenery and life along the river and in the Northern Song capital of Bianliang (modern Kaifeng, Henan province) on the day of the Qingming Festival. Some of these large umbrellas are clearly held open with a pin or small stick inserted horizontally just below the runner; some smaller models are shown closed.[20] There is also at least one parasol of fringed silk on a long stick, apparently carried over a person of rank who is not visible. Blue-green silk parasols had initially been restricted to princes of the Chinese imperial family. Such proscriptions were difficult to enforce, however. By the 13th century almost all government officials

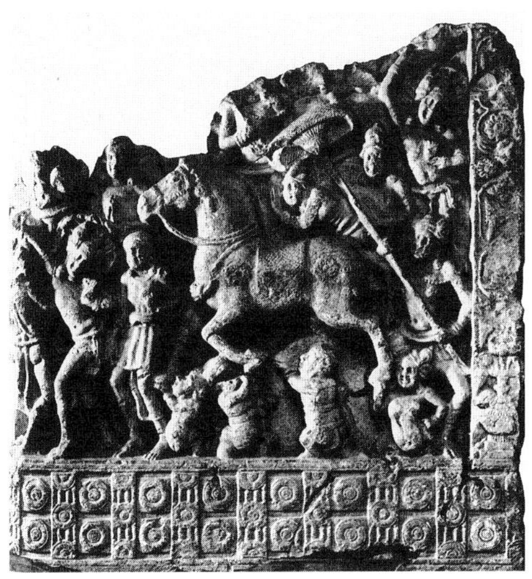

Fig. 47. The Great Departure, *a scene from the life of the Buddha, 2nd century* A.D. *Limestone relief. Amarâvatî Stupa, India*
Photo: Eliot Elisofon, Life Magazine
© Time Warner, Inc.

were using silk parasols as signs of prestige. According to historian Jacques Gernet:

> From the end of the tenth century permission was granted to certain officials to carry these parasols; then it was granted to women of the palace when they paid visits to town. In 1012 a faint effort was made to stem the tide; only members of the imperial family were to have rights to the parasol. A little later, there was not a single official who did not strut about with his parasol.[21]

The ordinary rain umbrella also appears in Chinese paintings. In *Landscape in Wind and Rain*, a 13th-century Southern Song hanging scroll, a man on a mountain path leans into the rain with his umbrella as he heads toward a temple complex (fig. 49). For the Chinese artist the little figure going about his business amidst the grandeur of a mountain scene signifies rusticity, a genre touch that is incidental in terms of the overall composition. Given the Southern Song concern with the perfect moment, however, the open umbrella serves as a marker to remind the viewer of the element of rain, which is reinforced by the diagonal wash of ink sweeping down from the upper right.

The First Japanese Umbrellas

The umbrella was almost certainly introduced to Japan from the mainland, but its early history is vague. Until the 17th century, most Japanese never used an umbrella. They made do with water-repellent straw rain capes (*mino*), oiled paper raincoats (*kappa*) or broad-brimmed round hats (*kasa*). Hats, tied under the chin, were made of such things as sedge, straw, bamboo skin and cypress bark. "Hat" is written, appropriately enough, with the Chinese character (*kanji*) for "standing" placed beneath another meaning "bamboo." In Japan, however, this "hat" character was also used for "umbrella," likewise pronounced *kasa*; by the 10th and 11th centuries the addition of a prefix, as in *ôgasa* (large umbrella) or *mikasa* (honorable umbrella), clarified its alternate meaning.

At some point "umbrella" came to be written with a Chinese character resembling four people standing under a tent on a stick (Ch. *san*). This character, which is the one used for "umbrella" today, can be read not only as *kasa* but also as *karakasa*, a word known to have been in use by 1000, although its etymology is uncertain. *Kara* means China or Korea and may refer to the foreign origin of the umbrella, but it can also mean a stick (in the sense of "a hat on a stick") or a mechanical device, such as a slide for opening and closing the umbrella. The earliest Chinese word for cover, canopy or umbrella (Ch. *gai*) was written with a different character; since early times this has been read by the Japanese as *kinugasa* (silk parasol).[22]

Umbrellas in Japanese art predate textual references. Unglazed earthenware cylinders and hollow sculptures known as *haniwa* (clay ring) decorated the tombs of the ruling class during the 4th to 7th centuries. One of the largest and most elegant *haniwa* from the early 4th century represents a ceremonial parasol or sunshade (fig. 50). Parasol *haniwa* were generally positioned at a sacred place at the center or corner of the tomb and faced the house *haniwa*.[23] Round or square in shape, they are sufficiently stylized to make it difficult to tell what the objects represented were really like. Presumably the functional prototype was covered with silk, as were contemporary Chinese parasols (see fig. 48).

The Japanese tombs with *haniwa* also contained bronze mirrors, symbols of power for the aristocracy. A unique Japanese example is decorated on the back

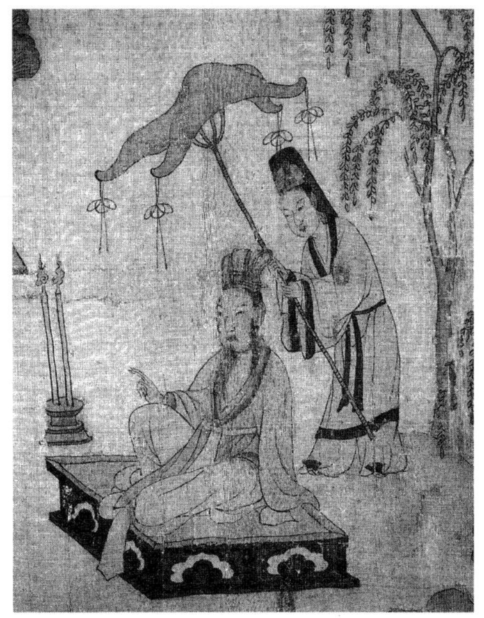

Fig. 48. Artist unknown, Nymph of the Luo River *(detail), Song dynasty, 12th-13th century. Handscroll; ink and color on silk. H. 9 7/16 in. (24 cm.). Freer Gallery of Art, Arthur M. Sackler Gallery, Washington, D.C.*

This scroll illustrates a famous 3rd-century prose poem and is a faithful copy of a composition associated with the painter Gu Kaizhi (ca. 344-ca. 406). In this detail from the last section of the scroll the poet is seated on a dais with a pair of lighted candles beside him to indicate that the time is night; the silk parasol is obviously intended not as a sunshade but as an emblem of status.

with four houses (fig. 51). An open parasol with a very long stick stands in front of the dwelling with a raised floor—an emblem of the high rank of the person who lived there. A much smaller parasol stands beside the pit dwelling opposite.[24] Wall paintings from Takamatsuzuka, a late-7th-century tomb excavated in Nara prefecture, are among the earliest paintings in Japan to depict the costumes of elite men and women of the period. The occupant of the tomb, probably a Korean aristocrat in service at the Japanese court, is shown standing beneath a tall, tasseled silk canopy on a long stick held by an attendant.[25]

The first written record of umbrellas in Japan is found in the *Nihon shoki* (Chronicle of Japan), an official history of Japan completed in 720. It mentions two crown princes during the reign of Emperor Seinei (480-84) who entered the imperial residence in a carriage or palanquin (*kuruma*) under a blue parasol.[26] The parasol was used by the upper classes both as a sunshade to protect their light skins (a matter of concern in Asia as well as in the West) and as an emblem of status. Poems in the 8th-century *Man'yôshû* (Collection of ten thousand leaves), Japan's first poetry anthology, mention silk parasols or canopies (*kinugasa*). For example, Kakinomoto no Hitomaro (active ca. 685-705), describing the prince's return from hunting, likens the full moon to his personal canopy:

> Our mighty lord,
> having caught the sky-traversing moon
> in his net,
> makes it his silken canopy![27]

The *Nihon shoki* also relates that a parasol was brought to the Japanese court as part of a diplomatic mission in A.D. 552. Hoping to enlist support in battle against a neighboring kingdom, the ruler of the Korean kingdom of Paekche sent gifts to the emperor of Japan. They included one gilt-bronze statue of the Buddha Shakyamuni, Buddhist texts, a banner, and a parasol or canopy.[28] This citation in the *Nihon shoki* is the first recorded contact between Buddhism and the Japanese court. The Korean banner and canopy must have been intended for installation over the altar in a temple.

The Umbrella in the Heian Period (794-1185)

Like everything else in Japan, umbrella usage was subject to endless rules and regulations. Even as early as the Heian period, social status determined the color, size and decoration of an umbrella, probably on the basis of Chinese precedents. A 9th-century compendium of rituals lists the colors appropriate for *kinugasa*, the silk brocade parasols carried by umbrella bearers. The crown prince's umbrella had a purple cover lined in dark purple-red—purple and red were expensive dyes reserved for the court—with tassels at the four corners. For imperial princes the tasseled cover was purple, lined in vermilion. Courtiers' umbrellas were lined in vermilion, with deep green covers for the First Rank, indigo (*kon*) for the Second and Third Ranks, and blue (*aoi*) for the Fourth. Only courtiers of the First Rank were allowed tassels.[29]

The *Engi shiki* (Procedures of the Engi era), fifty volumes of government regulations from the early 10th century, also mentions umbrellas in its endless lists of ritual paraphernalia. Among the ceremonial articles for the Shrine of the Great Deity at Ise, for example, the *Engi shiki* cites two silk umbrellas covered with lavender damask, lined with scarlet damask, the top notch and rib tips covered with brocade and hung with lavender braided tassels.[30] It also notes that umbrellas with long sticks could only be used by senior courtiers of the Third Rank and above. Among the luxury items in the possession of a princess

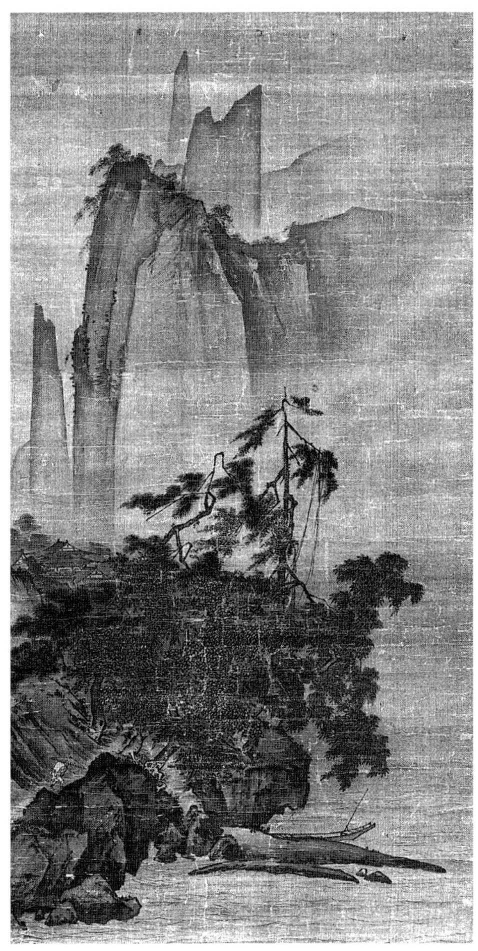

Fig. 49. Attributed to Ma Yuan, Landscape in Wind and Rain, *Southern Song, 13th century. Hanging scroll; ink and color on silk. Seikadô Collection, Tokyo*

consecrated to the Kamo Shrines were two large umbrellas (*ôgasa*) with lacquered sticks and cord ties.[31] During the enthronement ceremony, when the emperor entered, one court noble with the rank of carriage attendant carried the imperial sedge umbrella; one member of the Kobe clan of *sukune* rank (a hereditary order of nobility) and one member of the Kasatori (umbrella-bearer) clan of *atae* (chieftain) rank together carried the cords of the umbrella and pushed themselves forward on their knees as they performed their duties.

The Kobe and Kasatori cited in the *Engi shiki* were hereditary groups of umbrella bearers.[32] A gentleman never carried his own umbrella. Throughout the medieval period, umbrellas were for the most part restricted to the social elite and especially to men, namely courtiers, warriors and priests. In the Heian period upper-class women rarely ventured out of doors, unless it was in an ox-drawn carriage, and thus had little need of rain gear. In illustrated handscrolls dating from as early as the end of the 12th century, one often sees long-stick umbrellas (*nagaegasa*) stored in protective white cloth bags and carried like spears by umbrella bearers or servants, ready for emergency use.

What we now think of as a typically Japanese umbrella (*wagasa*) evolved in the mid-Heian period. Such umbrellas are shown for the first time in a set of early-12th-century scrolls in the Tokugawa Art Museum, Nagoya, illustrating *The Tale of Genji* (*Genji monogatari*), the novel written around the year 1000 by Murasaki Shikibu. Paintings of rain scenes that feature umbrellas accompany two chapters, "The Wormwood Patch" ("Yomogiu," chap. 15) and "The Eastern Cottage" ("Azumaya," chap. 50). These umbrellas appear to have large white covers with narrow, black-lacquered ribs and stretchers.

In "The Wormwood Patch" Prince Genji stops off on a rainy night in the fourth month to visit the reclusive Safflower Princess, a lady he had once courted ten years earlier (fig. 52). She lives in a now-dilapidated, gloomy mansion, the neglected grounds giving the appearance of a jungle. Genji's attendant, Koremitsu, who was always with him on such expeditions,

> beat at the grass with a horsewhip. The drops from the trees were like a chilly autumn shower.
>
> "I have an umbrella," said Koremitsu. "These groves shed the most fearful torrents."
>
> Genji's feet and ankles were soaking. Even in the old days the passage through the south gallery had been more obstacle than passage. Now the gallery had caved in, and Genji's entry was a most ungraceful one. He was glad there were no witnesses.[33]

The princess is not shown–she was no great beauty and preferred to hide behind bamboo blinds and curtains. Only her maid is visible peeking from behind the curtains on the veranda. Both men wear full-sleeved court robes and tall, lacquered gauze hats (*eboshi*) appropriate for informal attire. They are depicted with lowered heads, concentrating on their footing. Genji's large, ungainly black-lacquered shoes are not conducive to speedy movement.

It is a simple but dramatically effective composition. The artist conveys the contrast as well as the expectant tension between the protagonists, Genji and the unseen princess, by placing them in opposite corners, divided by the empty expanse of the garden, which forms a large parallelogram. The initial impact of the illustration depends on this space separating the men on the left from the maid on the right; the viewer is given an all-encompassing bird's-eye view, an

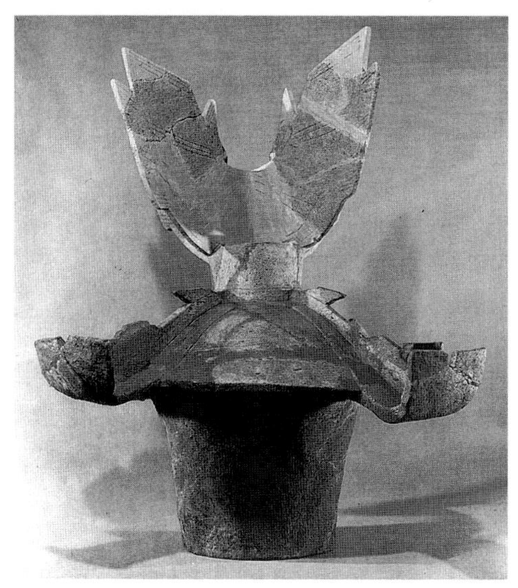

Fig. 50. Parasol Haniwa, *early Kofun period (250-600), early 4th century. Clay. H. 36 5/8 in. (93 cm.). University of Kyoto*

elevated vantage point that Japanese artists tend to favor. Strong black accents demarcate the triangular configuration at the lower left, balancing the diagonal of the veranda. The umbrella frames Genji like a spotlight, emphasizing his role as the hero arriving to rescue the lonely princess and make her dreams come true. When the umbrella became popular in the 18th century, artists often exploited it as a stylized design element in a very similar fashion, placing it in one corner, slanted on a diagonal, framing the face and towering coiffure of a beautiful woman (see no. 14).

The Japanese artist is typically more concerned with design than with realism: Genji's umbrella is tilted up at an awkward angle to allow us a view of the interesting patterns formed by the ribs and stretchers. Above all, we should note that Genji is not holding this umbrella. The long stick emerges from behind his left shoulder, implying an unseen umbrella bearer.

The cover of Genji's umbrella appears to be of paper rather than silk. This would reflect the new importance of paper in the Heian period, the golden age of papermaking in Japan. Paper was invented in China around the mid-2nd century B.C. and introduced to Japan by the 5th century. By the 11th century, with the flowering of the courtly culture that produced the refined world of the *Tale of Genji*, there was increased demand for official papers and luxuriously decorated sheets for poetry, diaries and the like, made primarily from the bark fibers of the paper mulberry (*kôzo*). One innovation of this age was the production of colored papers from vat-dyed pulp.[34] Such colored papers were later used for umbrella covers.

Sei Shônagon, a lady-in-waiting to Empress Sadako during the last decade of the 10th century, was a contemporary of Murasaki Shikibu. In *The Pillow Book* (*Makura no sôshi*), her informal volume of essays, impressions and lists, she gives an eye-witness account of a scene reminiscent of Genji's visit to the Safflower Princess:

> "There was a man in the corridor early this morning who had no business to be here," I heard one of the ladies-in-waiting say. "His servant was holding an umbrella over him when he left." I was listening to her story with interest when suddenly I realized that she was talking about a visitor of mine. He was admittedly a gentleman of rather low rank, but he was perfectly acceptable and there was no reason why I should not receive him. I was still feeling rather put out when a letter came from Her Majesty, with a message that I was to reply at once. Opening it in great excitement, I found a drawing of a large umbrella. One could see nothing of the person underneath except the fingers round the handle. Below were written the words, "Since dawn first shed its light over Mount Mikasa's peak." [35]

The literal meaning of Mikasa (a mountain in the former capital of Nara) is "three umbrellas" or "three hats," clearly a reference to Shônagon's visitor. The empress suggests that rumors have been spreading about him since dawn. Embarrassed, Shônagon responded by drawing a picture of rain falling and by capping the empress's poem with this riposte:

> My name, though innocent of rain,
> Has long been spattered by unfounded tales.

An umbrella nearly identical to that in the Genji painting is shown in the now-damaged frontispiece of the "Medicinal Herbs" chapter of the Kunô-ji Lotus Sutra, an illustrated Buddhist text (fig. 53).[36] Two Heian noblemen are caught in a sudden spring shower. Rain is depicted in the form of streaks of black ink

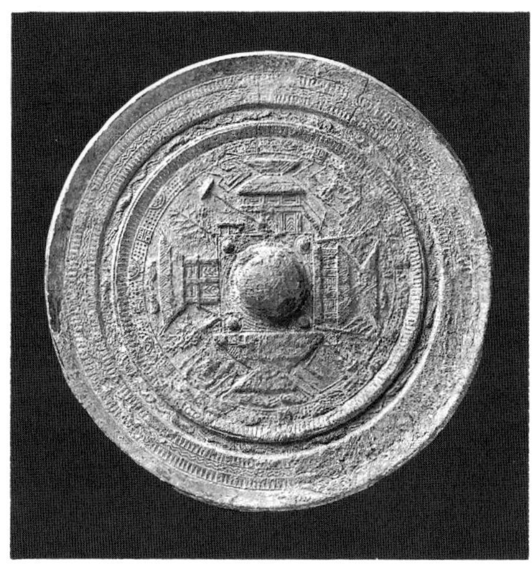

Fig. 51. Mirror, early Kofun period (250-600), late 4th century. Bronze. Diam. 9 1/4 in. (23.4 cm.). Excavated at Samida Takarazuka tomb, Nara prefecture. Imperial Household Collection, Tokyo

issuing from dark clouds, and dripping from the branches of the tree and over the rim of the umbrella cover. The effect is heightened by the thin strips of silver leaf and tiny gold-leaf particles that are scattered over the entire surface of the scroll.

The courtier holding the umbrella hovers solicitously over his more formally attired master. With his right hand, he grasps the stick just below the knob where the stretchers meet the stick. There is no indication that this umbrella was collapsible; the stick itself may actually have been detachable.

Although this painting of two gentlemen in the rain might well be a scene from daily life in the 12th century, here, in the context of the Lotus Sutra, it has religious meaning. It appears to illustrate one of twenty-eight poems (inspired by the twenty-eight chapters of the Lotus Sutra) composed by the poet Fujiwara Shunzei (1114-1204), who may even have participated in the production of these scrolls (the set was sponsored by courtiers in the circle of retired emperor Toba [1103-1156; reigned 1107-23]). In chapter 5 of the Lotus Sutra, the Buddha is likened to a great cloud from which the rain of the Buddhist law falls to nourish all plant—and, by analogy, human—life in the universe. Shunzei's allegorical interpretation is titled with a phrase from this chapter: "There is not 'this' or 'that' to me. There is no one I love or hate":

Harusame wa	The spring rain falls
kono mo kano mo no	on grasses and trees
kusa mo ki mo	both here and there
wakazu midori ni	and making no distinction
somuru narikeri	dyes them all green.

The painting is in reality a hidden poem-picture of the sort that appealed to the sophisticated courtier. To give just one example, the three (*mi*) birds (*tori*) flying overhead could be "read" as the word *midori* (green). The poetic association gave the image a layer of meaning beyond the sheer beauty of its formal composition.

The *Hajiki*, or Spring

Both closed and open umbrellas are shown in many 13th-century narrative handscrolls. The set of twelve scrolls painted in 1299 to document the life of Ippen (1239-1289), an itinerant holy man who traveled throughout the country preaching at shrines and temples, includes scenes of rain in which Ippen and his followers wear raincoats of oiled black paper and carry small, black paper umbrellas. Caught in a sudden downpour at Ono temple in Shimotsuke province, for example, Ippen and his companions run for cover using capes and umbrellas to protect their backpacks (fig. 54).[37] Two folded umbrellas have been deposited on the veranda. Similar umbrellas serving as parasols on sunny days are seen elsewhere in the set. A few smaller models appear to be made of sedge or rush. Sometimes a large pin is shown inserted through the stick just below the runner; these umbrellas were obviously collapsible.

The pin is the predecessor of the spring (*hajiki*), a practical closure apparatus which, according to Hiroshi Yabushita, may have been introduced by an enterprising Japanese merchant returning from a trip to the Philippines in 1594 with one thousand umbrellas and one thousand candles. There is no way of knowing what these imported umbrellas looked like; they are first mentioned more than a century later in the Japanese commentary in the 1712 *Wakan sansai zue* (Japanese-Chinese illustrated assemblage of the three components of the universe), a condensed version of the Chinese Ming-dynasty (1368-1644) illustrated encyclopedia *Sancai tuhui*, first published in 1607 (see no. 3).[38] The innovation of a spring would have made it worth carrying them back from the Philippines in such quantity, and the umbrellas could have been Chinese. Chinese traders were active in the Philippines at the same time as Spanish merchants, beginning in the second quarter of the 16th century, and it is thought that umbrellas were being imported to Japan from south China by the 16th century (the Chinese early proved themselves adept at mass production). It is also possible that the thousand umbrellas exhibited some novel European features. Colorfully fringed silk parasols, some with fanciful top notches, are portrayed in many early-17th-century Japanese screen paintings that depict the arrival of the Portuguese carracks at Nagasaki on the west coast of Kyûshû, the southernmost of the four main islands of Japan, between 1571 and 1640. Both pins and springs are shown holding open these Namban ("Southern Barbarian") sunshades, which are carried over the European captains by their servants on formal occasions.[39] On the other hand, illustrations in a contemporary account by the Dutchman Jan Huygen van Linschoten (1563-1616) of parasols borne over Portuguese colonists in Goa, where the carracks began their voyage to Macao and Japan, depict for the most part rather conventional covers without any fringe. They are neither as decorative nor as carefully observed as the models on Japanese screens. Some show a pin inserted below the runner, but there are no stretchers indicated in these rather schematized renderings of exotic customs.[40]

In December 1614 the English seaman William Adams (1564-1620), who spent the last twenty years of his life in Japan, sailed from Hirado, near Nagasaki, bound for Siam, but bad weather forced him to put in at the Ryukyus (Okinawa) and then return to Hirado. On the way back, he stopped at the Gotô Islands, near Hirado, and sold some gunpowder and three "kitasols"—*quitasol* is the Spanish word for parasol—for 6 *mas*.[41] These kitasols were presumably Chinese, and hence of interest to the inhabitants of the Gotô archipelago.

If we assume that the parasols shown in Namban screens were not purely the product of the Japanese artist's imagination (no two are alike), it is still difficult to know what influence, if any, the sight of these foreign novelties had in Japan. There is no doubt, however, that spectacular festival umbrellas, layered with bold fabrics and crowned with enormous artificial peacocks, peonies and butterflies, made a dramatic appearance in narrative screens dating from the first decade of the 17th century (fig. 55).[42] These umbrellas were so large that they were carried like floats on wooden frames, each resting on the shoulders of a group of strong men.

The Umbrella in the Edo Period (1615-1868)

Once the use of a spring to hold the runner in place was adopted by Japanese craftsmen around 1600, umbrellas could be opened and closed much more quickly and efficiently. The rapid growth of centers of urban wealth in the early 17th century, after the establishment of peace by the Tokugawa regime in 1615, also contributed to the spread of the umbrella as both rain gear and fashion accessory among the common people, men and women alike.

Late-16th- and early-17th-century Japanese genre paintings with panoramic views of Kyoto show women of means with red umbrellas held over their heads by female servants, but men and women are also seen carrying their own umbrellas (fig. 56). An early example of the proliferation of the umbrella occurs in the pair of late-16th-century folding screens known as *Scenes In and Around the Capital* (*Rakuchû rakugai-zu*) from the Takahashi collection in the National

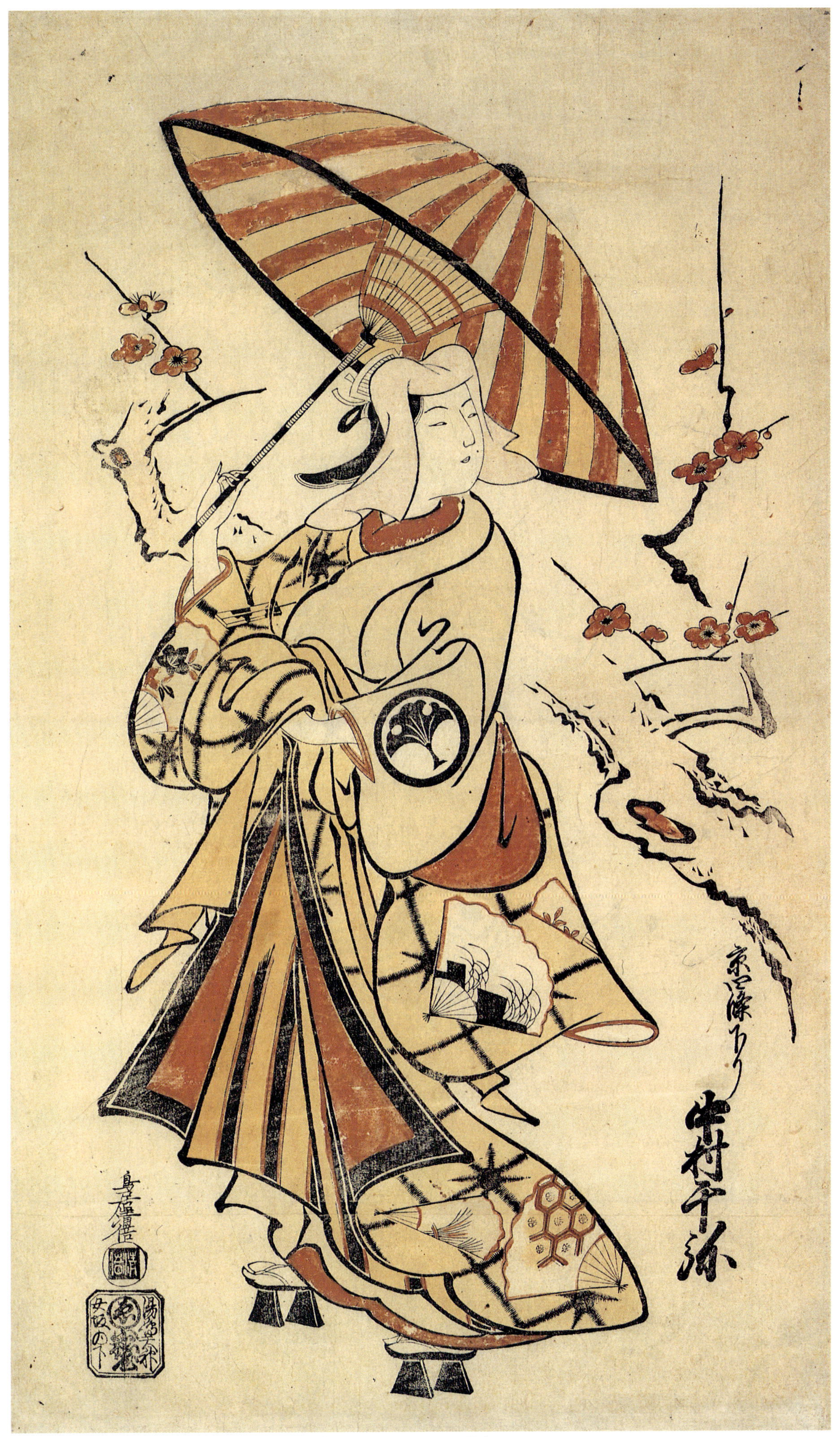

No. 61. Torii Kiyomasu I, *The Actor Nakamura Senya as Tokonatsu,* 1716

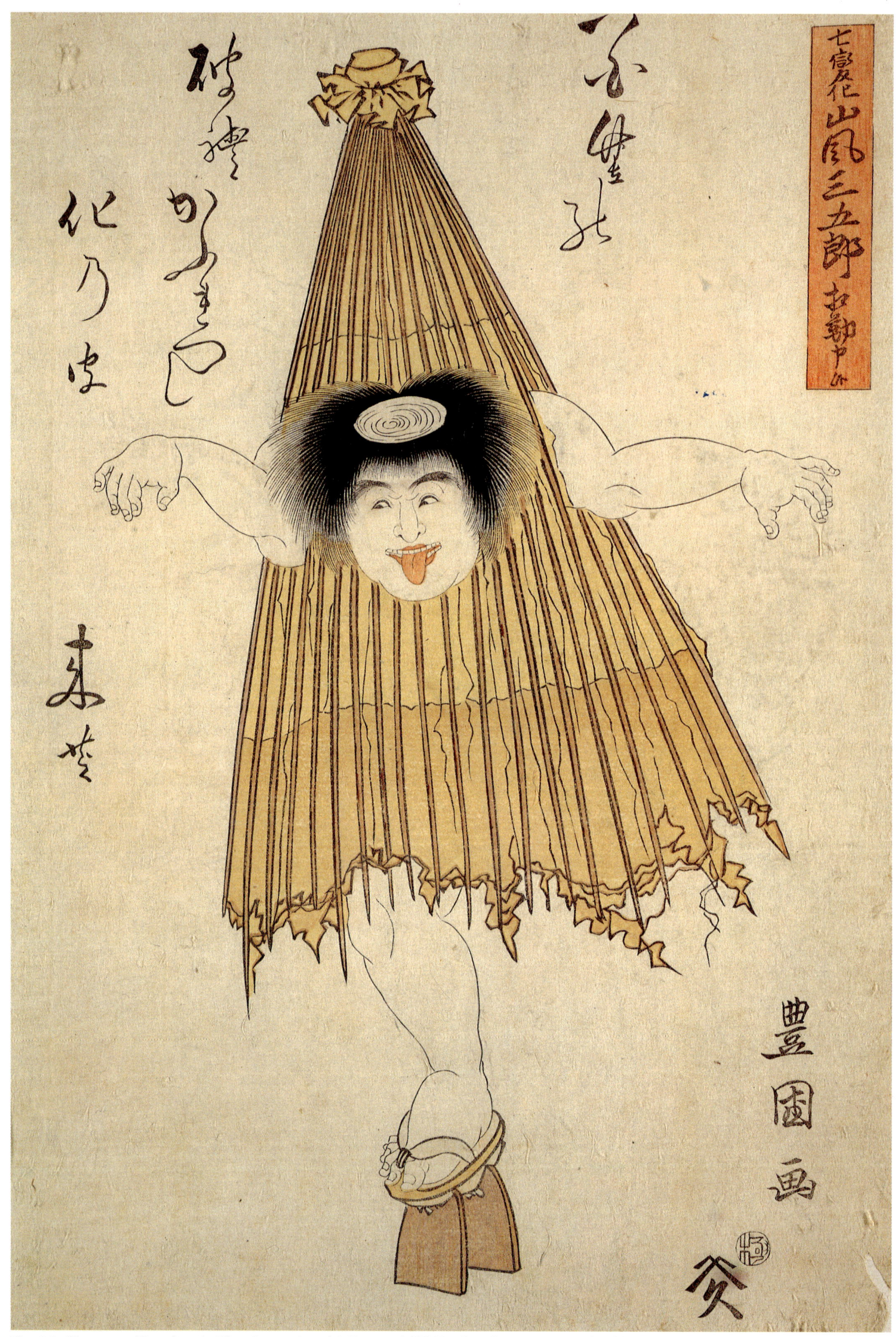

No. 92. Utagawa Toyokuni, *The Actor Arashi Sangorô III Performing as an Umbrella Monster,* ca.1810

Museum of Japanese History, Chiba prefecture. The painting includes men with black umbrellas and a group of ladies parading near Nijô Castle with small sunshades. Most of the sunshades are red, but one is yellow and one is blue with red polka dots.[43]

Umbrellas must still have been something of a rarity, however, for they are scarcely mentioned by the Portuguese Jesuit João Rodrigues (1561?-1633) in his very detailed account of life in Japan, *História da Igreja do Japão* (History of the Church of Japan); Rodrigues lived in Japan for thirty-three years, from 1577 until 1610. The etiquette of umbrella usage does appear, however, in his discussion of the courtesies required in an encounter on the road:

> When a man wearing clogs meets a noble who is not wearing them and he speaks to him, he asks his lad for his sandals and wears these while he is talking. If he does not have sandals with him and is not able to take off his clogs because of the mud, he removes his toes or the part containing the big toe from the straps of the clog, for this is the equivalent of taking off his shoes, and says, "Pardon me, your Honour, because I am high up." While speaking he bows slightly and if he is carrying a sunshade in his hand, he puts it slightly to one side as a sign of respect while he is talking to the person.[44]

Specialized umbrella makers are pictured in Japanese art for the first time around 1600. By the late 17th century the umbrella was widely used, at least in the big cities–Osaka, Kyoto and Edo. Yet it was still novel enough to serve as the centerpiece of an erotic tale, "The Umbrella Oracle," by the irreverent humorist Ihara Saikaku (1642-1693), in his "Tales from the Provinces" (*Saikaku shokoku-banashi*), which was written in 1685. Saikaku tells of a temple in the province of Kii (modern Wakayama prefecture, south of Osaka), where twenty paper umbrellas, repaired every year, were hung beside the temple for use by parishioners unexpectedly caught in the rain or snow; not one had ever been lost. One day in the spring of 1649, however, a villager borrowed an umbrella and had it blown out of his hands by a violent "divine wind" emanating from the shrine on Tamazu Isle. It landed finally in a remote hamlet in Kyûshû whose inhabitants had never seen an umbrella, where it aroused considerable speculation among the learned men and elders.

> Finally one local wise man stepped forth and proclaimed, "Upon counting the radiating bamboo ribs, there are exactly forty. The paper too is round and luminous, and not of the ordinary kind. Though I hesitate to utter that August Name, this is without a doubt the God of the Sun, whose name we have so often heard, and is assuredly his divine attribute from the Inner Sanctuary of the Great Shrine of Ise, which has deigned to fly to us here!"

Filled with awe, the villagers built a shrine and installed the umbrella as its god. At the time of the summer rains, the deity demanded a beautiful young maiden as an offering and threatened to inundate the earth with torrential rains if the request was not granted. The village maidens strongly protested this cruel demand. They doubted they could survive even one night with such a god,

> for they had come to attach a peculiar significance to the odd shape which the deity had assumed.
>
> At this juncture a young and beautiful widow from the village stepped forward, saying, "Since it is for the god, I will offer myself in place of the young maidens."

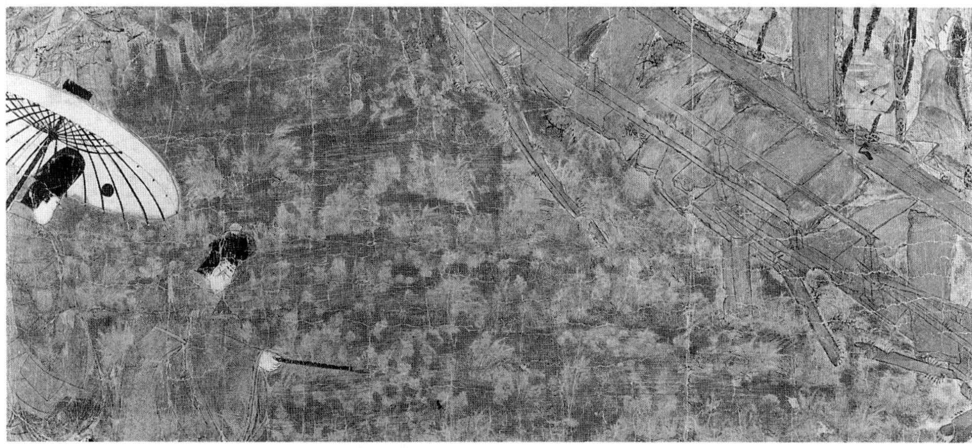

Fig. 52. Artist unknown, The Wormwood Patch, *from* The Tale of Genji, *late Heian period (794-1185), early 12th century. Detached segment of an illustrated handscroll; ink and color on paper. 8 1/2 x 19 in. (21.5 x 48.2 cm.). Tokugawa Art Museum, Nagoya*

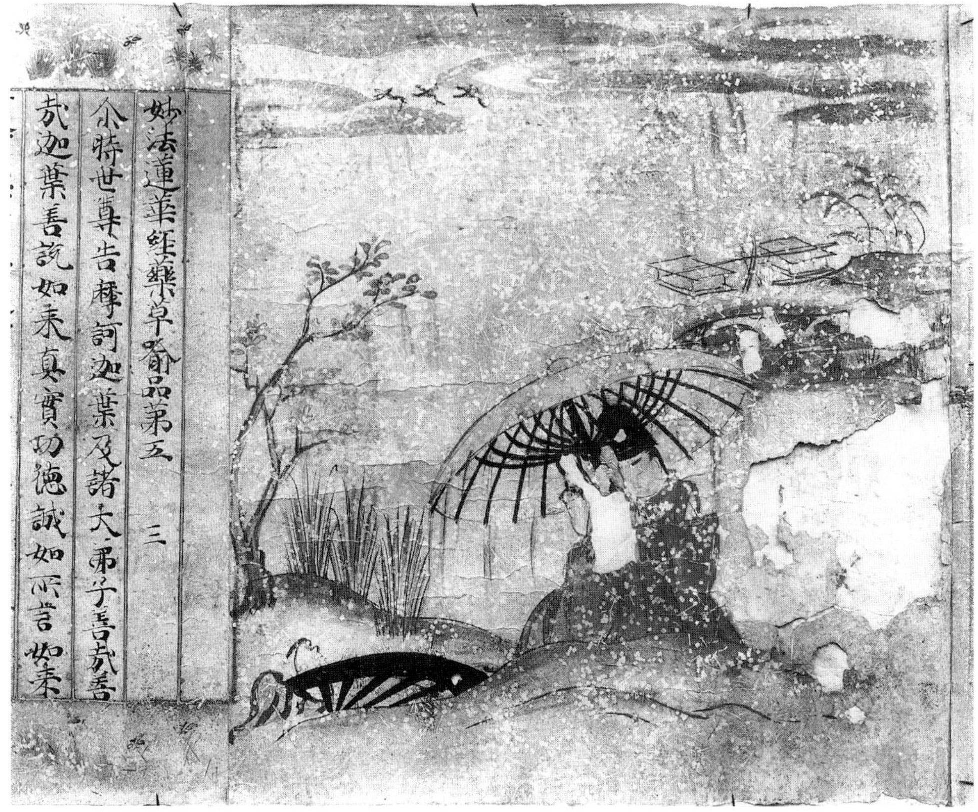

Fig. 53. Artist unknown, Frontispiece to "Medicinal Herbs," chapter 5 of the Kunô-ji Lotus Sutra, late Heian period, ca. 1141. Handscroll; ink, color and gold and silver leaf on paper. 10 x 8 3/8 in. (25.5 x 21.3 cm.). Mutô Haruta Collection, Hyôgo Prefecture

> All night long the beautiful widow waited in the shrine, but she did not get a bit of affection. Enraged, she charged into the inner sanctum, grasped the divine umbrella firmly in her hands and screaming, "Worthless deceiver!" she tore it apart, and threw the pieces as far as she could! [45]

The phallic shape of the closed umbrella did not escape the notice of Japanese artists when the woodblock print came into its own in the 18th and 19th centuries (fig. 57).[46]

The proliferation of umbrella types in the 18th century reflects the development of an essentially bourgeois culture, one in which people of wealth were not averse to going about on foot and carrying their own parasols. As a result, the umbrella infiltrated every aspect of Japanese art. In the hands of a geisha at night or when shared by two lovers it became a symbol of romance (nos. 14, 66, 67). It was a graceful prop on the Kabuki stage (nos. 61, 68, 72, 74, 75), and a decoration on samurai sword guards (nos. 89, 99, 100) and knife handles (nos. 21, 22, 81, 90); it could even be found in miniature form on netsuke (nos. 79, 88). The umbrella also appeared as a design element on fabric (no. 95), and sets of crossed umbrellas were presented in designers' catalogues as possible choices for a family crest (nos. 96, 97). It was typical of the playful humor of Edo Japan that even a sake bottle could adopt the form of a closed umbrella (nos. 106, 107). Hokusai, who was adept at subverting expectations, turned umbrellas into landscape elements in his "One Hundred Views of Fuji" (no. 2), while in the *Manga* he showed an eccentric Chinese, labeled *Sanfeng zi* (Master of Umbrella and Wind), using an umbrella as a boat (fig. 58). This may be a witty allusion to an obscure Northern Song painter whose name is pronounced the same, although it is written with entirely different characters reading either Master of the Three Insanities or Master of the Three Winds.

In Japanese art, broken and tattered umbrellas came to evoke a poignant image of fragility and the inevitable passage of time, not unlike that of falling cherry blossoms or scattered maple leaves. A damaged umbrella could signify that something fierce had happened—a fight or an unexpected storm, perhaps (nos. 72, 104). Old umbrellas could also be a little frightening. There is an ancient belief that an umbrella has a spirit of its own, as the painter-poet Yosa Buson (1716-1783) hints in these two haiku:

Furugasa no *basa to tsukiyo no* *shigure kana*	Oh, the winter rain on a moonlit night when the shadow of an old umbrella shudders.[47]
Bake sô na *kasa kasu tera no* *shigure kana*	It may transform itself, this umbrella lent by a temple, in the winter rain.[48]

In Japanese folklore, umbrellas were among a number of inanimate objects that might assume a demonic existence (no. 91). The umbrella monster, once impersonated by Kabuki actors (no. 92), even survives to this day as a comic-book spook (no. 94).

The Element of Rain

Sayo shigure *tonari e hairu* *kasa no oto*	On an umbrella, a patter of raindrops, but it enters next door; the evening darkens. —Ranran (1642-1689)[49]

The themes of rain and snow and the emotions associated with the four seasons are explored over and over again in classical Japanese poetry, and those literary themes reverberate in the woodblock prints of the Edo period. Japan is in a rain zone, a fact reflected in the vocabulary of its people. The oppressively long rain of June, the fifth month in the old lunar calendar (the *tsuyu*, or plum rain), is also the rain of longing. *Nagaame* (long rain) shares etymological roots with the ancient word *nagameru*, to lose oneself in reverie. This association, deeply rooted in Japan's culture and climate, underlines the evocative nature of rain as an artistic image. In a land where the four seasons might well include a fifth, the continuous rain of early summer, a literary tradition evolved to celebrate the variety of rain throughout the year in a wide range of descriptive terms, each with specific emotional nuances.[50] *Harusame*, the soft rain of spring; *samidare*, the "fifth-month rain," or early summer shower; *haku'u*, the "white rain" of a sudden daytime shower; *yûdachi*, an evening squall, especially in summer; *yau*, night rain; *shigure*, the chilling rain of autumn and early winter; *kirisame*, a drizzling, misting rain; *koriame*, ice rain—all are words that evoke rich poetic responses and that have inspired generations of painters and printmakers. The umbrella proved to be an effective compositional device with which to convey these emotional nuances.

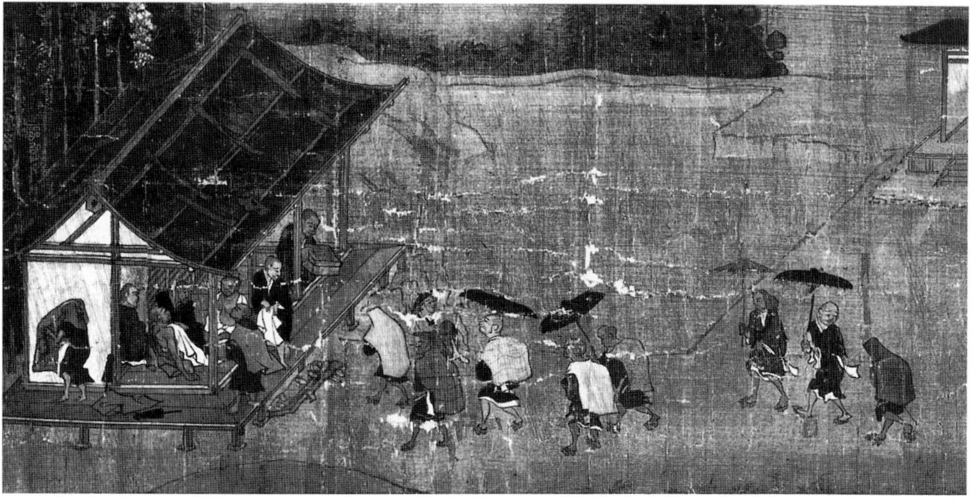

Fig. 54. En'i (active late 13th century), Rain at Ono Temple, *detail from the* Pictorial Biography of Saint Ippen *(* Ippen hijiri-e*), scroll five, section two, Kamakura period, 1299. Handscroll; ink and color on silk. H. 14 7/8 in. (37.7 cm.). Kankikô-ji, Kyoto*

Rain at different times of the year is the unifying theme of a mid-18th-century triptych by Torii Kiyohiro (no. 62). Three pairs of actors in assumed roles are shown under umbrellas, and each has an accompanying haiku. The poems progress from spring rain (*harusame*) on the left, through a summer evening squall (*yûdachi*) at the center, to the first cold showers of autumn (*hatsu shigure*) on the right. In the center panel the actor Nakamura Tomijûrô I (1719-1786) is depicted in the role of the Heian poetess Ono no Komachi, with Sanogawa Ichimatsu (1722-1762) as the servant (fig. 59). The haiku inscribed around the two actors alludes to one of the incidents for which Komachi is famous:

Yûdachi ya	A summer downpour—
saritote wa mata	this, yet again, must be
uta no toku [51]	the blessing of poetry's power.

Legend has it that Emperor Junna (823-33) called upon Komachi to compose a poem as a prayer for rain during a period when the country was suffering from drought and disease. She went to the imperial garden, the Shinsen-en in Kyoto, recited her poem, wrote it on a poem slip, and cast this into the pond. Immediately there was a heavy downpour that continued for three days. The poem attributed to her is probably an apocryphal work of the Muromachi period (1333-1573):

Kotowariya	This may be the land
hi no moto nareba	that lies beneath the sun, but
teri mo sen	its light torments us.
saritote wa mata	Surely what we call this earth
ame ga shita to wa	lies also under the rain.[52]

The 9th-century poetess was such a celebrated figure (beautiful and brilliant, yet cold-hearted and cruel to her lovers) that a cycle of seven variations on themes dealing with her life evolved, one being that of Komachi praying for rain (*Amagoi Komachi*). The "Seven Komachi" cycle was elaborated first as a series of Nô plays. It was then published as a text for the puppet theater in 1677 and performed by Takeda Izumo at the Takemoto puppet theater in Osaka in 1727. There were several Kabuki versions, as well.[53] The Edo-period poet Enomoto Kikaku (1661-1707) is said to have reenacted the scene of Komachi praying for rain at the Mimeguri Shrine on the banks of the Sumida River in Edo.[54]

In 18th-century prints Komachi is often shown about to launch a toy sailboat bearing the slip of paper on which she has written her poem. In the Edo period, when the classics were appropriated by cosmopolitan townsmen, the legend of Komachi became widely popular, and she is typically represented not in multi-

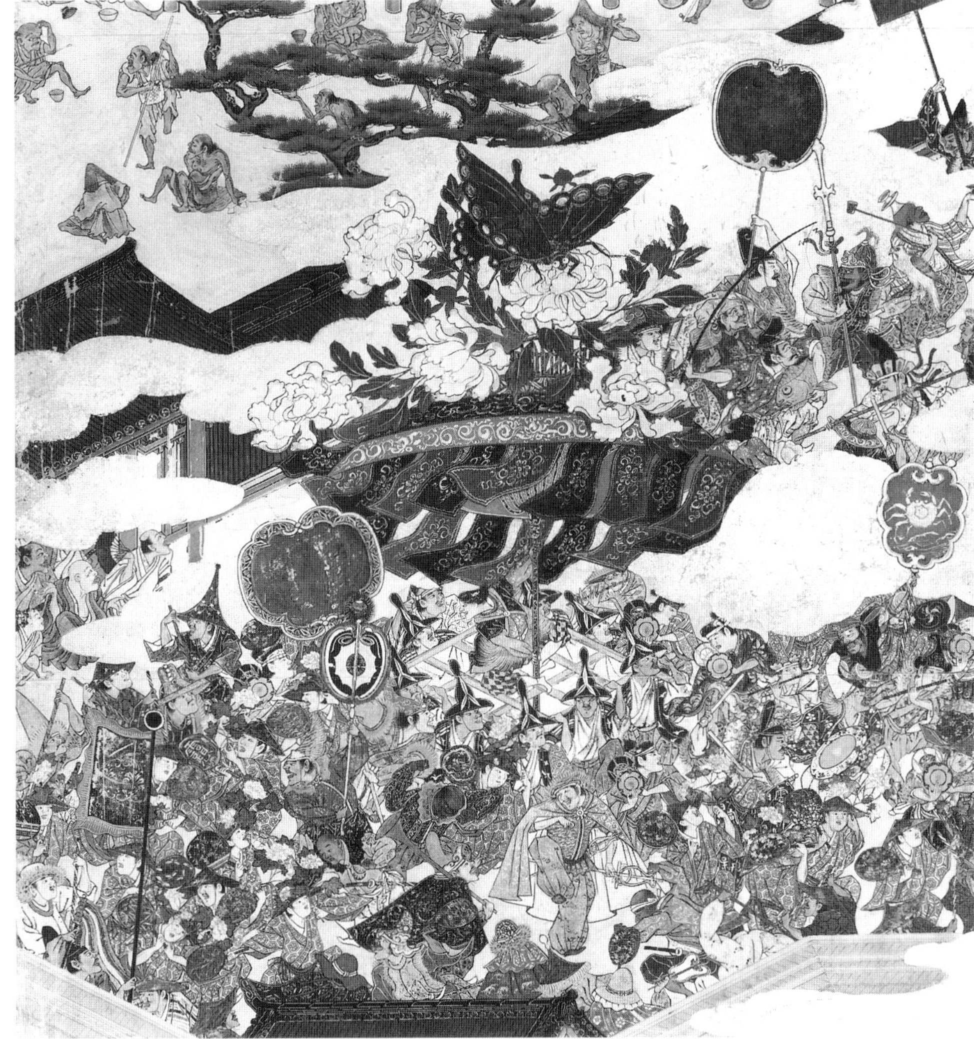

Fig. 55. Artist unknown, Hôkoku Festival *(detail showing a festival umbrella), Momoyama period (1573-1615), early 17th century. Pair of six-panel screens; ink, color and gold leaf on paper. Tokugawa Art Museum, Nagoya*

The Hôkoku Festival was first celebrated at the Hôkoku Shrine in Kyoto in 1604 to commemorate the seventh anniversary of the death of the military warlord Toyotomi Hideyoshi (1537-1598).

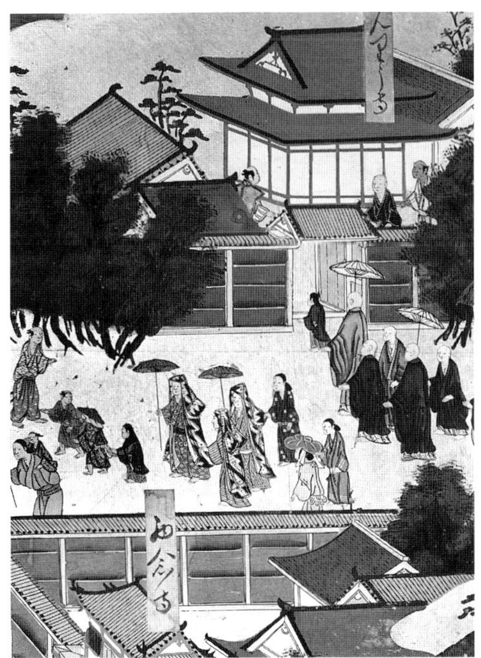

Fig. 56. Artist unknown, Scenes In and Around the Capital *(detail showing monks and women with umbrellas near Tenryû-ji temple on the western outskirts of Kyoto), Edo period, mid-17th century. Pair of six-panel screens; ink, color and gold leaf on paper. The Mary and Jackson Burke Foundation*

layered Heian-period costume but in the chic attire of a contemporary beauty. Rain and an umbrella are essential to her iconography. In some cases she holds a splendid *janome* (no. 63). In more dignified versions, a young servant walks behind her with a *nagaegasa*, seen as appropriate to the status of a Heian court lady or a Yoshiwara courtesan of rank. It was said that *jorô* (prostitutes) could use court umbrellas because they were *jorô*, a Heian term written with different characters meaning ladies-in-waiting of high rank.

Codification of the Umbrella

The first attempt to put the Japanese umbrella into its historical context is a brief entry in the *Wakan sansai zue*, the illustrated encyclopedia completed in 1712 by Terashima Ryôan, an Osaka physician, which mentions the one thousand umbrellas from the Philippines (see no. 3). A serious and detailed description of umbrella types was included in the *Morisada mankô*, a copiously illustrated treatise on Edo-period manners and customs by Kitagawa Morisada (b. 1810), completed in 1853. This manuscript was not published until 1928, when it appeared as *Ruijû kinsei fûzoku-shi* (History of modern customs). It is a typical product of the late Edo rise of historical consciousness and the concomitant compulsion to categorize information. Many of the imaginative umbrella types familiar from the 18th-century prints are absent; perhaps they were no longer in vogue. Morisada's text on umbrellas was expanded in 1930 by a solitary but dedicated historian of the subject, Takazu Daisaburô, in his *Nihon wagasa hôkan* (Handbook of Japanese umbrellas). Takazu was writing on behalf of Japan's umbrella wholesalers in an effort to educate the public about a craft endangered by cheap Chinese imports and Western-style umbrellas.[55]

These texts allow us to draw some conclusions about the specialized designs and shapes of umbrellas available in the late Edo period (diag. 4, p. 35). In view of the Japanese penchant for finely drawn distinctions in social status, for example, it is not surprising that umbrellas varied according to gender, rank, and even geography (Kyoto and Osaka versus Edo, or modern Tokyo). The *janome* (snake's-eye) type with black, brown, or indigo paper and a white center band came into fashion around the Genroku era (1688-1703); orange and red *janome* seem to have become popular much later. Among men, the *janome* was rarely used by the samurai class but was favored by monks and doctors.[56] In the Osaka-Kyoto region, *janome* were used by women of samurai status; their umbrellas, always held by female servants, had long sticks and large covers. In Edo, however, even if a woman had two or three servants, she carried her own umbrella, and the stick was accordingly shorter. By the 19th century, when people first took the trouble to record such things, courtesans of high rank used an indigo and white *janome* with a long stick (see no. 49); because their umbrellas were similar in scale to those used by government officials, they were carried by male servants.[57]

A dark indigo and white umbrella was favored by the intelligentsia—Confucian scholars and doctors—around the Shôtoku era (1711-15). The blue and white *momiji* (maple-leaf) umbrella appeared in the Kyôhô era (1716-35): the blue paper was limited to the top section only. Conversely, the *yakko* (spear-bearer) *janome* umbrella, originally used only in Edo, had a dark band around the rim, leaving the rest of the paper white. There were small children's umbrellas (*kogasa*), some of them decorated with portraits of Kabuki actors, painted parasols (*e-higasa*) for women, expensive extraslim umbrellas (*hosogasa*) that could be slipped through the sash of the kimono when not in use, and, of course, the sturdy and inexpensive everyday *bangasa*. The latter were first made by the Daikokuya, a shop in Osaka, in the second decade of the 18th century and were later diffused throughout the country (nos. 17-20). During the mid- to late 17th century, the long-stick parasol painted with bird and flower designs was very popular with women, to judge from contemporary genre paintings of scenes in and around Kyoto (see no. 47).

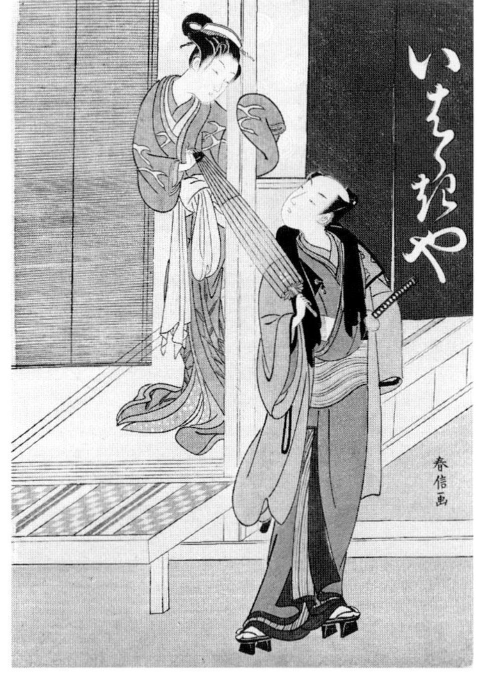

Fig. 57. Suzuki Harunobu (1724-1770), Courtesan of the Ibarakiya Detaining a Young Man, *Edo period, ca. 1767-68. Color woodblock print;* chûban. *The Minneapolis Institute of Arts, Bequest of Richard P. Gale*

The Tokugawa shogunate legislated a rigidly stratified class system, and there were regulations governing the use and color of umbrellas. Since umbrellas with long sticks (*nagaegasa*) had been used by the social elite since early times, the sight of commoners enjoying the same luxury may have seemed presumptuous or threatening to the ruling class. *Nagaegasa* were temporarily prohibited in 1718. In Kyoto in 1749, parasols (*higasa*) were banned for a year, and in Edo in 1791 umbrellas made with blue silk and paper were temporarily proscribed for commoners (the city magistrate announced that doctors and monks had objected to women using such umbrellas to protect their newly elaborate coiffures).[58]

There were complex rules for the military and for court nobles using *tsumaoregasa* ("clipped-fingernail" umbrellas), long-stick models with ribs curved at the tip and covered with red, black or white paper. These were presented as gifts to the shogun when daimyo, or feudal lords, came to the capital, and were required at official events. The "Buke tôji shôzoku-shô" (Summary of warrior clothing), written in 1840, records that court nobles were permitted vermilion umbrellas with black-lacquered ribs and sticks.[59] Daimyo used black, vermilion-lined umbrellas with vermilion sticks, probably in imitation of Chinese precedents: it seems more than coincidental that high-ranking Ming-dynasty officials were entitled to black gauze umbrellas with a red silk lining. Others in the Japanese warrior class used vermilion umbrellas with black-lacquered ribs and sticks.

The ceremonial long-stick umbrella wrapped in a storage bag is called a *sannai-gasa or fukuroiregasa* (umbrella in a bag). Storage bags for umbrellas even had their own set of rules. A white linen bag tied with leather cords was appropriate for formal occasions. Government officials, including the shogun, used black velvet bags. Only the highest-ranking daimyo were permitted purple ties; others had black. Some lower-ranking military families were not allowed to use a bag at all.[60]

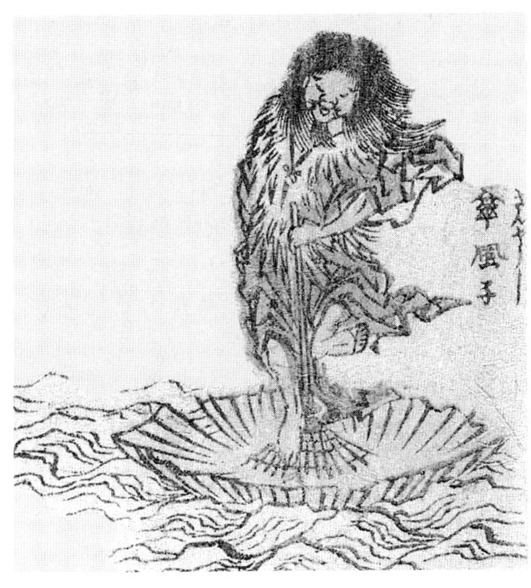

Fig. 58. Katsushika Hokusai (1760-1849), Sanfeng zi *(*Master of Umbrella and Wind*). From* Manga *(Book of humorous sketches), Vol. 3, 2nd ed., Edo period, ca. 1828 or later. Color woodblock-printed illustrated book. Page: 8 7/8 x 6 3/16 in. (22.5 x 15.7 cm.). The Metropolitan Museum of Art, Rogers Fund, 1931*

The Earliest Surviving Japanese Umbrellas

The earliest surviving umbrellas known at present in Japan are sets of daimyo umbrellas in the Tokugawa Art Museum, Nagoya. Part of the lavish trousseaux of Tokugawa brides, they have red paper covers painted with gold floral motifs and long wood sticks lacquered black with gold designs. They are stored in bags made of red wool (*rasha*) with a crest. A parasol of status and two umbrellas (the latter measuring almost 8 feet in length) with peony and arabesque designs were part of the trousseau of Lady Tsunagimi (1785-1847), adopted daughter of Tokugawa Munechika IX of the Owari branch of the Tokugawa, when she married Konoe Motomae in 1808 (fig. 60). Three parasols and two umbrellas with chrysanthemum and twig patterns were brought by Lady Sachigimi of the Konoe family to the Owari branch of the Tokugawa family when she married Owari Tokugawa Nariharu XI in 1836.[61]

Ironically, the largest group of antique Japanese umbrellas to survive today is in the West, specifically in Holland, where they were acquired as contemporary ethnological artifacts, part of collections formed by Europeans working in the Far East. The Dutch were the only Westerners allowed to remain in Japan after 1639, and they established their small trading mission, an outpost of the Dutch East India Company, on Dejima, a tiny artificial island in Nagasaki harbor.

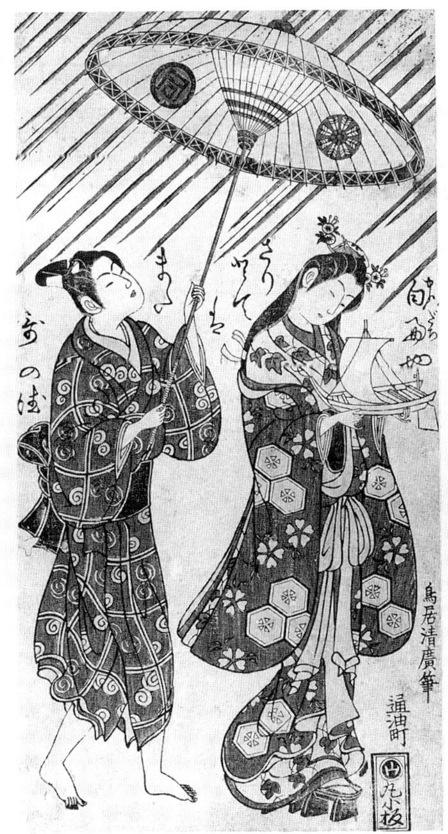

Fig. 59. Torii Kiyohiro (1708-1776), Nakamura Tomijûrô I as Ono no Komachi and Sanogawa Ichimatsu as Her Servant *(see no. 62), Edo period, early 1750s. Color woodblock print; center panel of a* hosoban *triptych. The Metropolitan Museum of Art, Gift of Estate of Samuel Isham, 1914*

As a result of this relationship, there are now nineteen early-19th-century umbrellas in the Rijksmuseum voor Volkenkunde (National Museum of Ethnology) in Leiden (see nos. 16, 48). These include nine of the *janome* type as well as ten with long sticks (*nagaegasa*), although none of the latter is as impressively long as the daimyo examples in the Tokugawa collection mentioned above. Some were brought back by Jan Cock Blomhoff (1779-1853), who resided in Dejima from 1809 to 1813 as warehouse master and from 1817 to 1823 as head of the trading station. Others came from the collection of Johan Frederik van Overmeer Fisscher (1800-1848), attached to the factory between 1819 and 1829 first as a secretary and then as warehouse master. Within two or three years of their return from Japan, both men sold their collections to King Willem I (1772-1843) for the Koninklijk Kabinet van Zeldzaamheden (Royal Cabinet of Rarities) in The Hague.

Another collector was Philipp Franz von Siebold (1796-1866), a German pioneer of Japanese studies in Europe, who served the Dutch government as a physician (and information gatherer, or de facto intelligence agent) in Nagasaki from 1823 until 1829. He was permitted to buy a house on the outskirts of Nagasaki, where he taught Western medicine and treated Japanese patients, accepting ethnographic and art objects as payment. Von Siebold made one trip to Edo in 1826. While there he lectured and demonstrated European therapy and surgery to an audience consisting of everyone from feudal lords to doctors and townsmen. In exchange he received a wide variety of gifts.[62] Upon his return to Europe, von Siebold established himself and his large collection of Japanese paintings, prints and artifacts, including umbrellas, in Leiden. This collection was purchased by the government in 1837. In 1862, the Siebold Museum was renamed the

National Museum of Ethnology. The Blomhoff-Fisscher collections were moved to the museum in 1883.

It is also worth noting that quite a few traditional umbrellas made for export in the Meiji era have been preserved in Leiden and in other Western museums. There are five late-19th-century umbrellas in the Peabody and Essex Museum in Salem, Massachusetts, which houses the collection of America's pioneer Japanologist, Edward Sylvester Morse (1838-1925).[63]

The Western Umbrella in Japan

The impact of the Western umbrella in Japan as a symbol of foreign ways is described by the educator and journalist Fukuzawa Yukichi (1835-1901) in his autobiography. Fukuzawa participated in the first government mission to America in 1860 aboard the *Kanrinmaru*. To illustrate a point about xenophobia in Japan at the time, he tells the following story:

> In San Francisco Captain Kimura bought an umbrella as a curiosity—we called it *kômori-gasa* (bat umbrella) because of its shape and to distinguish it from the Japanese umbrella. The officers of the ship had gathered around to look at it, and were discussing what might be the result, should the captain carry this strange object out in the streets of Edo back in Japan.
>
> "There is no doubt about it," said one of them. "He would be cut down by a *rônin* [a masterless samurai] before the captain could reach Nihombashi from his home in Shinsenza." So we generally decided that the only thing the captain could do with his new possession was to open it and look at it in his home. Such were the times. Any person who showed, by any will or deed, any favor towards admitting foreigners into Japan—indeed, any person who had any interest in foreign affairs—was liable to be set upon by the unrelenting *rônin*.[64]

Such an attitude proved to be short-lived. At first the curious imports were seen only in the hands of foreigners living in Yokohama, the treaty port that opened in 1859 (see no. 109), but after the Meiji Restoration of 1868, the Western umbrella became a kind of status symbol for samurai wishing to appear modern and civilized (no. 111). It could, after all, be used for both sun and rain, and as a cane. Moreover, it was thin, lightweight (thanks to steel ribs, which replaced whalebone and cane in the 1840s), and durable. One reason the Japanese changed so quickly in the Meiji period (1868-1912), adopting Western laws, clothing, and technology, was in reaction to the inequitable treaties imposed by Western powers; the Japanese wanted to show that they were, in fact, "civilized" and deserved to be treated as equals. "Civilization and enlightenment" (*bummei kaika*) was the slogan for the 1870s. There was a tremendous outburst of energy and enthusiasm for all things Western.

Japan's willingness to accept Western learning and culture is not surprising. It reflects a long history of fascination with anything new and foreign. In the past, this had meant the absorption of continuous waves of influence from China and Korea and even, in the late 16th century, from Europe. Such adaptability, combined with widespread education, a common language, large urban commercial centers with a skilled labor force, a strong secular tradition, and a rising agricultural surplus, helped ease Japan's transition from a feudal society to the modern world.

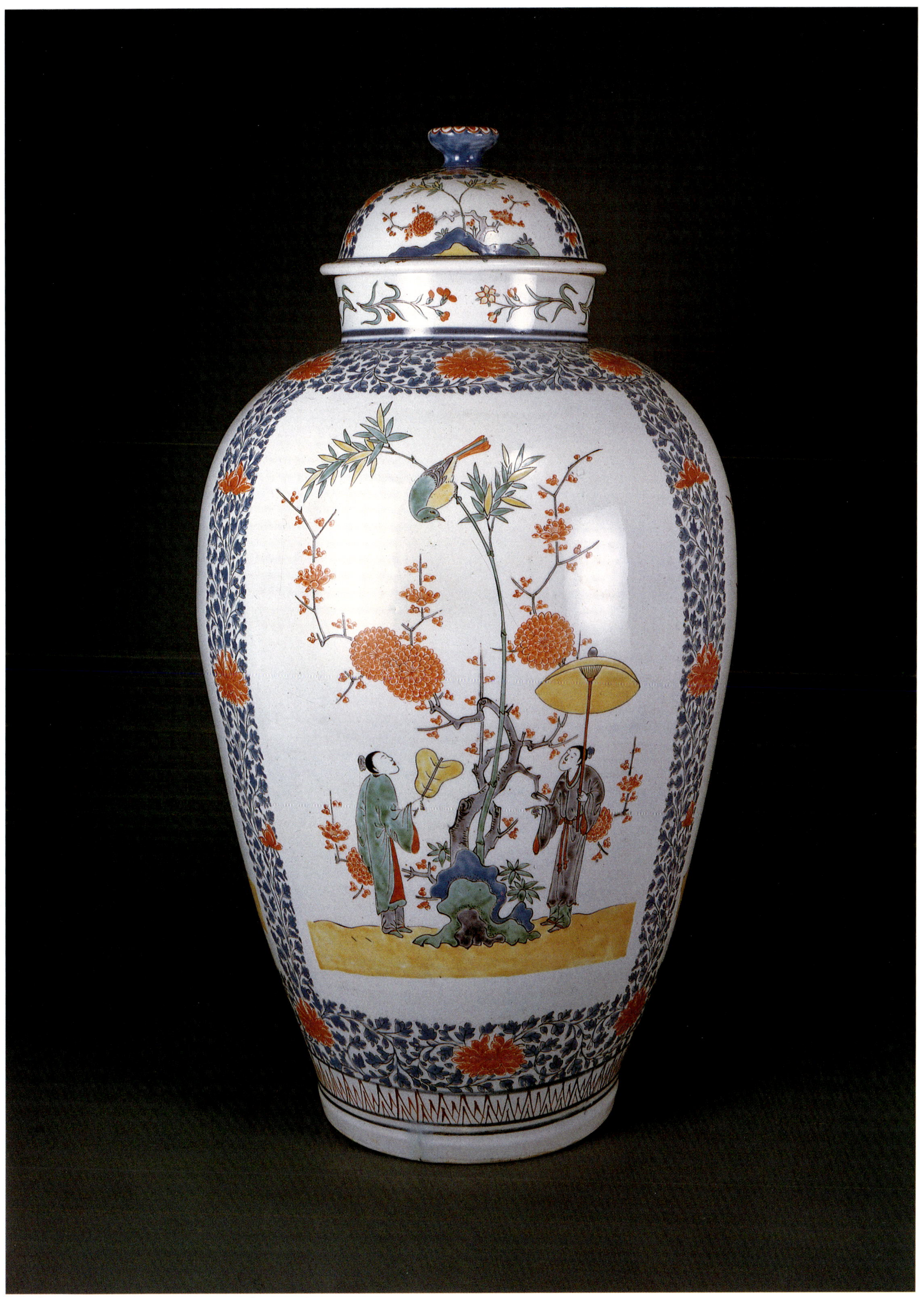

No. 122. Covered Jar, Arita ware, late 17th century

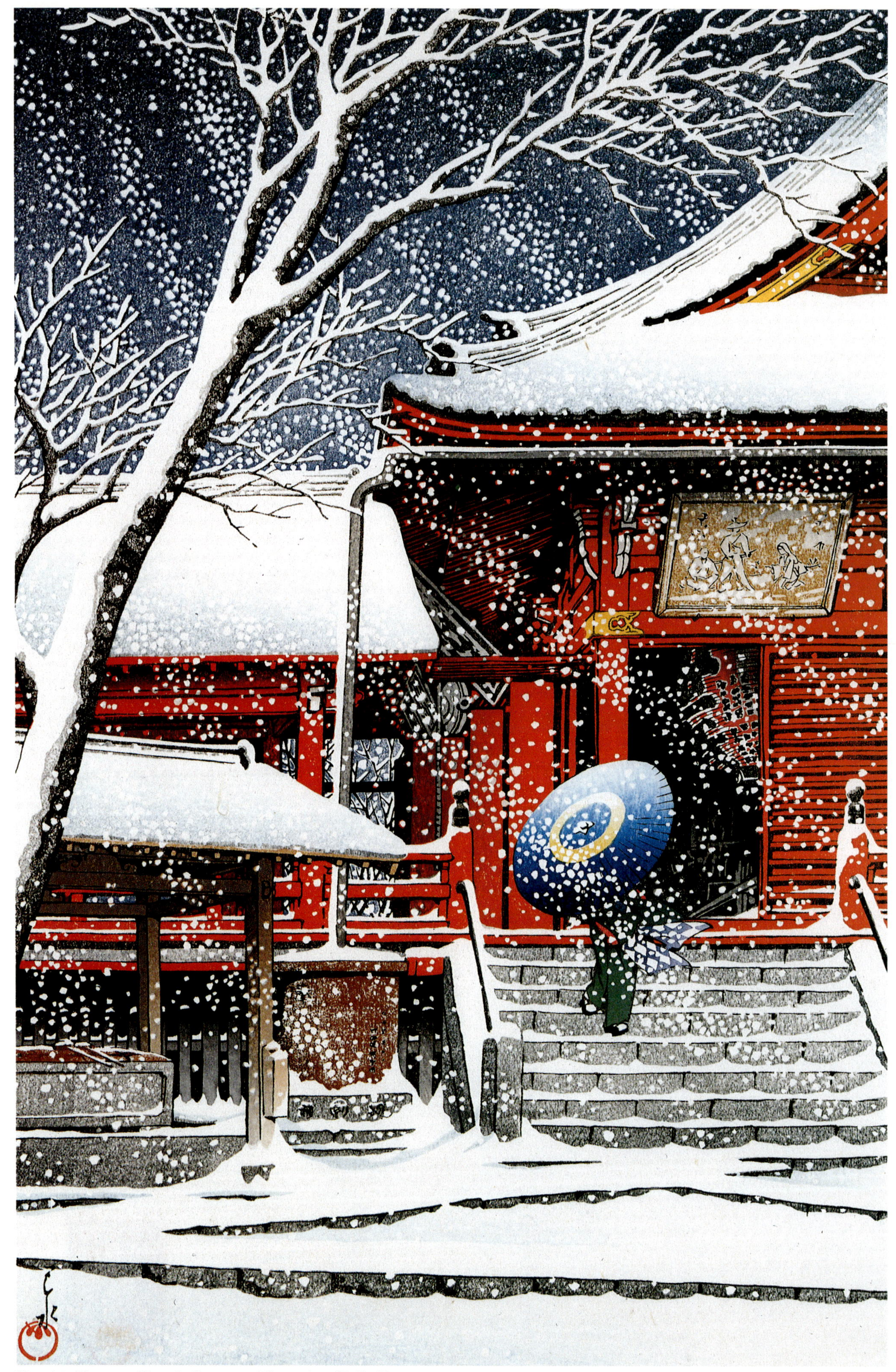

No. 44. Kawase Hasui, *Snow at Kiyomizu Hall, Ueno*, 1929

No one publicized Western civilization more effectively than Fukuzawa, who began as a student of Dutch learning but wisely turned his attention to English and gained a reputation as a translator. Following his first overseas trip in 1860, he was recruited for an official shogunal mission to Europe in 1862 and in 1867 was again ordered to accompany a delegation to America. Armed with first-hand information, he quickly published several books that established him as a serious authority on Western matters. *Seiyô ishokujû* (Western clothing, food and homes) appeared in 1867 on the eve of the Meiji Restoration as a guide to Western customs and manners. Fukuzawa's advice was aimed at young samurai of low rank who, like himself, were eager to rise in the hierarchy of the emerging New Japan. The book contains fundamental kinds of information for which there was obviously a desperate need. The author teaches his bewildered readers how to eat, dress, and even urinate in proper Western style. Each illustration has Chinese characters as well as phonetic symbols (*katakana*) for an approximation of English pronunciation. The umbrella, for example, has the character reading *kasa* (or *karakasa*) and also the phonetic symbols reading *omuburera* (fig. 61).[65] The useful information in Fukuzawa's manual soon filtered down to schoolchildren throughout the country in the form of illustrated woodblock-printed English primers such as the *Eiji kunmô zukai* (Illustrated manual of English instruction) of 1871 (no. 110).

The title of an 1881 triptych by Hiroshige III, *Additional Famous Places in Tokyo: View of Benten on Nakanoshima in Shinobazu Pond, Ueno Park* (no. 112; fig. 62), does not identify the real subject (the imperial family out for a stroll), but mentions only Nakanoshima, an island in the center of Shinobazu Pond where a Shinto shrine to the goddess Benten was built. By tradition, portraits of royalty were privately dedicated to Buddhist temples. This centuries-old taboo was hard to break. It was a full ten years into the Meiji period before print artists began to picture the emperor, presumably in response to the changing political climate, but even then he was never identified by name in the title of a print.[66] As a determined group of business entrepreneurs and government officials began to transform Japan into an industrial capitalist society, the emperor was presented to his people in a more human and personal guise.

Ueno, site of the Kan'ei-ji, the family temple of the Tokugawa shoguns, was converted to a park in 1873 at the suggestion of a Dutch physician—the very notion of public parks was introduced from the West.[67] Western dress modeled on European uniforms had been mandated for civil servants such as police, postmen, and railroad employees, and for the military in the early 1870s at the same time that Western formal wear was established for government officials. Emperor Meiji (1852-1912), who adopted his Western-style uniform in 1872, is posed in Hiroshige's print in a rather awkward bowlegged stance—he is said to have been uncomfortable in Western clothing in the early days. The empress did not abandon traditional court robes until the fall of 1886, when she abruptly switched to Western dress. She and her ladies-in-waiting, however, had taken to the Western umbrella much earlier. Clara Whitney saw the empress and her suite pass in open barouches in 1876:

> All the ladies carried umbrellas (foreign ones), which they kept well down over their faces to prevent their being stared at, I suppose. Her Majesty . . . was dressed in lovely rose-colored silk with a magnificent crest on the back. . . . They say her face is very sweet, but she kept her umbrella so low that we could not see it.[68]

The idea that the emperor and empress would stroll under the cherry blossoms in a public park is a delightful fantasy; it is unlikely that they ever walked together even in the privacy of the palace grounds—the emperor was not

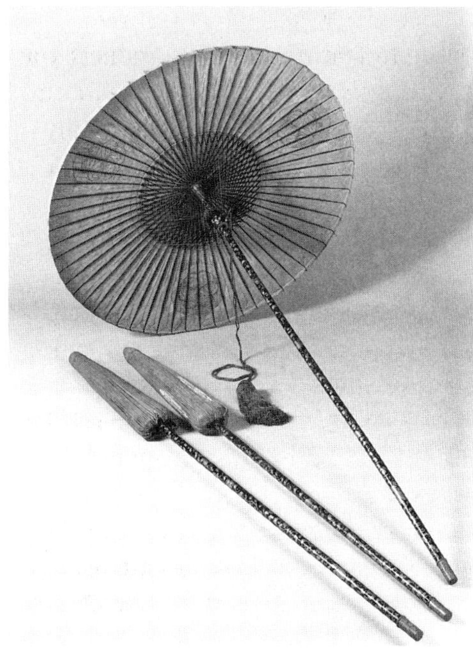

Fig. 60. Set of umbrellas from a Tokugawa wedding trousseau, Edo period, 1808. Tokugawa Art Museum, Nagoya

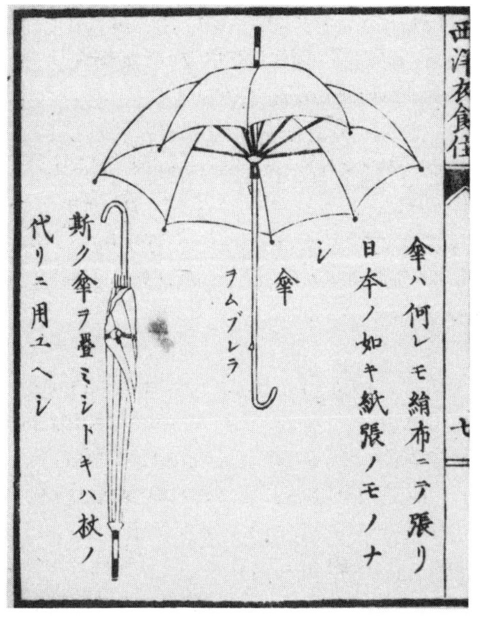

Fig. 61. Umbrella. *From Fukuzawa Yukichi,* Seiyô ishokujû *(Western clothing, food and homes), 1867. Woodblock-printed illustrated book. Keiô University Library, Tokyo*

The text reads: "Umbrellas are all made of silk. There are none made of paper in the Japanese manner. An umbrella, when folded, can also be used as a cane."

"enlightened" when it came to equality of the sexes. In Hiroshige's print, only the French silk parasols are believable. The imperial family became the embodiment of Japanese modernity in the 1880s. They were presented as enlightened role models, adopting Western customs and clothing, setting the pace, always up-to-date. *Imamekashisa* (up-to-dateness) has been a cherished virtue in Japan ever since the early Heian period, when the capital moved from the old Buddhist center of Nara to Kyoto. *Imamekashisa* was as important to the Meiji elite as it was in the 11th century to the urbane courtiers of Murasaki's *Tale of Genji.* Even so, in a rather charming touch, Hiroshige envisages his Western parasols as umbrellas of status, held by the ladies-in-waiting over the emperor, empress, and infant prince.

The Japanese Umbrella and the West

In the West from about the mid-17th century the vogue for Japanese objects was a manifestation of an infatuation with the exotic East, a fashion known as "chinoiserie." Curiosity about the Orient was stimulated by the importation of hundreds of thousands of Chinese blue and white porcelains first by the Portuguese in the 16th century and then by the Dutch in the 17th. The Japanese began to produce export wares in both blue and white and enamels for the Dutch East India Company around 1660, but Europeans at that time could not distinguish between China and Japan and it was common to identify everything as Chinese. Adding to the confusion was the fact that some Arita potters painted Chinese-style figures on their ceramics; in at least one example a figure is holding a parasol (no. 122).

Reacting to the vogue for chinoiserie, the Dutch East India Company commissioned the Amsterdam artist Cornelis Pronk (1691-1795) in 1734 to create designs for export porcelain to be made and painted in China and Japan.[69] One of his drawings features a Chinese noblewoman whose maidservant holds a fringed silk umbrella over her head (no. 123a). This might be a loose interpretation of the parasol with a long, fringed-silk border that is held over male officials depicted on 17th-century Chinese Transitional wares.[70] Another source for chinoiserie images of parasols could have been illustrations in European travel books, such as those by van Linschoten and Arnoldus Montanus (1625?-1683), neither of whom actually reached the Far East. (Montanus, who never even left Europe, invented an amusing fringed parasol carried so low over the head of a Japanese lady that a window grille is necessary for her to see out.)[71] In any case, Chinese dinner services with Pronk's *Parasol Ladies* survive in abundance but Japanese examples are less common. The Dutch East India Company ultimately decided against manufacture in Japan because the wages of the porcelain makers in the small factories at Arita were too high. There do nonetheless exist a small number of dinner plates and a saucer with the *Parasol Ladies* pattern which were unmistakably made in Japan (no. 123). These are presumably the remnants of services commissioned by the Dutch supercargos.

Chinese parasols were popular in France by the early 18th century and were favored by that arbiter of taste, Madame de Pompadour, mistress of Louis XV. Intricately carved ivory sticks for parasols were imported from China in the early 19th century, and chinoiserie subjects were often painted on white silk covers.[72] Japanese umbrellas, however, did not come to the attention of the Western public until the International Exhibition held in London in 1862. As part of its effort to transform itself into a modern nation by fostering trade and technological development, Japan participated in thirty-six overseas exhibitions between 1862 and 1910, when the Anglo-Japanese exhibition was held at the White City in London. Umbrellas and other contemporary Japanese crafts probably became

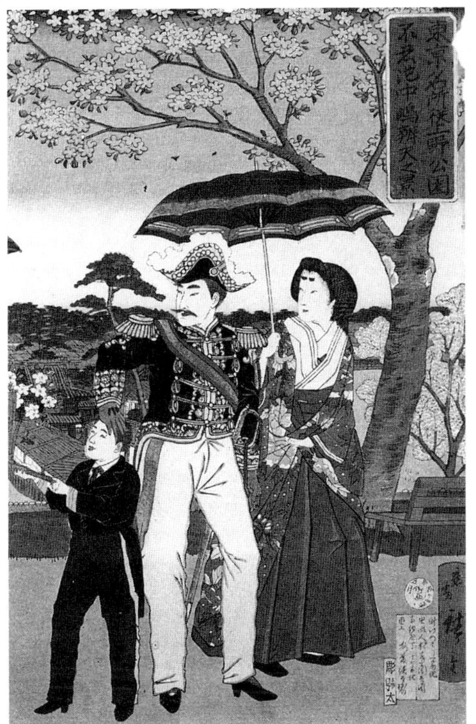

Fig. 62. Utagawa Hiroshige III (1843-1894), Additional Famous Places in Tokyo: View of Benten on Nakanoshima in Shinobazu Pond, Ueno Park *(no. 112; detail), Meiji period, 1881. Color woodblock print; triptych. The Metropolitan Museum of Art, Gift of Lincoln Kirstein, 1959*

readily available from 1868, when a commercial treaty was signed between Great Britain and Japan. The most famous store to feature Oriental products was Arthur Liberty's East India House, which opened on Regent Street in London in 1875. Japanese umbrellas were in fashion in the late 1870s and 1880s, in part because they were new and exotic, but also because they were inexpensive. A Liberty's employee remembers selling two cases of them at 1 shilling each.[73]

The French painter and etcher James Tissot (1836-1902) is typical of the first generation of European artists to be caught up in the cult of Japan. He began to purchase Japanese art in Paris as early as 1864, but its influence was not assimilated in his compositions until after he moved to London in 1871. Between 1878 and 1881 he did many portraits of his lover, Kathleen Newton (1854-1882) and her children, posing in the garden of his London home with a Japanese parasol (nos. 126, 127; fig. 63). At times Mrs. Newton holds it, framing her face in the manner of a courtesan by Utamaro; at other times it simply rests on the grass, fully opened. With these images Tissot re-creates an "earthly paradise," recording a happy existence with a bourgeois Eve in a 19th-century Eden.[74]

Although most Americans were first introduced to Japanese arts and crafts at the 1876 Philadelphia Centennial Exhibition, there were enterprising dealers in Chinese and Japanese art to be found on both Broadway and Fifth Avenue in the 1870s. The four thousand items collected by British designer Christopher Dresser in Japan, for example, were offered for sale by Tiffany and Company in New York in 1877.[75] At a time when crafts in general were held in high esteem, the Orient was a fresh discovery. The most ubiquitous Japanese art objects were fans—it was the rare middle-class American family that did not own one. There were nearly two dozen Japanese import houses in New York alone, but A. A. Vantine and Co. on Broadway and 18th Street dominated the market during the boom of the 1880s. Vantine, advertising itself as "Importers from the empires of Japan, China, India, Turkey, Persia and the East," produced an illustrated catalogue that vividly documents the trade with Japan.[76] The introductory sales pitch promotes the Japanese as the most "cultivated, artistic people":

> At the present time when the dilettante justly mourns the decline of handicrafts . . . caused by the constantly increasing use of machinery as a creative force, in Japan, the hand of the humble workman is still guided by his mind, or rather by an inherited freedom of touch that prevents the tiresome uniformity or sameness so common to ordinary productions.[77]

Vantine stocked paper umbrellas up to 18 feet in diameter (intended as a "lawn tent"—the double handle could be unscrewed), and sold smaller painted parasols with a 5-foot diameter in cases of five for 85 cents. The catalogue notes that such parasols "are largely used for fire places and ceilings," that is, attached to hanging light fixtures, a statement that can, in fact, be documented with views of contemporary American interiors (fig. 64). The wealthy New York doctor William A. Hammond decorated the walls and ceiling of his Japanese Bedroom with textiles, fans, miniature Japanese parasol covers, porcelains, and a frieze of woodblock prints; small parasols were affixed to the chandelier (fig. 65).

Western interest in ethnography and the customs of the East created a demand for photographs of Japanese craftsmen in the late 19th century (nos. 4, 5, 7, 18). Kusakabe Kimbei, who apprenticed with the Austrian photographer Baron von Stillfried in Yokohama (see no. 26), bought most of the latter's stock in the 1880s and worked until 1912. The well-known photograph of an umbrella maker attributed to Kimbei shows a specialist in *bangasa* in the process of smoothing down a sheet of paper he has just trimmed and pasted onto the frame before him (fig. 66). Carefully posed in the photographer's studio, the

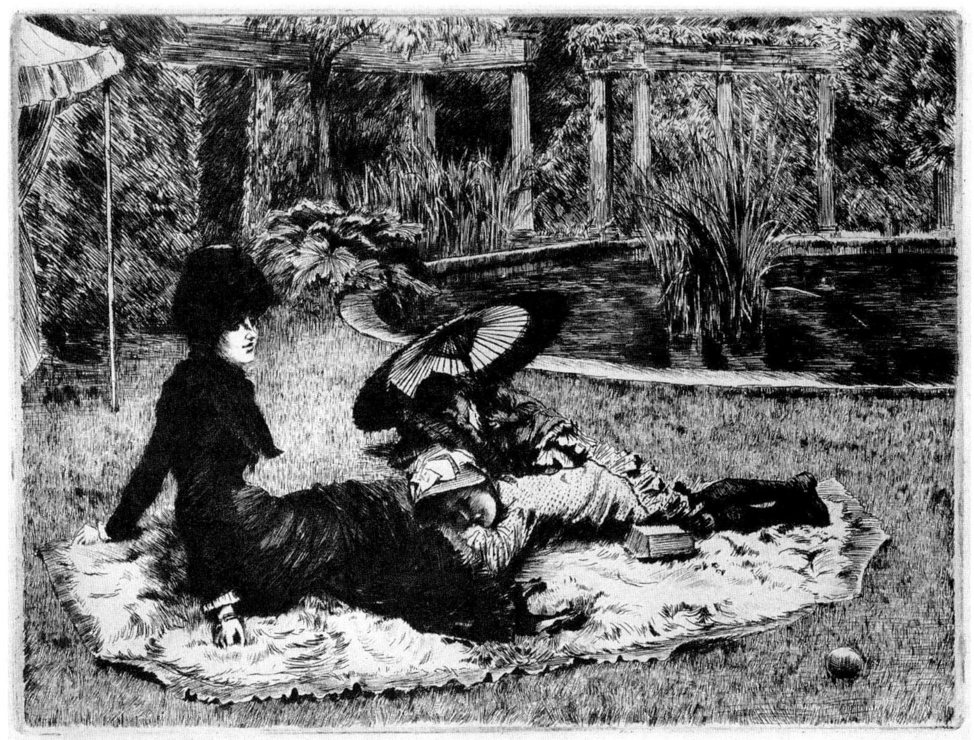

Fig. 63. James Jacques Joseph Tissot (1836-1902), On the Grass (Garden Party), *1880. Etching and drypoint. 7 3/4 x 10 5/8 in. (19.7 x 27 cm.). The Metropolitan Museum of Art, Gift of Otto F. Langmann, 1956*

scene includes umbrellas in every stage of manufacture and almost every type of tool. On the floor at the right rear is a basket with *shimewa*, small paper-wrapped bamboo rings that slide around a closed umbrella to keep it tightly shut. In the right foreground are four bamboo umbrella sticks with shaved nodes resting on closed umbrella skeletons that are waiting to be covered. A roller on the floor at the center may be used for applying paste to the thin strips of reinforcing paper at the center and around the rib tips, or it may be for lacquering the ribs. A triangular tool called a *maikiri*, a gimlet for punching holes in the ribs and stretchers (today a machine is used for this purpose), stands upright on its round wooden head between the roller and the paste bowl, whose wooden lid lies to the left of the roller. The whole is a painstakingly composed documentary for the Western armchair traveler.

The taste for things Japanese—Japonisme, as the French called it— continued well past 1900. For many, Japan still retained a mysterious allure by virtue of having been closed to the outside world for several centuries. Some were attracted by Japan's new status as a world power following its victories in the Sino-Japanese (1894-95) and Russo-Japanese (1904-5) wars. As knowledge of Japanese culture and arts grew in the West, it was color prints that often had the most significant impact. They were endlessly fascinating both in their subject matter and in their use of line and flat planes of color to create stunning graphic designs. The medium itself became a stimulus for artists, especially those touched by the Arts and Crafts movement.

Helen Hyde and Bertha Lum, American graphic artists who went to Japan to live and work during the first decade of this century, both exploited the exotic Orient to the fullest. Using the medium of the woodblock print, they avoided scenes of modern Tokyo and chose instead to focus on more nostalgic themes, stereotypes of the old Japan that no doubt appealed to them and to their Western clientele. Both took special pleasure in depicting kimono-clad figures shielding themselves against the onslaught of rain and snow with traditional paper umbrellas (nos. 129, 130).[78]

Among Japanese artists at the beginning of the century, the status of the individual woodblock print was in great flux, many of its former functions assumed by

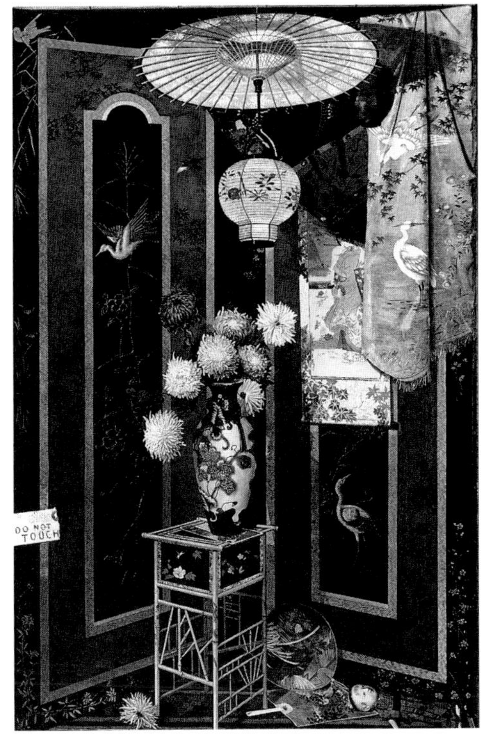

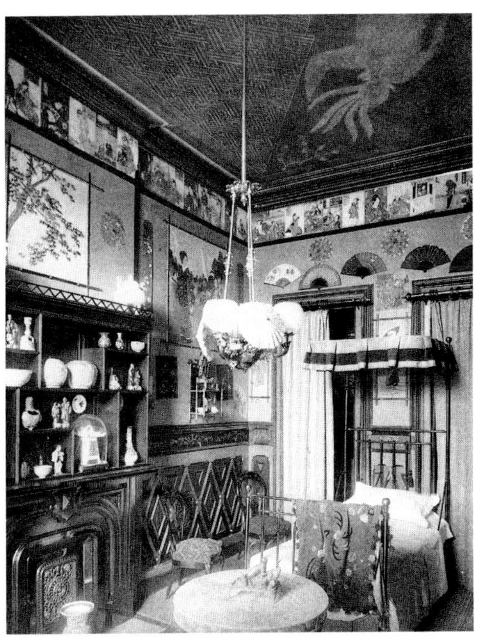

Fig. 64. John Haberle (1856-1933), American. Japanese Corner, *1898. Oil on canvas. 81 x 52 in. (205.7 x 132.1 cm.). Gift of Mr. and Mrs. Chauncey Steiger, Museum of Fine Arts, Springfield, Mass.*

Fig. 65. Dr. William A. Hammond's Japanese Bedroom, Fifty-fourth Street, near Fifth Avenue, New York City, ca. 1883. From Artistic Houses *(1883). Courtesy of the Wadsworth Atheneum, Hartford, Conn.*

photography, chromolithography, and newspapers. Two movements in printmaking developed as a result: the "creative print" (*sôsaku hanga*) and the "new print" (*shin hanga*). Adherents of the creative-print movement believed that artists should perform the entire process themselves, carving and printing as well as creating the images. Although influenced by Western art, many, including Mizushima Nihou, Maekawa Sempan and Takei Takeo, continued to work in the woodblock technique, selecting subjects related to contemporary experience (nos. 117-119). Mori Yoshitoshi converted the stencil-dyeing technique into a fine-art medium (no. 6). Ultimately this group brought Japanese graphic arts into the international arena.

Shin hanga artists were traditional in their approach and more commercially oriented. They worked in close collaboration with publisher and artisans in an adaptation of the old system of print production, and drew on time-honored subject matter—beautiful women in rain and snow, actors, and famous scenic spots. Watanabe Shôzaburô (1885-1962), one of Japan's leading print publishers and dealers, initiated the new-print movement in an effort to revive the creative spirit of the ukiyo-e tradition. Hoping to attract the same wealthy Japanese clientele that had supported fine mica-ground prints by Utamaro in the 18th century, Watanabe sought artists who would design new, modern ukiyo-e. In the spring of 1915 he finally found his man, a foreigner. At a Tokyo department-store exhibition Watanabe saw watercolors by the visiting Austrian painter Fritz Capelari (1884-1950). Among the landscapes were two that depicted Japanese genre subjects. Watanabe immediately recognized that Capelari's sense of composition and color might lend itself to the type of image he hoped to promote. *Umbrellas*, the first sketch they turned into a print, shows girl students returning home in the rain, a scene in which Hokusai's influence can be clearly traced (nos. 131, 131a). By the end of 1915 Watanabe had published twelve color woodblock prints designed by Capelari.[79] Carefully supervising the block cutter and printer, they managed to create a kind of *shin hanga*, just as Watanabe had hoped. Watanabe's seal and Capelari's initials appear on all of the images.

Watanabe's collaboration with Capelari and with British printmakers Elizabeth Keith (1887-1956) and Charles W. Bartlett (1860-1940) stimulated the *shin hanga* movement, encouraging fine craftsmanship and popular imagery. Picturesque scenes of rain and snow in a painstakingly detailed realistic style were favorites. Itô Shinsui (1898-1972) and Kawase Hasui (1883-1957) were two *shin hanga* artists who collaborated successfully with Watanabe (nos. 27, 44, 45). Their prints, in which traditional umbrellas often appear, had commercial appeal in the West as well. By the late 1920s Watanabe and Kawaguchi, a rival publisher, were exporting *shin hanga* to New York by the thousands.[80]

The evolution of the Japanese umbrella follows a pattern often seen in Japanese art—adaptation and gradual transformation of an imported model. The end result is a product that is more elegant, subtle, and skillfully crafted than the original prototype. The umbrella, an essentially mundane, utilitarian object, was transformed by Japanese sensibilities into something alternately romantic, humorous, playful, dynamic, and even frightening. Torn umbrellas could assume a life of their own as monsters and ghosts. They can also evoke a melancholy sense of the impermanence of things and of life in general. From the time of the *Tale of Genji*, when a gentlemen caller arrived sheltered by an umbrella, there has been an element of intrigue and passion about it as well. In the Edo period courtesans en route to an assignation seemed even more beautiful against the backdrop of a gorgeous *janome*, and women were shown leaping from great heights to prove their love, with only an open umbrella to slow their descent. Nothing was more affecting than a man and woman walking together holding

Fig. 66. Attributed to Kusakabe Kimbei (1841-1934), Umbrella Maker, *Meiji period, ca. 1880. Albumen print*

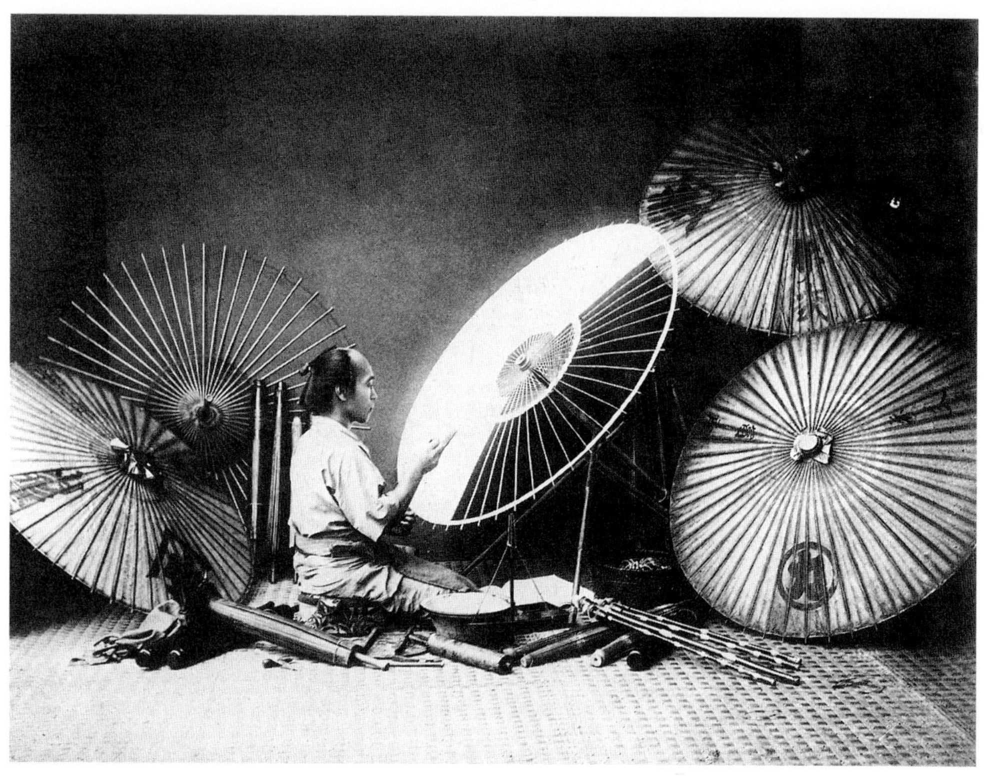

between them the stick of a single umbrella. The umbrella became—and remains—a familiar prop in Kabuki and Kyôgen dance performances. Literary themes relating to rain and snow were amplified by haiku inscribed around umbrella images on prints and paintings. The umbrella enhanced the persona of a man as much as that of a woman; it is said that the famous 17th-century warrior Miyamoto Musashi could fight with two swords while carrying an open umbrella. For the ambitious samurai on the eve of the modernization of Japan, a Western umbrella was emblematic of his status as a forward-looking leader.

The beauty of the traditional Japanese umbrella is indeed subtle. It has to do with smell, if the umbrella is freshly oiled, and with color—the translucent cover filters the light through indigo or red paper to create what Stephan Köhler calls "heaven on earth" or "private skies." It even has to do with sound—the "thunk" of the umbrella opening and the loud patter of raindrops on the taut paper cover.

The sensuous experience begins at the moment the user of the umbrella grasps its rattan-wrapped handle, which feels cool and smooth. There is no Western-style automatic opening device here. Since the oiled paper has a tendency to stick, the folds of the umbrella must first be shaken loose by twisting it two or three times in a left-to-right motion. As the umbrella is then pushed open, the user becomes conscious of its weight and mass, and of the fragility of its thin bamboo ribs and stretchers, reinforced only by thread and strips of paper. The weight increases, of course, if snow is falling, a sensation that underlies a familiar Japanese proverb:

Waga mono to *omoeba karoshi* *kasa no yuki*	As I think of it as mine the snow on my umbrella is light.

Rows of intricate silk embroidery on the stretchers add to the dazzling visual effect when one looks up into the open cover. The unique beauty of the Japanese paper umbrella derives from this rich sensory appeal.

Notes

1. Translated by Hiroaki Sato.
2. Takazu (1930), 35; and Miyamoto (1968), 219.
3. Katagiri (1985), 9.
4. Strommenger (1962), pl. 115.
5. Young (1981), 74-75, fig. 45 and pl. 32F,G.
6. Crawford (1970), 22.
7. Reflecting their history, the words "umbrella" and "parasol," with roots ultimately in Latin (*umbra*, shade; *sol*, sun), came into English from Italian, via French. Both originally had the sense of "sunshade" (cf. Fr. *ombrelle*, parasol).
8. Farrell (1985), 20-23. Farrell notes that the umbrella "has always been the poor relation of the frivolous, expensive parasol," and that its history is accordingly more difficult to trace in written sources; ibid., 23.
9. Weinstein (1978), 138 and nn. 18, 19.
10. Crawford (1970), 51.
11. Weinstein (1978), 143. For an illustration of two figures worshiping an umbrella set on an altar, from a railing medallion at Bodh Gayâ (ca. 100 B.C.), see Coomaraswamy (1935), pl. XIV. A relief carving of the scene "Adoration of the Stupa by Nâgas" at Amarâvatî shows a stupa crowned by multiple layers of small umbrellas; see Zimmer (1968), Vol. 2, pl. 97.
12. Illustrated in Huntington (1985), 150-151.
13. Biot (1851), 488. The *Zhou li* was written in the early Han dynasty but describes customs far more ancient. For a discussion of ancient Chinese cosmology, notably the "Heavenly Cover" school, see Needham (1965), Vol. 3, 210ff.
14. Umbrella references in the *Zhou li* are found in the chapters "Kao gongji" (Records of crafts and labor) and on the Xia dynasty. The commentary is cited in Morohashi (1974), 845.
15. The Changsha painting on silk, which measures 37.5 x 28 cm., was published in *Wenwu* (Cultural relics), no. 7 (1973), 3-4. See also Li (1985), 455, fig. 204 (the illustration is published upside down), and text, 444-445. For a Western Han (2nd century B.C.) wood tomb figurine riding in a horse-drawn chariot with parasol, see *Wenwu*, no. 12 (1972), 13, fig. 7. These Chou and Han references were generously provided by Professor Elizabeth Childs-Johnson, Hamilton College.
16. Lim (1987), 116, pl. 28. The chariot canopies may have been color-coded according to rank, in keeping with Chinese fastidiousness for detail. The *Hou Han shu* (History of the Later Han) cites both blue and white examples.
17. Needham (1965), Vol. 4, part 2, 70. Needham also makes note of the collapsible chariot-umbrella ribs of Wang Mang's time recovered from the tomb of Wang Kuang at Korean Lolang (ibid., 71). For the Lolang example, see Harada and Komai (1937), pls. XIX and XX.
18. Akiyama and Matsubara (1969), fig. 187. A canopy suspended over the Buddha replaced the umbrella in later Buddhist art, but a silk parasol is one of the eight Buddhist emblems that often appear in later Chinese decorative arts.
19. Ibid., pls. 123, 124.
20. Gugong bowuyuan (Palace Museum) Editorial Committee (1981), 71.
21. Gernet (1962), 128.
22. The *Iroha jirui shô*, an influential Japanese-language dictionary compiled in the late Heian period by the courtier Tachibana Tadakane (active late 12th century), defines *gai* as *kinugasa*; see *Koji ruien* (1984), 427. The *Koji ruien* is a compendium of references from books written before 1867; part 2 of Vol. 54, 365ff, contains a section on umbrella citations. See also Morohashi (1974), 845. For *karakasa*, see Takazu (1930), 1.
23. Information regarding the placement of parasol *haniwa* was given by Hiroshi Yabushita, Gifu City Museum of History. The author is indebted to Mr. Yabushita, an archaeologist, for pointing out this reference and many others pertaining to the early history of umbrellas in Japan. Mr. Yabushita, who is the de facto historian of Gifu umbrellas, served as instructor and patient guide to the author during the course of this project, and generously shared his research. The most spectacular example of a parasol *haniwa* was excavated from the Anderayama tomb, Uji City, Kyoto prefecture, and is now in the collection of the University of Kyoto (see fig. 50); see also Tokyo National Museum (1973), figs. 7-10. Weinstein, who notes that parasol *haniwa* were placed facing houses, also cites their possible cosmological significance; Weinstein (1978), 174.
24. Pearson (1992), 226.
25. Ibid., 272. For an illustration of the umbrella, see Uehara (1982), pl. 6.
26. *Koji ruien* (1984), 431.
27. *Manyôshû* (1965), 48. In the same anthology, the poet Kume no Hironawa writes that a large leaf held by servants over their masters who are hunting in the fields looks like a blue *kinugasa*.
28. *Nihon shoki* (1952), 76-77. For a translation, see *Nihongi* (1956), 65.
29. *Ryô no gige* (Commentary on administrative laws) is a ten-volume book of rituals completed in 833 that annotates the 8th-century Yôrô Penal and Civil Codes; see *Koji ruien* (1984), 429. Reference supplied by Hiroshi Yabushita.
30. Bock (1972), Vol. 1, 140.
31. Ibid., Vol. 2, 20.
32. Ibid., Vol. 2, 50-51, n. 252.
33. Murasaki (1976), Vol. 1, 299-300 (Edward Seidensticker's translation). Murasaki uses the word *mikasa* (honorable umbrella). Modern editions of the novel (the original manuscript does not survive) write the word with the honorific prefix *mi* (or *on*) followed by the character for *kasa* or *karakasa*; see Murasaki (1959), 155; and Murasaki (1979), 253.
34. For a survey of Japanese papermaking, see Brian Hickman, "Washi," in *Kodansha Encyclopedia* (1983), Vol. 8, 233-234.
35. Morris (1967), Vol. 1, 198, Vol. 2, nn. 866, 867. Shônagon used the word *ôgasa* (large umbrella). The original manuscript does not survive; modern editions of the text print the Chinese character meaning "large" for *ô* and Japanese phonetic symbols for *kasa*. For a second reference to a courtier with an umbrella bearer on a rainy day, see ibid., Vol. 1, 108. Elsewhere Shônagon also used the word *karakasa*, presumably in phonetic script.
36. This sutra was dedicated at the Anrakujû-in, but later entered the collection of Kunô-ji temple, for which it is named. For a fuller discussion of this painting, see Meech-Pekarik (1977), 61-62.
37. For a translation of the text accompanying the painting, see Kaufman (1980), 353. Illustrated in Miya (1971), color offset pl. 7.
38. See above, p. 22. See also Terashima Ryôan (1983), Vol. 1, 353.
39. Sakamoto and Ide (1982), nos. 37, 54, 68, 70.
40. See van Linschoten (1596), plates between pages 44-45, 46-47, 58-59. The author is indebted to Gunhild Avitabile for this reference.
41. See Pratt (1931), Vol. 1, 109. Pratt transcribed these trading accounts of the English factory at Hirado in the 1820s. The author is grateful to Michael Cooper, S.J., Sophia University, Tokyo, for this reference and for general counsel on matters pertaining to the "Southern Barbarians." For kitasols, see *Oxford English Dictionary*, s.v. *kittisol* (obsolete, with numerous variant spellings). Meaning "umbrella" or "parasol," the word is defined as usually associated with the East Indies and China, and specifically as a Chinese umbrella of bamboo and oiled paper. It is difficult,

however, to be sure what Adams's transactions involved, since the word had dropped out of current use by the time it was last recorded in 1875.

42. An earlier version of the *Hôkoku Festival* screen illustrated here was painted by Kano Naizen (1570-1616), who is believed to have visited the port of Nagasaki where the Portuguese landed. Naizen documented huge, brocade-covered festival parasols in his screen, painted in 1606 for the Hôkoku Shrine, Kyoto; illustrated in Takeda et al. (1978), pls. 15, 16.
43. See Kobayashi (1987), 19-24.
44. Cooper (1973), 181.
45. Keene, ed. (1955), 354-356. The translation is by Richard Lane, who points out that the sun deity, although normally a goddess, Amaterasu, was popularly believed about this time to be a god. For another umbrella story by Saikaku, see "Umbrellas in an Ill Wind that Blew Their Lives to Shreds," in Ihara Saikaku (1981), 51-54.
46. The image alludes to the story of the demon Ibaraki, whose arm was cut off by a warrior, Watanabe no Tsuna (953-1024), and who then returned in human guise to snatch it back. The arm of Harunobu's courtesan is hidden inside her kimono sleeve.
47. Translation by Timothy Screech, University of London.
48. Blyth (1952), 216.
49. Ibid., 231.
50. The author is indebted to Hiroshi Onishi, The Metropolitan Museum of Art, for information on rain terminology.
51. On the print the characters for "summer downpour" are *hakuu,* but the *furigana* (phonetic symbols) to the side read *yûdachi.* In theory these words are translated as "daytime shower" and "evening squall" respectively, but in practice they are sometimes synonymous.
52. Waterhouse (1964), 82. Waterhouse points out that the poem depends on two puns. *Hi no moto* means "beneath the sun" and also "Japan"; *ame ga shita* means "that which is beneath the sky"—the earth—as well as "in the rain."
53. Ibid., 297, 302.
54. Yamaguchi (1983), 78; and Genshoku ukiyo-e daihyakka-jiten henshû-iinkai, ed. (1982), Vol. 6, fig. 284.
55. For the *Wakan sansai zue*, see n. 38 above; for *Morisada mankô*, see Kitagawa (1989). The author is indebted to Joseph Seubert for locating a copy of Takazu (1930).
56. In Britain in the early 18th century, when it was still chiefly a woman's accessory, "the only men who could use the umbrella with impunity were doctors and clergymen whose professional duties took them out in the rain"; Farrell (1985), 24. For matters pertaining to Western umbrellas the author is much indebted to the expertise of British costume historian Jeremy Farrell, Museum of Costume and Textiles, Nottingham. For umbrella nomenclature, see ibid., 91.
57. Takazu (1930), 20-22.
58. Ibid., 18, 29-30.
59. This work exists only in manuscript. Portions are cited in *Koji ruien* (1984), 442.
60. Kitagawa (1989), 380; and Takazu (1930), 19-20.
61. See Koike and Chikamatsu (1991), nos. 35 and 123.
62. Sugimoto and Swain (1978), 338-343; see also Vos (1987), 21-23. The von Siebold collection of prints in Leiden is well known; see Narazaki et al., eds. (1978). There are three types of paper umbrellas among the early (pre-Meiji) examples in the Siebold, Blomhoff and Fisscher collections in Leiden: a) ten long-stick parasols with black, red, white, yellow and blue covers, most painted with floral designs, L. 48 1/8-65 in. (122-165 cm.); they have bamboo sticks except for a few luxury items with lacquered wood sticks, brass fittings, and velvet storage bags; b) five medium-length banded *janome* with black, brown, and possibly indigo covers, L. 35 in. (89 cm.); c) four *janome* with short sticks, L. 30 3/8-33 1/8 in. (77-84 cm.). Information regarding the Leiden umbrellas was graciously provided by Matthi Forrer, Rijksmuseum voor Volkenkunde. The interest in Japanese umbrellas in Holland is further documented by an illustration in an 1841 catalogue published by the Dutch curio dealer Dirk Boer (1803-1877). Boer's shop in Scheveningen apparently featured five life-sized dolls representing a Japanese feudal lord with his family and attendants. One male doll has both a sword and a fully opened paper umbrella awkwardly thrust through his obi, a bizarre sight; see van Dam (1987), 19.
63. One umbrella was accessioned in 1898, and five predate 1909. This information was provided by Michelle Tolimi in the museum's Department of Ethnology. For an illustration see Hosley (1990), 77, no. 52.
64. Fukuzawa (1966), 122.
65. This book is fully translated and illustrated in Meech-Pekarik (1986), 65-71.
66. The author is grateful to the publisher of *Asian Art* for permission to draw on material that has already appeared in print; see Meech (1993), 2-4.
67. Waley (1984), 159.
68. Whitney (1979), 86. See also Meech-Pekarik (1986), 112-114.
69. For a definitive study of the Pronk designs, see Jorg (1980), 15ff.
70. Kilburn (1981), fig. 12, no. 41; and Little (1983), nos. 20, 51. An interesting variation on the parasol theme occurs on a French ewer of 1650-80 in the Victoria and Albert Museum, London, decorated with a design of a European gentleman holding a fringed parasol over a Chinese figure; see Carswell (1985), 41, fig. 18.
71. Montanus (1670), 77; for van Linschoten see n. 40 above.
72. Farrell (1985), 26, 28, and 41.
73. Ibid., 75.
74. See Wentworth (1984), 125-153.
75. Halén (1987).
76. Hosley (1990), 44-45.
77. *Illustrated Catalogue of A. A. Vantine and Co., Importers . . .* ([1880]), 4. There is a copy of this catalogue in the Winterthur Museum; the author is indebted to William Hosley, Wadsworth Atheneum, for the reference.
78. For more on Lum and Hyde, see Meech and Weisberg (1990), 101-125, 127-156.
79. Watanabe Tadasu, ed. (1974), 143-144; also Watanabe Shôzaburô (1936), 8. According to the Austrian Thieme-Becker, Capelari, who trained at the Vienna Academy, set sail for Shanghai in 1911 with a commission to paint the harbor. After living in China, Japan and Java, he returned to Europe in 1922. He was in Japan a second time prior to 1932; see also Pantzer (1990), 34. The author is grateful to Johannes Wieninger, Österreichisches Museum für Angewandte Kunst, Vienna, for these references. For the *shin hanga* movement and Japonisme in the graphic arts, see Stephens (1993).
80. Watanabe and others gave the impression of exclusivity by numbering their editions, but would in fact oblige clients by reprinting an edition when it sold out.

Catalogue

Glossary of words not defined in the catalogue entries

Kaô: written seal

Nanako: raised dot ground

Shakudô: alloy of copper and gold, patinated black

Shibuichi: alloy of three parts copper to one of silver

Woodblock-Print Terms

Beni-e: "red picture"; print hand-colored with deep pink pigment derived from the safflower, popular ca. 1720-40

Benizuri-e: "red printed picture"; two-color print, generally deep pink and green, popular ca. 1740-55

Chôôban or *nagaban:* very long, large print

Chûban: medium-sized print

Pillar print (*hashira-e*): very tall, narrow print said to have been displayed on a wooden pillar

Hosoban: small, narrow print

Ôban: large print

Ôôban: extralarge print

Surimono: deluxe, limited-edition print often commissioned by a poetry club

Toshidama: literally, "year jewel," a circular seal used by the Utagawa school

Urushi-e: "lacquer picture"; hand-colored print that imitates the appearance of black lacquer by the application of clear glue to areas printed in black ink, popular ca. 1720-40

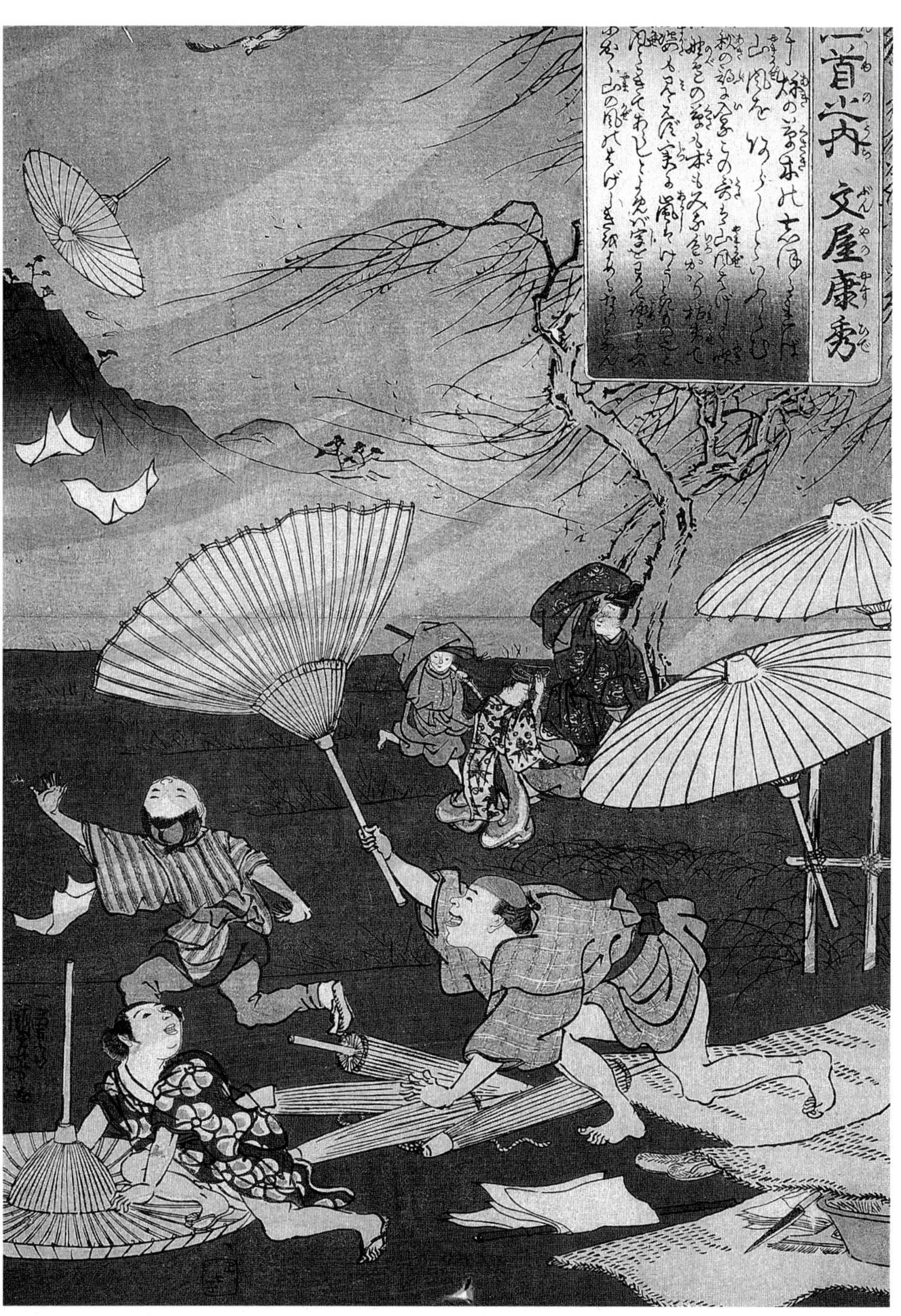

1. Utagawa Kuniyoshi (1797-1861)
The Poet Bunya no Yasuhide
Series: One Hundred Poets
Edo period, ca. 1840
Signed: Ichiyûsai Kuniyoshi ga
Publisher: Ebiko
Color woodblock print; vertical *ôban*
13 1/4 x 9 1/2 in. (33.7 x 24.1 cm.)
Museum of Fine Arts, Springfield, Massachusetts, Raymond A. Bidwell Collection, 60.D05.204

An umbrella maker and his assistants see their precious wares blown inside out and into the sky on a windy day. Sheets of paper fly off like white egrets. On the mat in the lower right corner are a bowl (*suribachi*) for mixing paste and a paste brush (*noribake*), as well as a stack of white paper for covering the umbrella, together with a paper-cutting knife.

Kuniyoshi's image is closely modeled on a picture in Tamba Tôkei's woodblock-printed book "Famous Views of the Province of Settsu," dated 1796-98. Tokei shows oiled umbrellas planted in holes to dry in the garden of an umbrella maker. A strong wind has lifted some of the umbrellas into the sky.[1]

Kuniyoshi has some finished umbrellas tied on a wooden stand to dry; presumably they have just been oiled for waterproofing. If so, it is not clear why the paper pasting and the oiling processes are shown together in this way. The artist may have been confused about the stages of umbrella making. On the other hand, this may represent the final stage of the paper-pasting process, in which the umbrella is left open for several hours so that the paste can dry. The artist errs in showing the ribs of the inverted umbrella as concave—they should be straight.

This contemporary genre scene is juxtaposed with a portrait of the 9th-century court poet Bunya no Yasuhide in the background. Yasuhide's poem is from an anthology compiled by Fujiwara no Teika (1162-1241) in the 13th century, *Ogura hyakunin isshû* (Ogura collection of single poems by one hundred poets), the best-known collection of poems in all Japanese history:

Fuku kara ni
aki no kusa ki no
shiorureba
mube yamakaze o
arashi to iuramu

The plants and trees of autumn
shrivel in its gusts—
"wind from the mountains,"
so rightly called a tempest.[2]

1. Suzuki (1992), 207, fig. 23.
2. Translation by John Carpenter. This is a calligraphic punning poem: the character for *arashi* (tempest or storm) is formed by combining the characters for "mountain" and "wind" (*yamakaze*).

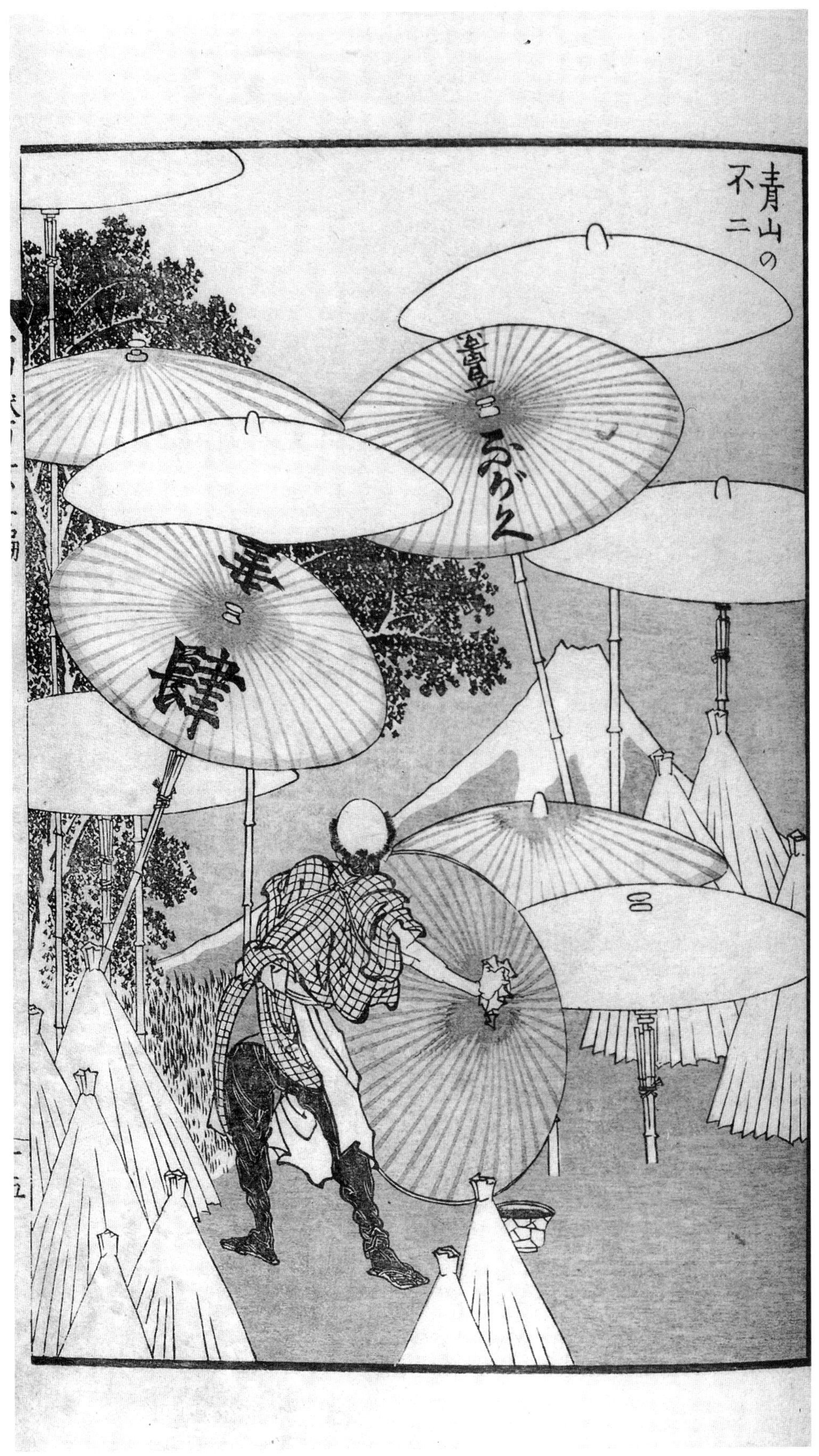

2. Katsushika Hokusai (1760-1849)
Fuji from Aoyama
From *Fugaku hyakkei* (One hundred views of Fuji), Vol. 3
Edo period, ca. 1849
Color woodblock-printed illustrated book
Publisher: Eirakuya Tôshirô
Page: 8 5/16 x 6 3/16 in. (21.1 x 16.2 cm.)
Ravicz Collection

An umbrella oiler is waterproofing paper umbrellas in the Aoyama district in Edo (now a fashionable section of the Minato ward in Tokyo.) Rotating the umbrella, which is supported on a metal stand, he applies hot oil with a handful of shredded rags (for a view of this process today, see fig. 10); a bucket of oil is visible on the ground to his right. The finished umbrellas are set out to dry in his yard. Some are tied fully open atop long bamboo poles; others are planted half-open in holes in the ground. Two umbrellas with writing on them appear to be *bangasa*; one is inscribed "Bookstore" and the other announces the title of the book, "One Hundred Views of Fuji." Several have top notches (*atama rokuro*) with an indentation for tying on a protective paper cap (*kappa*) after the umbrella is finished.

Hokusai seems to have made a mistake in the depiction of the half-open umbrellas planted in the ground: the paper layers wrapped around the top notch should have been smoothed down in the preceding step of the process, when the paper was pasted onto the frame. The oiler would not be able to work on an umbrella in this condition.

In this witty composition the umbrellas create a landscape of their own. The cones of the half-open umbrellas echo the shape of Mount Fuji; those that are open and elevated resemble clouds passing overhead. The three-volume "One Hundred Views of Fuji," printed in black and gray, is considered one of Hokusai's masterpieces.[1] A work of his old age, it documents his obsession with Fuji, and his preoccupation with the Taoist belief in Fuji as the secret source of immortality.

Hokusai was far from the first artist to succumb to the mysterious allure of this mountain. Nearly a century earlier Ike Taiga (1723-1776) had set out to produce a series of one hundred paintings of Fuji, and there were others before and after with the same compulsion. "From the beginning of cultural memory," writes art historian Melinda Takeuchi, "the Japanese have held the majestic volcano to be a living divinity. Fuji's eternal form, unearthly in its immense scale, presides serenely over the surrounding landscape and dwarfs the human realm."[2]

1. The first two volumes, known as the "Falcon Feather" edition, were published in 1835, when the artist was seventy-five. The gray blocks for the third volume were not prepared until immediately prior to its publication, which is generally believed to have been in 1849, the year of Hokusai's death; Forrer (1985), 172-173. Hokusai may have connected *kasa* and Aoyama in his mind because of the famous pine known as *kasamatsu* (umbrella pine) in the garden of the Ryûgan-ji temple in Aoyama; *Edo meisho zue* (1919-20), Vol. 4, 276.
2. Takeuchi (1992), 52.

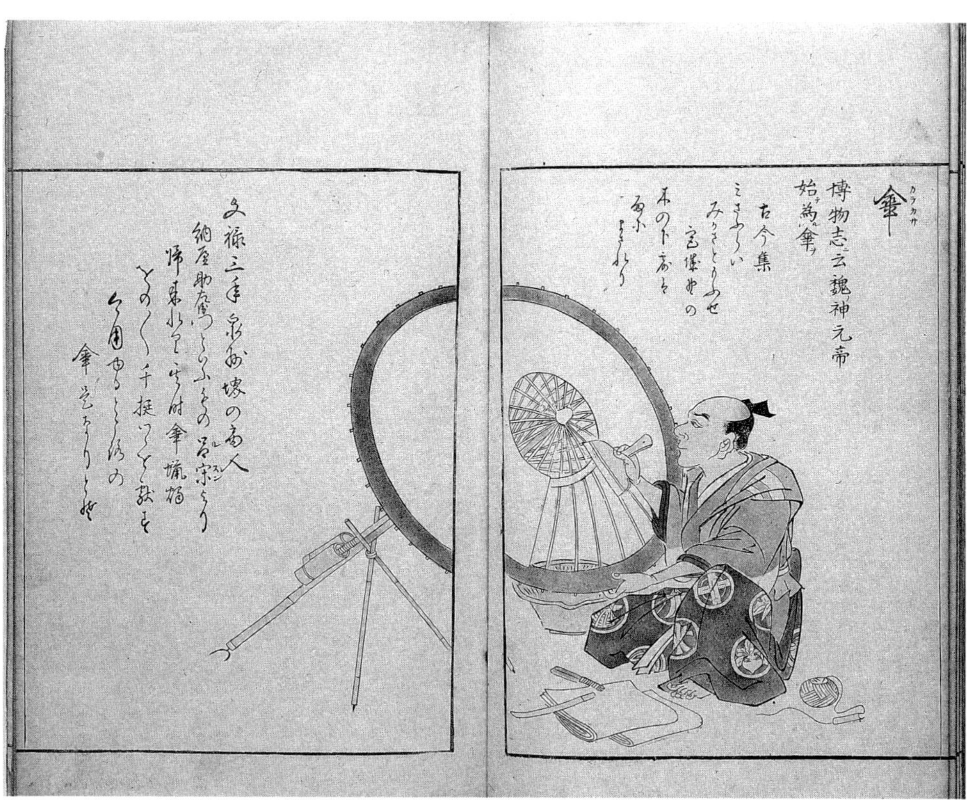

3. Tachibana Minkô (active mid-18th century)
Umbrella
From *Saiga shokunin burui* (Various classes of artisans in colored pictures), Vol. 2
Edo period, 1770
Signed: Gyokujuken Tachibana Minkô; sealed: Tachibana Masakatsu
Publisher: Uemura Tosaburô and Sawa Isuke, Edo
Woodblock-printed illustrated book with stencil-printed color
Page: 11 7/8 x 8 3/8 in. (30.2 x 21.3 cm.)
Former collections of Henri Vever, Edmond de Goncourt, and Hayashi Tadamasa
Ravicz Collection

Instead of a simple workman's costume, this umbrella maker wears the kimono of a samurai. In the early Edo period impoverished samurai often turned to umbrella making for extra income; splitting bamboo for ribs and pasting paper onto a frame or skeleton were skills they could easily master.

The umbrella is raised on a simple bamboo tripod called a *kasaharidai* (umbrella-spreading stand) of the type used in the Tokyo region; Gifu craftsmen employ a box-type stand (see fig. 1). The short hairs on the paste brush are also typical of Edo; the brushes used in Gifu have long hairs. With the bowl (*suribachi*) for mixing paste by his right knee, the umbrella maker applies paste to the bamboo ribs before fitting on the next section of heavy white paper. The paper is rectangular and will be trimmed to size after it has been fastened to the skeleton. Gifu umbrella makers precut their paper into wedges, which align more or less with the rim (see fig. 6). The first and more difficult method, probably typical of Edo craftsmen, yields more accurate results.

The artisan rotates the umbrella with his left hand. Lying on the ground by his left foot are two cutting tools and the extra sheets of paper he needs to finish the cover. The tools are a little different from one workshop to the next because they are usually made by the craftsmen themselves. At the side is a ball of thread, used to strengthen the frame around the outer edge and the inner ring before paper is applied.

In applying the paper, the umbrella maker begins with thin strips at the sensitive areas that most need strengthening, the rib tips and the joints where the stretchers meet the ribs. A portion of the reinforcing strip at the center (*nakaokigami*) is still visible here. This umbrella, with its decoration restricted to a narrow blue outer band, is of a type known as a *yakko-gasa*, or "spear-bearer umbrella."

Minkô's two-volume book depicts twenty-eight craftsmen, including a potter, a swordsmith, a papermaker and a metalworker. The image with the umbrella maker is titled *Karakasa*, or *Umbrella*, and its text, copied from the illustrated encyclopedia of 1712, *Wakan sansai zue*, begins by attributing the invention of the umbrella to the Chinese emperor Yuan (reigned 260-64) of the Wei Dynasty in the Three Kingdoms period.[1] There follows a poem from the *Kokinwakashû* (Collection of early and modern Japanese poetry), an anthology compiled by Ki no Tsurayuki and others around 905:

Misaburai
mikasa to môse
Miyagino no
ko no shita tsuyu wa
ame ni masareri

Suggest to your lord,
attendants, that he wear his hat,
for beneath the trees
of Miyagino the dew
comes down harder than rain.[2]

The account concludes with the often-told story of Naya Sukezaemon, a merchant from the city of Sakai (just south of present-day Osaka), who returned from a journey to Luzon (the Philippines) in 1594 with one thousand candles and one thousand umbrellas. The umbrellas used today, the story goes, are of this type.

1. Terashima Ryôan (1983), Vol. 1, 353, bottom.
2. McCullough (1985), 244.

4. Photographer unknown
Umbrella Maker
Meiji period, ca.1880-90
Hand-colored albumen print
8 1/8 x 10 5/8 in. (20.6 x 26.9 cm.)
Collection of Ken Jacobson

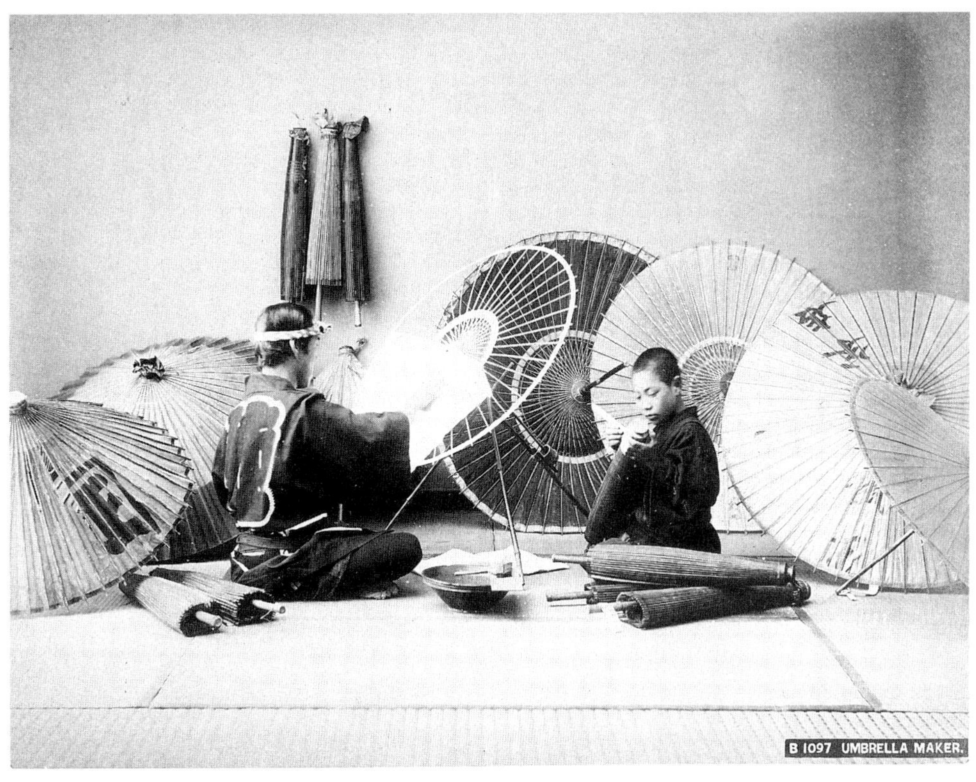

This umbrella maker is concerned solely with pasting paper onto the frame; there are no superfluous tools in sight in his immaculate workshop. Propped on the floor at the far right are an inscribed *bangasa* and a small blue parasol. At the far left is a torn *bangasa*, perhaps waiting to be stripped so that its frame can be reused. *Bangasa* are stacked on the tatami mat.

The craftsman, with a pile of precut papers in front of him, has just begun to paste the individual sheets onto the skeleton of a small parasol supported on the usual tripod stand. He has already applied the thin strips of paper needed for extra strengthening around the outer edge and the center, i.e., the *nokigami* and the *nakaokigami*. His paste pot and brush are by his right knee. A young assistant uses a bamboo implement to push in the paper and make clean valleys, as they are called, between the ribs of a finished umbrella.

5. Photographer unknown
Umbrella Maker
Meiji period, ca.1890
Hand-colored albumen print
3 1/2 x 5 1/4 in. (8.9 x 13.3 cm.)
Herbert F. Johnson Museum of Art, Cornell University, Gift of Dr. and Mrs. Henry D. Rosin, 84.120.247

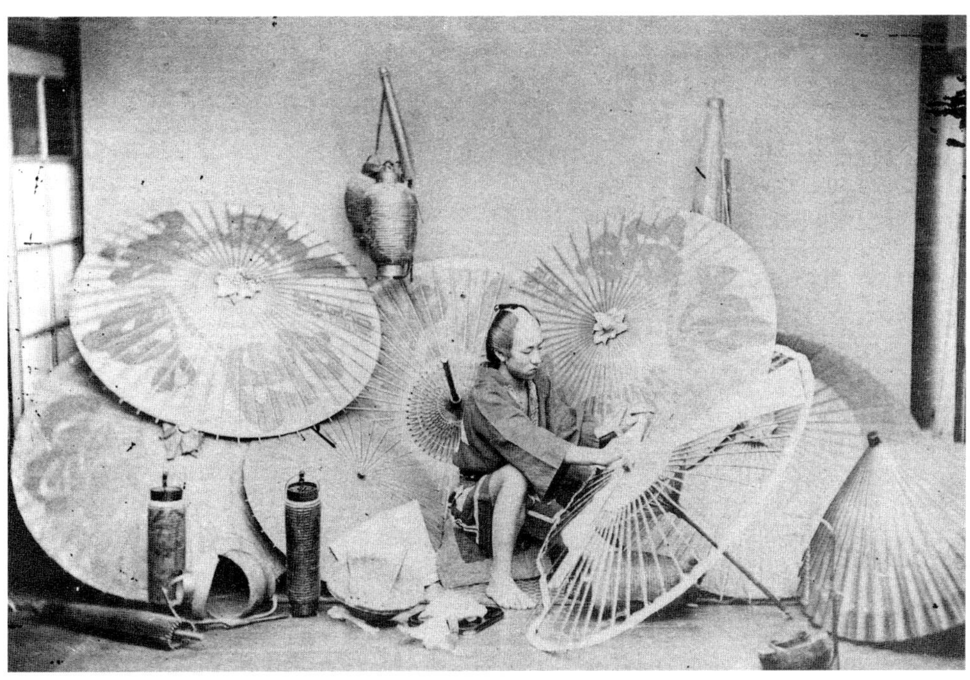

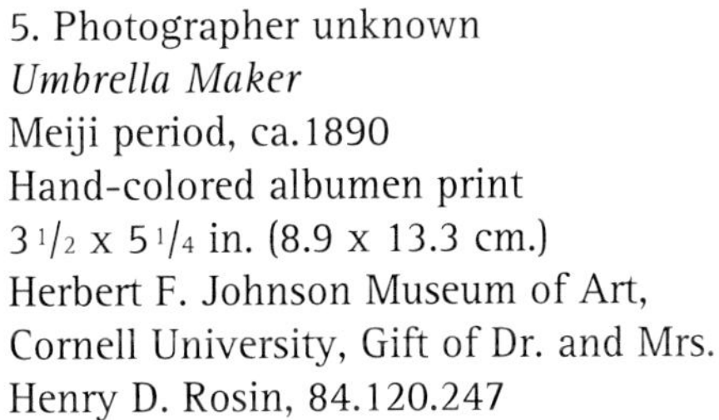

This craftsman may be a model posed in the photographer's studio. It appears that the paper has not been pasted on correctly: the thin outer strip hangs loose, there is no center strip (*nakaokigami*), and the large cover sheets (*hiragami*) are being applied in a haphazard manner. On the other hand, it may be that the man is pasting paper onto an old, recycled umbrella skeleton. Some of the umbrellas and lanterns around him look used, and the *bangasa* in the back has its protective paper cap (*kappa*), an element that would not appear in the studio of an artisan making new umbrellas. As for the odd placement of the *hiragami*, these larger sheets of cover paper are sometimes pasted in the course of production onto warped ribs, in order to straighten them. The technique is used today even for new umbrellas if the ribs are bent.

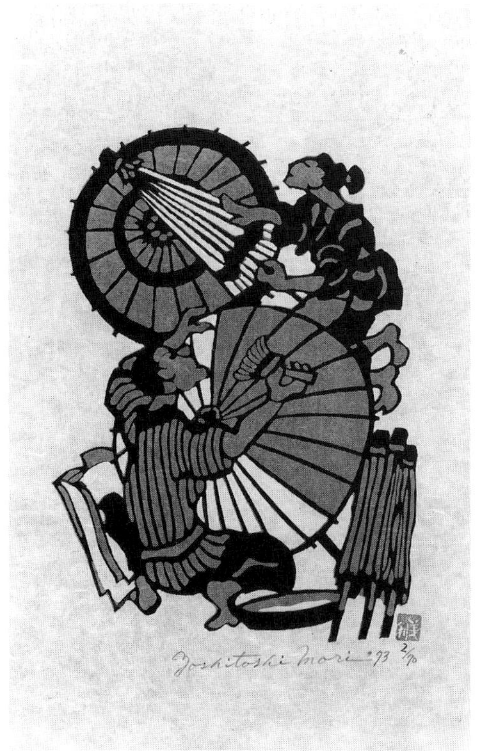

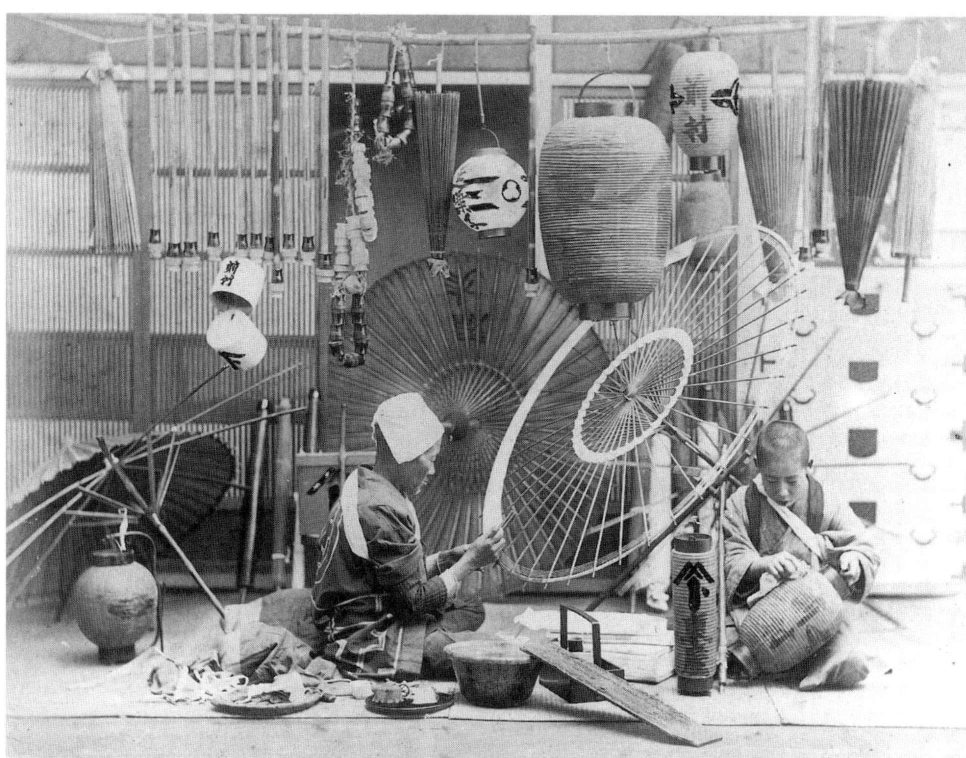

6. Mori Yoshitoshi (b.1898)
Umbrella Maker
Shôwa period, 1973
Signed and numbered: Yoshitoshi Mori; 2/70; sealed: Yoshitoshi
Stencil-colored print
20 1/2 x 13 1/2 in. (52.1 x 34.3 cm.)
Collection of Griffith and Patricia Way

This is one of a series of prints depicting artisans at work. The umbrella maker is shown smoothing paper onto the bamboo frame. Mori had apparently never seen an umbrella being made; in practice the craftsman always rotates the umbrella, which is supported on a stand (Mori's umbrella seems to rest on the floor), so that he is working on the lower half, closest to him, and has no need to reach up (see nos. 3, 4). Loose sheets of paper are stacked to the left; to the right is the paste bowl. Mori includes a decorative assemblage of open and closed umbrellas. At the back a woman, probably the artisan's wife, is pushing the paper into the valleys of a half-closed finished umbrella.

For thirty years Mori was a designer and dyer of cloth for kimono, the traditional Japanese dress. At the same time he became involved in the study and revival of the folk-art traditions of Japan, including stencil printing. He combines his knowledge and skills to make his own creative stencil prints, using earthy, natural colors.

7. Photographer unknown
Umbrella Maker
Meiji period, ca. 1880-90
Hand-colored albumen print
8 x 10 1/2 in. (20.3 x 26.7 cm.)
Ukiyo-e Books, Leiden, The Netherlands

Late-19th-century photographs of umbrella makers often show workshops such as this one, in which both lanterns and umbrellas were produced. Here, the craftsman, in the preliminary stages of affixing the thin strip of reinforcing paper (*nokigami*) to the outer rim of an umbrella frame, smoothes the paper down with a bamboo pincer (*hera*). The strip around the center (*nakaokigami*) is already in place. Rows of fine threads, called spider's threads (*kumoito*), are visible around the edge of the frame; these reinforcing threads were commonly used until the 1940s. On the floor is a large bowl (*suribachi*) for paste and a long rectangular paste board (*noriita*), the latter used to support the strips of paper when paste is applied to them. Discarded paper has piled up to the left. Also visible are a small tea set and a smoking set beside the *noriita*.

On the right the assistant is working on a lantern. On the floor to the extreme left is the skeleton of an umbrella with ribs and stretchers joined together, but without the additional binding threads. Hanging overhead are some finished umbrellas and lanterns, as well as bamboo sticks to which the top notch and runners have already been attached (the latter appear as black). Several strings of top notches and runners (*rokuro*) hang on the wall.

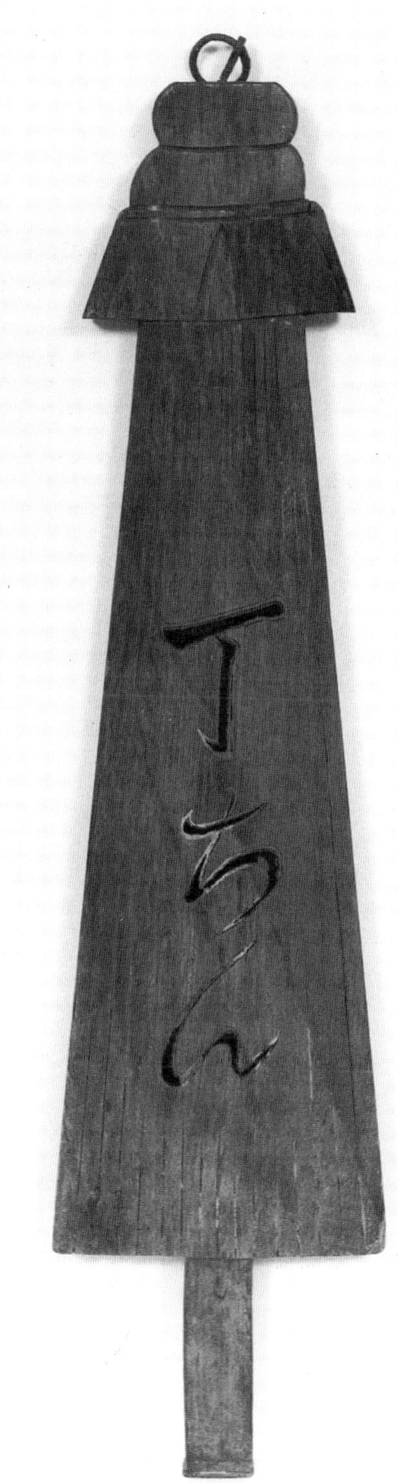

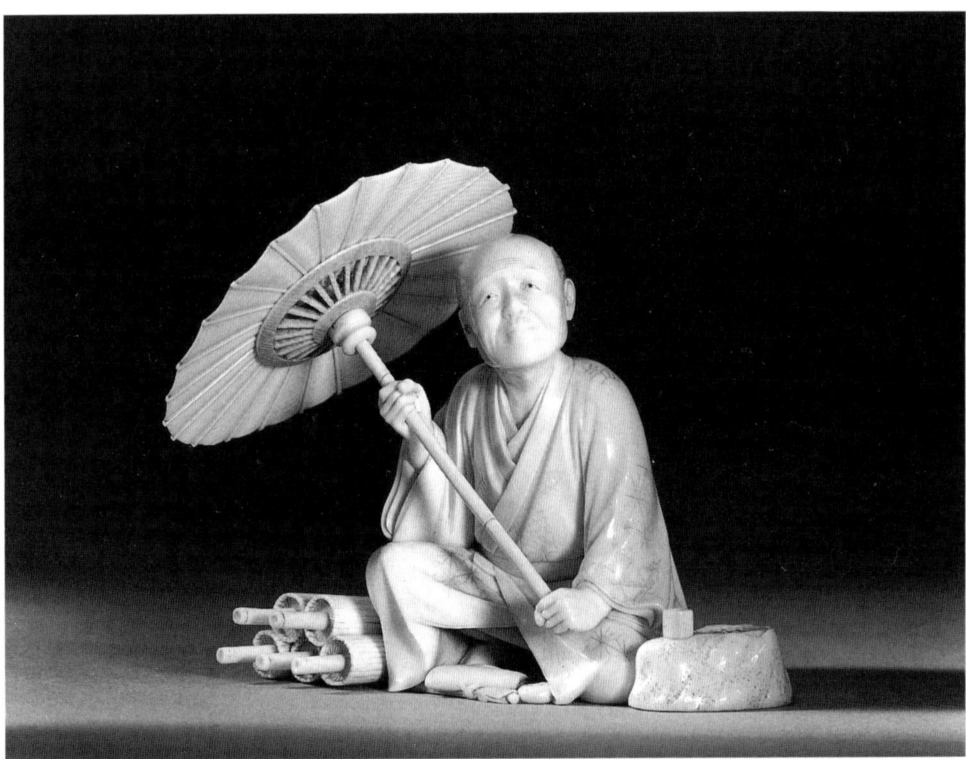

8. *Shop Sign* (*kanban*)
Edo period, 19th century
Wood with black lacquer
36 x 9 in. (91.4 x 22.9 cm.)
Collection of William Green, promised gift to Mead Art Museum, Amherst College

The traditional wooden signboard (*kanban*) often relied on shape alone to convey its message, but in this case, because the shop sold two products—lanterns and umbrellas—a written message was necessary. The word "Lantern" (*chôchin*) is inscribed on the front of the sign, which is in the shape of an ordinary *bangasa* with a paper cap tied on the top.

The materials for making umbrellas and lanterns are basically the same—paper and bamboo—and in some districts they were often produced by the same craftsman. The shop advertised by this particular sign, however, was probably not in Gifu. There were umbrella makers in Gifu from the 18th century on, but lantern makers came later, in the early 19th century, and worked separately.

9. *Umbrella Vendor*
Meiji period, late 19th century
Signed: Shizuo
Okimono; ivory
Figure: $2\frac{1}{2}$ x 3 x 2 in. (6.4 x 7.6 x 5.1 cm.); umbrella: $2\frac{1}{2}$ x $2\frac{1}{4}$ in. (6.4 x 5.7 cm.)
Denver Art Museum, Gift of Mr. and Mrs. George A. Argabrite, 1979.294ab

The smiling umbrella vendor offers his wares to a potential customer. His smoking implements—pipe and tobacco pouch—lie on the ground in front of him. At one side is a hibachi with pieces of charcoal set in the ashes. A small empty cup sits on the rim of the hibachi, perhaps to hold charcoal for lighting the man's pipe.

This work is a tour de force of technical virtuosity, the ivory carver showing off his skill at miniaturization. In the open umbrella, executed as a separate piece, he paid attention to such minute details as the protective paper cap tied on top, the stretchers carved in the round, and the thin strips of paper used to strengthen the area where the stretchers meet the ribs and the area just above the runner, i.e., the *nakaokigami* and *temotogami*.

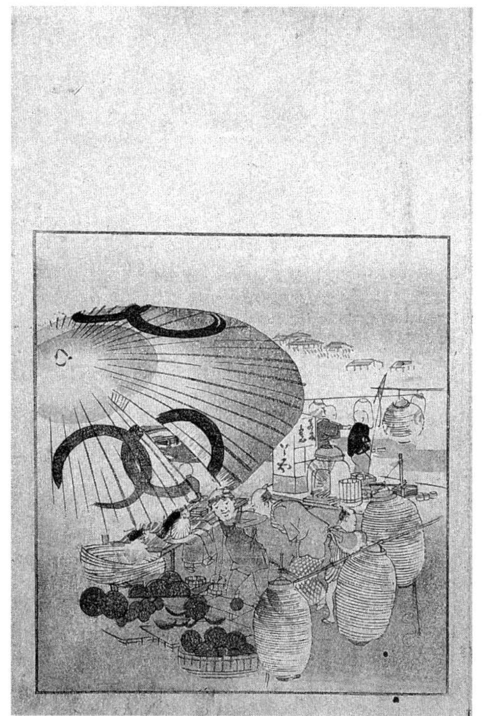

10. Tanaka Nikka (Kyûhodô, d. 1845)
Melon Vendor
From *Kyûhodô gafu* (Book of sketches by Kyûhodô), compiled by Ikeda Kyûka, Vol. 2
Edo period, 1856
Publisher: Ikeda Kyûka
Color woodblock-printed illustrated book
Page: $11^{13}/_{16}$ x $7^{3}/_{4}$ in. (30 x 19.7 cm.)
Ravicz Collection

An oversize umbrella (*ôgasa*) is used as an awning by a fruit seller on the bank of a river on a summer evening; two intersecting rings represent his *yago*, or commercial trademark. A tea vendor is visible toward the back, and the space shared by the two men is strung with festive paper lanterns. A torn strip in the umbrella affords the glimpse of a distant bridge.

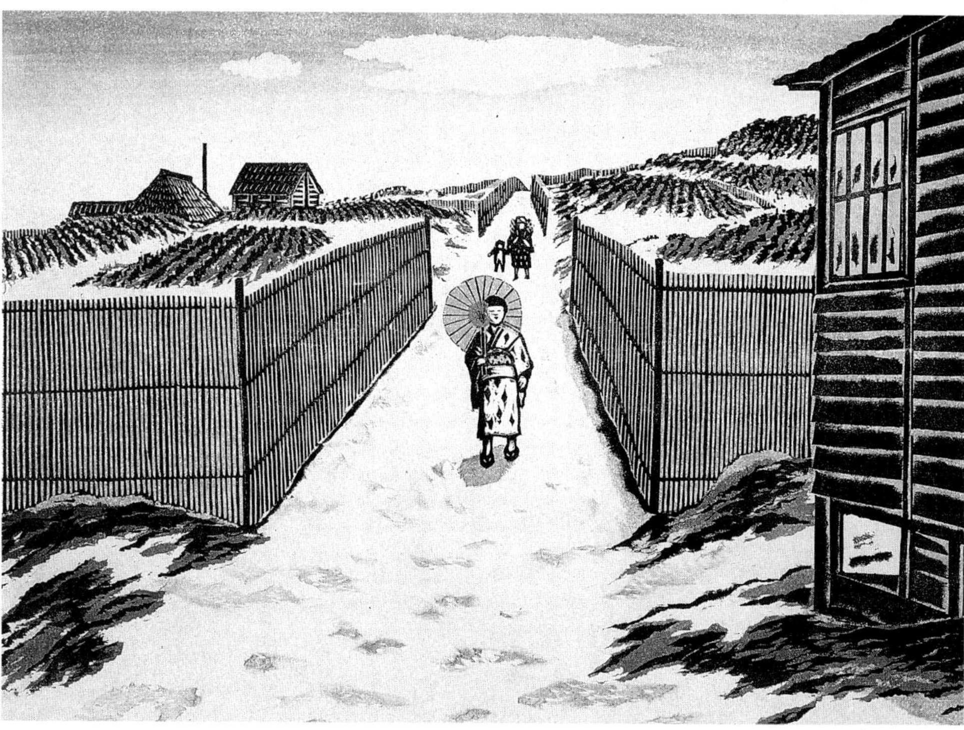

11. Henmi Takashi (1895-1944)
Paper Parasol
Shôwa period, 1930s
Color woodblock print
$14^{3}/_{8}$ x $17^{7}/_{8}$ in. (36.5 x 45.5 cm.)
The Art Institute of Chicago, Clarence Buckingham Fund, 1979.640

A little girl wearing a cotton summer kimono holds a small red parasol (*higasa*), the focal point of the composition. There are farmhouses in the background and a Western-style building (probably a schoolhouse) in the foreground. In this sandy area near the seashore, fences are used to keep out sand drifts.

Henmi was a self-taught printmaker who supported himself as an accountant for the Lion toothpaste company in Tokyo. His style is quiet, personal and deceptively simple.

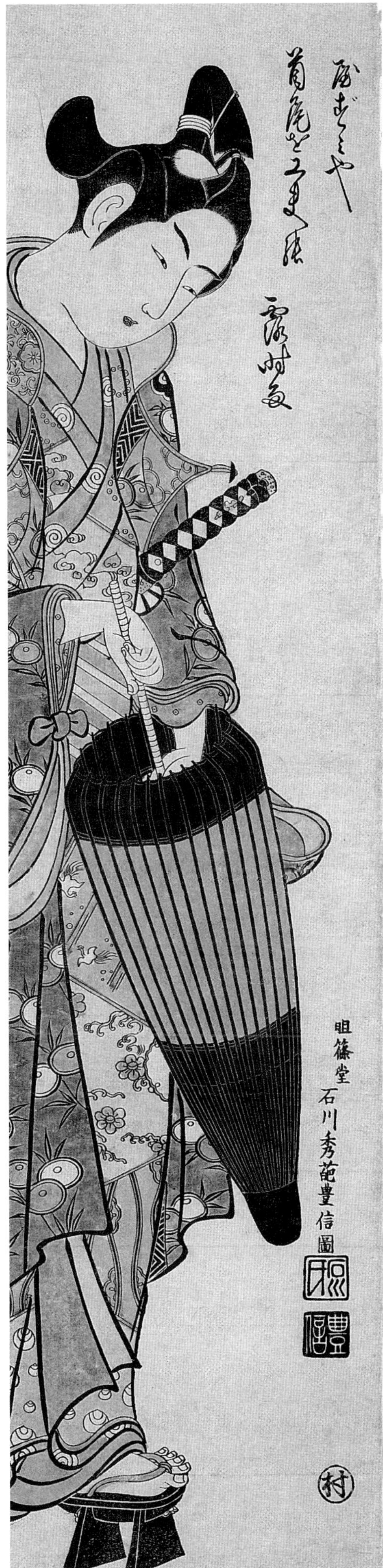

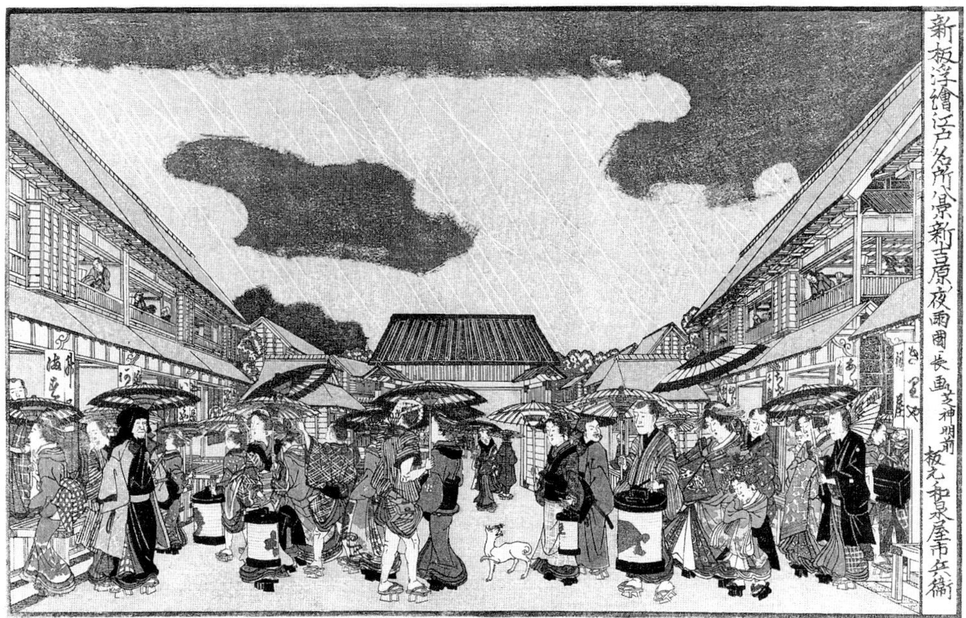

12. Ishikawa Toyonobu (1711-1785)
Young Man Opening an Umbrella
Edo period, early 1740s
Signed: Tanjôdô Ishikawa Shûha Toyonobu zu; sealed: Ishikawa Uji; Toyonobu
Publisher: Murataya Jirobei
Hand-colored woodblock print; wide pillar print
25 1/2 x 6 in. (64.8 x 15.2 cm.)
The Metropolitan Museum of Art, Ledoux Collection, Harris Brisbane Dick Fund and Rogers Fund, 1949, JP3108

This handsome youth, wearing high rain clogs, or geta, and a showy raincoat, has given his large *janome* a slight twist before reaching in to push it open. The initial twist is needed to loosen the stiff oiled folds of the umbrella, and ultimately extends its life. Men point an umbrella up to open it; young women and *wakashû* (young actors or male prostitutes) point it down.

The poem is one of romantic longing in the cold autumn rain:

Heyazumiya
shubi o kufû no
tsuyu shigure

A young man still residing in his
parents' home
in autumn showers contrives
opportunities.[1]

1. Stern (1969), 92; "to rendezvous with his beloved" is the implication of the last line.

13. Utagawa Kuninaga (d.1827)
Picture of Evening Rain in the New Yoshiwara
Series: New Edition of Perspective Views of Eight Famous Places in Edo
Edo period, early 19th century
Signed: Kuninaga ga
Publisher: Izumiya Ichibei
Color woodblock print; horizontal *ôban*
10 1/16 x 15 1/8 in. (25.5 x 38.5 cm.)
Collection of William Green, promised gift to Mead Art Museum, Amherst College

In the main street—the Naka-no-chô—of the Yoshiwara (known as the New Yoshiwara after it was rebuilt following a fire in 1657), the first house on the right is the Kiriya, followed by the Ômiya and the Chitoseya. On the left is the Masuya. These are *hikite-jaya*, teahouses from which clients were guided to the brothels. Most of the umbrellas are of the *janome* (snake's eye) type, but there are a few simple *bangasa* carried by servants holding lanterns and by the tradesman at the far right who is delivering a large box of food. The Great Gate, closed at night to keep the women from leaving, is visible at the end of the street. A contemporary view of the Naka-no-chô, looking in the other direction, is given by Shûchô (no. 31).

Although Kuninaga's title includes the name of the print series, this image is in fact the only one known.

14. Kitagawa Utamaro (1753?-1806)
Night Rain
Edo period, ca.1796
Signed: Utamaro hitsu
Publisher: Moriya Jihei
Color woodblock print; vertical *ôban*
15 1/8 x 10 1/4 in. (38.5 x 26 cm.)
The Art Institute of Chicago, Gift of Mr. and Mrs. Gaylord Donnelley, 1968.158

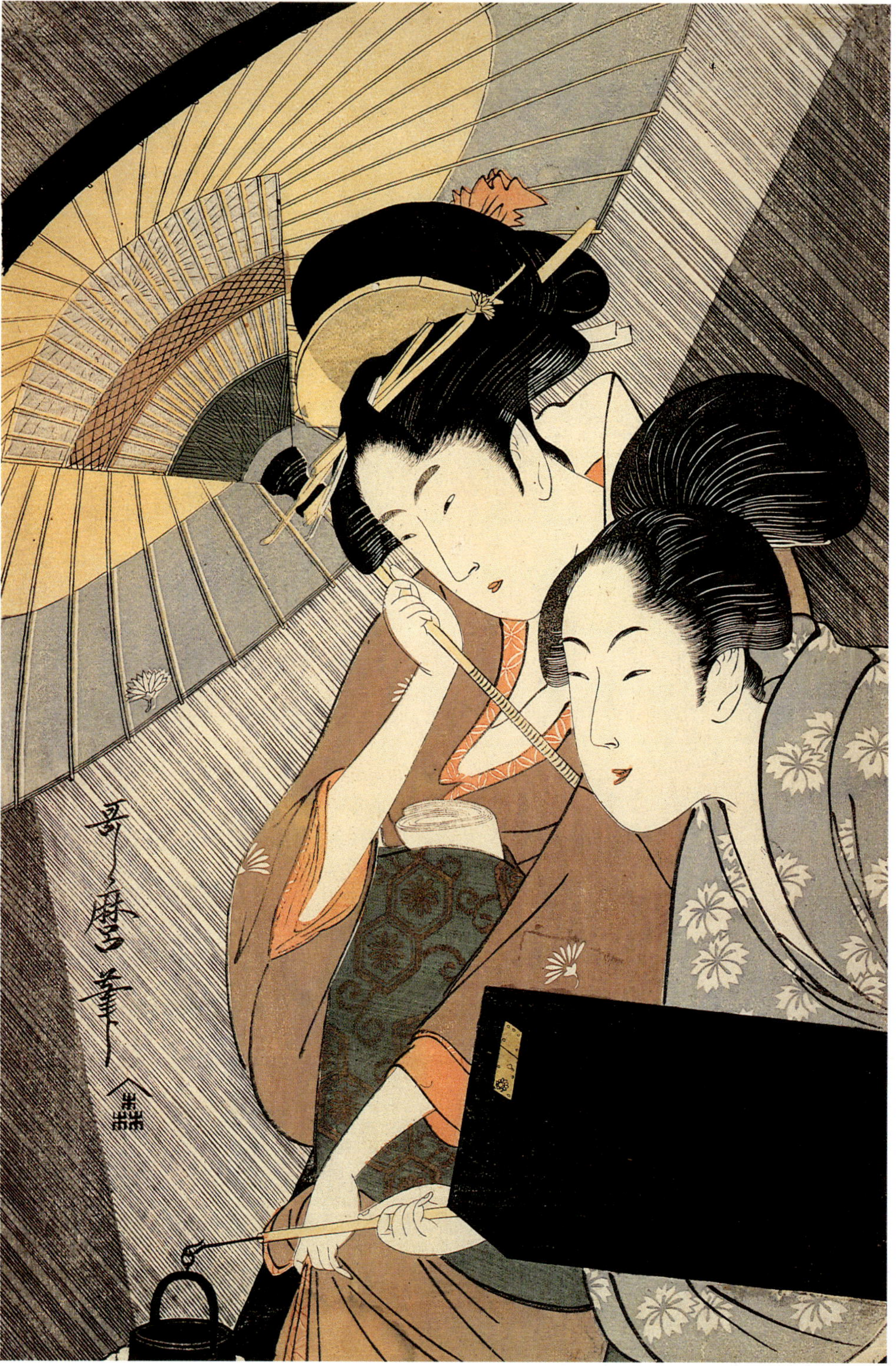

Karakasa ni
oshimodosaruru
shigure kana

As I walk in the winter rain,
the umbrella
presses me back.
—Shiseijo (active 19th century)[1]

Accompanied by her maid, a geisha hurries through the night to her next engagement. She bends forward, tilting her umbrella low against the driving rain. Unlike *yûjo*, low-class prostitutes who catered to men's sexual needs, geisha were supposed to restrict themselves to social and cultural pursuits. The maid, or *hakoya* (box carrier), holds the shamisen box under her left arm and a lantern in her right. A triangular wedge of light cast by the lantern illuminates the interior of the umbrella. The women's pale skin and feminine curves stand out against the surrounding darkness. Artificial illumination of a scene was a popular new technique learned from the West, and Utamaro was one of the first Japanese artists to use it effectively.

This may be a *yakko* umbrella: there appears to be only one band of color. The design embroidered on the stretchers with purple threads (*kagari ito*) is in the pattern called *hitotsu nawa* (single rope) or *kasumi* (mist). This cross-stitching is purely decorative and has no function; an inexpensive *bangasa*, for example, never has any *kagari ito*.

The geisha's crest appears on her kimono and is painted on the outer edge of the umbrella. Crests are shown on umbrella covers from as early as the Kyôhô era (1716-35).

1. Blyth (1952), 119.

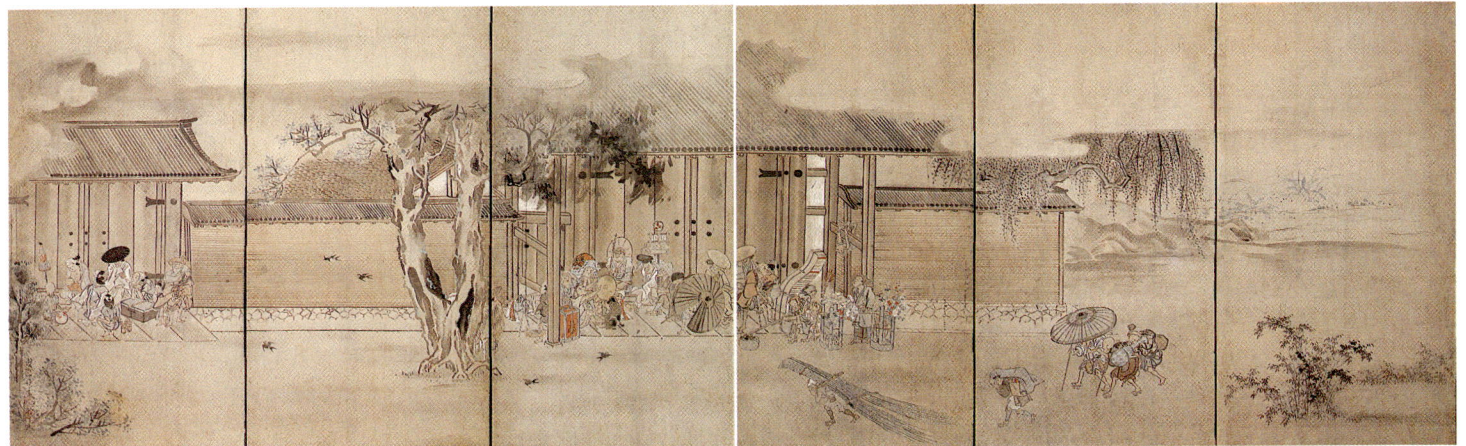

15. Hanabusa Itchô (1652-1724)
Taking Shelter from the Rain
Edo period, ca.1710-15
Signed: Hanabusa Itchô; sealed: Shuzai San'un Senseki Kan; Aimoko
Single six-panel screen; ink and color on paper
37 1/16 x 122 3/8 in. (94.1 x 310.8 cm.)
The Mary and Jackson Burke Foundation

Itchô was an unconventional artist with a gift for incisive observation of ordinary people. Here a motley group takes refuge from a sudden summer downpour in the roofed gateways of a samurai mansion. There are itinerant entertainers, street merchants, nuns, pilgrims, children, a samurai and a nursing mother. Moisture-laden rain clouds hover overhead as a few stragglers rush for shelter.

Most of the travelers have relied on the old rain-gear staple, a broad-brimmed hat. At the right a blind monk-entertainer with a *biwa* strapped to his back grasps the arm of a companion carrying a handsome umbrella, a *bangasa*. The bored and frustrated group inside the main gateway includes a young boy who peeks through the gaping hole in a torn *bangasa*—a humorous touch. A man wearing a straw rain cape (*mino*) stands by his horse beneath the tree. Propped against one of the doors in the secondary gateway at the far left is a pretty little red and white parasol.

16. *Umbrella*
Edo period, 1820s
Paper, bamboo and silk threads
L. 32 3/4 in. (83.3 cm.)
Rijksmuseum voor Volkenkunde, Leiden, The Netherlands, Collection of Philipp Franz von Siebold, No. 1-1388

This indigo umbrella can be securely dated to the 1820s, when it was acquired in Japan by Philipp Franz von Siebold, a German doctor working for the Dutch government.

There are some early-19th-century umbrellas of status for members of the military elite in the Tokugawa Art Museum (fig. 60), but this example was for a commoner's everyday use. It is finely made, probably a form of *janome*, with sixty ribs, spider's threads (*kumoito*) around the rim, and many bands of multi-color embroidery on the stretchers.

16a. Detail showing embroidered stretchers

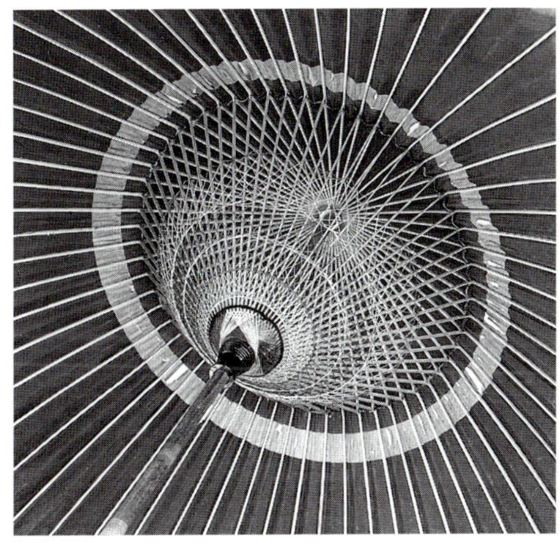

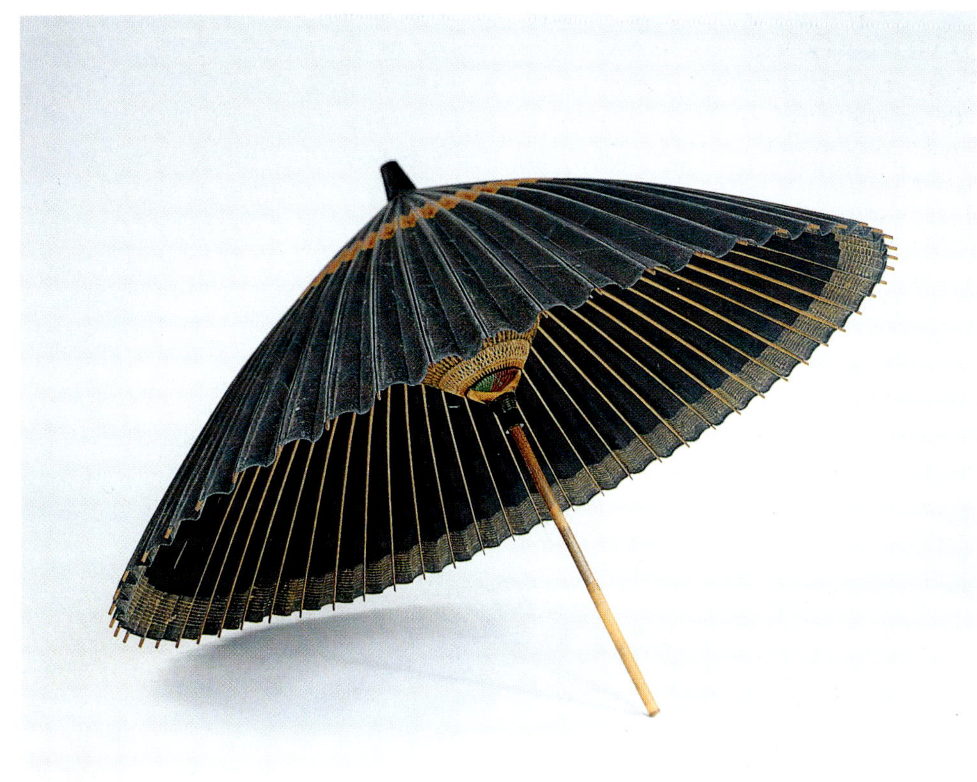

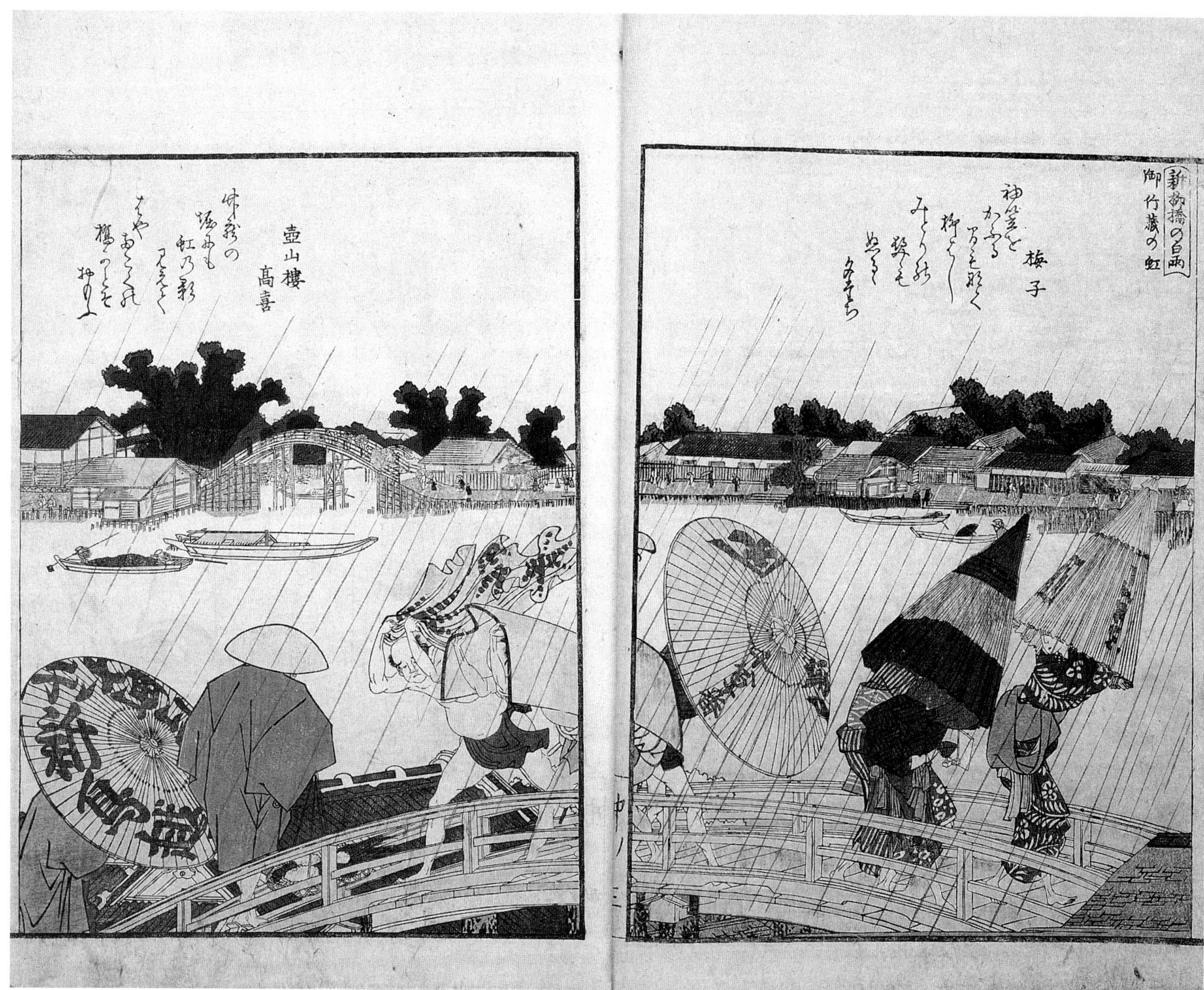

17. Katsushika Hokusai (1760-1849)
Sudden Shower at New Willow Bridge: Rainbow at Otakegura
From *Ehon Sumidagawa ryôgan ichiran* (Picture book of a panoramic view of both banks of the Sumida River), Vol. 2
Edo period, ca. 1801-6
Color woodblock-printed illustrated book
Page: 10 3/8 x 7 1/8 in. (26.4 x 18.1 cm.)
Collection of Geoffrey Oliver

In this three-volume book of *kyôka*, or humorous verse, Hokusai creates a continuous panorama of the four seasons along the banks of the Sumida River.[1] He follows the river as it runs through the center of Edo up to its northern extremities in the Yoshiwara, focusing on the activities of the middle and lower classes on the near shore. Each double-page illustration stands alone but is also contiguous with the adjacent compositions, as in the unfolding of a horizontal handscroll. The most striking scene is the sudden shower, shown here. It is contrived, perhaps, in the carefully chosen variety of rain gear, but it takes us onto the streets of the vibrant world of Edo.

Two figures are almost hidden behind their open *bangasa*. The barefoot women at the far right are sensibly sheltered under half-closed umbrellas, a *bangasa* and a fancier *janome*; Hokusai's attention to the volumetric modeling of the individual folds of these umbrellas is impressive. Two seminaked porters make do with simpler means—one uses a small mat, the other his cotton jacket. A raincoat and broad-brimmed hat protect a vegetable peddler.

All three *bangasa* here are shown with protective paper caps and are inscribed. "Shintorigoe[-chô]," a place name in Edo, in the Sanya district, is written on the umbrella at the left. The middle one, probably a rental umbrella, is numbered "1,810." The syllable *ban* (number) in the word *bangasa* derives from the fact that these cheap umbrellas were often numbered by rental shops for purposes of identification. Shops and inns would always have their trademarks, or *yagô*, placed on their umbrellas as well—in this case the character *dai* (large) is inscribed under a peak.[2] A later print by Kuniyoshi (no. 19) also features a numbered umbrella.

The poem on the right is signed by Baishi:

Sodegasa o
kaburu ma mo naku
Yanagibashi
midori no kami mo
nururu yûdachi

Not even time
to raise one's sleeve
against the rain—
a sudden downpour
drenches our hair
as we cross Willow Bridge.

Sodegasa (sleeve hat) refers to use of the broad sleeve of one's kimono as a shield against the rain. "Sleeve-hat rain" (*sodegasa ame*) is, in fact, a light drizzle that does not call for an umbrella.

The poem on the left is signed by Kozanrô Takaki:

Takegura no
hori ni mo niji no
kage miete
haya Ryôgoku no
hashi ka to zô omou

Seeing the light of a rainbow
over the canal
near the Bamboo Storehouse—
at first I wondered,
could it be Ryôgoku Bridge?[3]

The poet takes pleasure in confusing a real rainbow (not depicted) with the famous Ryôgoku Bridge, arched like a rainbow, which appears in the two double-page spreads preceding this one. Otakegura (literally, "Bamboo Storehouse"), just north of the bridge, was originally a place for storing building materials.

1. Hokusai's name is mentioned in the preface to volume 1. The Oliver example is undated, but one in the Ryerson collection published by Senkakudô in Edo and Maekawa Zembei in Osaka is dated 1806. The colophon of the example in the Museum of Fine Arts, Boston, is signed Hokusai Tokimasa (or Tatsumasa), a name the artist used from 1799 to early 1804.
2. For Hokusai's use of inscriptions on *bangasa* to make a humorous or erotic point, see Forrer and Keyes (1979), 51, fig. 24; and Lane (1989), figs. 208, 219.
3. Translations by John Carpenter.

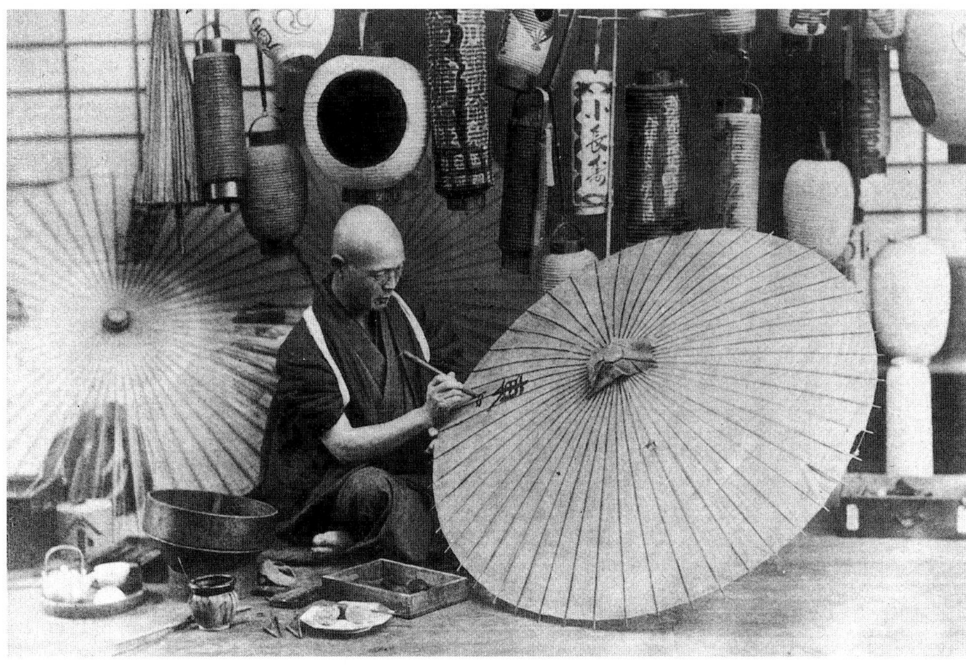

18. Photographer unknown
Sign Writer
Meiji period, ca.1890
Hand-colored albumen print
3 1/2 x 5 1/2 in. (8.9 x 14 cm.)
Herbert F. Johnson Museum of Art, Cornell University, Gift of Dr. and Mrs. Henry D. Rosin, 84.120.248

This craftsman specializes in painting designs and writing shop names on umbrellas and lanterns. He has completed the character for "East" on an ordinary *bangasa*, very like the ones depicted by Hokusai and Kuniyoshi earlier in the century (nos. 17, 19). A modern example of a *bangasa* similarly identified bears the name—"Nishibu shôten" (Nishibu Shop)—and address of a store in Gifu City (no. 18a).

Bangasa are inexpensive, only one-fifth the cost of a *janome*. They are more simply and crudely made than other types of umbrella. The cover is of plain white paper, which soon turns yellow from the oil used for waterproofing, the wide ribs are unlacquered, and the short handle is thick and consequently rather heavy. *Bangasa* were first made in Osaka around the year 1711.

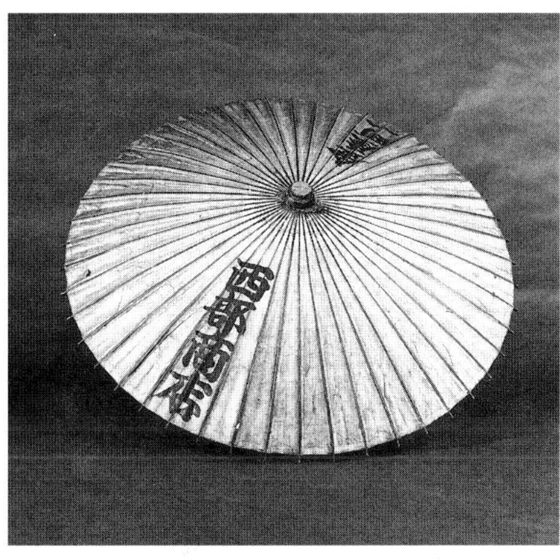

18a. *Bangasa*, Gifu, early Shôwa period, ca. 1930-60. Paper and bamboo. L. 30 in. (76 cm.). Gifu City Museum of History

Somewhat damaged by wear, this *bangasa* has forty-eight ribs, a plain bamboo stick, and a single metal spring.

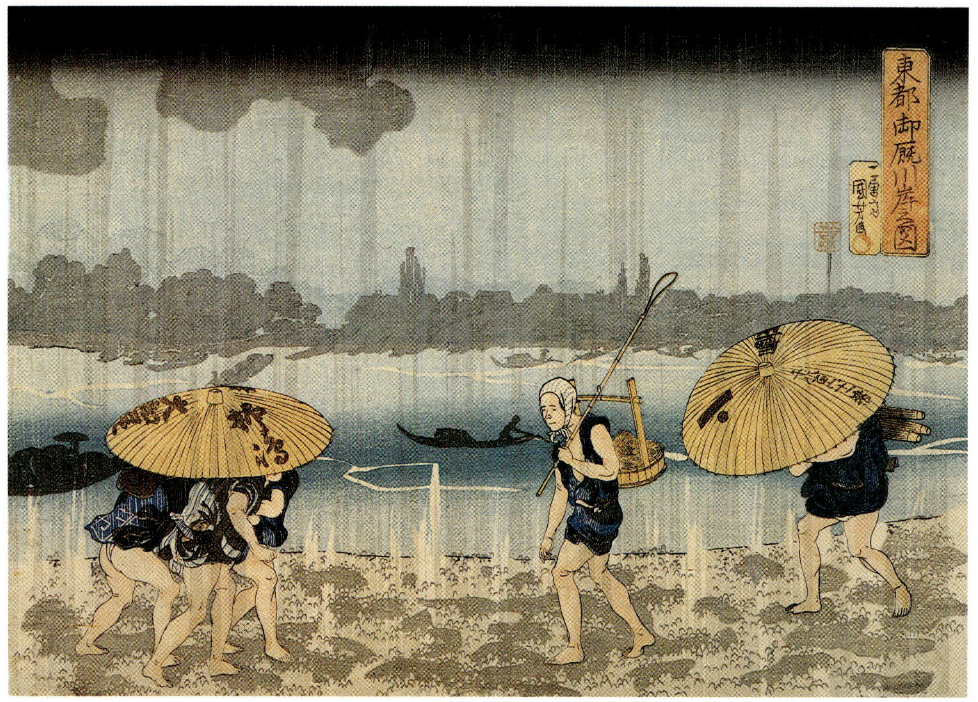

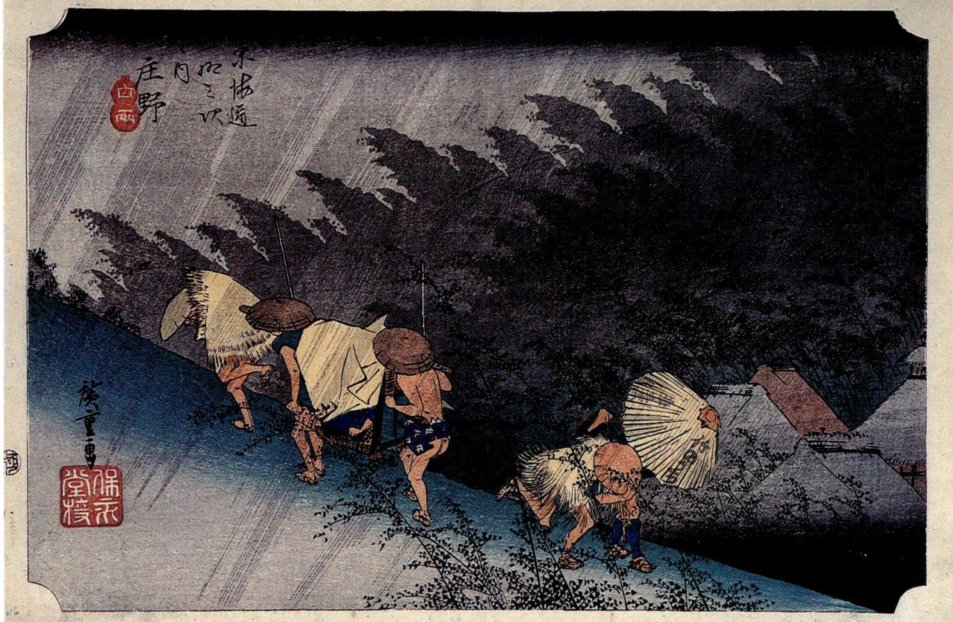

19. Utagawa Kuniyoshi (1797-1861)
View of the Ommaya Embankment in the Eastern Capital
Edo period, ca. 1834
Signed: Ichiyûsai Kuniyoshi ga; artist's *toshidama* seal
Publisher: Yamaguchiya Tôbei
Color woodblock print; horizontal *ôban*
$10\,^{1}/_{4}$ x $14\,^{5}/_{8}$ in. (26 x 37.1 cm.)
The Metropolitan Museum of Art,
H. O. Havemeyer Collection, Bequest of
Mrs. H. O. Havemeyer, 1929, JP1805

Along the bank of the Sumida River at Miyoshi-chô in Asakusa, a suburb of Edo (now Tokyo), there is a sudden, intense downpour. Only the fisherman at the center, his catch in a bucket slung from his pole, seems oblivious to the weather. The three barefoot laborers at the left huddle under one *bangasa* on which is written the name of a restaurant or shop, Yamatoya at Yanagishima. The man at the right carries several extra umbrellas under his arm; he may be a vendor, or he may have been sent by a busy restaurant or inn to take extra umbrellas to customers in a boat on the river (figures dimly visible in a boat at the left wear rain hats). His own umbrella is inscribed "1,861," a number not too distant from that used by Hokusai on a *bangasa* thirty years earlier (no. 17). Kuniyoshi cleverly incorporates the mark of his publisher, Yamaguchiya Tôbei, on this umbrella, a common conceit (see no. 20).

The artist experiments here with Western perspective, noticeable in the reduction in scale from foreground to background.

20. Utagawa Hiroshige (1797-1858)
Shôno: Driving Rain
Series: Fifty-three Stations of the Tôkaidô
Edo period, 1833-34
Signed: Hiroshige ga
Publisher: Hoeidô (Takenouchi Magohachi) and Senkakudô
Color woodblock print; horizontal *ôban*
$9\,^{1}/_{2}$ x $14\,^{7}/_{8}$ in. (24.1 x 37.8 cm.)
Print Collection, Miriam and
Ira D. Wallach Division of Art, Prints and Photographs, The New York Public Library, Astor, Lenox and Tilden Foundations

This image was regarded as a masterpiece during the artist's lifetime and retains an almost incredible cross-cultural popularity even today. There was nothing remarkable about the mountain hamlet of Shôno, and so the artist chose to evoke the mood and atmosphere of a sudden heavy shower, a hazard familiar to any traveler. One traveler lucky enough to be carried in a palanquin shields himself by using his raincoat as a curtain. A peasant in a traditional straw rain cape (*mino*) with a hoe over his shoulder races downhill heading for home, while another points his fragile paper *bangasa* into the wind; written on its cover are the title of the series and the name of the publisher.

When Hiroshige made his first trip down the Tôkaidô in 1832, sketching on his way, there was already a large body of illustrated guidebooks devoted to the pleasurable theme of domestic travel along this famous highway. His prints are a record of the journey, on the order of a souvenir for both city dwellers and visitors from the provinces. The Tôkaidô series of 1833-34 became an overnight best-seller, and was issued in perhaps as many as ten thousand impressions, exceptional for the period. Prior to the 20th century, Japanese woodcuts were not numbered and were probably published in groups of a few hundred at a time, to be reprinted according to demand.

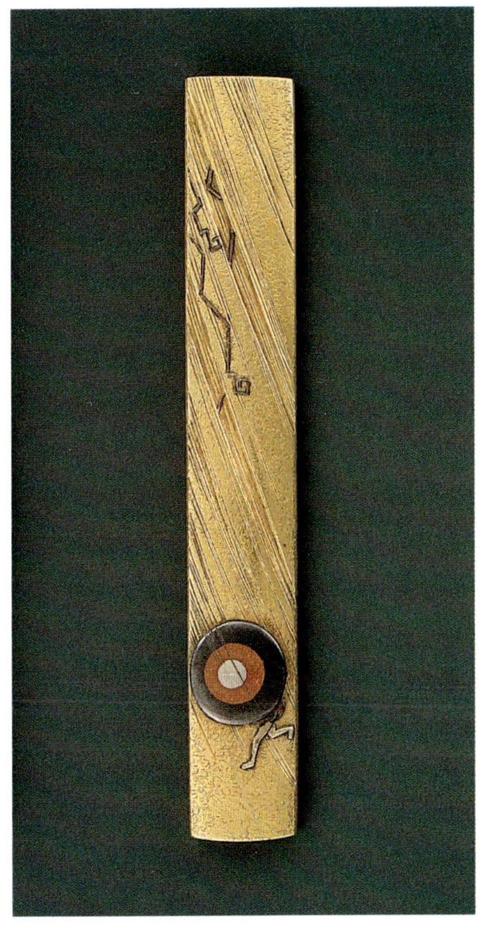

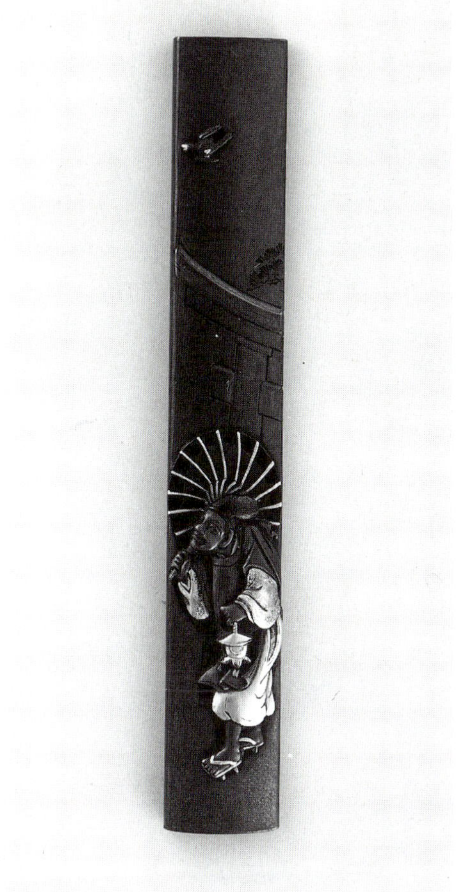

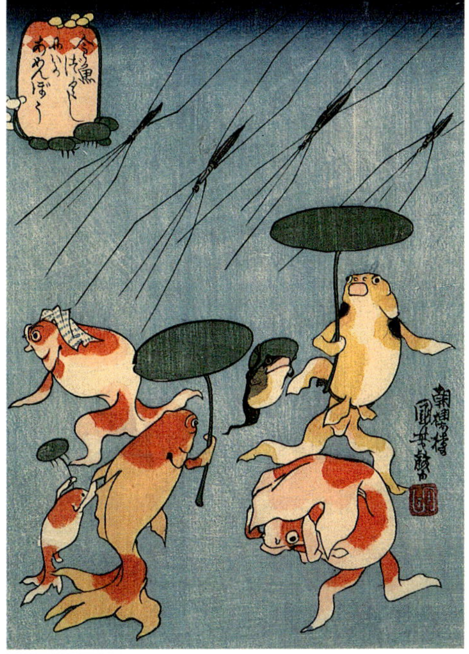

21. *Knife Handle* (*kozuka*): Running figure with umbrella
Nara school; Edo period, late 18th century
Signed: Yasuchika III [Tsuchiya Yasuchika, d. 1778]
Silver, copper and *shakudô* inlaid on gilt *shibuichi* ground, incised (front); white *shibuichi* (back)
Approx. 3 13/16 in. x 9/16 in. (approx. 9.7 x 1.5 cm.)
The Metropolitan Museum of Art, Gift of Herman A. E. and Paul C. Jaehne, 1943, 43.120.505

The greater part of the front of the handle is incised with lines representing flashes of lightning and driving rain, making the plight of the small, barefoot figure running for cover at the bottom seem all the more urgent.

22. *Knife Handle* (*kozuka*): Shrine attendant and cuckoo
Late Edo period, mid-19th century
Gold, copper and *shakudô* on *shibuichi* plate, with incised carving
L. 3 3/4 in. (9.5 cm.)
The Metropolitan Museum of Art, H. O. Havemeyer Collection, Bequest of Mrs. H. O. Havemeyer, 1929, 29.100.1288

A shrine attendant, with an open umbrella in his right hand and a lantern in his left, looks up at a cuckoo, symbol of the arrival of summer and the rainy season. The gate of the shrine and a pine tree are carved on the reverse.

23. Utagawa Kuniyoshi (1797-1861)
Sudden Rain of Water Striders
Series: Collection of Goldfish
Edo period, late 1830s
Signed: Chôôrô Kuniyoshi giga; sealed: Kuniyoshi
Publisher: Murataya Jirobei
Color woodblock print; vertical *chûban*
8 3/4 x 7 3/16 in. (20.2 x 18.3 cm.)
Musées Royaux d'Art et d'Histoire, Brussels, 2109

The goldfish in Kuniyoshi's print are taking cover from a downpour of water striders, long-legged insects of the *Gerridae* family that skim the surface of freshwater ponds. Three of the fish have hoisted lily pads as makeshift umbrellas.

Kuniyoshi often depicted animals and insects in anthropomorphic form, sometimes with satirical intent.

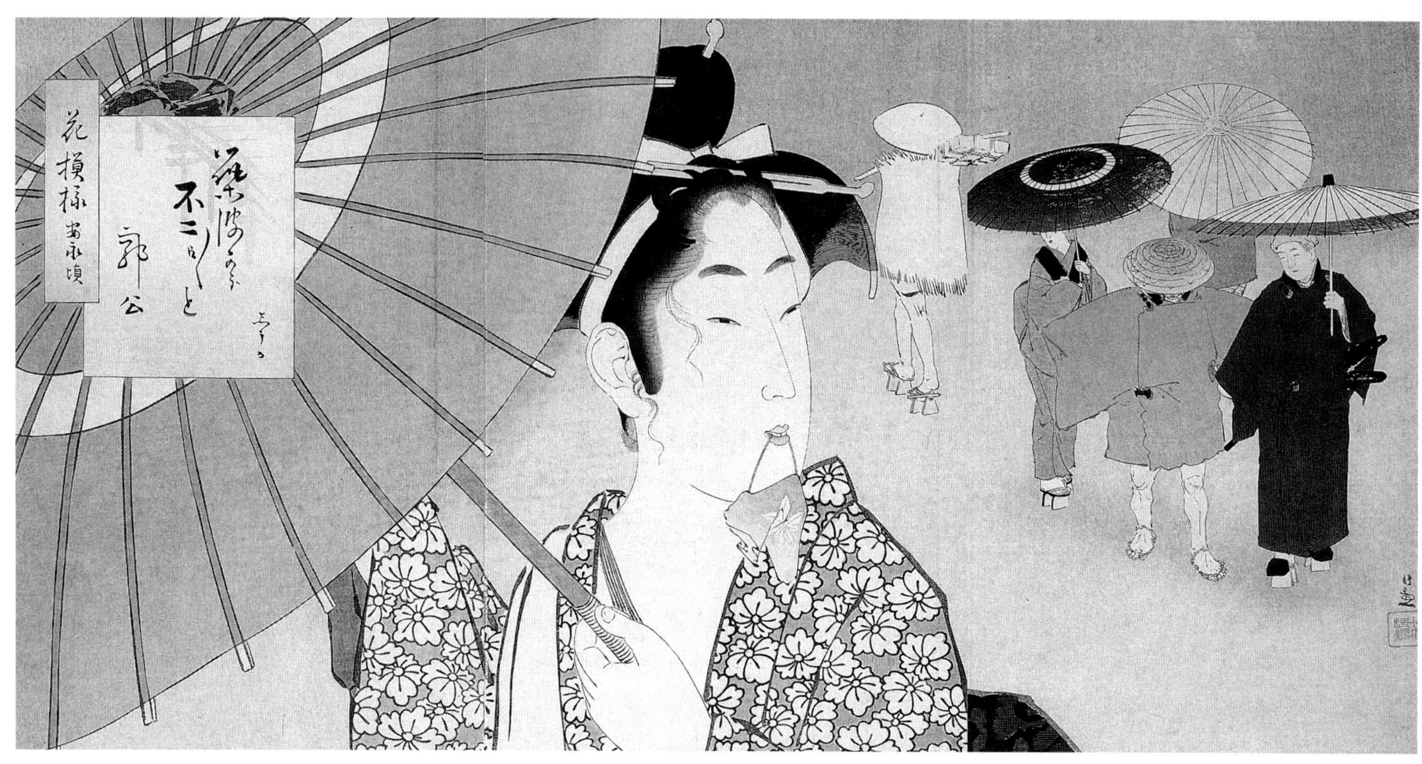

24. Kobayashi Kiyochika (1847-1915)
The An-ei Era
Series: Flower Patterns
Meiji period, 1896
Signed: Kiyochika; sealed: Kobayashi Kiyochika
Publisher: Takegawa Seikichi
Color woodblock prints; triptych, vertical *ôban*
Together: 15 3/8 x 28 3/8 in. (39.1 x 72.1 cm.)
Collection of Robert O. Muller

Returning from the public bathhouse, a fashionable young woman is caught in a shower. Her hair is tied up and a wet bath towel is slung over her shoulder. While opening her handsome *janome* umbrella, she holds her small drawstring *nuka-bukuro* (rice-bran bag)—a soap equivalent—in her teeth. The background tableau shows a variety of rain gear supposedly in use during the An-ei era (1772-80).

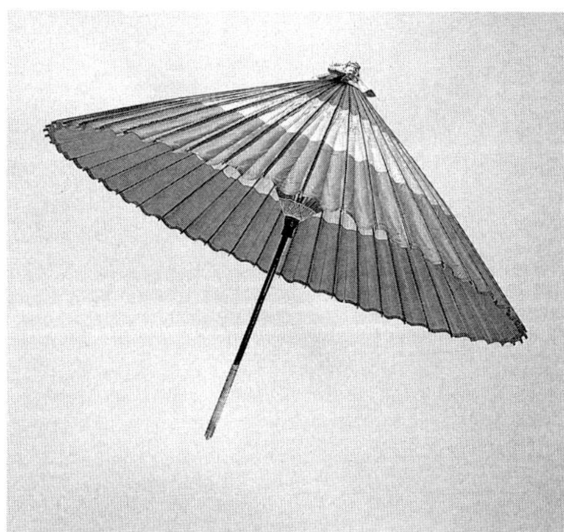

25. Janome *Umbrella*
Gifu, Shôwa period, 1950s
Paper, bamboo, wood and silk threads
L. 28 3/4 in. (73 cm.)
Gifu City Museum of History

This slender *janome*, from the shop of the Gifu umbrella wholesaler Fujisawa Tôgo (b.1903), has forty-eight ribs and a very broad center band. The wood stick is painted black and has two wood springs.

26. Baron von Stillfried (1839-1911), Austrian
Wind Costume
Meiji period, 1870s
Hand-colored platinum albumen print
8 x 10 in. (20.2 x 25.4 cm.)
H. Kwan Lau Collection, New York

Posed in the photographer's studio, the woman holds a traditional *janome* umbrella with a wide white center band; in modern versions this band is often narrower. Wires attached to her clothing create the effect of wind, and streaks scratched on the negative give the illusion of rain.

It is ironic that in the late 19th century the camera, a Western import, documented the rapidly vanishing traditions of old Japan, while the woodblock print, a native Japanese art form, recorded modernization and a flood of Western imports (see, for example, no. 112). Lucrative business with

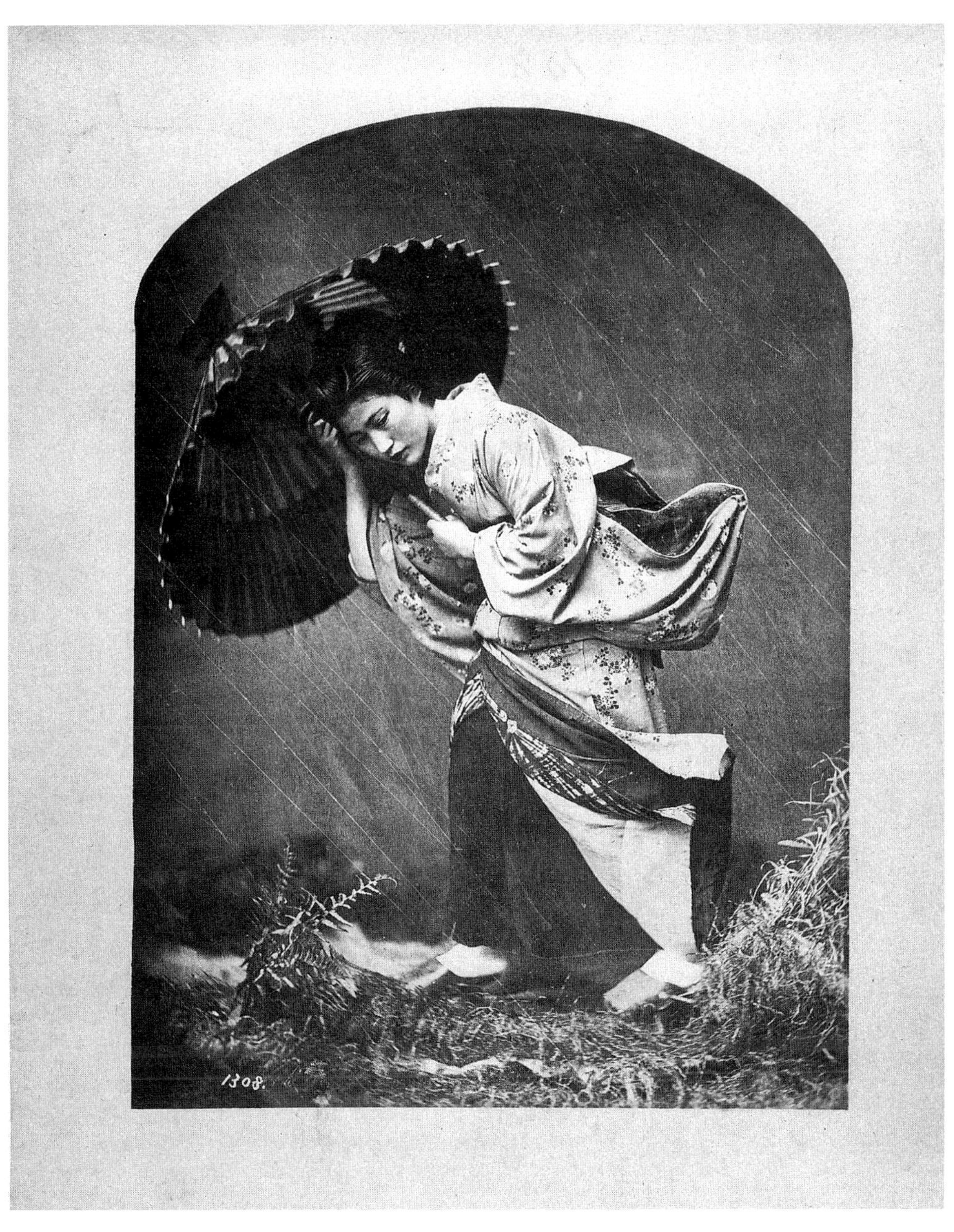

foreigners and the armchair traveler, in particular, lured commercial photographers to Yokohama from the early 1860s. The Austrian artist and photographer Raimund Baron von Stillfried und Rathenitz established his own studio in Yokohama in 1870. In 1877 he bought out the cosmopolitan photographer Felice Beato (1825-1904) (see no. 41) and continued in business until 1885, when he returned to Vienna.

27. Itô Shinsui (1898-1972)
Passing Rain
Taishô period, 1917
Signed: Shinsui; sealed: Shinsui
Publisher: Watanabe Shôzaburô, Tokyo
Color woodblock print
$17\frac{5}{16}$ x $11\frac{7}{8}$ in. (44 x 30.2 cm.)
Collection of Robert O. Muller

Silhouetting the nape of the neck, the artist emphasizes the traditional Japanese beauty spot, but he models the *janome* umbrella with a rounded volume that betrays an assured command of Western techniques.

The collaboration between the young Shinsui and his publisher, Watanabe Shôzaburô (1885-1962), began in 1916, at the start of the "new-print" (*shin hanga*) movement, an effort to revive the themes and craftsmanship of the ukiyo-e print.

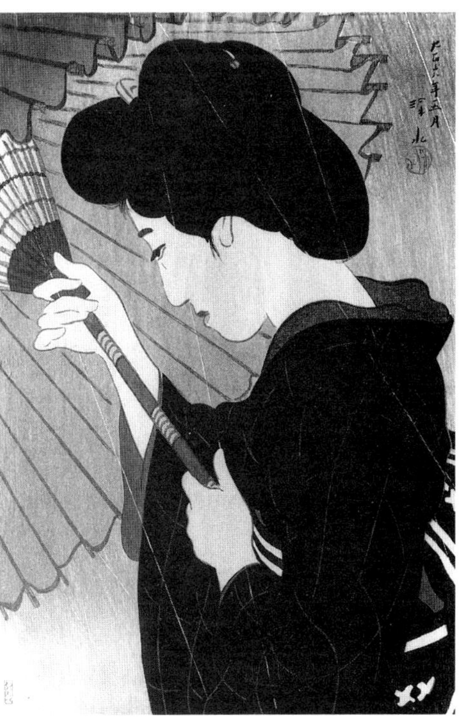

Color plate, p. 27

28. Nishimura Shigenaga (1697-1756)
The Actor Arashi Wakano as a Woman Walking in the Snow
Edo period, ca. 1725
Signed: Nihon gakô Nishimura Shigenaga hitsu; seal: Shige
Publisher: Igaya
Woodblock print with hand-painted pigments, *urushi-e*; *hosoban*
13 3/8 x 6 1/4 in. (34 x 15.9 cm.)
The Metropolitan Museum of Art, The Howard Mansfield Collection, Purchase, Rogers Fund, 1936, JP2657

Walking through deep snow in high geta, the actor pauses to admire the early blossoms on a plum tree. Snow has mounded on his umbrella, which is of the small type that seems to have been in vogue in the early 18th century. The stretchers are elegantly embroidered with threads of several colors, and a row of X's decorates the border of the cover. This border design is not described in any of the scanty Edo-period literature about umbrellas and thus has no fixed nomenclature, but it is quite prevalent in 18th-century woodblock prints. It seems likely that the design was made with threads, rather than painted, and it may have been a precursor of the use of spider's threads (*kumoito*).

The artist made a mistake in showing a band of rattan wrapped around the stick just below the bent-wire spring. This would have prevented the umbrella from closing. The rounded stretchers also seem too bulky for the size of the umbrella.

The actor's crest appears both on his umbrella and on the sleeve of his robe. Arashi Wakano I (d. 1728) was a small and very beautiful female impersonator (*onnagata*) who became famous for a role he performed in 1723, and who died a few years later, while still in his twenties. He may be shown here in a 1725 performance of *Oguri chôseiten* at the Nakamura theater in Edo.[1]

1. Meech-Pekarik et al. (1979), no. 68.

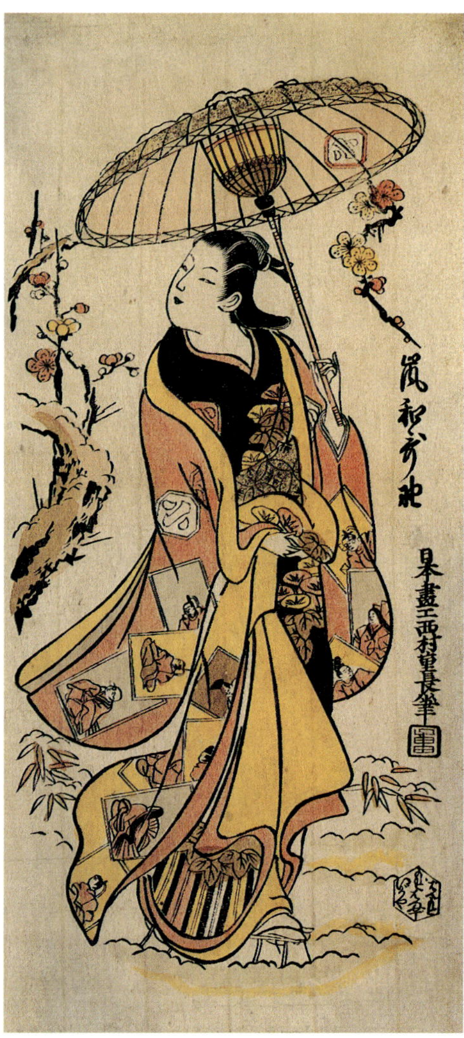

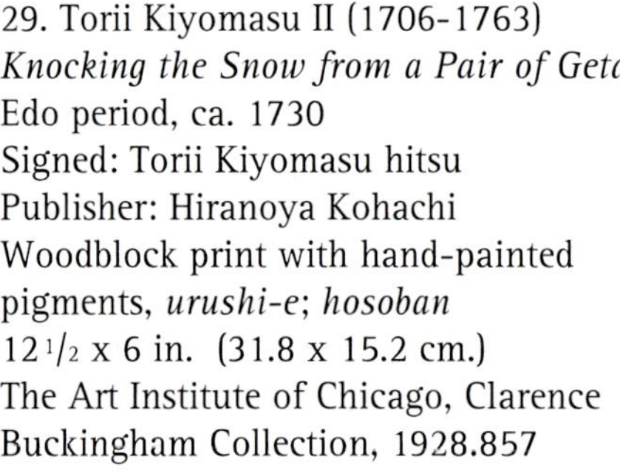

29. Torii Kiyomasu II (1706-1763)
Knocking the Snow from a Pair of Geta
Edo period, ca. 1730
Signed: Torii Kiyomasu hitsu
Publisher: Hiranoya Kohachi
Woodblock print with hand-painted pigments, *urushi-e*; *hosoban*
12 1/2 x 6 in. (31.8 x 15.2 cm.)
The Art Institute of Chicago, Clarence Buckingham Collection, 1928.857

A young male servant uses the handle of his fan to clear snow from his mistress's clogs. The provocative pose of a man bending low enough to be able to look up a woman's skirt appealed to ukiyo-e print artists, and the theme was reworked in many variations.

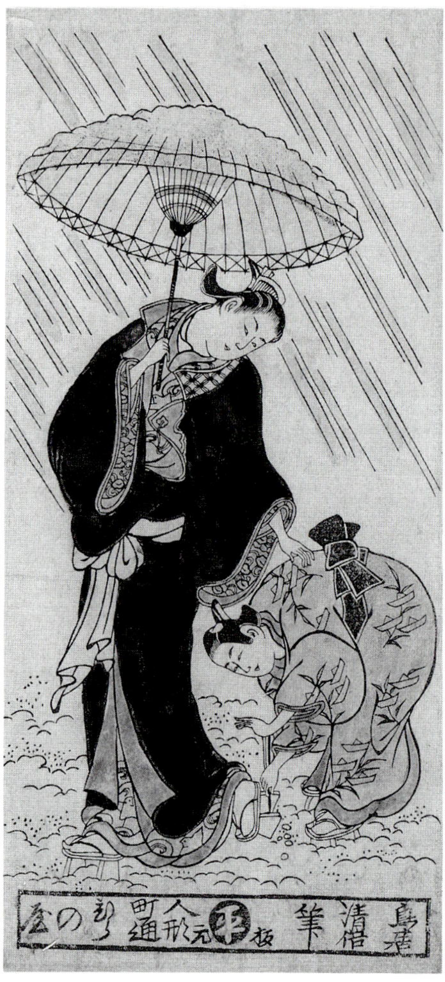

The bell-shaped form of the umbrella stretchers is typical for the first half of the 18th century. There are two bands of embroidered threads on the stretchers. The spring (*hajiki*) is metal; one made of bamboo or ivory would be depicted as solid. Today there is both an upper and a lower spring (*ue-hajiki* and *shita-hajiki*) on the stick of a *janome* umbrella (see diag. 1*l*,*m*). This seems to be an innovation of the late 19th or early 20th century. The lower spring allows the umbrella to be carried more easily half-closed against heavy rain or snow. There were, however, some large umbrellas with long sticks in the Edo period that used a double spring, placed on opposite sides of the stick at the same height. For our purposes, the single *hajiki* seen in woodblock prints is referred to as the spring.

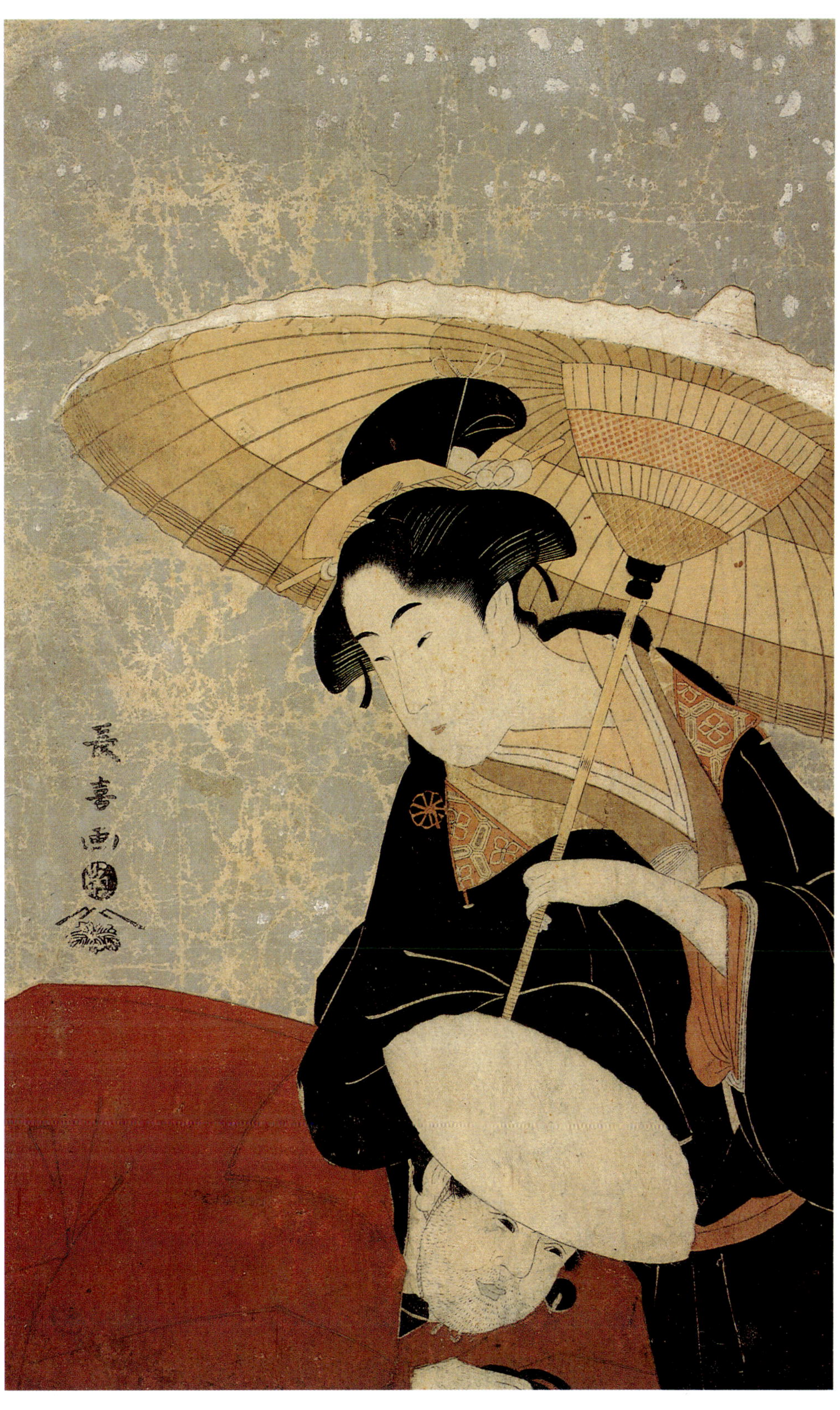

30. Eishôsai Chôki (active late 18th-early 19th century)
Beauty in the Snow
Series: untitled (beauties of the four seasons)
Edo period, ca.1794
Signed: Chôki ga
Publisher: Tsutaya Jûzaburô
Color woodblock print; vertical *ôban*
15 x $9\frac{1}{2}$ in. (38 x 24 cm.)
Honolulu Academy of Arts, Gift of James A. Michener, HAA 21,759

This is the winter scene from an untitled set of prints of the four seasons. White pigment (*gofun*) is dabbed over the mica ground to suggest snow. In the foreground, an ugly manservant bends low to clear the snow from the high wooden clogs worn by his mistress, a young beauty in a heavy black winter coat. She steadies herself by leaning on his back. In her left hand she holds the rattan-wrapped handle of a very large blue and white *janome* umbrella (the blue has faded); the white paper has, as usual, turned yellow from oiling. Two dark spots on the bamboo stick are nodes that have been shaved. The metal spring is visible just below the black-lacquered runner. The stretchers are embroidered with decorative blue and red cross-stitching. The artist, with no concern for realism, simplifies and flattens his design by filling in the nonembroidered portions of the stretchers with solid bands of color. Five lines of spider's threads (*kumoito*) circle the rim of this high-quality umbrella. *Kumoito* were used on Gifu umbrellas until just after the Second World War.

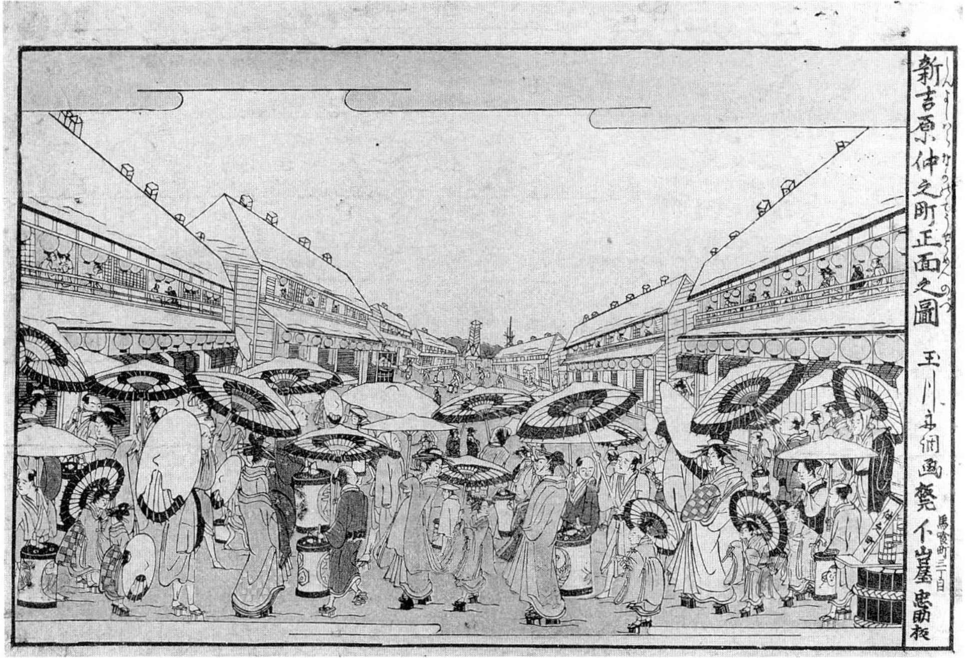

31. Tamagawa Shûchô (active ca.1790-1803)
Picture of Naka-no-chô in the New Yoshiwara
Edo period, ca. 1800
Signed: Tamagawa Shûchô ga
Publisher: Yamaguchiya Chûsuke
Color woodblock print; horizontal *ôban*
9 3/4 x 14 3/4 in. (24.8 x 37.5 cm.)
Collection of William Green, promised gift to Mead Art Museum, Amherst College

The signboard in the lower right corner is inscribed "Naka-no-chô," the name of the street running the length of the Yoshiwara district from the main gate. At the end of the street is the watch tower. (Kuninaga's *Picture of Evening Rain in the New Yoshiwara* [no. 13] shows Naka-no-chô from the other direction.) The scene is bustling with courtesans and their attendants; by the mid-19th century there were over ten thousand women in service in the Yoshiwara.

The umbrellas shown are all of the *janome* type. Those with long sticks are carried by male servants; the very small ones are held by little girls, who are apprentice courtesans (*kamuro*).

32. Ippitsusai Bunchô (1723-1792)
The Courtesan Chôsan of the Chôjiya
Series: untitled (love letters)
Edo period, ca.1770
Signed: Ippitsusai Bunchô ga;
sealed: Moriuji
Color woodblock print; *hosoban*
12 3/4 x 6 in. (32.4 x 15.2 cm.)
The Metropolitan Museum of Art, Purchase, Rogers Fund, 1936, JP2412

The message on the love letter in the upper left corner reads: "To Chôsan, the lady of the Chôjiya, from one she knows." The courtesan Chôsan, a famous Yoshiwara beauty, moves very slowly through thick powdery snow en route to her next assignation. The pavement in the brothel district is uneven, her black-lacquered clogs are high enough to make her unsteady even in good weather, and her robe is long and cumbersome. She is followed, outside the print area to the left, by a male servant, who holds the long-stick umbrella (*nagaegasa*) that protects Chôsan—and apparently her young companion too—from the snow. The *kamuro* seems uncertain as to whether she needs to open her own umbrella.[1]

The crane crest of the Chôjiya, the House of Cloves, appears on the courtesan's robe and on the umbrella, which serves here both in its functional capacity and as a badge of rank.

1. Kobayashi (1991), 149.

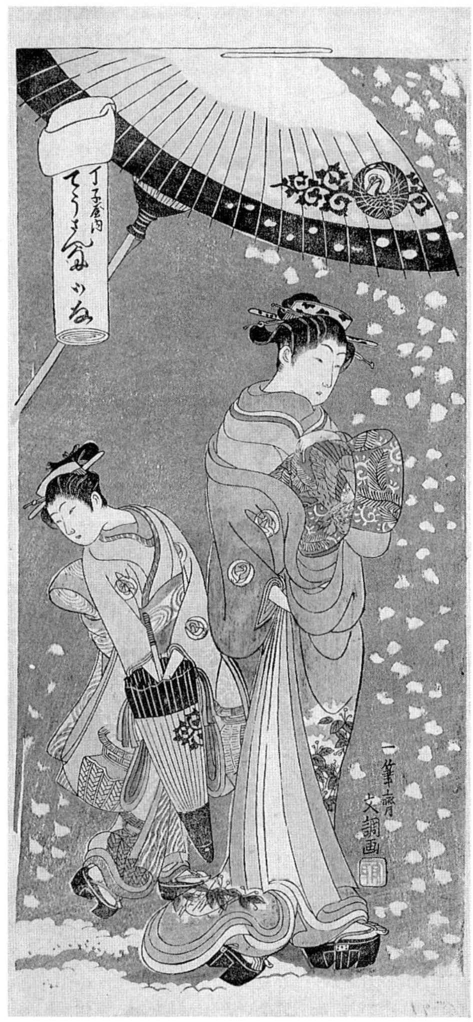

Color plate, p. 28

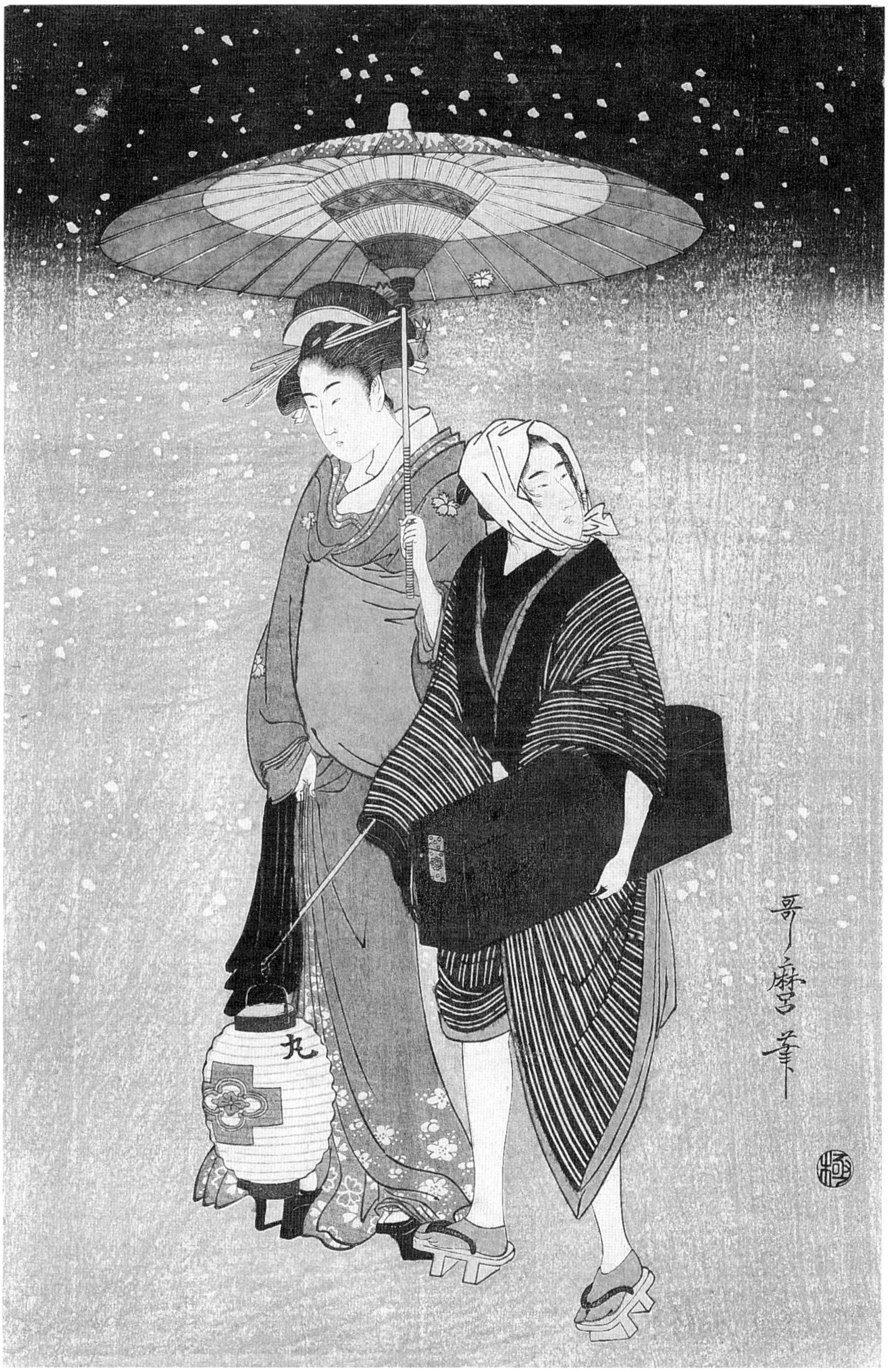

33. Kitagawa Utamaro (1753?-1806)
A Geisha and a Male Attendant in Snow
Edo period, ca.1796
Signed: Utamaro hitsu
Publisher: Tsutaya Jûzaburô
Color woodblock print; vertical *ôban*
$14\frac{5}{8}$ x $9\frac{5}{8}$ in. (37.1 x 24.4 cm.)
The Metropolitan Museum of Art,
H. O. Havemeyer Collection, Bequest of
Mrs. H. O. Havemeyer, 1929, JP 1665

Geisha were called into the licensed brothel quarters to entertain courtesans and their guests. As night falls, this geisha is on her way to an appointment at a nearby restaurant. Her floral crest appears on her robe and on the edge of her *janome* umbrella. A young male attendant carries the box with her shamisen and lights the way with a lantern.

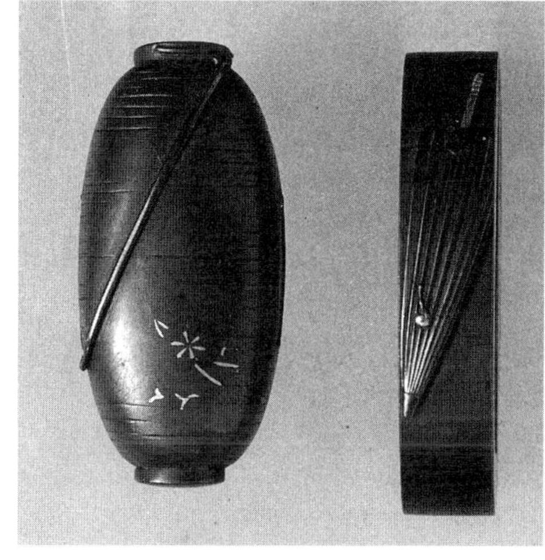

34. *Sword Fittings* (*fuchi-kashira*)
Late Edo period, 19th century
Fuchi: Umbrella with snail
Shibuichi ground carved in relief with *shakudô*, and inlaid with gold and silver
L. $1\frac{1}{2}$ in. (3.8 cm.)
Kashira: Lantern
Shibuichi ground inlaid with gold and copper
L. $1\frac{5}{16}$ in. (3.4 cm.)
The Metropolitan Museum of Art,
H. O. Havemeyer Collection, Bequest of
Mrs. H. O. Havemeyer, 1929, 29.100.1342ab

Fuchi-kashira are a pair of metal sword fittings which form the collar and cap of the hilt. This *fuchi* is carved on the front with an umbrella to which a snail has attached itself; on the back are a cuckoo in silver relief and a sickle moon inlaid in silver. The *kashira* takes the shape of a paper lantern with a design of plum blossom and pine. The combination of lantern and *janome*—the accoutrements of a geisha and her attendant en route to a rendezvous—suggests a night scene in the Yoshiwara.

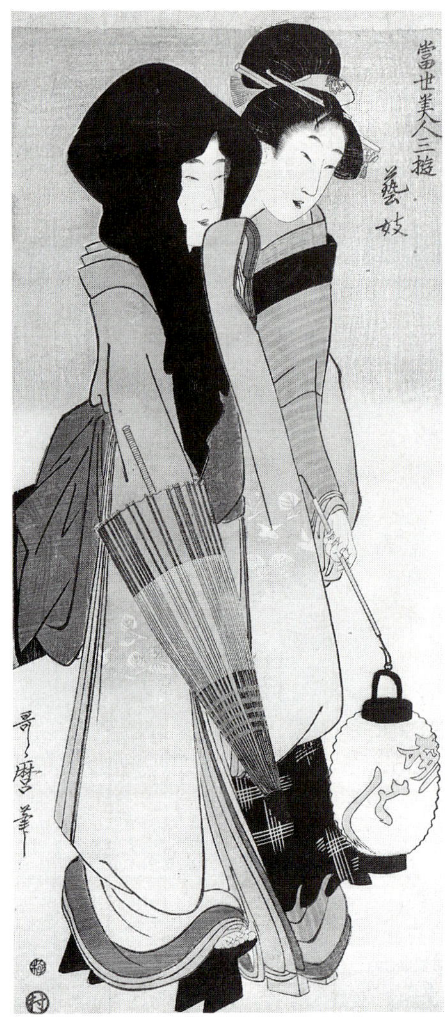

35. Kitagawa Utamaro (1753?-1806)
Pleasures of Modern Beauties: Geigi
Edo period, ca.1798-1800
Signed: Utamaro hitsu
Publisher: Marumura
Color woodblock print; *chûôban*
$20\frac{3}{4}$ x $9\frac{1}{2}$ in. (52.7 x 24.1 cm.)
The Metropolitan Museum of Art,
H. O. Havemeyer Collection, Bequest of Mrs. H. O. Havemeyer, 1929, JP1664

It has stopped snowing, and a geisha (also called *geigi*) with high wooden clogs and bare feet, wearing a winter hood, has closed her *janome* umbrella. Her maid illuminates their path with a lantern bearing the name of their establishment, Yanagibashi.

36. Janome *Umbrella*
Gifu, Shôwa period, 1980
Paper, bamboo and silk
L. $32\frac{1}{2}$ in. (82.5 cm.)
Gifu City Museum of History

This *janome* reproduces a style popular from the Meiji period to the beginning of the Shôwa, that is, from the 1870s to the 1920s. The ribs at the top of the umbrella are lacquered yellow-green, and decorated with thin lines running horizontally in concentric circles. The color of the cover is a persimmon brown (*shibu-cha*) with a white center band. There are fifty ribs and the stick, which has two springs, is made of a special kind of bamboo called Shinohara. The handle is wrapped with rattan. The umbrella was commissioned by Miyajima Rizô from the shop of Fujisawa Tôgo in Gifu.

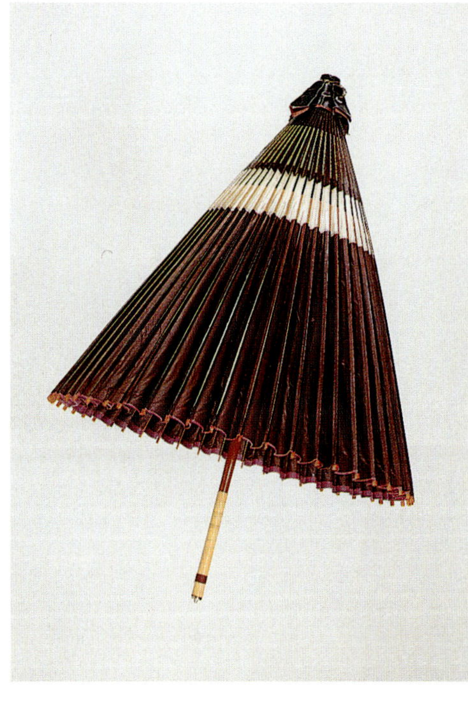

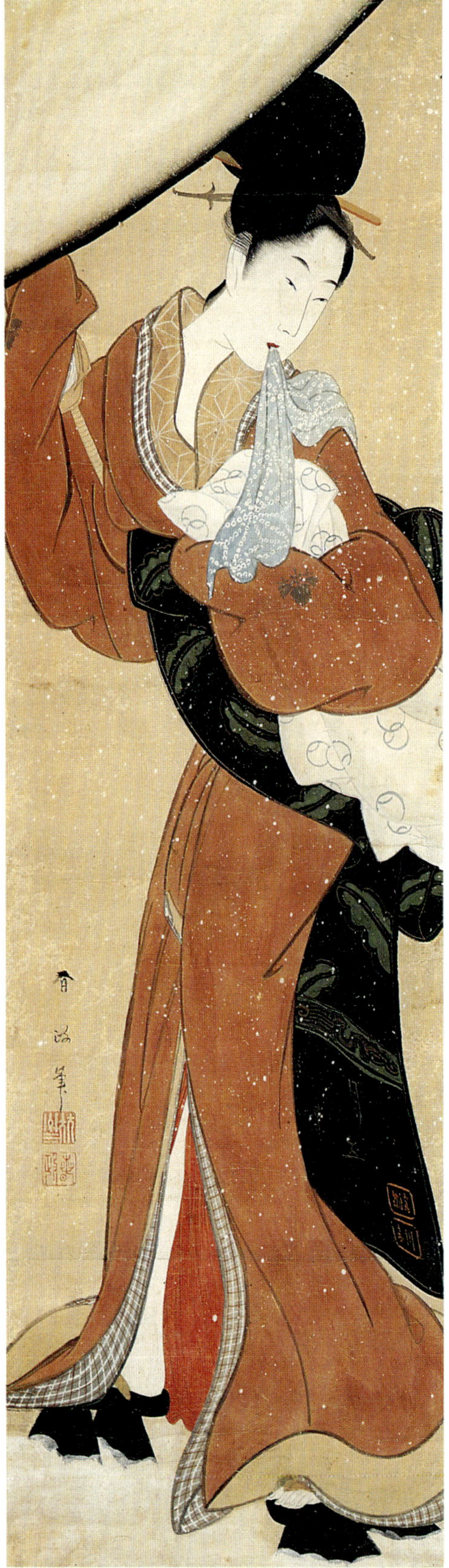

37. Koikawa Harumasa (active 1800-20)
Woman with Umbrella
Edo period, early 19th century
Signed: Harumasa hitsu; sealed: Kitagawa in; Harumasa
Hanging scroll; ink, color, gold and silver pigments on paper
$40\frac{9}{16}$ x $10\frac{7}{8}$ in. (103 x 27.6 cm.)
The Cleveland Museum of Art, The Kelvin Smith Collection, Given by Mrs. Kelvin Smith, CMA 85.257

A young woman hurries home from the local bathhouse, braving the elements. To judge by its thin, rattan-wrapped handle, her umbrella is of high quality and may be a *janome* type, but only the dark edge of its cover is visible beneath the snow. Still immaculately coiffed, she carries her wet towel in her teeth because her hands are occupied with the umbrella and with a bundle containing her change of clothing. Her hands are covered to keep warm, but her feet are exposed; presumably she does not have far to go. The pose shows off the sensuous lines of her long white neck and her bare legs. In Japanese images of beautiful women, bare feet and a towel held between the teeth both have erotic overtones.

38. Utagawa Hiroshige (1797-1858)
Beauty in the Snow
Edo period, 19th century
Signed: Ryûsai; sealed: Hiroshige
Hanging scroll; ink and color on silk
31 1/8 x 12 1/2 in. (79.1 x 31.8 cm.)
The Metropolitan Museum of Art, The Howard Mansfield Collection, Purchase, Rogers Fund, 1936, 36.100.22

Walking with difficulty along the embankment of a river—presumably the Sumida River in Edo—this woman may be on her way to meet a lover at a teahouse, or she may be heading for a small boat, by far the easiest mode of transportation given the weather conditions (white pigment sprinkled on the surface of the painting suggests the falling snow). The lady is bundled against the cold in a cloak, and her hair and cheeks are protected by a dark winter hood called *okôso zukin* (high-priest hood), after one of this type that appears on a famous statue of the 13th-century priest Nichiren. Her kimono is subdued and on her feet are split-toed linen socks (*tabi*), an article of clothing not worn by courtesans. Her right hand is covered for warmth but with the left she raises the hem of her kimono, revealing a suggestive glimpse of her red undergarment.

Rattan is wrapped around most of the stick of the woman's snow-covered umbrella, which may be a *janome*; or it may be of the *yakko* type, with only a thin outer band of color.

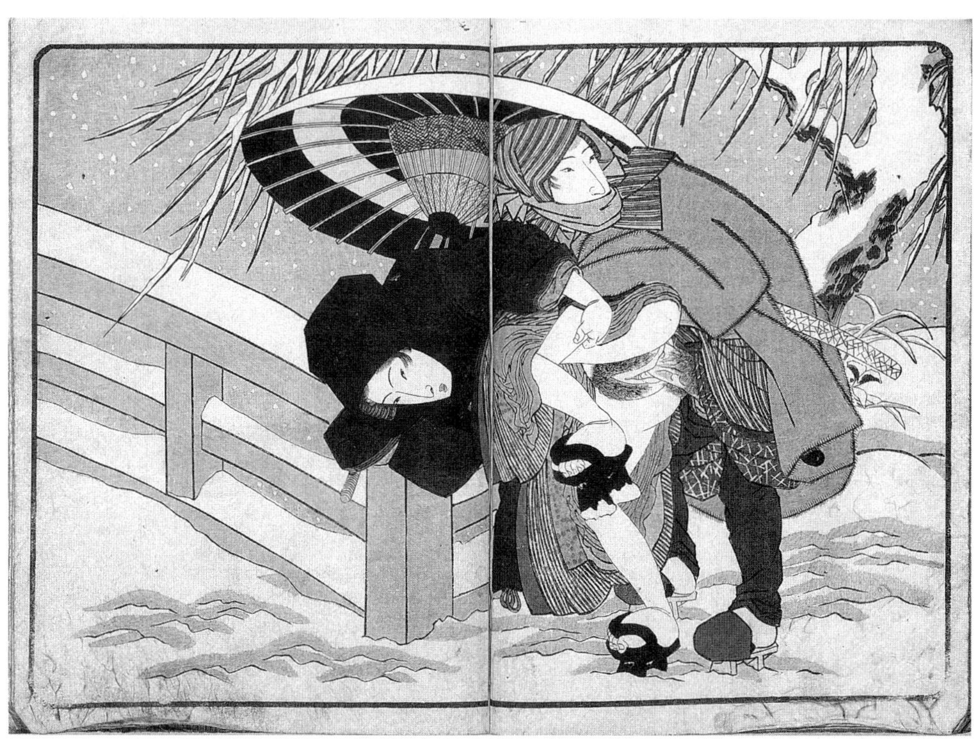

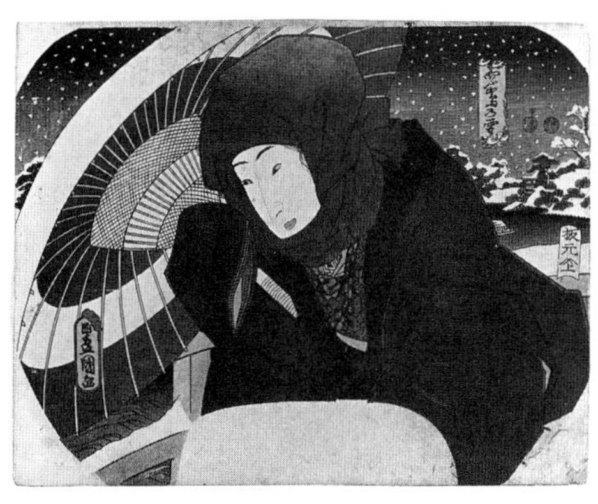

39. Utagawa Kunisada (1786-1864)
Snow at Mukôjima
Edo period, 1843-47
Signed: Toyokuni ga
Publisher: Iseya Sôemon
Color woodblock print; fan shape
9 x 11 13/16 in. (22.9 x 30 cm.)
Elvehjem Museum of Art, Gift of Abigail and John H. Van Vleck, 80.2626

Mukôjima is an island in the Sumida ward in Edo (present-day Tokyo), on the opposite side of the Sumida River from the Yoshiwara pleasure quarters. The artist has placed his signature as though it were a crest on the edge of the woman's snow-covered *janome*.

40. Utagawa Kunisada (1786-1864)
Pillow Bridge
From *Shiki no nagame* (Singing of the four seasons), Winter volume
Edo period, ca. 1829
Color woodblock-printed illustrated book
Page: 10 x 7 1/4 in. (25.4 x 18.4 cm.)
Ravicz Collection

A husband and wife and their servant are returning home after a visit to Inari Jinja, or the Fox Shrine, in Edo. The wife suddenly realizes that she has left behind the souvenir she purchased, and the servant is sent back to fetch it. While waiting for her to return, the amorous couple finds a way to keep warm. The husband, wrapped in a furry coat, watches out for the maid, while his wife holds their *janome* umbrella.

The Pillow Bridge scene is one of eight illustrations in the winter volume of a four-volume erotic work celebrating love in the four seasons.[1] Its accompanying poem reads:

Yuki no hada
misete mo suso o
Makurabashi
shiranami nagasu
Suda no kawazoi

Snow-white skin
bared as skirt is rolled up
at Pillow Bridge—
white waves cascade
along the Suda River.

Makurabashi, or Pillow Bridge, an appropriate location for a sexual encounter, crosses a canal a few steps from the Sumida River (referred to in the poem by its colloquial abbreviation, Suda) in the Honjo district.[2]

1. The first two volumes have cover titles that read *Shun-ka-shû-tô: Shiki no nagame*, which might be translated as "Spring–Summer–Autumn–Winter: Singing of Love in the Four Seasons." One would expect the first word in the main title–*shiki*–to be written in two characters meaning "four seasons," but instead the author has playfully inserted a pun by using the character *shiki*, which can also be read *iro* or *shoku*, meaning "love" or "sex." The second two volumes (Autumn and Winter) have the more predictable title *Shiki no nagame* or "Singing of the Four Seasons." According to the preface, the first volume came out at the end of the Bunsei era (1818-29). See Shibui (1933), nos. 83, 84. The author is grateful to Kakehi Mariko, Gifu City Museum of History, and to John Carpenter for their assistance in interpreting the text and title of this book.
2. The canal leads eastward from the Sumida past the southern extremity of Sumida Park toward the Nakagawa, or Naka River. Yaomatsu, a famous Edo restaurant, stood at Makurabashi. The author is grateful to Edward Seidensticker for pinpointing the location of this bridge.

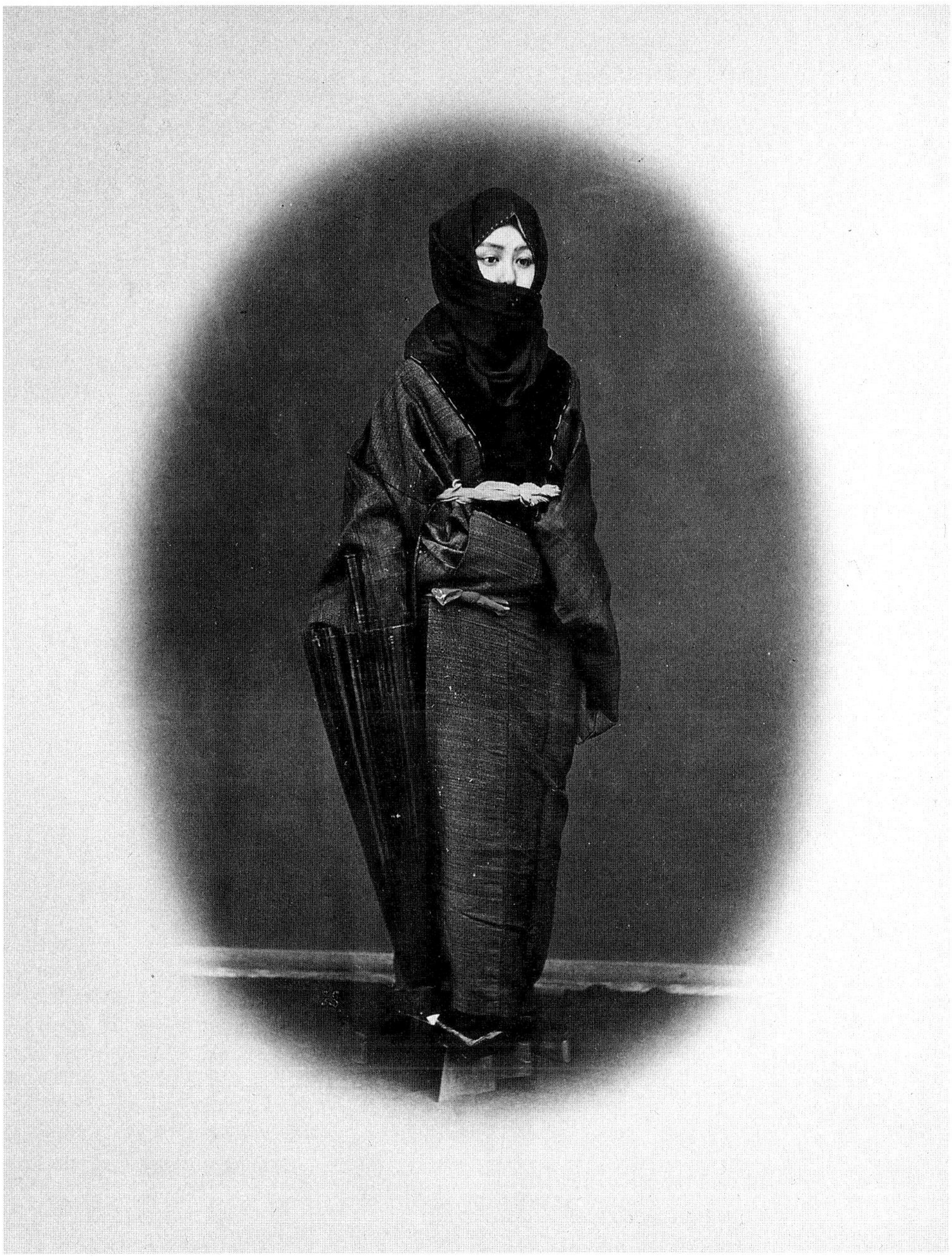

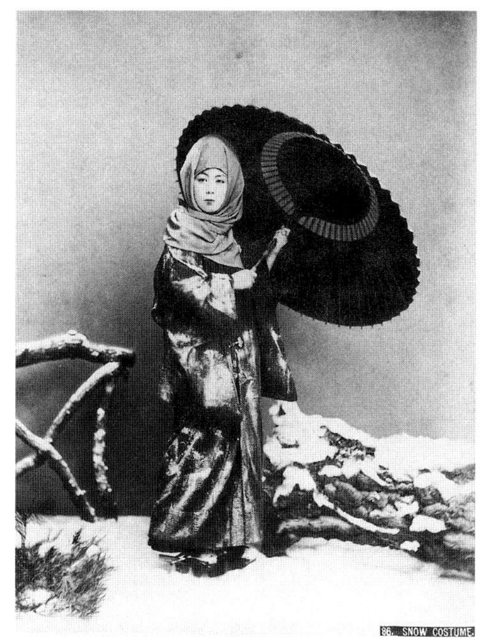

42. Photographer unknown
Snow Costume
Meiji period, ca.1880-90
Hand-colored albumen print
10 x 7 3/4 in. (25.4 x 19.7 cm.)
The Jane Voorhees Zimmerli Art Museum, Rutgers, The State University of New Jersey, 1987.0638

The woman in this studio photograph holds a *janome* umbrella with sixty ribs. There was a time when umbrellas were made with as many as eighty to one hundred and twenty very thin ribs.

41. Attributed to Felice Beato (1825-1904), British (born Venice)
Snow Costume
Meiji period, 1870s
Hand-colored albumen print
10 1/4 x 8 in. (26 x 20.3 cm.)
Collection of Mr. and Mrs. Joel H. Frankel

Swathed in a dark snow hood and winter coat, the young woman wears very high snow clogs. Mysterious and alluring, she is posed to great effect in the artist's studio in Yokohama, with the traditional costume and paper umbrella that were guaranteed to please a foreign audience. The color of her umbrella, which appears as black in the photograph, would in reality have been either gray-black, known in umbrella shops as *hatoba* (pigeon wing), or dark purplish-gray, *hatoba nezumi* (pigeon-wing mouse).

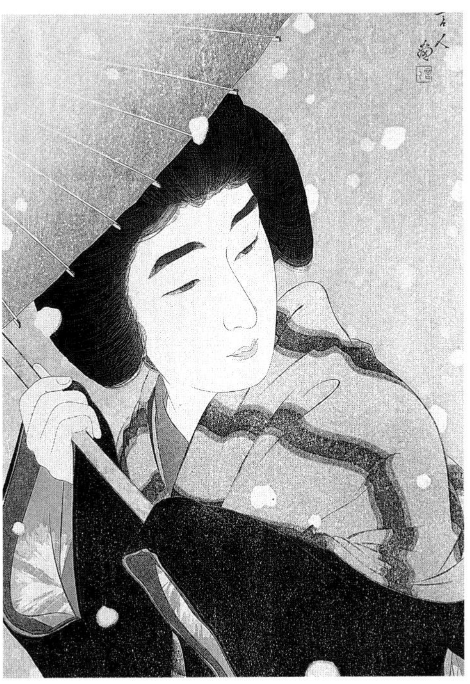

43. Torii Kotondo (1900-1976)
Peony Snow
Shôwa period, 1934
Signed: Kotondo ga; sealed: Kotondo
Publisher: Ikeda
Color woodblock print
18 1/4 x 11 5/8 in. (46.4 x 29.5 cm.)
Collection of Robert O. Muller

Kotondo was the eighth-generation head of the Torii family of print artists, which had specialized in actor prints since the late 17th century (see nos. 61, 62, 67). His own preference, however, was for romantic images of beautiful women in traditional costume, in this case recalling the words of a Japanese proverb: "See a woman at night, from a distance, or under an umbrella" (*Yome, tôme, kasa no uchi*).

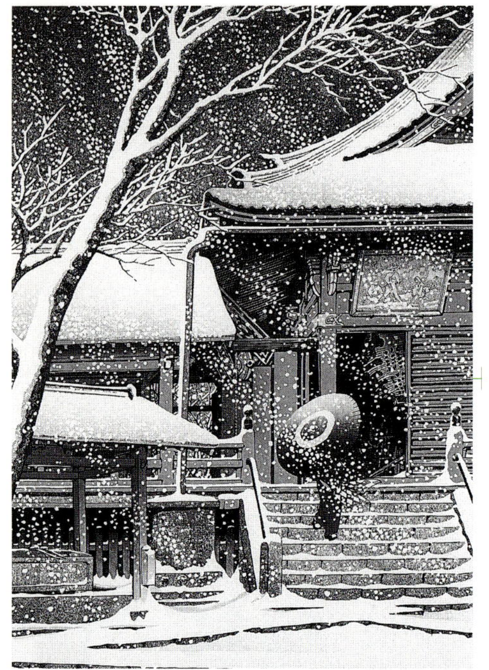

44. Kawase Hasui (1883-1957)
Snow at Kiyomizu Hall, Ueno
Shôwa period, 1929
Signed: Hasui; sealed by the artist
Publisher: Kawaguchi and Sakai, Tokyo
Color woodblock print
$15^{7}/_{8}$ x $10^{3}/_{4}$ in. (40.3 x 27.3 cm.)
Collection of Robert O. Muller

A kimono-clad figure, shielded against the driving snow by a *janome* umbrella, descends the steps of Kiyomizu Hall in Ueno Park, in the suburbs of Tokyo. The hall was one of the city's famous sites, and Hasui treats the scene in a deliberately picturesque fashion.

See color plate, p. 56.

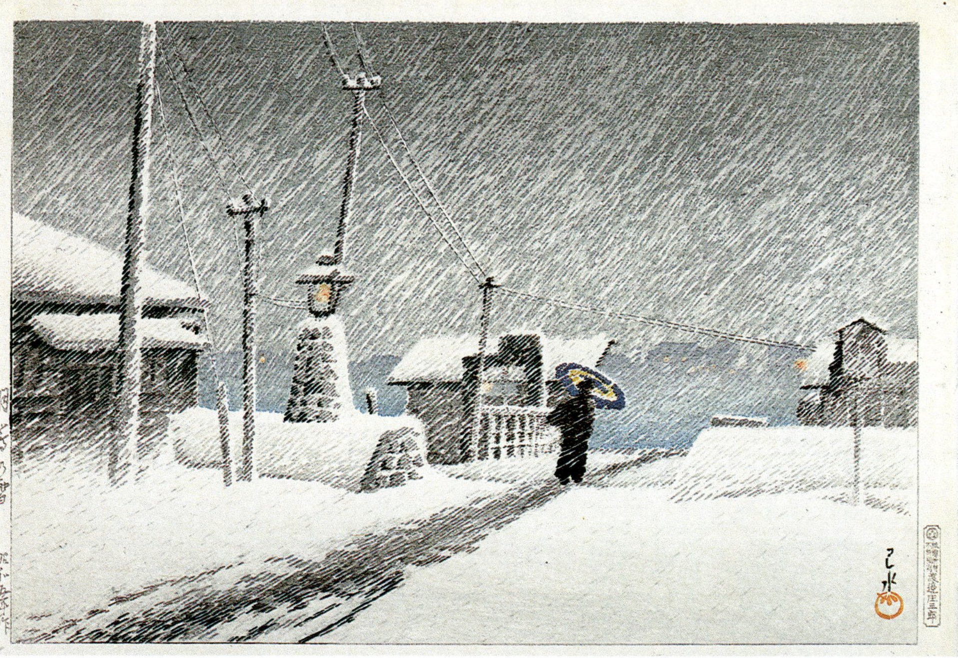

45. Kawase Hasui (1883-1957)
Snow at Tsukijima
Series: Twenty Views of Tokyo
Shôwa period, 1930
Signed: Hasui; sealed by the artist
Publisher: Watanabe Shôzaburô
Color woodblock print
$10^{1}/_{2}$ x $15^{7}/_{16}$ in. (26.7 x 39.2 cm.)
Lawrence and Bessie Weinberg Collection, Chicago

A bleak winter night in modern Tokyo is given a romantic touch by the solitary pedestrian's traditional *janome* umbrella. The scene evokes a haiku by Yaha (1662-1740):

Karakasa no
hitotsu sugiyuku
yuki no kure

An umbrella—one alone—
passes by:
An evening of snow.[1]

1. Blyth (1952), 257.

46. Janome *Umbrella*
Gifu, Shôwa period, 1975-85
Paper, bamboo and silk threads
L. $32^{1}/_{2}$ in. (82.5 cm.)
Gifu City Museum of History

This indigo and white *janome*, commissioned by Miyajima Rizô from the shop of the Gifu umbrella wholesaler Fujisawa Tôgo, reproduces a style popular from the Taishô period through the first half of the Shôwa, that is, from 1912 to the 1940s. With a diameter when opened of 48 inches (121 cm.), its large size makes it a man's umbrella. Its fifty ribs are lacquered reddish-brown, and the bamboo stick, with two wood springs, is painted the same color.

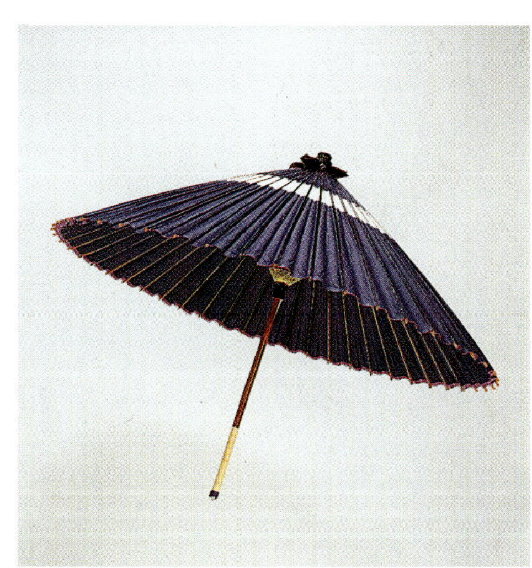

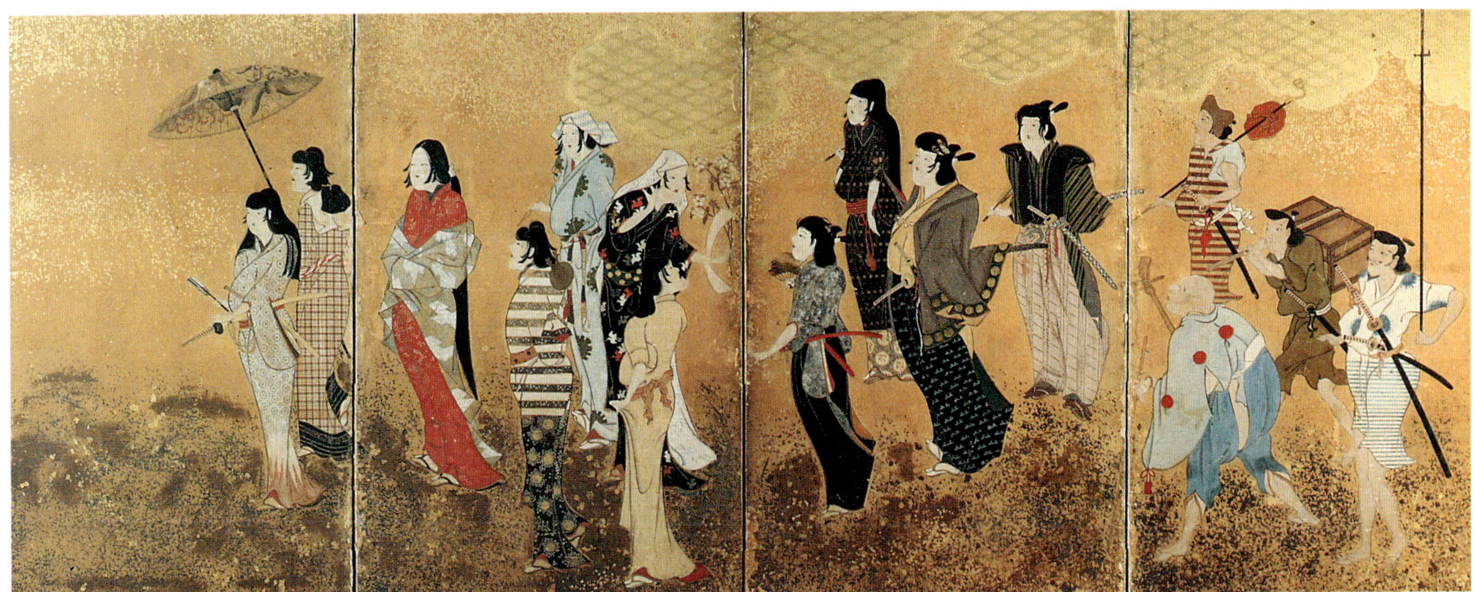

47. Artist unknown
Cherry-Blossom Viewing Picnic
Edo period, first half 17th century
Right half of a pair of four-panel screens; ink, color, gold pigment, and gold and silver leaf on paper
33 3/4 x 86 1/2 in. (85.7 x 219.7 cm.)
The Brooklyn Museum, Gift of Mr. Frederic B. Pratt, 39.87

This painting, the right half of a pair of screens, takes an intimate look at the frivolities of contemporary life in 17th-century Kyoto. The subject is ambiguous, however: women are dressed as men, and the men are overtly feminine. On the left half of the screens (in the Yahata collection in Tokyo) a young man armed with a pair of samurai swords dances for a group of admiring women picnickers on a spring outing. The procession on the Brooklyn screen approaches this festive gathering, led by a seductive young woman wearing samurai swords. One theory is that she and her female companions are simply bathhouse girls, the lowest class of prostitutes, who washed and entertained their customers.[1] The women are indeed brazen and bold, charged with sensual energy. They are tall, sinuous figures, whose buttocks and thighs are conspicuously outlined by the clinging fabric of their robes.

On the other hand, the girl in the lead, who has her own umbrella bearer and an entourage, may be a rising new star from the Kabuki stage making her public debut.[2] She is trailed by a group of prostitute-entertainers, three samurai dandies, a blind shamisen player, a buffoon with an ostentatiously long pipe, a footman with a picnic box, and a lance bearer. During its initial development in the early years of the 17th century, Kabuki was a burlesque of song, dance and farce presented by female entertainers and prostitutes. The ladies of the licensed qarters advertised their feminine charms from the stage. Okuni, promoter of Women's Kabuki, appeared on stage as a young man wearing two swords; perhaps the dancer on the left screen is in reality a woman taking the role of the "Dashing Playboy" in an impromptu Women's Kabuki skit. The modish young men on the Brooklyn screen have powdered faces and wear their hair pulled back over their shaved pates in the manner of *wakushû*, young actors or male prostitutes.

The umbrella (no. 47a), a lightweight parasol with a long stick (*sashikake higasa*), is in any case ultrachic and perfectly suited to this unconventional group from the Kyoto demimonde. The design painted on the cover has a fashionable continental flavor; the motif of two phoenixes chasing one another is familiar from Chinese porcelain decoration of the Wanli period (1573-1620).[3] Foreign imports in clothing and accessories were a sign of style and good taste: the tobacco pipe represents a custom introduced around 1600 by the Dutch, and the tall young man strutting in the second panel from the right wears ballooning trousers reminiscent of Portuguese costumes. Even the trim mustache and goatee of the lance bearer at the end of the procession can be said to emulate European models.

The parasol cover may be transparent silk, since the design shows through on the underside. There are three rows of reinforcing threads (*kumoito*) around the rim, a sign of superior workmanship. The long stick (the bottom reappears behind the bearer's right knee) is lacquered black and is wrapped with numerous bands of rattan, possibly to cover the bamboo

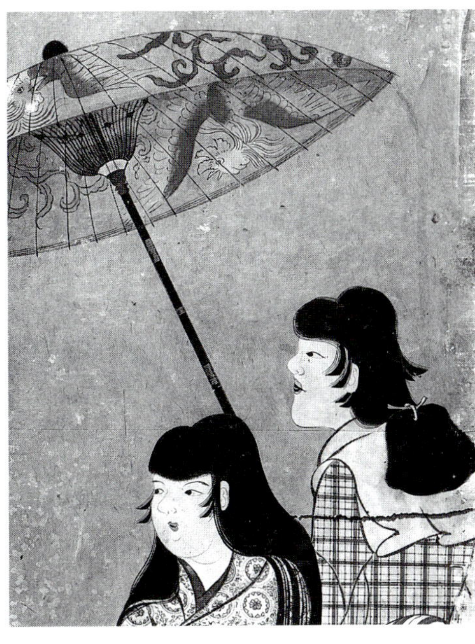

47a. Detail showing parasol

nodes. The stretchers are decoratively shaped, as is often the case with parasols, but they lack any embroidered decoration. There appear to be knobs or holes in the ribs into which the stretchers are inserted. It may be that this type of umbrella was not collapsible; there is certainly no indication of a spring or pin.

1. Murase (1990), 169.
2. Goodwin (1988).
3. See Valenstein (1989), fig. 28.

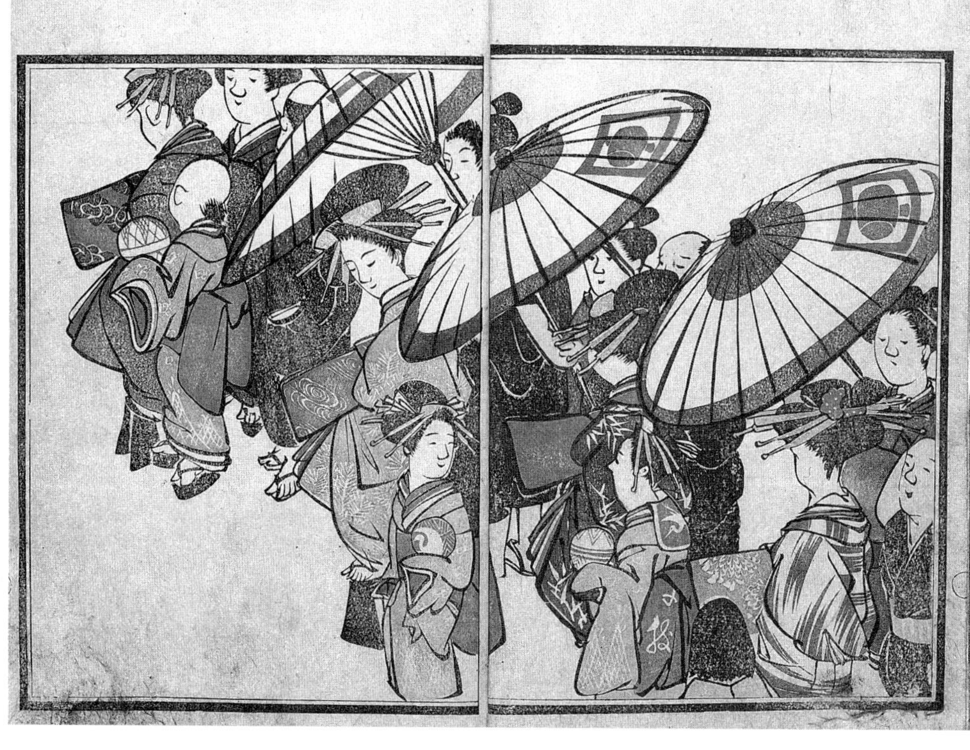

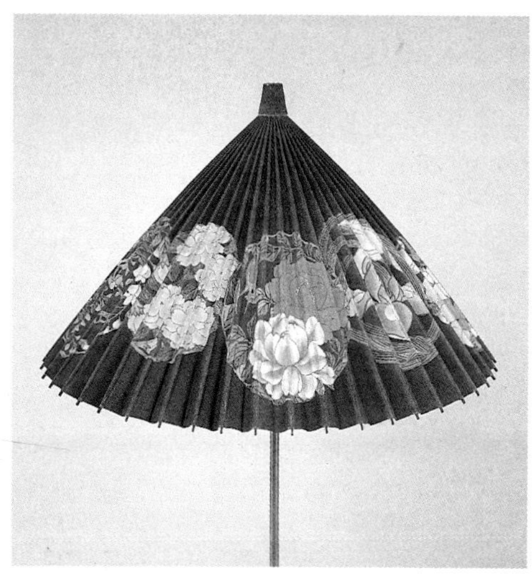

Color plate, p. 18

48. *Parasol*
Edo period, 1810-30
Paper, bamboo, lacquered wood and silk threads
L. 65 in. (165 cm.)
Rijksmuseum voor Volkenkunde, Leiden, The Netherlands, Blomhoff-Fisscher Collection, No. 360-6546

Members of the Dutch settlement on the island of Dejima in Nagasaki were permitted by the Japanese government to purchase merchandise for export to Europe. Lacquer and porcelain (see nos. 122, 123) were always favorite acquisitions. Johan Frederik van Overmeer Fisscher (1800-1848), stationed at Dejima in the 1820s, and Jan Cock Blomhoff (1779-1853), who was there around 1810 and again around 1820, returned to Holland with collections of Japanese art and artifacts that included umbrellas. Their collections were purchased by the king and were later deposited in the Rijksmuseum voor Volkenkunde (National Museum of Ethnology), Leiden.

This rather showy parasol was probably carried over a lady of means. The bright blue cover is painted with rondels of blossoms: iris, peony, cherry, plum, wisteria, laburnum, magnolia and hydrangea. The long stick (only part of which is shown in the photograph) is lacquered red and there is a single spring.

49. Saitô (or Aoi) Shûho (1769-1859)
Procession of Courtesans
From *Kishi empu* (Mr. Aoi's chronicle of charms), Vol. 1
Edo period, 1803
Publisher: Ueda Uhei and Murakami Sakichi, Osaka
Color woodblock-printed illustrated book
Page: 10 1/16 x 7 1/16 in. (25.6 x 17.9 cm.)
Former collection of Henri Vever
Ravicz Collection

The irreverent Kyoto artist shows a New Year's procession of courtesans, accompanied by maids on their right and young apprentice courtesans (*kamuro*) on their left, in Shimmachi, the licensed pleasure quarter of Osaka. Male servants carry the long-stick umbrellas, which bear the mallet crest of the Daikokuya brothel. Meiji-period photographs document similar processions (no. 49a).

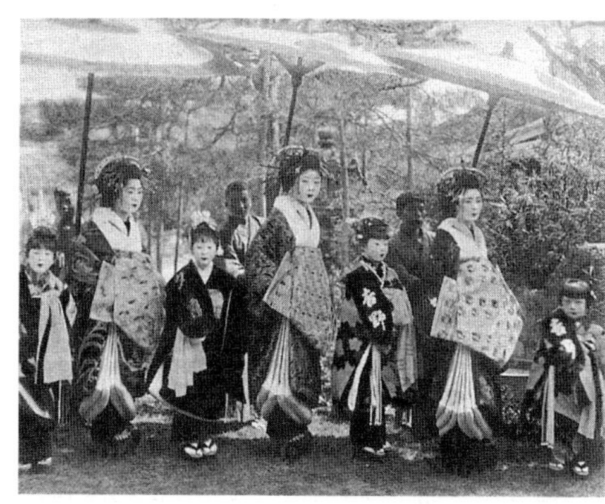

49a. Photographer unknown, *A Procession of Courtesans and* Kamuro, Meiji period, 1890s. Albumen print. Yokohama Archives of History

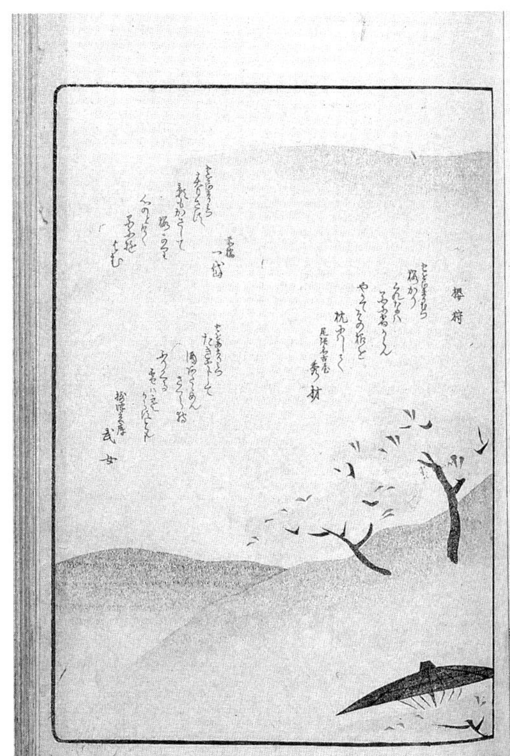

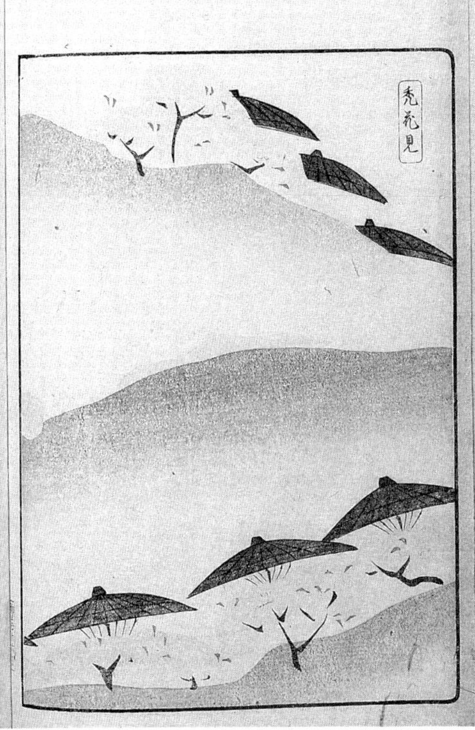

50. Kabocha Sôen (d.1846)
Kamuro *Viewing Cherry Blossoms*
From *Ryûkô meibutsu-shi* (Record of noted attractions of the Willow District)
Edo period, 1834
Signed: Kabocha Sôen hitsu; sealed: Bunrô (Tower of learning)
Privately published by Kurokawa Harumaru
Color woodblock-printed illustrated book
Page: 11 x 7 in. (27.9 x 17.8 cm.)
Ravicz Collection

The blue parasols belong to a procession of unseen apprentice or child courtesans (*kamuro*) on a cherry-blossom viewing excursion in the environs of the Yoshiwara, the licensed pleasure quarters on the outskirts of Edo (here referred to politely as the "Willow District"). The preceding illustration in the book is labeled "Cherry Blossoms in the Naka-no-chô," the heart of the Yoshiwara. The illustrations thus move from the center of the brothel district to the surrounding countryside.[1] The parasols are of the type with long sticks (*nagaegasa*) used for escorting both courtesans and *kamuro*, shown, for the sake of a clever composition, as if floating above the treetops. A late-19th-century photograph presents a more conventional view of similar umbrellas (no. 51).

The "Record of Noted Attractions of the Willow District," an illustrated anthology of *kyôka* poems, was commissioned by the prominent *kyôka* master and National Learning scholar Kurokawa Harumaru (1799-1866),[2] also known as Sensôan (Asakusa Hermitage) III, the head of the Tsubo-gawa poetry group. He seems to have invited all his students to contribute poems and no doubt collected a small fee from each of them. Addresses beside the names of the poets throughout the book reveal that they come from all over the country—an indication of how *kyôka* masters tried to spread their influence and supplement their income. A *kyôka* (literally, "mad verse") is a witty poem in thirty-one syllables that came into its own in the early Edo period and appealed to a broad spectrum of society.

The illustrator, Sôen (who also went under the names Murata Ichibei, Kabocha II or Kabocha Motonari), was a poet, painter and puppeteer. As a poet he studied *kyôka* under Sensôan III, and was responsible not only for the illustrations in this volume but for arranging the poems as well, which explains why image and verse work together more effectively here than in most *kyôka* books. The very last verse in the volume is his, an indication of respect.

The sequence of poems and illustrations, following traditional convention, is governed by the seasons: the opening scene shows courtesans making their New Year's visits (*nenrei*). The artist has cleverly selected poems to go with each image that would tie *meibutsu* (noted attractions, or famous products) to a seasonal topic. Here the theme is *sakuragari* (hunting for cherry blossoms), a phrase included in each of the three poems on the left-hand page. Other "noted attractions" of the Yoshiwara mentioned in the poems are the umbrella, the pillow and sake.

The first poem is by Shûzai of Nagoya, in Owari province:

Sakuragari
kurenaba hana ni
yadokaran
yagate sono ne o
makura ni wa shite

If twilight descends
while on our cherry blossom hunt,
we will lodge amid flowers.
The roots of the trees then
will become our pillows.

The second poem is by Ittai of Maebashi, in Gumma prefecture:

Haru hi sasu
kage mo kasa shite
sakuragari
kokoro nodokeku
hana ni asobamu

Though the spring sun glares
we carry umbrellas
in our search for cherry blossoms.
We frolic amid flowers
with tranquil hearts.

The implication here is that courtesans, reputed to have skin as white as snow, do not want to risk a sunburn, hence the parasols. The word *hana* (flower) in the last line can refer both to the evanescent beauty of prostitutes and to cherry blossoms in the context of the Yoshiwara.

The final poem is by the poetess Takejo from Settsu, in Hyôgo prefecture:

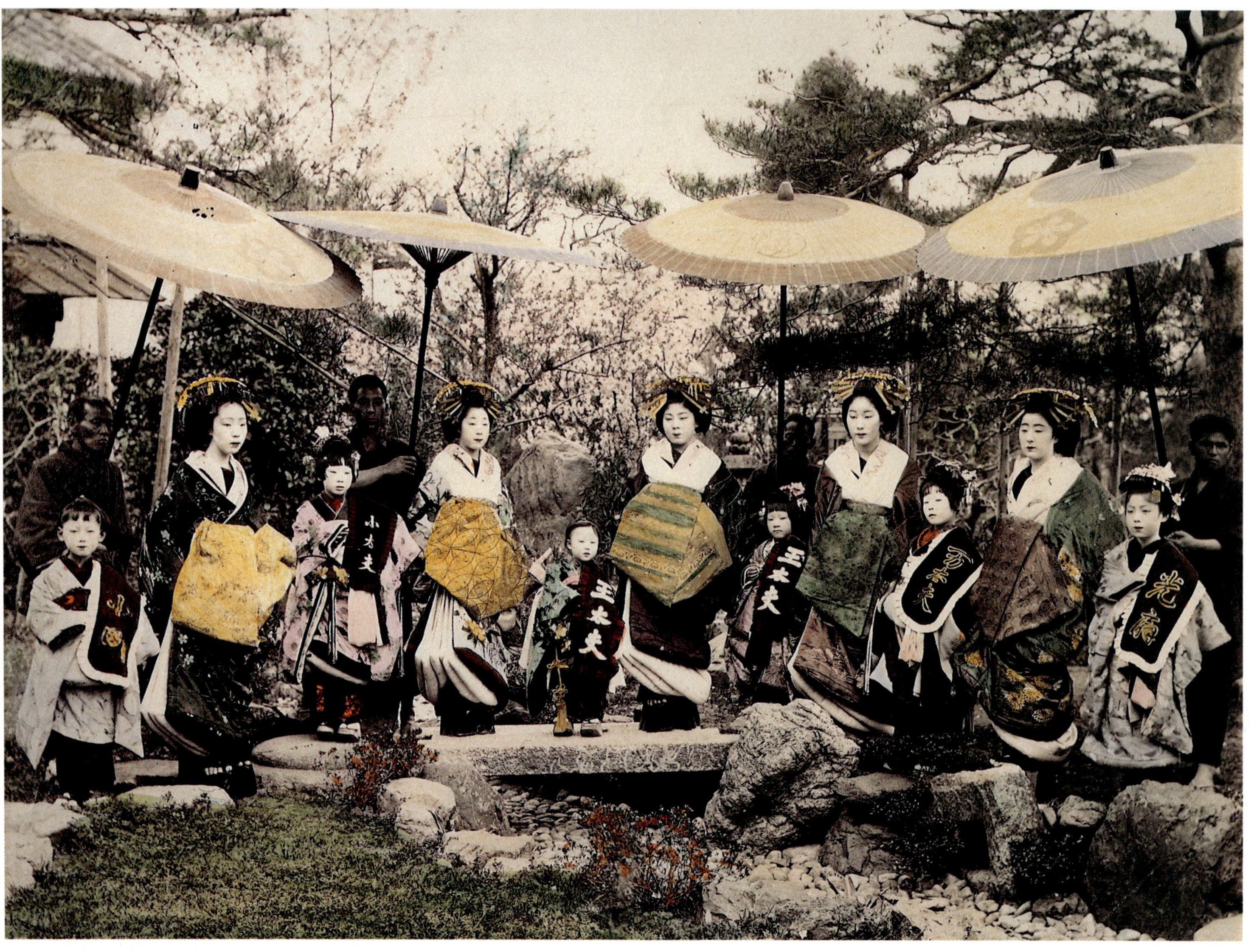

Takibi shite
sake atatamen
sakuragari
furikuru yuki wa
samukarazu to ya

We make a bonfire
to heat the wine
as we hunt for cherry blossoms.
Snow begins to flutter,
but why doesn't it feel cold?[3]

The reference to snow is a poetic conceit dating back to the classical period, when the falling, scattering cherry blossoms were compared with flurries of snow. Drinking sake under the blossoms is a favorite Japanese custom, both then and now.

1. During the cherry-blossom season *kamuro* and *shinzô* (teenage courtesans) were allowed out of the Yoshiwara to visit nearby Ueno, Asukayama and Mukôjima; De Becker (1971), 231. For a procession of Yoshiwara courtesans through hills covered with blossoming cherry trees on a fan print by Hiroshige, see Suzuki (1970), pl. 66.
2. National Learning (*kokugaku*) is the name given to the philological study of Japanese classical literature and ancient writings that began in the 17th century with the aim of identifying peculiarly Japanese cultural elements.
3. Translations and commentary by John Carpenter, Columbia University.

51. Photographer unknown
Courtesans and Kamuro
Meiji period, 1890s
Hand-colored albumen print
8 x 10 1/2 in. (20.3 x 26.7 cm.)
Collection of Christer von der Burg and Chris Uhlenbeck

Five high-ranking courtesans (*oiran*) and their child attendants pose among cherry blossoms in the garden of a teahouse in the Yoshiwara. Alone their umbrella bearers, as befits their lowly status, have not been tinted in this hand-colored photograph. The women are weighed down with the usual paraphernalia of a courtesan's dress: a large number of oversize hairpins, many layers of padded brocade gowns, a large obi tied in the front, and ungainly black-lacquered clogs. Their feet, as was customary in their profession, are bare.

The young beauty at the center must have had the highest ranking in the group; she is flanked by two little girls. All the *kamuro* wear banners over their shoulders identifying them with their respective mistresses.

52. Utagawa Kokunimasa (1874-1944)
Hell Courtesan
Meiji period, ca. 1900
Signed (on right lantern): Ryû-a
Six-panel folding screen (right half of a pair)
Ink, color and silver leaf on paper
68 1/8 x 137 13/16 in. (173 x 350 cm.)
Collection of Penelope Mason

This stately procession of a courtesan and her attendants reveals them in the skeletal form they will assume after death. Symbols of the transience of human existence, the skeletons are Buddhist in inspiration. Legend has it that Jigoku (Hell) was the house name of a courtesan in Takasu-chô, Osaka, who was befriended by the eccentric Zen priest and poet Ikkyû (1394-1481). The iconoclastic Ikkyû, who had a predilection for finding virtue in the midst of vice, scorned the hypocrisy of his supposedly devout colleagues and indulged himself in sensual pleasures, claiming to have spent ten years in the brothels. On his first encounter with Jigoku, he composed the opening stanza of a linked verse (*renga*):

Kikishi yori
mite osoroshiki
Jigoku kana

Though I had heard
all about "Hell,"
seeing the real thing—
more daunting still!

The Hell Courtesan's beauty was *osoroshiki*, which can mean "frightening," as in the case of the Buddhist hell, or "daunting," to describe the attractions of this femme fatale. Jigoku, a woman of many talents, immediately improvised the final stanza:

Iki-kuru hito mo
ochizarameyawa

Even the living who draw near
cannot but fall into the abyss![1]

Jigoku, cleverly alluding to the men who are ensnared by the beauty of courtesans, thus showed herself already enlightened in a worldly sense. Ikkyû was to direct her on the path to spiritual wisdom.

The story was updated by the popular writer and ukiyo-e artist Santô Kyôden (Kitao Masanobu, 1761-1816) in volume 4 of his 1809 *Honchô suibodai zenden* (Stories of drunken enlightenment in Japan), a source for many 19th-century images of the Hell Courtesan, and was widely popularized when the play *Ikkyû jigoku banashi* (Ikkyû's tale of hell) by the leading Kabuki dramatist, Kawatake Mokuami (1816-1893), was performed at the Ichimura theater in Tokyo in 1865.[2]

Jigoku (hell) became a general term for unlicensed prostitutes in the Edo period, and the grotesque possibilities of the association appealed to late-19th-century artists. In an 1889 print Yoshitoshi depicted a courtesan with scenes of hell on her outer robe, dreaming of a skeletal version of herself, with an attendant holding the skeleton of an umbrella over her head. This image or similar prints and paintings by Kawanabe Gyôsai (1831-1899) may well have inspired Kokunimasa's witty screen painting.[3] Here Jigoku and her young female attendants are clothed in skirts of green leaves and sashes of white blossoms. Wildflowers and grasses serve as hair ornaments. Two male attendants light their way with paper lanterns (instead of the name of the brothel, the artist's signature is written on one of them), and a third supports the long stick of the umbrella against his back. A few of the ribs of the umbrella have broken. Bringing up the rear is a teenage courtesan (*shinzô*) with a male attendant. The scene brings to mind the words Ikkyû wrote in 1457 in a work called *Gaikotsu* (Skeletons), describing his belief that the world is an illusion: "Remember that under the skin you fondle lie the bones, waiting to reveal themselves."[4]

1. Translation and interpretation of the poem are by John Carpenter.
2. Genshoku ukiyo-e daihyakka-jiten henshû-iinkai, ed. (1980-82), Vol. 4, 77 and Vol. 9, fig. 208.
3. Mason (1990), 58-63. Little is known about this artist, who is also called Baidô Kokunimasa and Ryûkei. He is best known for his prints depicting events in the Sino-Japanese and Russo-Japanese Wars. Ryû-a (Willow Frog) is the name he is said to have adopted when he began to study painting with Iijima Kôga (1829-1900).
4. Keene (1971), 240.

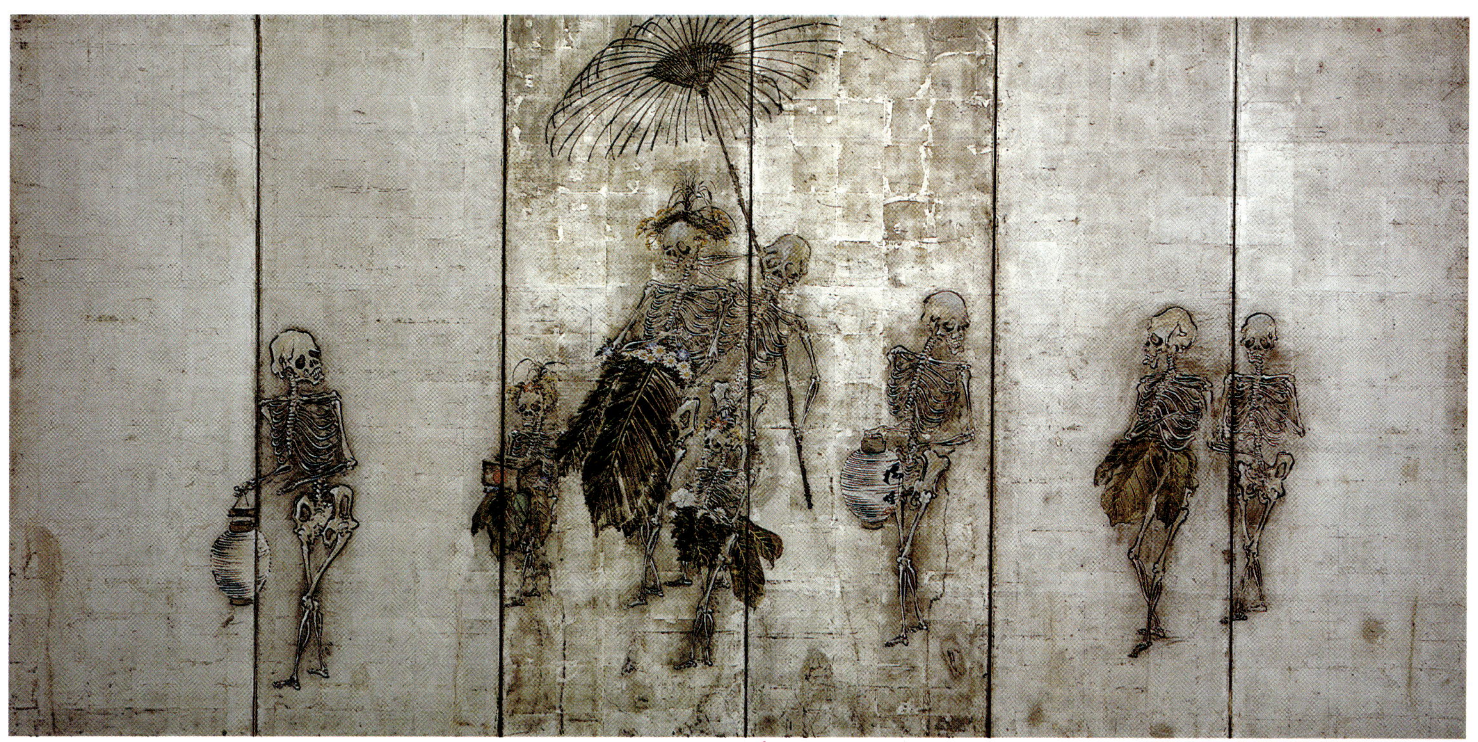

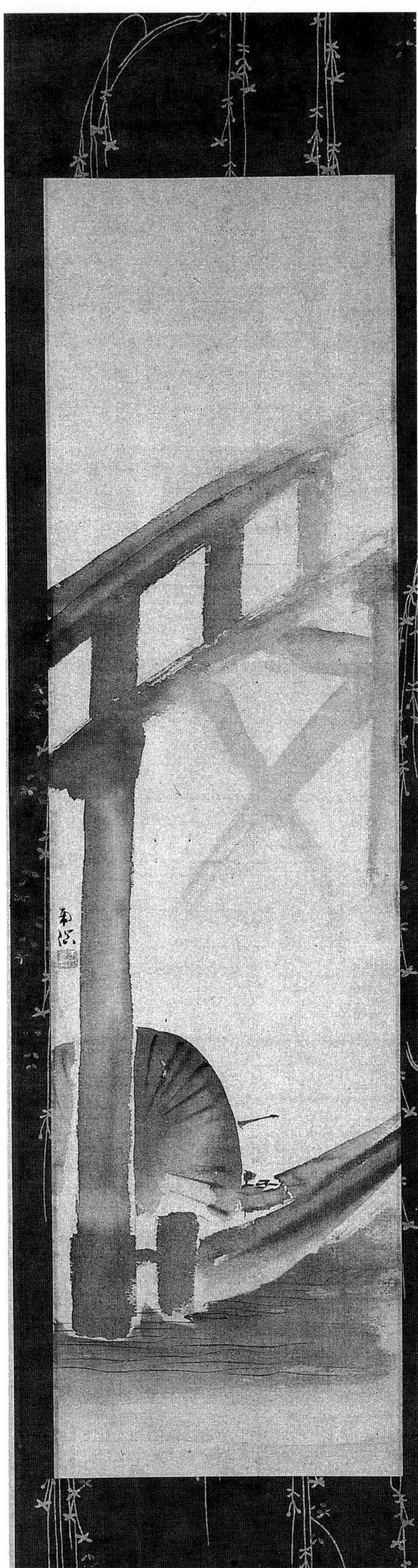

53. Haruki Nammei (1795-1878)
Boating Party Under the Ryôgoku Bridge
Edo period, early 19th century
Signed: Nammei; sealed: Haruki
Hanging scroll; ink and light color on silk
30 x 8 3/8 in. (76.2 x 21.3 cm.)
Collection of Robert O. Muller

An umbrella is tilted on its side to screen the occupant(s) of the boat from view and give them some privacy. We see only a tobacco set and a long pipe protruding from behind the cover. Perhaps a geisha or a prostitute from one of the unlicensed quarters of Edo is enjoying the cool breeze of a summer evening on the Sumida River with a client. Officially opened every summer with a display of fireworks at the Ryogôku Bridge, the river was crowded with the craft of pleasure seekers for the rest of the season. A contemporary print by Kunisada shows a similar scene at river level with a geisha on her way to a rendezvous (no. 53a). Unlike the highest-ranking courtesans, geisha were not entitled to umbrella bearers, but they could furnish their own lavish umbrellas, and use them on occasion as a shield from public scrutiny.

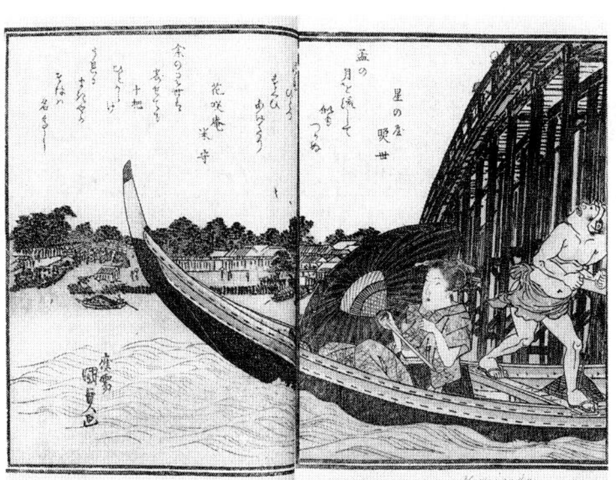

53a. Utagawa Kunisada (1786-1864), *Under a Bridge in Edo.* From *Uta no tomobune* (A friend's boat of verses), Edo period, ca. 1830. Color woodblock-printed illustrated book. The British Museum, London

54. Ôishi Matora (1794-1833)
Festival Dancers
From *Soga hyakubutsu* (Sketches of one hundred things), Vol. 1
Edo period, 1832
Signed: Ôishi Matora; sealed: Ayuchi no kôri kokyô [native of the district of Ayuchi, i.e., Nagoya]
Publisher: Bunkaidô (Tsurugaya Kyûbei), Osaka
Color woodblock-printed illustrated book
Page: 8 15/16 x 6 3/8 in. (22.7 x 16.2 cm.)
Ravicz Collection

A male servant holds a red parasol with a long stick (*sashikake-gasa*) over a child riding on the shoulders of a young woman. This is the "nanny parasol" (*ouba higasa*), borne as an indication of status over the head of a child carried by a nursemaid. Children of wealthy merchants often enjoyed this special treatment. Watching the street dance at the right are two samurai, their identities disguised with low-brimmed straw hats (*amigasa*) and masks; samurai were not eager to be recognized in the wrong part of town.

An amulet box (*tsutsu-mamori*) hangs inside the parasol. Perhaps the child is the eldest son and the amulet is for his protection.[1] Amulets were also suspended beneath umbrellas carried over the heads of high-ranking courtesans.[2] In the medieval period, when itinerant monks traveled with Buddhist paintings that they used for the edification of local audiences, they carried the paintings rolled up and suspended beneath their umbrellas.[3]

1. For *tsutsu-mamori* in paintings of children in the Kan'ei era (1624-43), see *Koji ruien* (1984), 458.
2. Takazu (1930), 18.
3. For an illustration, see Miya (1971), monochrome pl. 12.

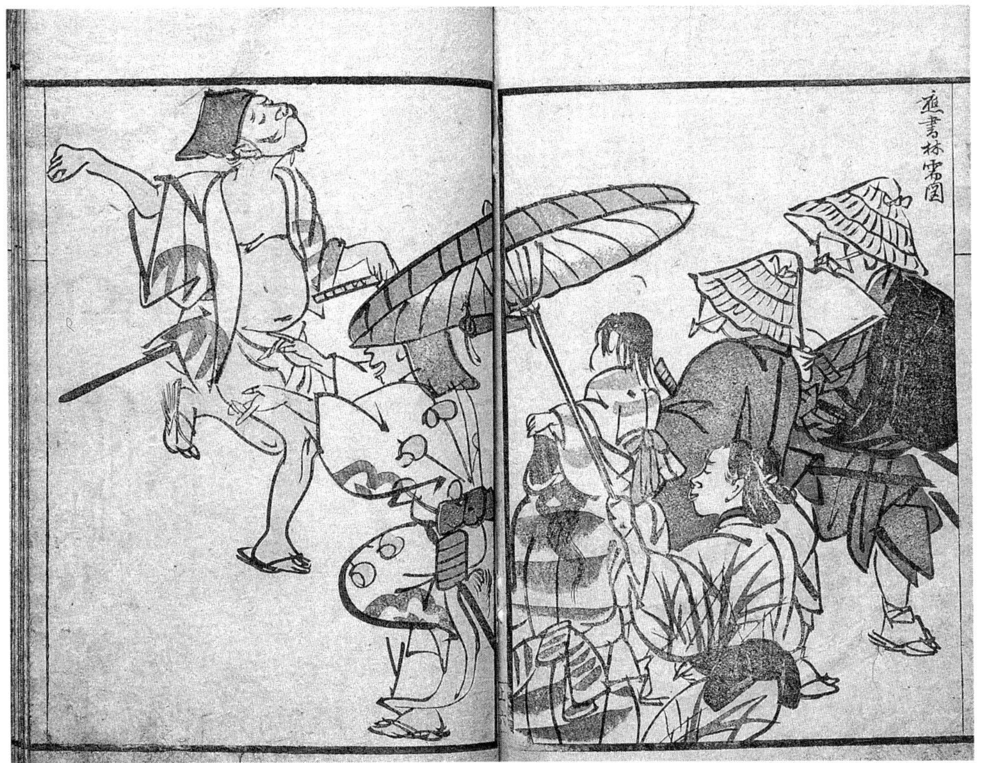

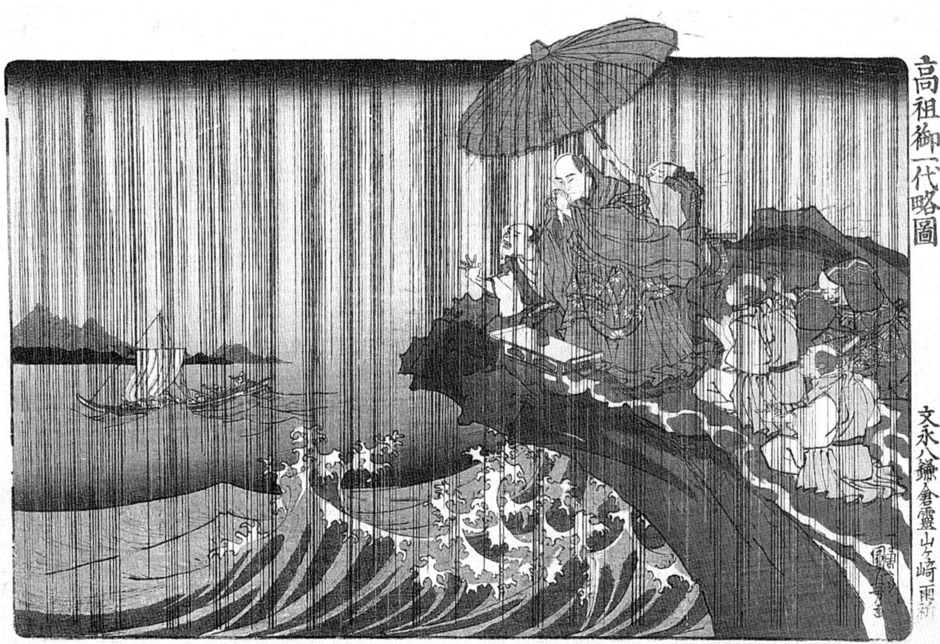

55. Utagawa Kuniyoshi (1797-1861)
Nichiren Prays for Rain on the Promontory of Ryôzengazaki in Kamakura in 1271
Series: Simplified Pictures of the Life of Nichiren
Edo period, ca. 1835
Signed: Ichiyûsai Kuniyoshi ga
Publisher: Iseya Rihei
Color woodblock print; horizontal *ôban*
10 1/4 x 14 3/4 in. (26 x 37.5 cm.)
The Metropolitan Museum of Art, Henry L. Phillips Collection, Bequest of Henry L. Phillips, 1940, JP2859

The umbrella of status here serves a useful purpose. On a rocky promontory overhanging the sea at Kamakura, where he lived and worked, the aggressive Buddhist monk Nichiren (1222-1282) is shown praying for rain after a long drought in 1271. Evidently, his prayers have already been granted. Nichiren stands before a small portable altar, while a disciple behind him struggles with the heavy, long-stick orange umbrella with tips that curve down (*tsumaore sashikake-gasa*), the type used by the upper classes and by monks. The artist emphasizes the size and height of the umbrella by allowing it to push through the border of the print into the margin.

This is one of a set of ten images of famous scenes from the life of Nichiren, founder of the Nichiren sect, published soon after his 550th memorial service.

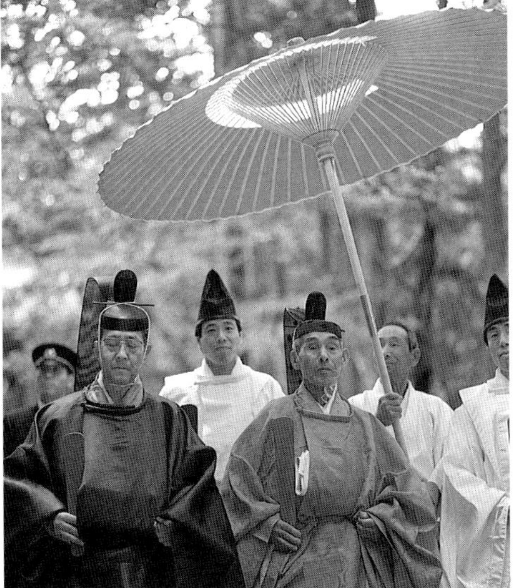

Color plate, p. 17

56. Stephan Köhler (b. 1959), German
Daisai Festival at the Hachiman Shrine, Hachiman
Heisei period, April 15, 1990
Ciba print
Courtesy of Stephan Köhler

An umbrella is carried over the head priest—Katô Masanao, age eighty-three, in red—during the annual spring festival of the Shinto shrine dedicated to the god of war in the village of Hachiman, Mugegawa-chô, Gifu prefecture. The umbrella, with its asymmetrical white band, was made by the German artist and photographer Stephan Köhler, whose essay on makers of the traditional Japanese umbrella appears earlier in this volume.[1] Köhler, who lives in Hachiman, donated the umbrella to the shrine, which was founded in A.D. 1200. The priests are wearing court robes and lacquered gauze hats in the style of classical Heian courtiers (see figs. 52, 53).

1. See also no. 135.

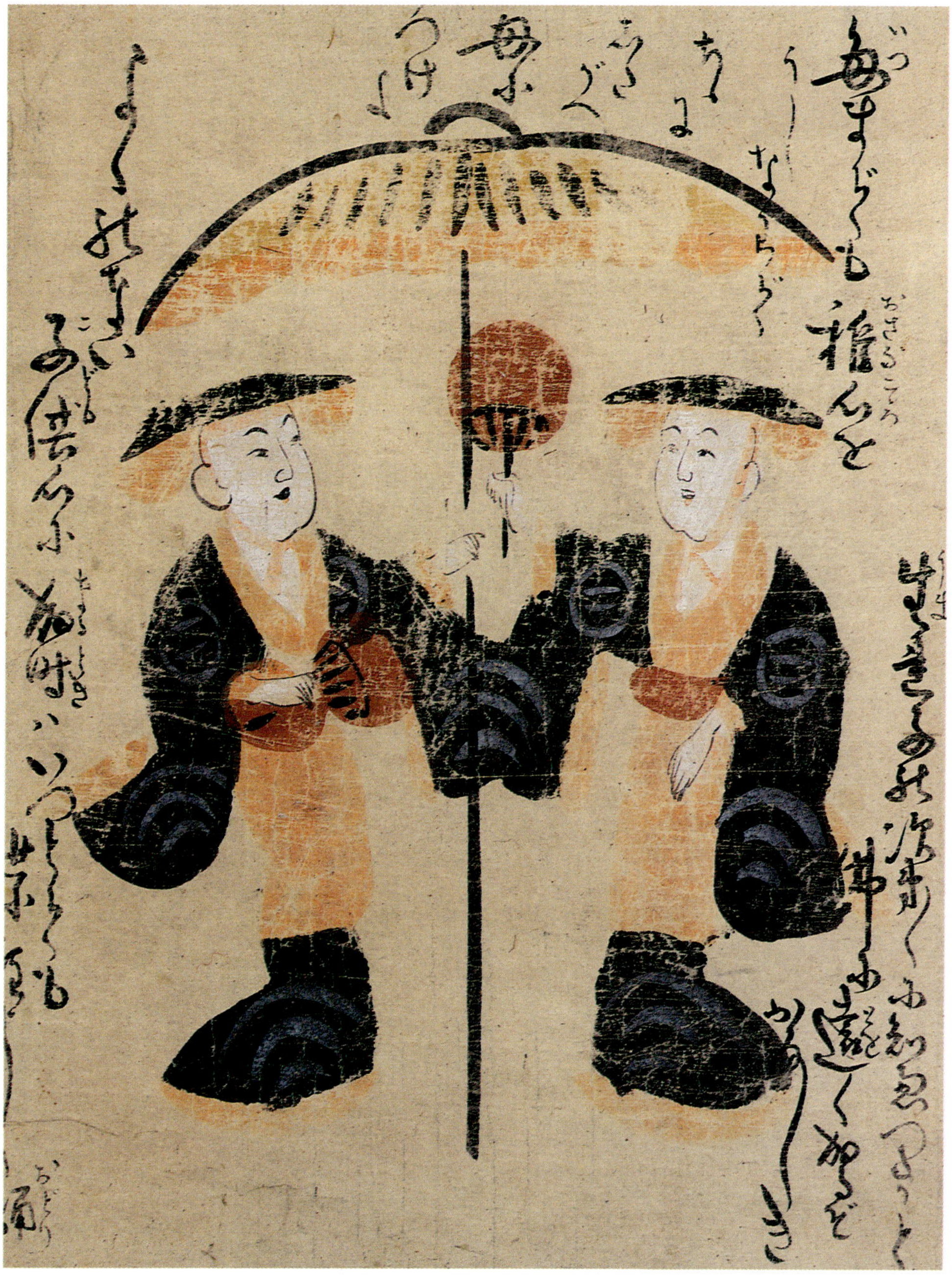

57. Artist unknown
Sumiyoshi Dancers
Edo period, ca. 1730
Hanging scroll, ink and color on paper
13 1/2 x 9 3/4 in. (34.2 x 24.6 cm.)
Collection of John and Kimiko Powers

The Sumiyoshi dance (*odori*) originated at Sumiyoshi Shrine in Settsu province (the present-day Osaka area) as part of the annual rice-transplanting (*otaue*) ceremony. During the Edo period the cult of the Sumiyoshi gods at branch shrines throughout the country became extremely popular. In its earlier stages the dance was performed by male priests, but later by groups of women as well. Their costume included round fans (*uchiwa*), distinctive red aprons, and wide-brimmed umbrella-like hats with veils that partially covered their faces. They danced around a *kasaboko* (umbrella spear), a festival umbrella retaining the shape of a spear at the top, held by a man who tapped out the beat for them on the stick of the umbrella (see no. 57a). The cover had a red cloth fringe and was decorated around its spear-headed top with pendent paper strips (*gohei*). (Fringed silk umbrellas are pervasive in Japanese religious and festival dances even today.) The female performers were often taken from the local brothels, which gave the dance erotic overtones, as did its association with agriculture and fertility rites. To judge by depictions in 18th- and 19th-century books, the women dancers abandoned themselves to the beat, swirling around the umbrella with gusto.[1]

Two women are shown here in a highly simplified, shorthand interpretation of the theme; one holds the large upright umbrella with a cloth fringe, the other dances. Their wide hats have cloth veils, and they wear aprons and hold round fans. The umbrella fringe and the veils and aprons are faded orange in color. The figures have the static symmetry of the ingenuous folk paintings made during the Edo period as cheap souvenirs for travelers in villages near the town of Ôtsu,

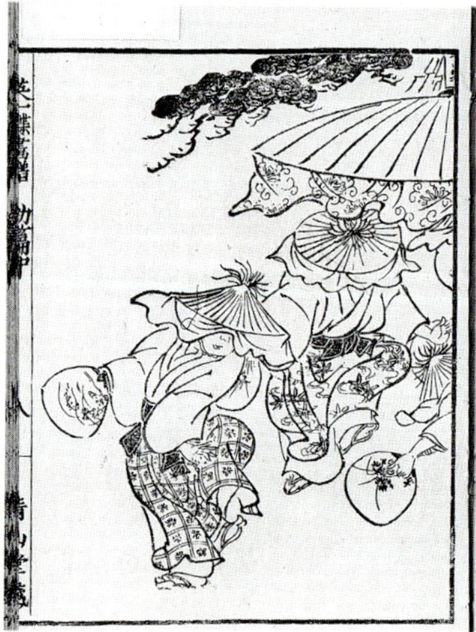

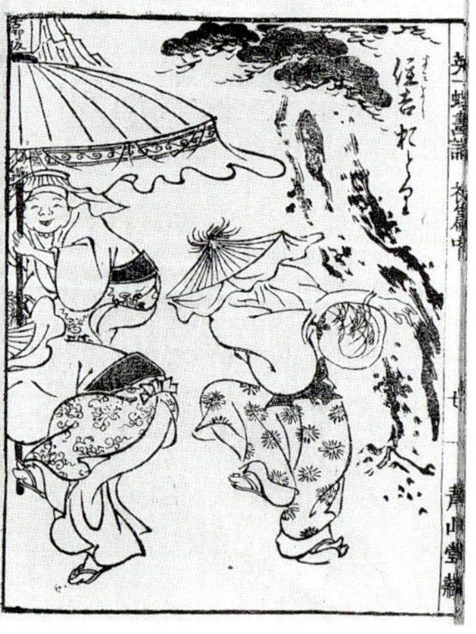

57a. Hanabusa Itchô (1652-1724), *Sumiyoshi Dance*. From *Gunchô gaei* (Drawings like a swarm of butterflies), Edo period, 1778. Woodblock-printed illustrated book. The British Museum, London

which lies eight miles northeast of Kyoto on the shore of Lake Biwa. Ôtsu paintings (*Ôtsu-e*) often have moralistic inscriptions; here three thirty-one-syllable poems frame the performers:

Itsu made mo
osana-gokoro o
ushinawade
chichi ni shitagae
haha ni natsuke yo

Umarego no
shidai shidai ni
chie tsuki[te]
hotoke ni tôku naruzo
kanashiki

Yoku no nai
kodomogokoro ni
naru toki wa
itsu tote mo yo ni
Sumiyoshi odori

Never lose the mind of a child;
Obey your father.
Be attached to your mother.

The infant gradually gains in wisdom,
Goes far from [the innocence of] the Buddha.
How sad!

When we regain the unselfish spirit of children,
There is always the Sumiyoshi dance.[2]

1. The dance is illustrated in Hasegawa Mitsunobu (active 1730-60), *Ehon otozashina kagami* (1739), Vol. 1; it is also shown in the woodblock-printed illustrated book by Nishimura Nantei (1775-1834), *Nantei gafu* (1804), Vol. 3.
2. Rosenfield and Shimada (1970), 351; *sumiyoshi* can also mean "to live in ease," giving an alternate reading for the last line of the third poem: "We will always live in ease."

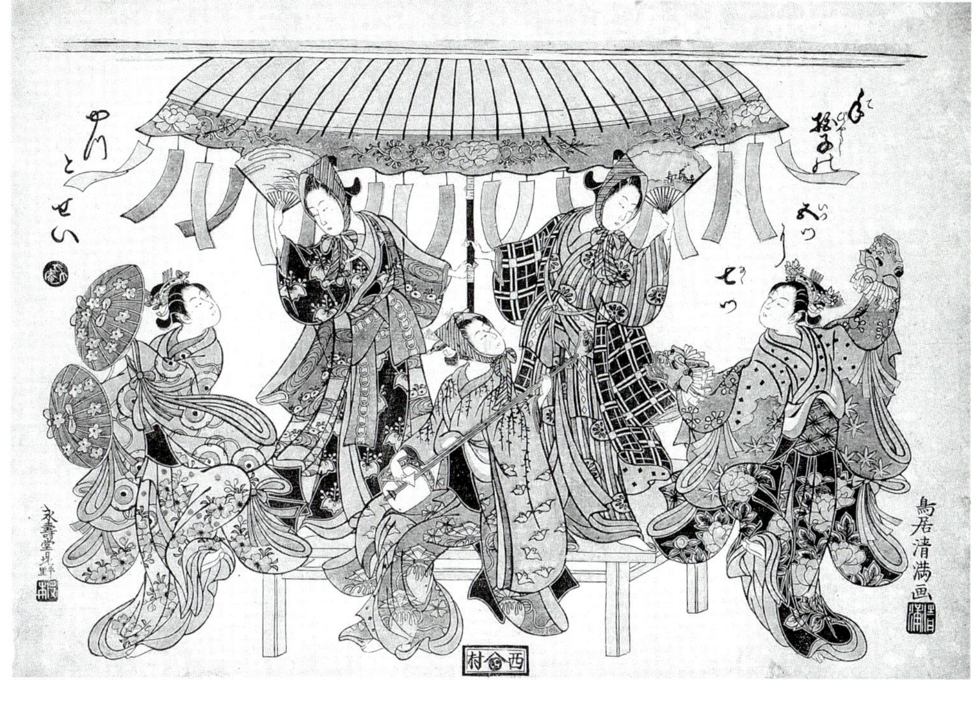

58. Torii Kiyomitsu (1735-1785)
Four Dancers and a Shamisen Player Under a Large Parasol
Edo period, early 1760s
Signed: Torii Kiyomitsu ga; sealed: Kiyomitsu
Publisher: Nishimura Eijudô
Color woodblock print, *benizuri-e*; horizontal *ôôban*
12 x 18 in. (30.5 x 45.7 cm.)
The Art Institute of Chicago, Clarence Buckingham Collection, 1925.1997

The dancers sway to the playful words of the song by Mokuan scattered across the top of the print: "Clapping our hands five, seven, eight times" (*Tebyôshi no itsutsu ni nanatsu yattosei*). These may be female performers at the late-summer Niwaka festival in the Yoshiwara.

59. Utagawa Kuniyoshi (1797-1861)
Picture of the Public Viewing of the Deity Tametomo in Ryôgoku: Children's Procession
Edo period, 1851
Signed: Ichiyûsai Kuniyoshi ga
Publisher: Sumiyoshiya Masagorô
Color woodblock prints; triptych, vertical *ôban*
Together: $14\frac{1}{2}$ x $29\frac{1}{2}$ in. (36.8 x 74.9 cm.)
Museum of Fine Arts, Springfield, Massachusetts, Raymond A. Bidwell Collection, 60.D05.637

Beginning on the fifth day of the fifth month of 1851, there was a two-month public viewing of the image of Tametomo Daimyôjin, the deity worshiped at the Kaikô-in Shrine on Hachijô Island in Izu province (now part of Shizuoka prefecture).[1] Kuniyoshi's triptych depicts the children's procession in the Ryôgoku district of Edo when the small portable shrine (*mikoshi*) housing the deity was paraded through the streets. The roof of the Kaikô-in is visible in the distance at the far right, and Ryôgoku Bridge can be seen at the upper left. At the center is the portable shrine, accompanied by a throng of children wearing orange scarves and headbands and carrying small parasols hung with banners reading "Children's Group."

Minamoto no Tametomo (1139-1177) was the great archer who was exiled to Ôshima, the large island off the coast south of present-day Tokyo in the bay of Atami, after his defeat in the battle of Hôgen in 1156. He ended up by subjugating the natives on this island as well as on six smaller islands, including Hachijô, where he is revered for having driven out the god of smallpox.

1. Suzuki (1992), no. 329.

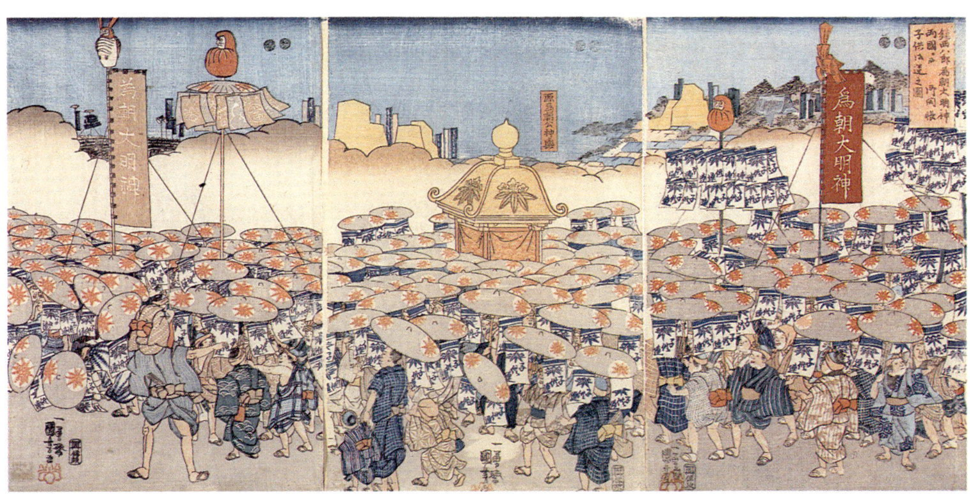

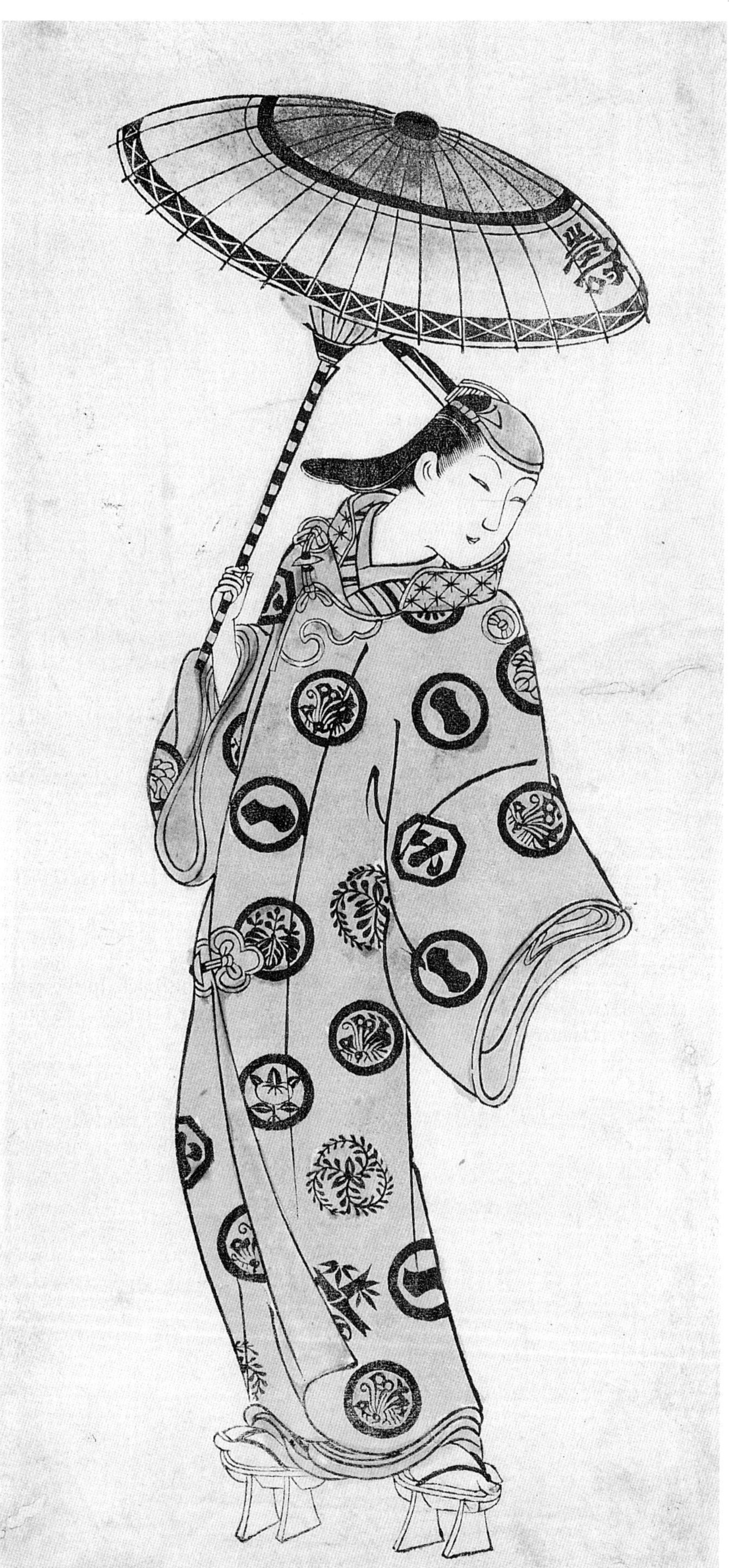

60. Attributed to Ishikawa Toyonobu (1711-1785)
A Dandy
Edo period, ca. 1728
Woodblock print with hand-painted pigments, *beni-e*; *hosoban*
12 5/8 x 5 7/8 in. (32.1 x 14.9 cm.)
The Metropolitan Museum of Art, Ledoux Collection, Harris Brisbane Dick Fund and Rogers Fund, 1949, JP3085

This fashionable young dandy wears a cap over the shaved front of his head, like that worn by *onnagata*, Kabuki actors in female roles, to disguise one obvious sign of masculinity in a society of unisex clothing. His raincoat with its Chinese-style fasteners and his petite parasol are both very stylish. The umbrella stick, lacquered in decorative horizontal stripes, has a metal spring at the top. Unlike the tall, narrow top notch (*atama rokuro*) on a modern Gifu umbrella, this one is as flat as a button.

The word *kotobuki* (felicitations) is written on the cover of the parasol; this may be the crest of the *onnagata* Sodezaki Kikutarô, who appeared on the Kabuki stage during the second and third decades of the 18th century.[1] On the dandy's coat are crests of six popular Kabuki stars, including that of the young *onnagata* Arashi Wakano (see no. 28).

1. Meech-Pekarik et al. (1979), no. 76.

61. Torii Kiyomasu I (active mid-1690s to early 1720s)
The Actor Nakamura Senya as Tokonatsu
Edo period, 1716
Signed: Torii Kiyomasu; sealed: Kiyomasu
Publisher: Komatsuya
Woodblock print with hand-painted pigments; *kakemono-e*
$23\frac{1}{16}$ x $12\frac{15}{16}$ in. (58.4 x 32.9 cm.)
Honolulu Academy of Arts, Gift of James A. Michener, HAA 20,497

This print commemorates a performance of the Kabuki play *Mitsudomoe katokuhiraki* at the Nakamura theater in Edo in the eleventh month of 1716. The *onnagata* Nakamura Senya, who appeared in the role of Tokonatsu, the wife of Higuchi Jirô Kanemitsu, had just moved from Kyoto to Edo. During this "face-showing" (*kaomise*) performance, his debut in Edo, he wore a purple head covering, carried an umbrella, and bowed to the audience.[1] He is shown here turning his head to look at a blossoming plum tree, while holding the umbrella in an affected stage gesture, as though it were weightless. The prominent use of a thin strip of black paper around the outer edge of this umbrella may be a special design for actors. The vertical stripes on the cover are often seen in early actor prints; generally speaking, umbrella designs in early hand-painted prints show great variety and imagination, defying strict categorization. The elegant stick is wrapped with many bands of rattan, but the artist made a mistake in showing the uppermost band abutting the runner or slide (*temoto rokuro*), which would have prevented the umbrella from closing (a metal spring is indicated just below the runner). This mistake was made quite often by print artists (see no. 28). The bell-shaped stretchers are typical of the early 18th century. Made of pliant bamboo, they could easily have been bent into shape when heated.

1. Genshoku ukiyo-e daihyakka-jiten henshû-iinkai, ed. (1980-82), Vol. 6, 46. Link (1980), 48, dates this print to January 1717.

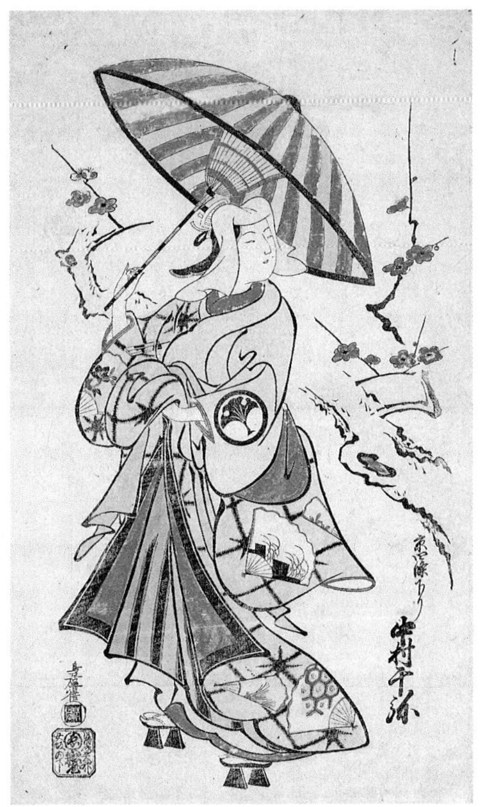

Color plate, p. 45

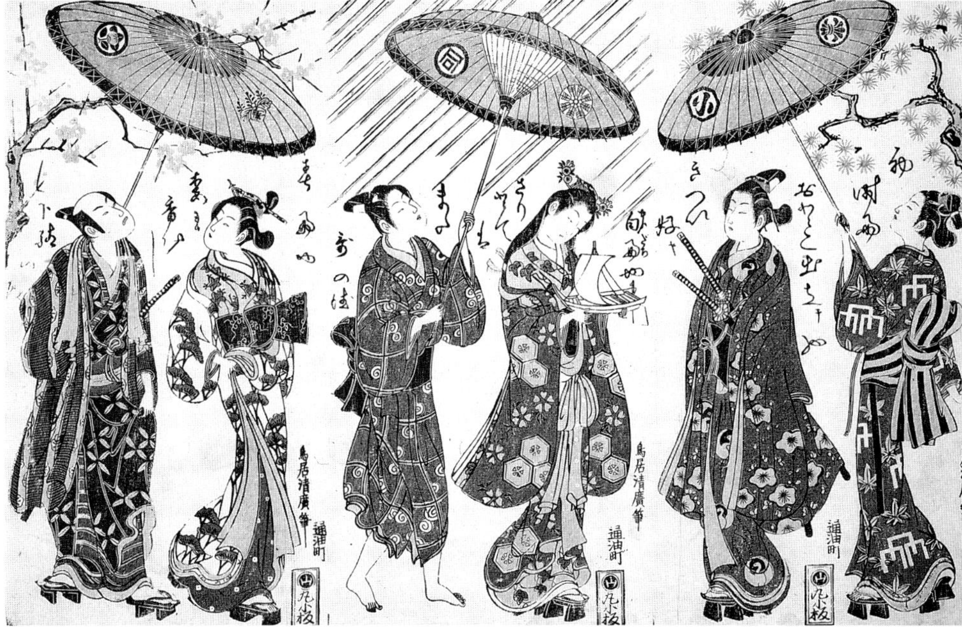

62. Torii Kiyohiro (1708-1776)
Three Umbrella Scenes
Edo period, early 1750s
Signed: Torii Kiyohiro hitsu
Publisher: Maruya Kohei
Color woodblock print, *benizuri-e*; uncut *hosoban* triptych
$11\frac{5}{8}$ x $17\frac{3}{16}$ in. (28.7 x 43.6 cm.)
Honolulu Academy of Arts, Gift of James A. Michener, HAA 21,655

Three pairs of popular Kabuki actors are shown in roles connected with spring, summer and autumn rain, the subjects of the accompanying haiku. The actors' crests appear on the umbrella covers overhead. In the left panel Ichikawa Kamezô holds an umbrella of status (*sashikakegasa*) over Nakamura Kumetarô in the role of a courtesan strolling under plum blossoms. Kamezô supports the weight of the umbrella against his back. In the center panel is Nakamura Tomijûrô I as the Heian poetess Ono no Komachi, who produced rain by the power of her verse, with Sanogawa Ichimatsu as the servant (see p. 50 and fig. 59). On the right Segawa Kikujirô, as a maid, holds an umbrella over Arashi Otohashi, who is dressed as a *wakashû*.[1]

1. Link (1980), 203, suggests that the pairs may not correspond with actual roles performed by the actors.

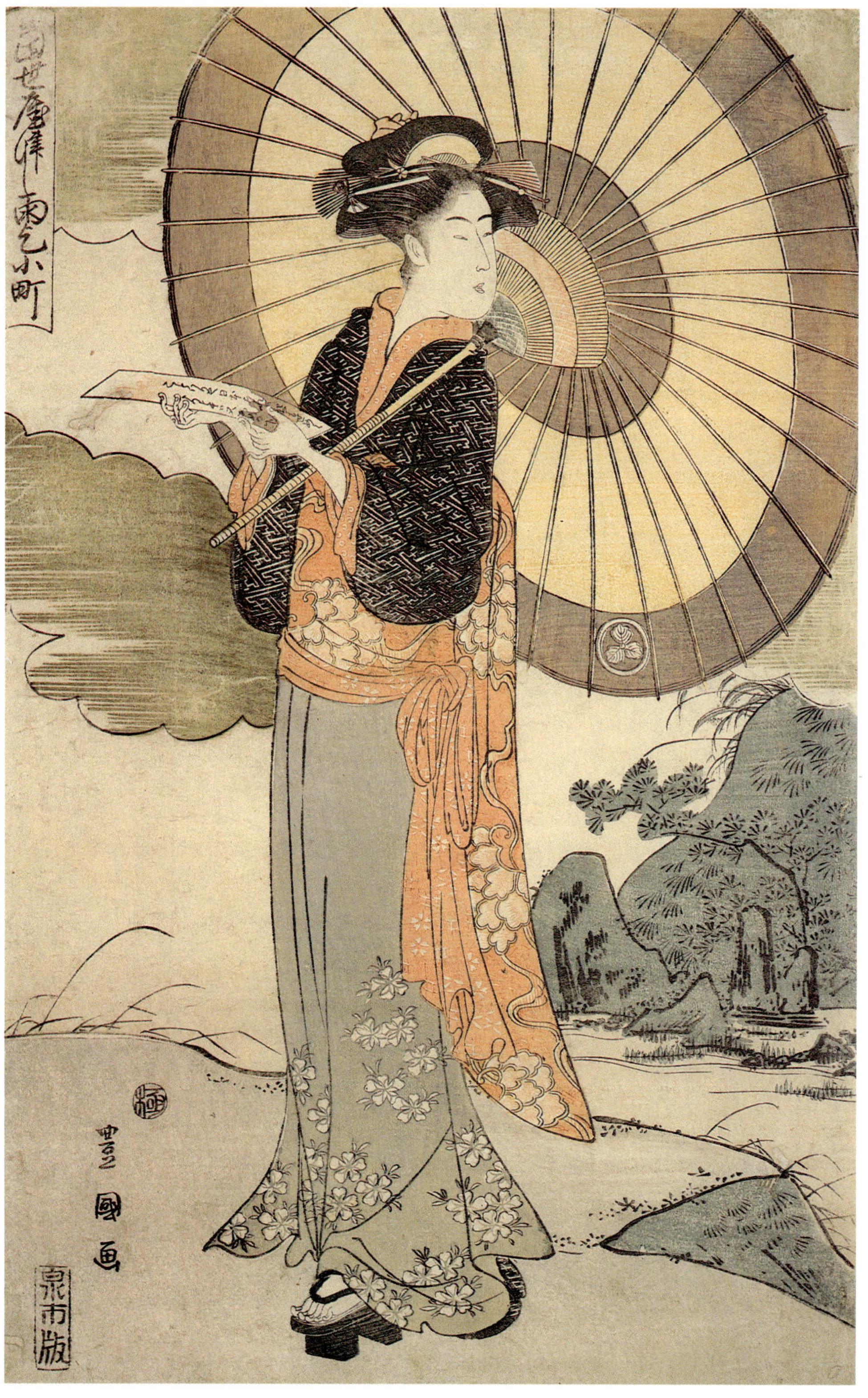

63. Utagawa Toyokuni (1769-1825)
A Contemporary Parody of Komachi Praying for Rain
Edo period, 1790s
Signed: Toyokuni ga
Publisher: Izumiya Ichibei
Color woodblock print; vertical *ôban*
$9\frac{5}{8}$ x $14\frac{3}{4}$ in. (24.5 x 37.6 cm.)
The Art Institute of Chicago, Clarence Buckingham Collection, 1925.3131

Ono no Komachi (see no. 62) is here represented by Takashima Ohisa, a popular teahouse beauty from the Ryôgoku district in Edo, whose crest appears on the rim of the umbrella and on her costume. A few words of Komachi's poem invoking rain are written on the poem slip in Ohisa's hands. The handle of the *janome* is wrapped with rattan, and several rows of spider's threads (*kumoito*) are visible at the edge of the cover. Decoratively embroidered threads embellish the stretchers in the single-rope pattern.

64. Isoda Koryûsai (active ca.1766-88)
Umbrella Jump
Edo period, ca. 1769
Signed: Koryûsai ga
Color woodblock print; pillar print
$27\frac{13}{16}$ x 4 in. (70.6 x 10.2 cm.)
The Metropolitan Museum of Art, Gift of Estate of Samuel Isham, 1914, JP884

Kiyomizu no butai kara tobioriru
To jump from the platform of Kiyomizu.
—Japanese proverb

At least four print artists depicted the umbrella jump in the 1760s (nos. 64, 64a, 64b, 65). None of the images is an actor print, but interest in the theme may have been spurred by several contemporary Kabuki and Bunraku plays set at Kiyomizu temple in Kyoto. The old saying that to make a tough decision is tantamount to leaping from the platform of Kiyomizu goes back to Heian times. The jump was also a way to test the future of a romantic liaison: if one survived, happiness was assured.

Koryûsai cleverly emphasizes the great height of the platform, which is already suggested by the pillar-print format, by segmenting the composition into three sequential parts. A band of clouds and a corner of the veranda mark the top, the young woman with her drapery swirling about her fills the center, and the cherry trees obscured by mist hint at the solid ground below. Expressively curled bare toes often have a sexual connotation in prints. One wonders what the artist had in mind here. Perhaps the woman is every man's fantasy—so passionately in love that she will risk her life for him.

The artist disregards rational laws of perspective in order to show the platform from above and the umbrella from below. This allows us to appreciate the structure of the elegant umbrella, including the rattan-wrapped handle, the yellow stick, the bent-wire spring, the slide, the stretchers and the two bands of embroidery, one red and one yellow.

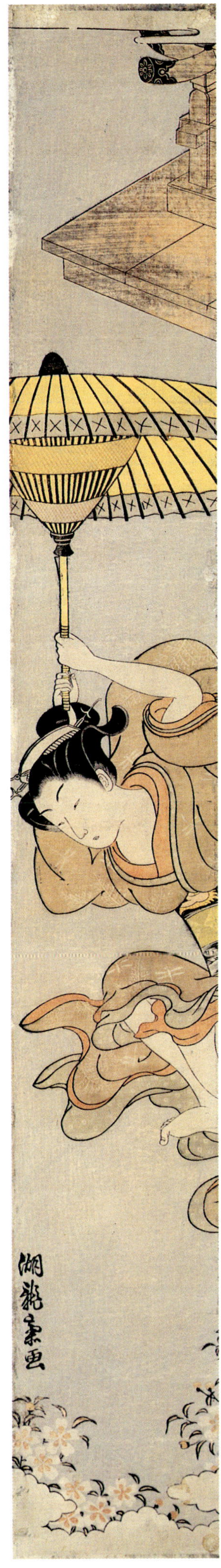

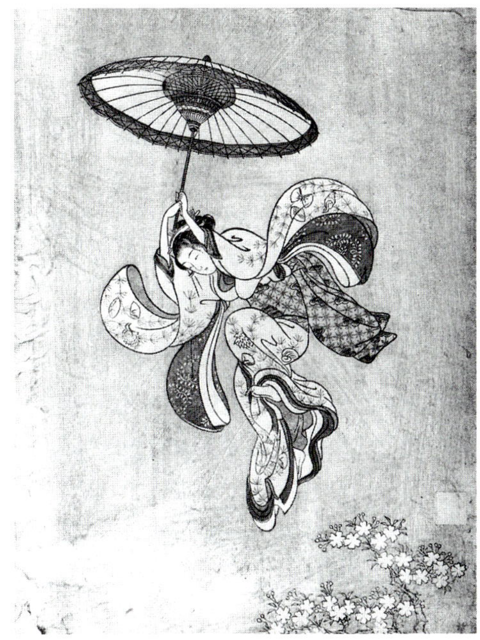

64a. Suzuki Harunobu (1724-1770), *Umbrella Jump*, Edo period, 1765. Color woodblock print; *chûban*. Courtesy Sotheby's, London

This is a calendar print for 1765, with the character *dai* (large) and the numerals of the long months (2, 3, 5, 6, 8 and 10) hidden in the seashell pattern on the young woman's kimono.

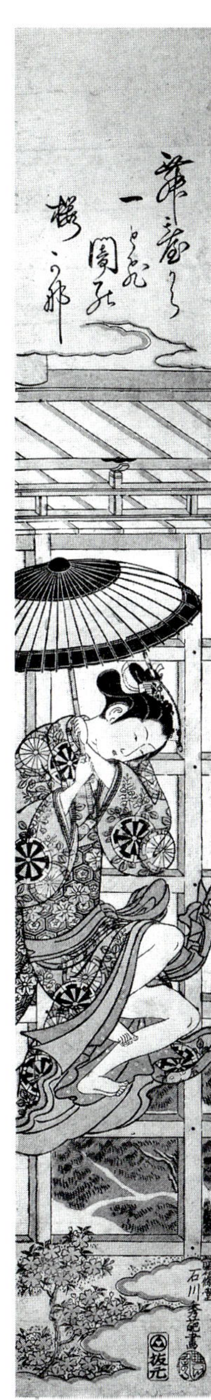

64b. Ishikawa Toyonobu (1711-1785), *Leaping from Kiyomizu Temple*, early 1760s. Four-color woodblock print, *benizuri-e*; pillar print. The Art Institute of Chicago, Clarence Buckingham Collection, 1925

The poem in the clouds above the platform reads: "A jump from the platform into the cherry blossoms of darkness" (Link [1980], 196).

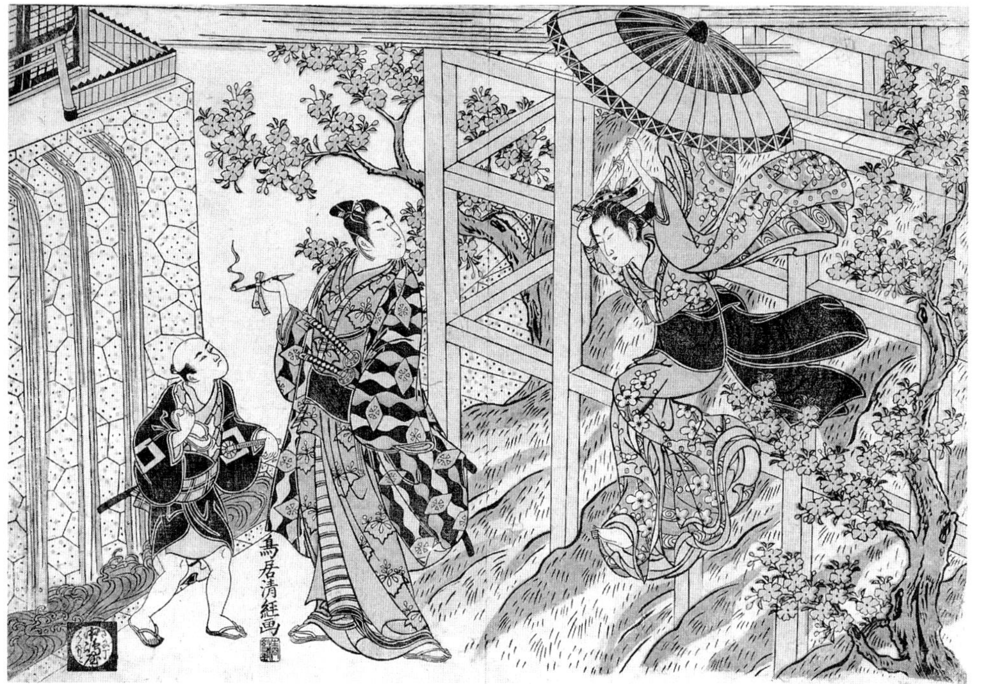

65. Torii Kiyotsune I (active 1757-79)
Umbrella Jump
Edo period, ca. 1764-65
Signed: Torii Kiyotsune ga; sealed: Kiyotsune no in
Publisher: Nakajimaya Izaemon
Color woodblock print, *benizuri-e*; horizontal *ôôban*
12 3/4 x 17 3/4 in. (32.4 x 45.1 cm.)
The Art Institute of Chicago, Clarence Buckingham Collection, 1939.2159

The wide wooden veranda of the main hall of the Kiyomizu temple in Kyoto is cantilevered over a cliff on the side of Otowa Hill, which is planted with cherry trees. The spectacular panoramic view from the veranda into the deep valley below is familiar to every tourist. A Tokyo newspaper recently reported on many actual incidences in the Edo period of people who jumped and lived to tell the tale, albeit with broken limbs. There was no mention, however, of the use of umbrellas as parachutes.[1] A Kiyomizu Hall was built in Ueno Park in Edo in the 17th century in imitation of the one in Kyoto (see no. 44). It was part of Kan'ei-ji, the family temple of the shogun.[2]

The young lady in Kiyotsune's print should have a stretcher and ambulance waiting for her—the umbrella is so small that it would rapidly turn inside out, doing nothing to break her fall. Instead, there is only her nonchalant samurai lover, smoking a pipe, and his servant thoughtfully holding her shoes. The Otowa Waterfall, where pilgrims stop to offer prayers at the base of the main hall, is shown on the left.

By the second half of the 18th century, Kiyomizu had taken on magical, mystical connotations. On the one hand it was a famous scenic place in Kyoto; on the other it was symbolic of some decisive event. The platform features, for example, in the well-known *Shin usuyuki monogatari* (New tale of Usuyuki), adapted for Kabuki within three months of its first performance as a puppet play in 1741. The servants play a key role in bringing together Princess Usuyuki and the handsome samurai she loves; perhaps the servant in Kiyotsune's print echoes such a role. Another Kabuki play set on the platform of the temple—*Kiyomizu Seigen rokudô meguri* (Priest Seigen of Kiyomizu and the six paths of rebirth) by Takeda Jizô—opened in the seventh month of 1762, two or three years before the date of this print.[3] Probably there were other plays on the theme that have long since dropped out of the Kabuki repertory. As it is, however, the jump itself is known only in one early-19th-century work by the Kabuki playwright Tsuruya Namboku IV (1755-1829).[4] In his *Onna Seigen* (or *Sumidagawa hanagoshozome*), a parodic version of a by-now mythic topic, the heroine becomes a nun after hearing of the death of her fiancé, jumps from the temple platform with an umbrella, survives the fall, and uses her closed umbrella to ward off an attack.

1. Joseph Needham points out that historians doubt whether the parachute was actually tried in practice in the West before 1778, when it was tested with animals. In China, however, there was the odd occurrence of a young man in Canton in the 13th century who stole an ornament from the minaret of a local Arab mosque and descended by leaping from the top holding on to two umbrellas, which were kept open by the wind, like wings; Needham (1965), Vol. 4, part 2, 594-595.
2. Waley (1984), 153-155; for illustrations of the Kiyomizu Hall in Edo in the early 19th century, see *Edo meisho zue* (1919-20), Vol. 5, 406, 428.
3. Shimonaka (1991), 242.
4. The author is indebted to Mark Oshima, Harvard University, for the references to *Shin usuyuki monogatari* and to Namboku.

66. Banki II (active early 19th century)
Umegawa and Chûbei
Edo period, ca. 1800
Signed: Banki hitsu
Color woodblock print; pillar print
23 9/16 x 4 1/2 in. (59.8 x 11.4 cm.)
The Metropolitan Museum of Art, H. O. Havemeyer Collection, Bequest of Mrs. H. O. Havemeyer, 1929, JP1827

The Kabuki play *Koi bikyaku yamato ôrai*, first performed in Osaka in 1757, is based on a true story of tragic love, although the exact details are no longer clear. It was adapted from the popular puppet play *Meido no hikyaku*, written by Chikamatsu Monzaemon (1653-1725) in 1711, which has been translated by Donald Keene as *The Courier for Hell*. Chûbei, a farmer's son, is adopted into the family of the Kameya courier service in Osaka. Although he has considerable business acumen, Chûbei is blinded by love for Umegawa, a beautiful prostitute from the Shimmachi pleasure quarters in Osaka, and tries to outbid a rich patron to release her from bondage. He steals the money needed, and at the end of the twelfth month the two lovers escape to Chûbei's native village in Yamato where they say farewell to his father. They are caught as they continue their flight and are sentenced to death. An alternate title for the play, "Umegawa and Chûbei," is written in the upper right corner of this print.

Shown here is the *michiyuki* (road-going), or elopement, scene on the way to Yamato, the couple's "road of love." "The tears they shed glaze the ice on their sleeves," and Umegawa's frozen sandals stick to her bare feet.[1] Chûbei leans protectively over her and carries the umbrella two-thirds closed to reduce the weight of the snow that has settled on the cover.

1. Keene (1961), 185.

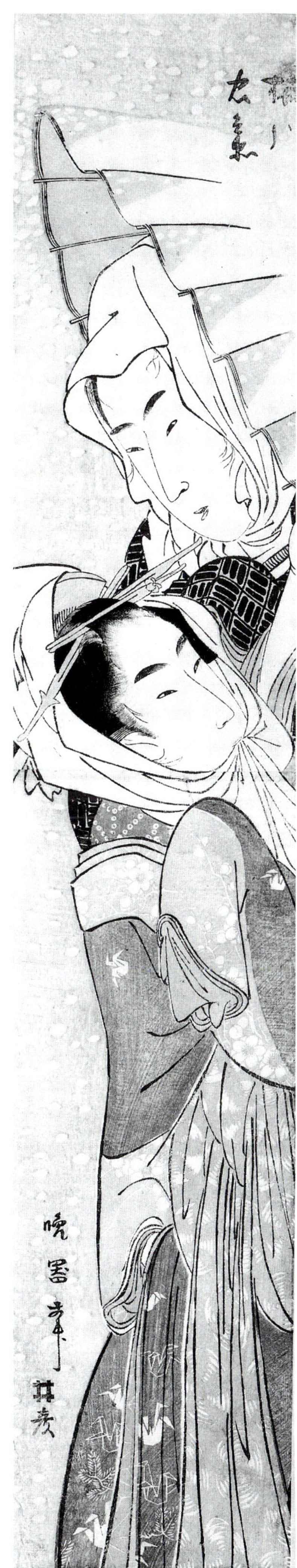

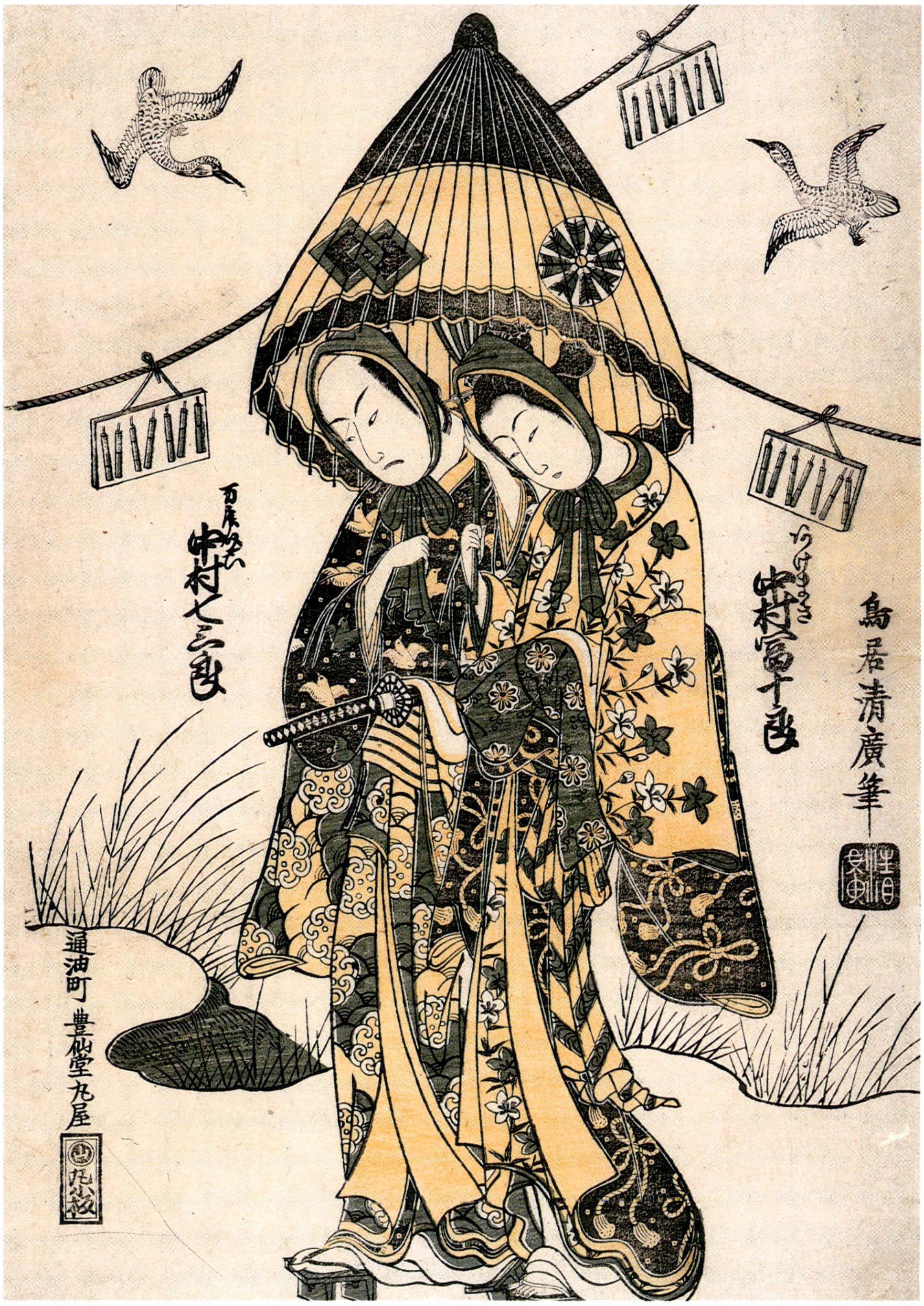

67. Torii Kiyohiro (active 1737-76)
Nakamura Shichisaburô II as Sukeroku and Nakamura Tomijûrô I as Agemaki
Edo period, 1753
Signed: Torii Kiyohiro hitsu; sealed: Kiyohiro
Publisher: Maruya Kohei
Color woodblock print, *benizuri-e*; vertical *ôôban*
16 3/4 x 11 1/2 in. (42.5 x 29.2 cm.)
The Brooklyn Museum, Gift of Louis V. Ledoux, 48.15.1

Shichisaburô and Tomijûrô (see no. 62) are shown as the lovers Yorozuya Sukeroku and Agemaki in the play *Meisho no yûgure* performed in the seventh month of 1753. This is the *michiyuki* (road-going) scene–always the most poetic and dancelike of a play. The couple, leaving to commit double suicide, walk through an autumn field hung with clappers (*naruko*) to scare away the birds.

Both figures clasp the stick of a single large *janome*, which is partially closed to convey a feeling of intimacy. An umbrella shared by two lovers is called an *aiaigasa* (literally, "sharing-together umbrella"). The actors' crests appear side by side on the cover. The crests on the umbrellas of courtesans and Kabuki actors may be painted, or they may be pasted cut-outs.

This play is rarely performed today, but it was the original love-suicide version of the story of Sukeroku and Agemaki. The later Edo version, known as "Sukeroku's Affinity for Cherry Blossoms of Edo" (see no. 68), retained only the names of the protagonists; the original story had been forgotten.

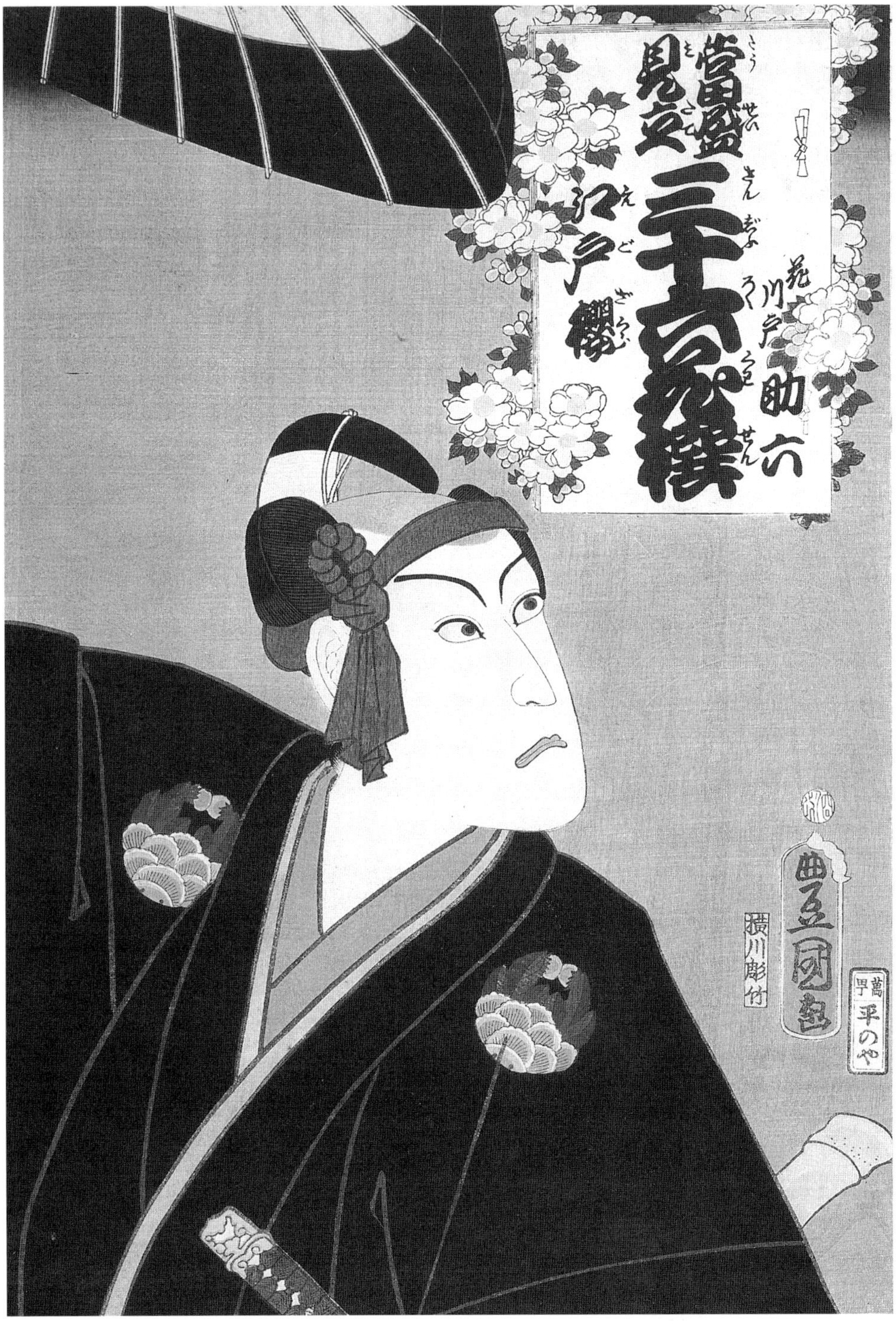

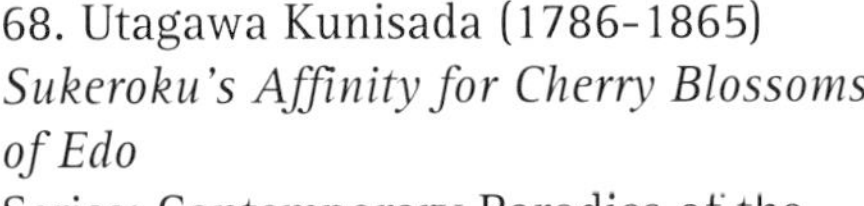

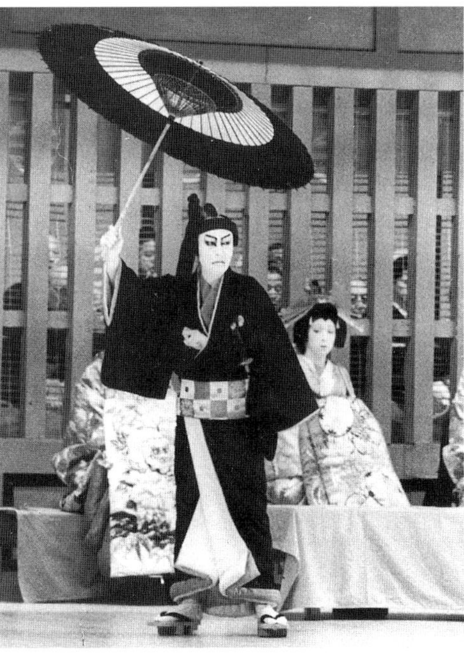

68a. Ichikawa Ebizô X (b. 1946) as Sukeroku. Photograph. Waseda University Tsubouchi Memorial Theater Museum

68. Utagawa Kunisada (1786-1865)
Sukeroku's Affinity for Cherry Blossoms of Edo
Series: Contemporary Parodies of the Thirty-six Poets
Edo period, 1861
Signed: Toyokuni ga
Publisher: Hiranoya
Color woodblock print; vertical *ôban*
14 1/16 x 9 13/16 in. (35.8 x 24.5 cm.)
Collection of Ayako Abe

The actor is Kawarazaki Gonjûrô, who became Ichikawa Danjûrô IX (1838-1903) in 1873. He was the fifth son of Danjûrô VII and inherited the title after an elder brother, Danjûrô VIII, committed suicide in 1854. He is shown in the role of Sukeroku from the famous play *Sukeroku yukari no Edo-zakura* (Sukeroku's affinity for cherry blossoms of Edo), written in 1713 and first staged by Danjûrô II, who achieved such fame in the part that it became a symbol of his family's skill. The peony crest of the Ichikawa family on the actor's robe would also have appeared on the indigo and white *janome* he carried onstage.

The single act of the play is set in the Naka-no-chô, the center of the licensed quarter in Edo (see nos. 13, 31), in front of the brothel of the celebrated courtesan Agemaki. Sukeroku, in love with Agemaki (a "cherry blossom" of Edo), is in search of his father's sword, which has been stolen by the vicious villain Ikyû, a wealthy patron of Agemaki. Hoping to pick a fight with Ikyû and retrieve the sword, Sukeroku announces himself offstage with the sound of his bamboo flute, a *shakuhachi*, then enters by the *hanamichi* (flower path), a raised passageway that joins the stage on the audience's left and passes through the auditorium.

Handsome, witty, elegant and brave, Sukeroku is the ideal man as imagined by Edo citizens. He presents himself to the audience by dancing on the *hanamichi* in a series of stylized poses with his open umbrella, as shown in this print and in a photograph of a recent performance (no. 68a). Sometimes he revolves it like a wheel, sometimes he is half hidden under the umbrella, partially closed. When the lyrics chanted by the musicians speak of seeing Mount Fuji and Mount Tsukuba through the blossoming willows and cherries along the Sumida River, he looks up into his umbrella, shaped like a triangular mountain peak. He swaggers and struts, conscious of his good looks. Sukeroku wears a black kimono with a single sword, and carries his flute (at one point he uses it as a weapon) tucked into the back of his obi. He is also known for his distinctive purple headband, tied on the right instead of the usual left.

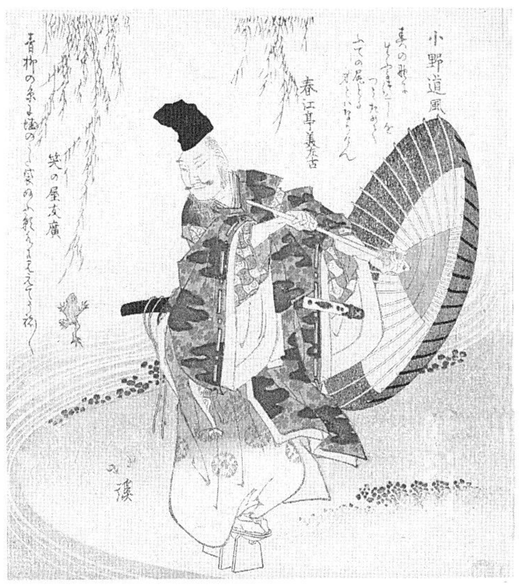

69. Totoya Hokkei (1780-1850)
Ono no Tôfû
Series: Gathering of the Elders of Poetry
Edo period, ca. 1825
Signed: Hokkei
Privately published by the Hanazono poetry group
Color woodblock print with brass and silver powder; square *surimono*
8 11/16 x 7 5/8 in. (22 x 19.4 cm.)
The Metropolitan Museum of Art, Gift of Estate of Samuel Isham, 1914, JP1035

The subject of this print was popularized by the mid-18th-century Kabuki drama *Ono no Tôfû aoyagi suzuri* (Ono no Tôfû and the green willow inkstone), a so-called dynasty piece with a semihistorical theme. A puppet play (*jôruri*) of the same name written by Takeda Izumo and others was first performed in 1754 at the Takemoto theater in Osaka. The script was immediately rewritten for Kabuki and had its premiere the next year at the Sawamura Kunitarô theater in Kyoto.

The play falls into the category known as *mikurai arasoi* (three ranks competing), dealing with power struggles among imperial princes at the Heian court. The main scene comes in the second act, set at the Tôji temple in Kyoto.[1] Ono no Tôfû (894-966), who was a celebrated Heian-period court calligrapher, is urged to join forces with an evil faction at court wishing to overthrow the emperor. Ono does not take the plot seriously, until he observes a frog trying over and over again to jump up into a willow tree. Displaying patience and perseverance, it finally succeeds. Ono realizes that the efforts against the government could also succeed if pursued with diligence. The Kabuki scene is known for Ono's long speech and fierce pose. He throws one villain into the pond, to be devoured by frogs, and renounces the wicked factions at court.[2]

Ono always appears in a tall black cap, or *eboshi*, and classical court robes (*kariginu*). His high rain clogs and *janome*, unknown in Heian times, add a stylish contemporary touch. The ribs of the umbrella are correctly shown as though lacquered black on the exterior.

Hokkei's *surimono* includes a *kyôka* poem by Shunkôtei Misako at the right, and another about the frog and willow branch by Eminoya Tomohiro at the left.

1. Shimonaka, ed. (1991), 87-88.
2. Bowers (1952), 162-163.

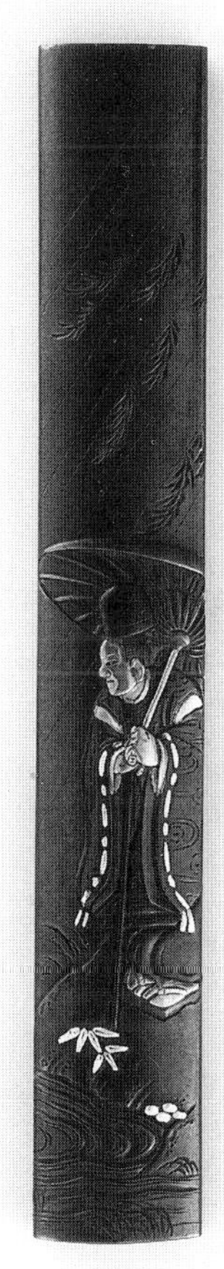

70. *Knife Handle* (*kozuka*): Ono no Tôfû
Signed: Katsufusa [d. 1869] at age 68; with *kaô*
Mito school, late Edo period, mid-19th century
Shibuichi plate with silver, gold and *shakudô*, incised
L. 3 3/4 in. (9.5 cm.)
The Metropolitan Museum of Art, Gift of Herman A. E. and Paul C. Jaehne, 1943, 43.120.321

Ono no Tôfû, holding an umbrella and leaning on a cane, stands beneath a willow tree beside a stream. He looks toward a frog incised on the reverse, shown leaping in the direction of a willow branch.

71. *Netsuke*: Frog as Ono no Tôfû
Late Edo period, late 18th-early 19th century
Wood with traces of lacquer and eyes inlaid with seeds
3 1/8 x 1 x 1 1/4 in. (8 x 2.6 x 3.1 cm.)
Los Angeles County Museum of Art, Lent by Raymond and Frances Bushell, L.85.28.107

The frog in the story of Ono no Tôfû here assumes the latter's accoutrements. It wears high rain clogs and the tall cap of a courtier and leans on an umbrella. An element of realism is supplied by the thin layer of red lacquer on the umbrella ribs and the clogs.

72. Tsukioka Yoshitoshi (1839-1892)
Ohatsu's Revenge
Series: Twenty-four Accomplishments of the Empire
Meiji period, 1881
Signed: Taiso Yoshitoshi hitsu;
sealed: Taiso
Publisher: Tsuda Genshichi
Color woodblock print; vertical *ôban*
13 1/8 x 8 7/8 in. (33.3 x 22.5 cm.)
Collection of Donna Levis

The *janome* umbrella in this print has been shredded when used by the heroine to defend herself in a sword fight. It is the final scene in the Kabuki play *Kagamiyama kokyô no nishiki-e*, popularly known as *Onna chûshingura* (Women's *Chûshingura*), written by Yô Yôdai in 1782 and based on a scandal that occurred in a daimyo palace in Edo earlier in the century; a jealous senior lady-in-waiting beat a lower-ranking attendant of the shogun's daughter with her sandal. In the play the villain, Iwafuji, humiliates Onoe, who commits suicide. Onoe's personal attendant, Ohatsu, kills Iwafuji in revenge; at the beginning of their fight she wards off the other woman's sword with an umbrella. Here she is shown wiping Iwafuji's blood from her own sword with her sandal—a fitting symbol of the humiliation her mistress once suffered.

The text panel above, by Tentendô Shujin, gives an account of the story.

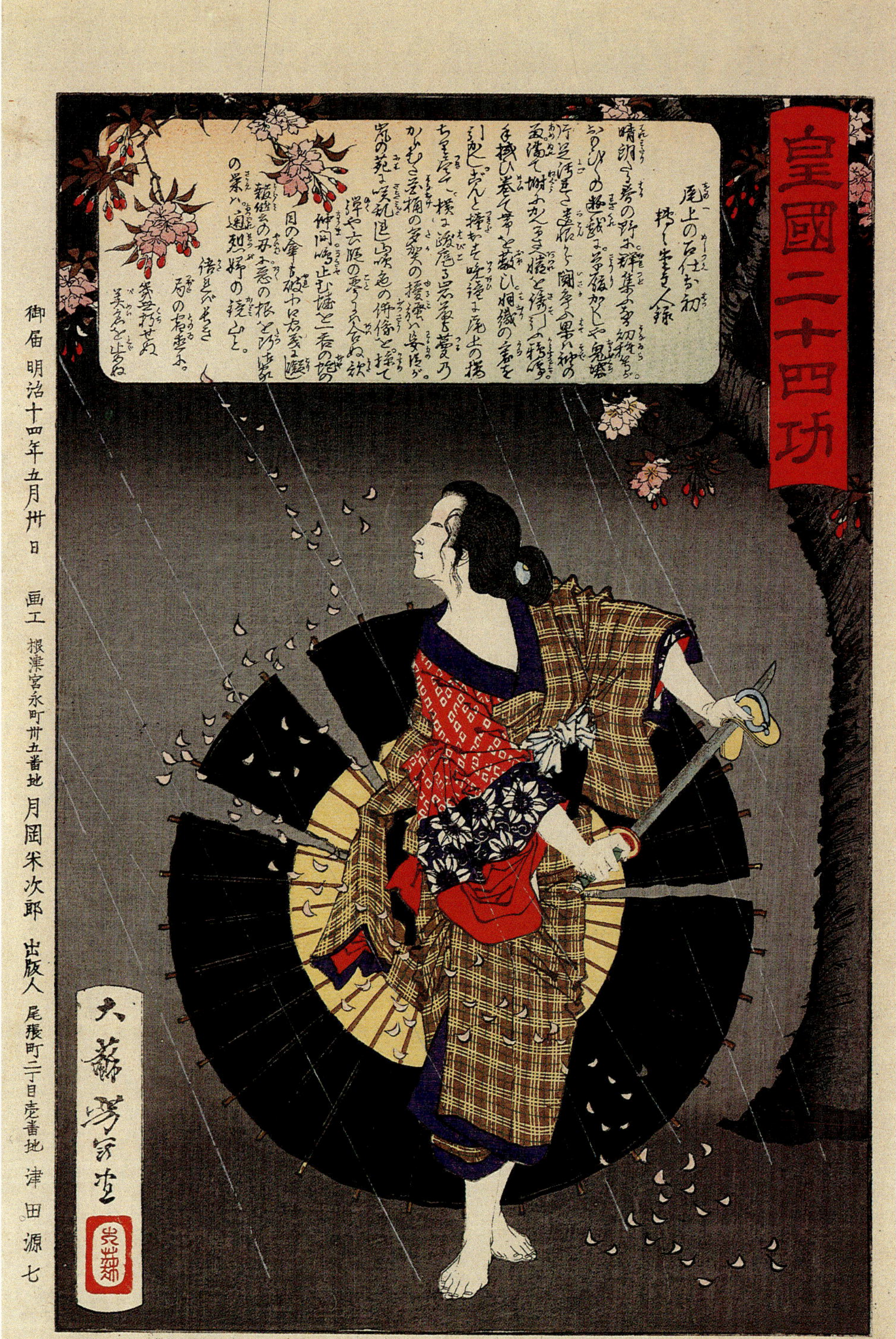

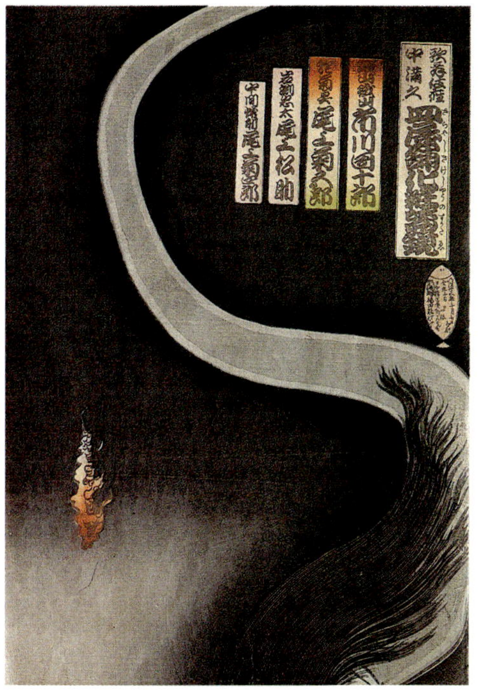
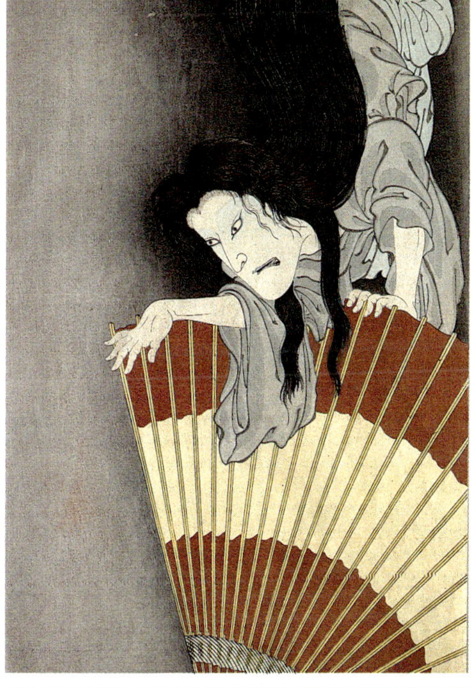
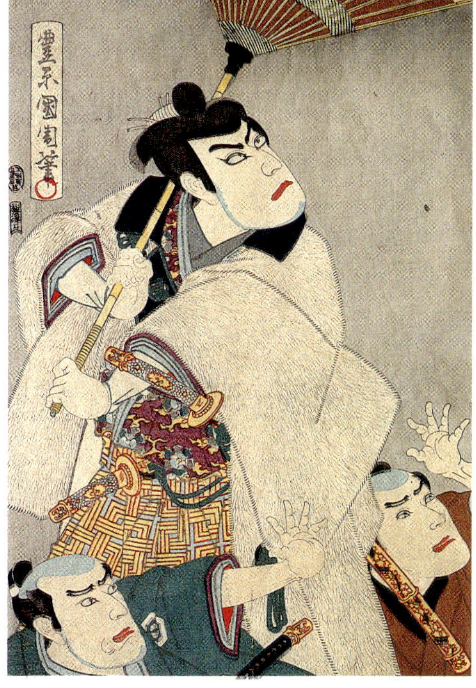

73. Toyohara Kunichika (1835-1900)
Ichikawa Danjûrô IX as Aoyama Tetsuzan
Meiji period, 1892
Signed: Toyohara Kunichika hitsu
Publisher: Fukuda Kumajirô
Color woodblock prints; vertical triptych, vertical *ôban*
Together: 48 7/8 x 9 5/8 in. (124.1 x 24.5 cm.)
Collection of Robert O. Muller

Ichikawa Danjûrô IX (see no. 68), holding the umbrella, stars as Aoyama Tetsuzan, the master who murdered his beautiful maid Okiku and threw her body down a well when she broke one of his dishes. Onoe Kikugorô V (1844-1903) takes the role of Okiku, whose ghost haunted her master by counting dishes one by one at night from the bottom of the well. The theme had its debut in 1741 in the puppet play *Banshû sarayashiki*, but was made popular by a number of Kabuki versions written during the 19th century when ghost plays were in vogue. The play illustrated here, *Sarayashiki keshô sugata kagami*, was written by Kawatake Mokuami and first performed at the Ichimura theater in Edo in 1863.[1]

In this scene the ghost of Okiku, in a long white gown, her loose black hair streaming behind her, comes to haunt Tetsuzan on a rainy night. Perceived as legless, Japanese ghosts are said to arrive from above, and it is possible that onstage the actor was lowered from overhead on wires. Danjûrô probably uses an acting technique called *renribiki* (entwined pulling), often employed in ghost plays: trying to flee, the haunted person turns his head and mimes as if being drawn backwards by the collar (no. 73a), an effect intensified by the reversed umbrella. Okiku's power seems to be forcing it into a funnel shape called the *asagao* (morning-glory) style. The reversed umbrella also reflects the panic of the person who opens it too fast and reverses it by mistake. A special umbrella is used for such scenes.

It is not clear in the print where the stretchers meet the ribs of this *janome*. (Kuniyoshi did a slightly better job of depicting an umbrella blown inside out; see no. 1.) In Gifu it is said that the most beautiful *janome* have stretchers that are one-third the length of the ribs.

1. Genshoku ukiyo-e daihyakka-jiten henshû-iinkai, ed. (1980-82), Vol. 4, 73; and Takahashi and Yoshida (1974), 131.

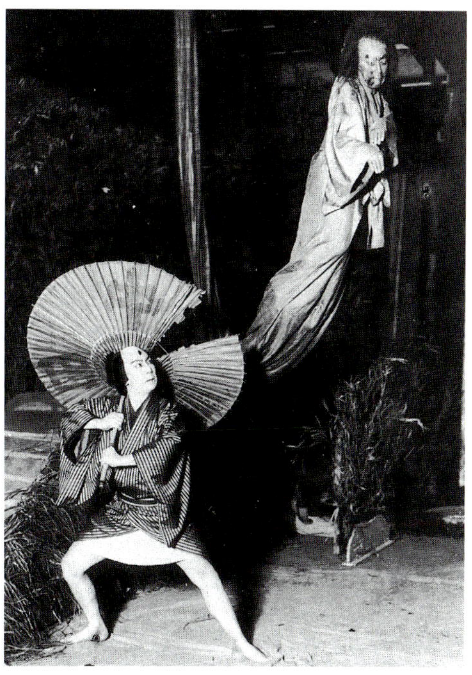

73a. Demonstration of the *renribiki* technique: the ghost of Hôkaibô prevents Shinza from escaping, in the play *Sumida gonichi no omokage*. Photograph. Waseda University Tsubouchi Memorial Theater Museum

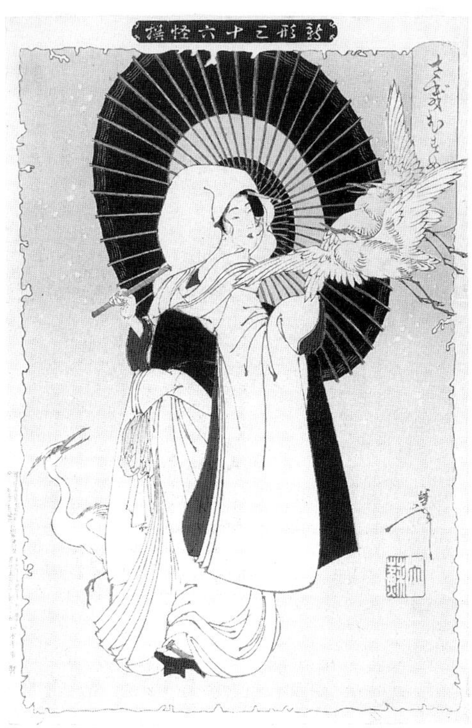

74. Tsukioka Yoshitoshi (1839-1892)
Heron Maiden
Series: Thirty-six Ghosts in New Forms
Meiji period, 1889
Signed: Yoshitoshi; sealed: Taiso
Publisher: Sasaki Toyokichi
Color woodblock print; vertical *ôban*
14 x 9 1/2 in. (35.7 x 24.2 cm.)
Philadelphia Museum of Art: Purchased with funds contributed by the E. Rhodes and Leona B. Carpenter Foundation, 1989.047.598

Sagi musume (Heron maiden) is a famous *nagauta*, a single-scene Kabuki song-and-dance form with musical accompaniment. It was first performed by Segawa Kikunojô II (1741-1773) in March 1762 at the Ichimura theater in Edo in the play *Yanagi ni hina shochô no saezuri*. The 1770 revival of *Sagi musume* at the same theater, again with Kikunojô, was commemorated in prints by Isoda Koryûsai and Bunchô, creating models for Yoshitoshi.[1]

Sagi musume evokes an old folk tale in which a wounded heron is rescued by a young man, and its spirit turns into a beautiful young woman. He falls in love and marries her, but when he realizes that she is none other than the heron he saved, she must disappear forever.

In this Kabuki dance, a ghost story, the actor first appears as the lonely spirit of the snow heron, transformed into a beautiful girl wearing a white outer kimono with a black obi and a white snow hood (*zukin*); holding an umbrella, she stands at the water's edge beneath a willow tree in the evening light, drenched by softly falling snow. The white robe is her wedding dress, the black sash signifies death. In the dance, her heron steps reveal her true nature. The actor assuming the role has to make several costume changes in the course of the performance. He later takes on the appearance of a city girl wearing a red kimono to reenact her tragic infatuation with a lover who did not reciprocate, and finally conveys her tragic death and suffering in hell.

The text that is chanted to the accompaniment of shamisen music includes the lines:

Our dissension was caused by
gusts of passion that
blew: yet on my umbrella
the snow is lying
deeply piled, where my longing,
as when thin wet snow
melts and vanishes, is like
a warm path of love![2]

Yoshitoshi may have selected this subject because the play, starring Danjûrô IX (see nos. 68, 73), had been revived in 1886, after a long period of neglect.

Onstage the actor would have used an umbrella with a translucent silk cover, a stylized version of the paper *janome*, but lighter and more appropriate for the graceful effects sought in Kabuki dances.

1. Waterhouse (1964), nos. 81, 82, appendix E, 306-307. See also Waterhouse (1982), Vol. 1, pl. 3, Vol. 2, pl. 411. Harunobu depicted several versions of *Sagi musume* in prints dating between 1766 and 1769; see Meech-Pekarik et al. (1979), no. 79.
2. Waterhouse (1964), 308.

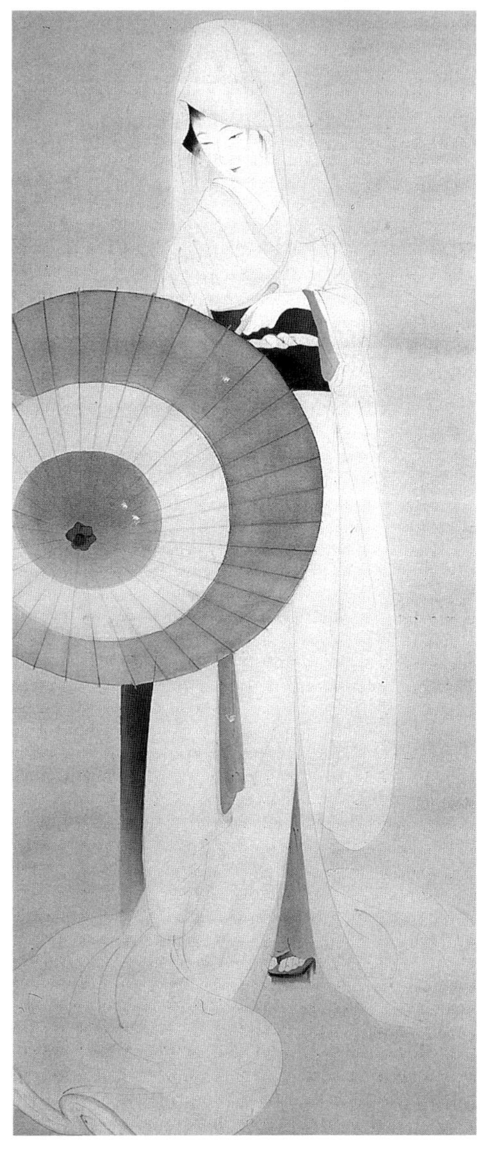

75. Yamakawa Shûhô (1898-1944)
Heron Maiden
Early Shôwa period, ca. 1930
Signed: Shûhô; sealed by the artist
Hanging scroll; color on silk
45 x 12 in. (114.3 x 30.5 cm.)
Collection of Patricia Salmon

A poignant and romantic figure, the doomed Heron Maiden stands in the snow holding a small *janome*, with a dainty protective cap tied onto the top.

76. Yabuta Takeshi (b. 1927)
Dance Parasol
Tokyo, Heisei period, 1991
Silk, paper, bamboo and wood
L. 37 3/8 in. (95 cm.); Diam. 51 1/8 in. (130 cm.), when opened
Collection of Yabuta Takeshi

A Kabuki umbrella is used on the stage only. It must be light, for ease of handling, but also durable enough to survive weeks of daily performances. Many factors have to be taken into account in its construction, and it is accordingly much more costly than an ordinary umbrella. A fine example, made to order for the specific play and to the proportions of the actor's body, has more ribs than is usual. The stick is very thin, to reduce the weight.

Sometimes more than one umbrella is used in a scene. During a fight sequence, for example, an actor might suddenly switch to a trick umbrella. In the "Heron Maiden" (nos. 74, 75), the actor starts with a translucent umbrella, and then goes to an opaque paper one when he needs to cover a costume change.

Today the finest Kabuki umbrellas are made by Yabuta Takeshi, a fourth-generation craftsman, who works alone in a tiny workshop in the Koiwa ward on the outskirts of Tokyo. He carves and lacquers the ribs of his umbrellas himself, and dyes his own paper. Only the top notches are ordered ready-made from Gifu. Each umbrella takes ten to fifteen days to complete and is a work of consummate artistry.

This umbrella was commissioned by the famous Kabuki actor Bandô Tamasaburô V (b. 1950) for the role of the Heron Maiden, which he performed at the National Theatre in London in October 1991. The cover is a transparent purple-gray silk dyed with ink (*sumi*). The top notch, the fifty ribs and stretchers, and the delicate stick are all lacquered black. There is a single wood spring, and a longer section of the handle is covered with rattan than would be the case with an ordinary umbrella. The rib-tip paper is purple, and the stretchers are elaborately embroidered with four bands of white silk threads.

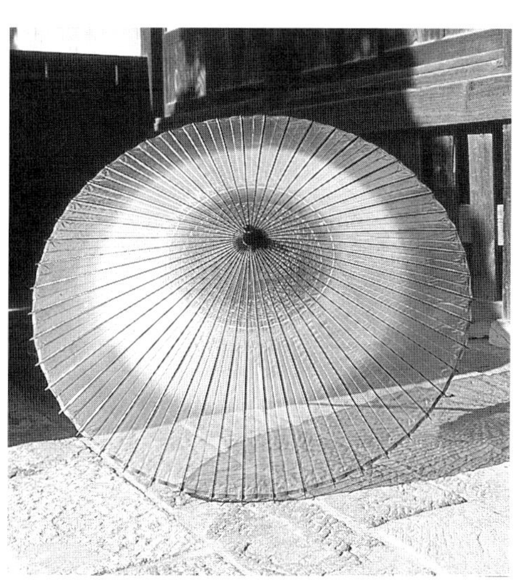

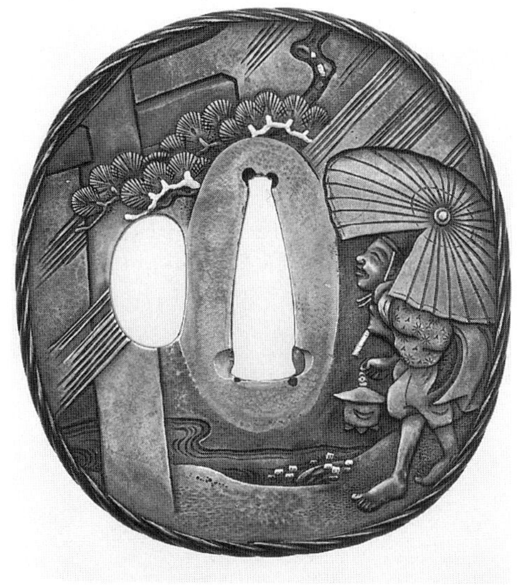

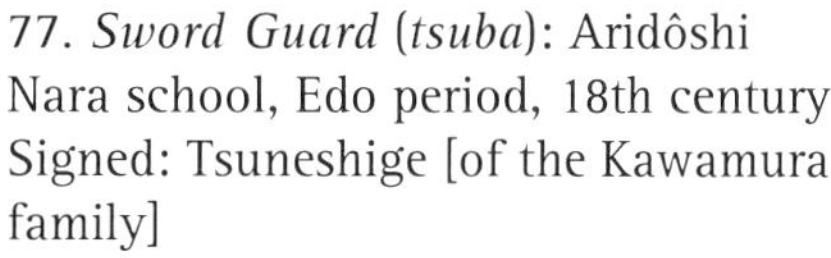

77. *Sword Guard* (*tsuba*): Aridôshi
Nara school, Edo period, 18th century
Signed: Tsuneshige [of the Kawamura family]
Inlay of gold, copper and *shakudô* on brass plate in the shape of a saddle flap (*aori*); rim cover added later
2 7/8 x 2 3/4 in. (7.3 x 7 cm.)
The Metropolitan Museum of Art, Gift of Edward G. Kennedy, 1932, 33.40.53

At the left is the gate of Aridôshi Shrine, near present-day Osaka, and to the right is the god Aridôshi as a shrine attendant holding a lantern and an umbrella, which protects him from a heavy downpour (indicated by diagonal streaks). The tear in the umbrella allows the artist to show its cover from above without hiding the attendant's face. The reverse of the *tsuba* depicts a pine tree by a stream.

The legend of Aridôshi ("Passage of the Ants"), which incorporates various old traditions, is recounted in a poem from the collected works of the early Heian poet Ki no Tsurayuki (868-945). One day when Tsurayuki was riding back to the capital his horse became ill. The local people explained that it was the doing of the irate god of that place, who had no shrine of his own. Tsurayuki then dedicated this poem to the god:

How could I have known
That in this cloudy, unfamiliar sky
There dwelt the Passage of the Ants?[1]

The god was appeased and the horse restored to health.

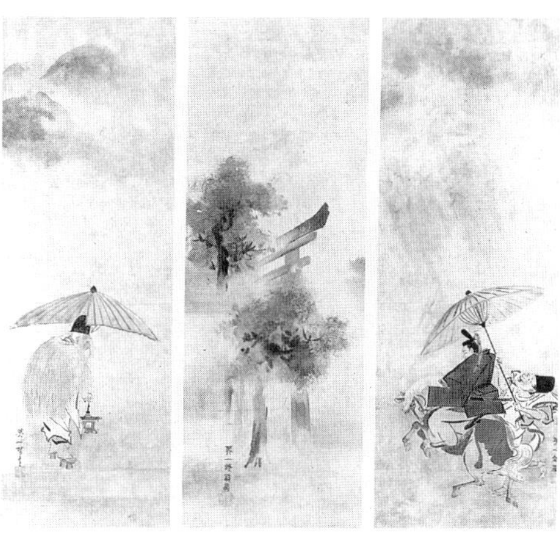

77a. Hanabusa Itchô (1652-1724), *Aridôshi*, middle Edo period. Set of three hanging scrolls; ink and color on paper. Private Collection

In *Aridôshi*, a Nô play by Zeami (1363-1443), the god is angered when Tsurayuki rides through the sacred precincts without dismounting. There is a heavy rainstorm and the horse refuses to go on. Aridôshi appears in the guise of a shrine attendant to say that the downpour is the direct result of Tsurayuki's own actions and to advise him to allay the god's wrath by reciting a poem. Tsurayuki dedicates his poem to the god, who is calmed and as a reward performs an auspicious Shinto dance. One well-known rendering of the subject is a set of three early-18th-century hanging scrolls by Hanabusa Itchô (no. 77a).[2] As in the many late-Edo sword-guard, netsuke, and ukiyo-e renditions of the theme, Itchô's Aridôshi wears a straw raincoat and carries an umbrella that is torn, an indication, apparently, of the severity of the storm.

1. Morris (1967), Vol. 2, 157; and Genshoku ukiyo-e daihyakka-jiten henshû-iinkai, ed. (1980-82), Vol. 4, 17.
2. Kobayashi and Sakakibara (1978), nos. 49-51.

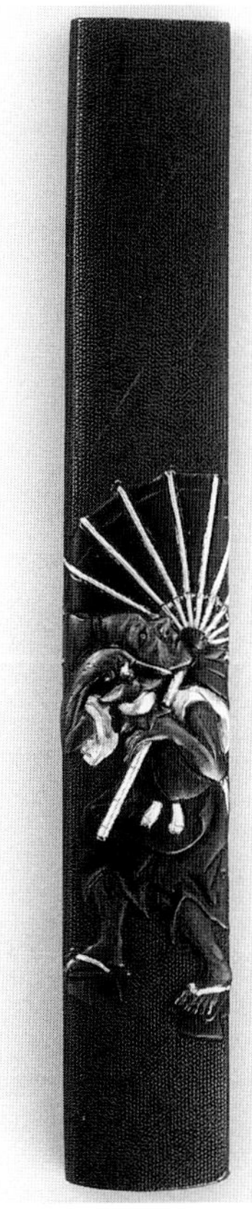

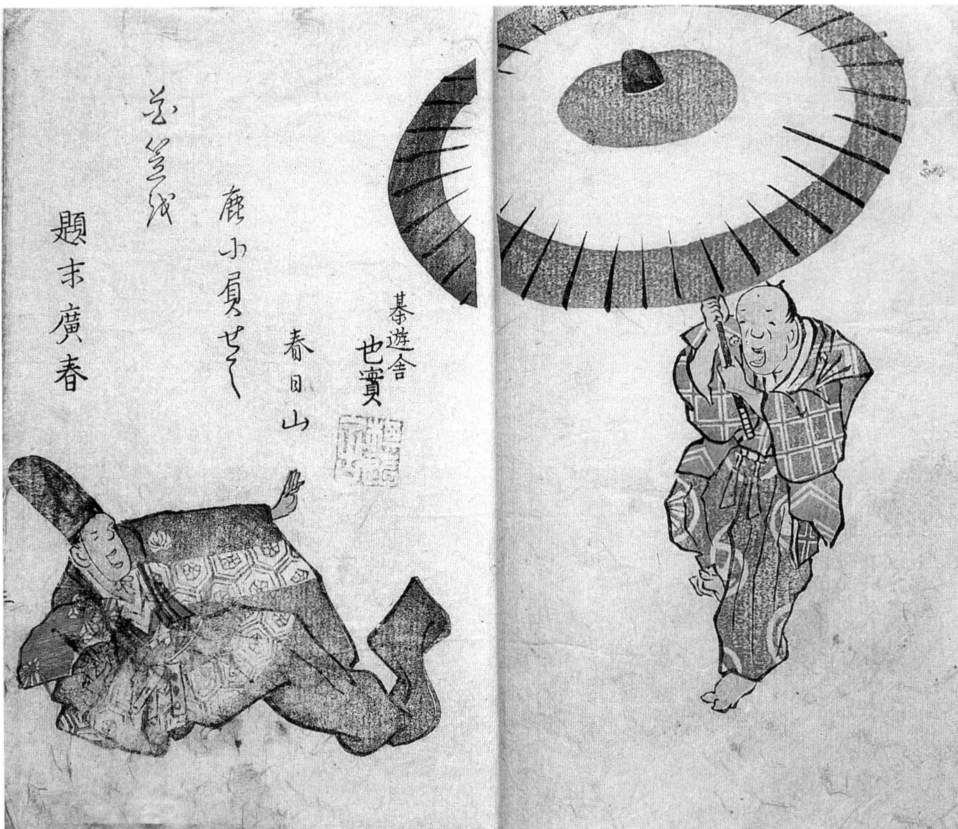

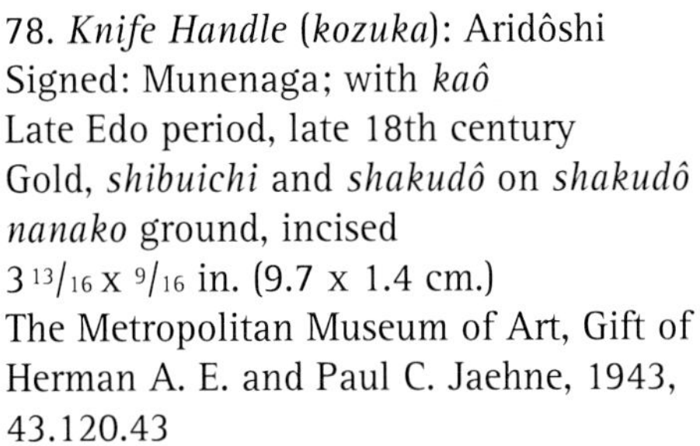

78. *Knife Handle* (*kozuka*): Aridôshi
Signed: Munenaga; with *kaô*
Late Edo period, late 18th century
Gold, *shibuichi* and *shakudô* on *shakudô nanako* ground, incised
3 13/16 x 9/16 in. (9.7 x 1.4 cm.)
The Metropolitan Museum of Art, Gift of Herman A. E. and Paul C. Jaehne, 1943, 43.120.43

The ribs of Aridôshi's umbrella are gold. Incised lines represent the rainstorm.

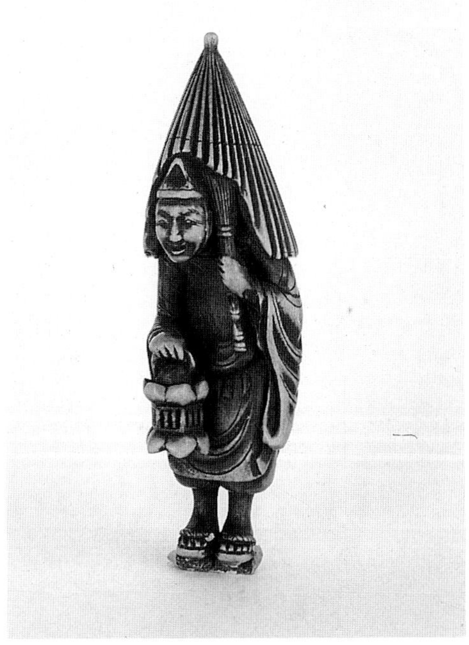

79. *Netsuke*: Aridôshi
Late Edo period, 19th century
Signed: Mitsuharu
Wood
2 7/8 x 7/8 in. (7.2 x 2.1 cm.)
Floyd Segel Collection

The artist has taken the trouble to incise a line around the middle of the miniature umbrella, indicating where the lower and upper sheets of paper meet. A netsuke is a toggle at the end of a cord holding a lacquer *inrô* (medicine container), which is suspended from the obi (see no. 86); it must be compact and smooth, so as not to catch on the wearer's clothing. For this reason, Aridôshi's umbrella here is shown nearly closed, but his head is visible through a gaping tear in the cover.

80. Maki Bokusen (1736-1824)
Suehirogari
From *Shiki sambasô* (*Sambasô* of the four seasons), compiled by Baijuken Itsujin
Late Edo period, 1813
Signed: Kyôgadô Bokusen; sealed: Hokutei sanjin, Bokusen
Publisher: Shôkadô (Matsuya Zembei), Nagoya
Color woodblock-printed illustrated book
Page: 8 3/4 x 6 1/4 in. (22.2 x 15.9 cm.)
Ravicz Collection

The subject is taken from the Kyôgen farce *Suehirogari* (An umbrella instead of a fan). A sublimely stupid servant, Tarô Kaja, is sent to the capital to buy a *suehirogari*—a special type of fan—as a present for a guest on New Year's Day. Without identifying it, his master explains that a *suehirogari* is made with strong paper from Mino, has polished ribs, a sturdy pivot which allows easy opening and closing, and a playful painted design (*zara-e*), meaning, too, a handle to strike with, like that of a fan. When Tarô Kaja reaches the capital and announces that he wants to buy a *suehirogari*, a dishonest umbrella vendor decides to take advantage of this ignoramus. Pointing out that his product has all the required attributes, he sells him an old umbrella at an exorbitant price. He also teaches Tarô Kaja a song about umbrellas and Mount Kasuga to make his lord feel good if he becomes unhappy. When a self-satisfied Tarô Kaja returns home, his very unhappy master chases him out. He then begins to sing and dance the mantralike ditty he was taught. The master comes out to watch, then joins in himself, and in the end rewards Tarô Kaja for his cleverness.[1]

This illustration shows the final dance, with the servant carrying an umbrella and his master a fan. The accompanying poem is a *kyôka* by Kiyusha Yajitsu entitled "*Suehiro* Spring" (*Suehiro no haru*):

Hanagasa o	Mount Kasuga—
shika ni owasete	flower umbrellas
Kasugayama	cover the deer.

Deer roam freely on Mount Kasuga, in Nara, which is covered with blossoming cherry trees in the spring and has the triangular shape of an open umbrella. The poem is derived from Tarô Kaja's song, which compares the open umbrella to Mount Kasuga, a hill beside Mount Mikasa; *mikasa* means "three hats" or "three umbrellas." The song concludes: "Putting up an umbrella is to act in accordance with the vows of the god, who has promised to save mankind. If others are going to open their umbrellas, I will do the same."

The *Shiki sambasô* illustrates scenes from Nô and Kyôgen plays, each accompanied by verse; *sambasô* is the traditional dance prelude to a theatrical performance. *Suehirogari* is an example of Waki Kyôgen, a class of Kyôgen that is placed first on a program and that has auspicious content intended to make the audience smile.

1. Kenney (1968), 251-252; and Kitagawa and Yasuda (1972), 66-80. This play is first documented in the *Tenshô kyôgen-bon*, the daily record book of a provincial Kyôgen performer dating from Tenshô 6 (1578).

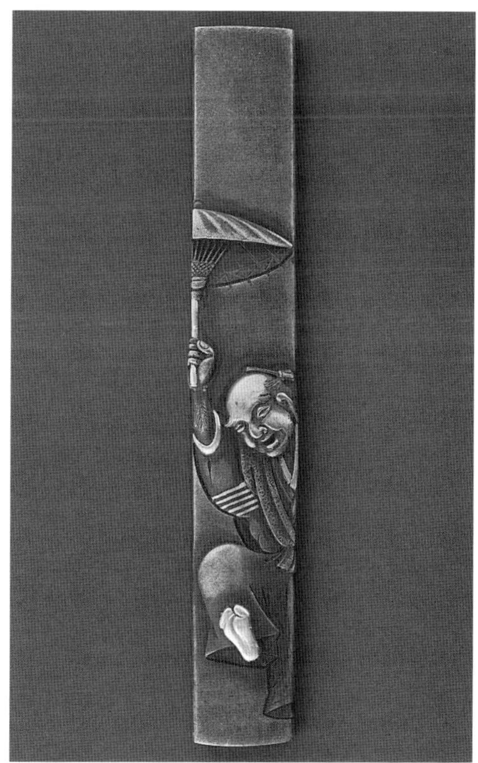

81. *Knife Handle* (*kozuka*): *Suehirogari*
Signed: Katsuryûken Naoyoshi [Iwama Naoyoshi]
Late Edo period, first half 19th century
Silver and two colors of gold inlaid on a *shibuichi* ground
3 7/8 in. x 9/16 in. (9.8 x 1.5 cm.)
The Metropolitan Museum of Art, Gift of Herman A. E. and Paul C. Jaehne, 1943, 43.120.55

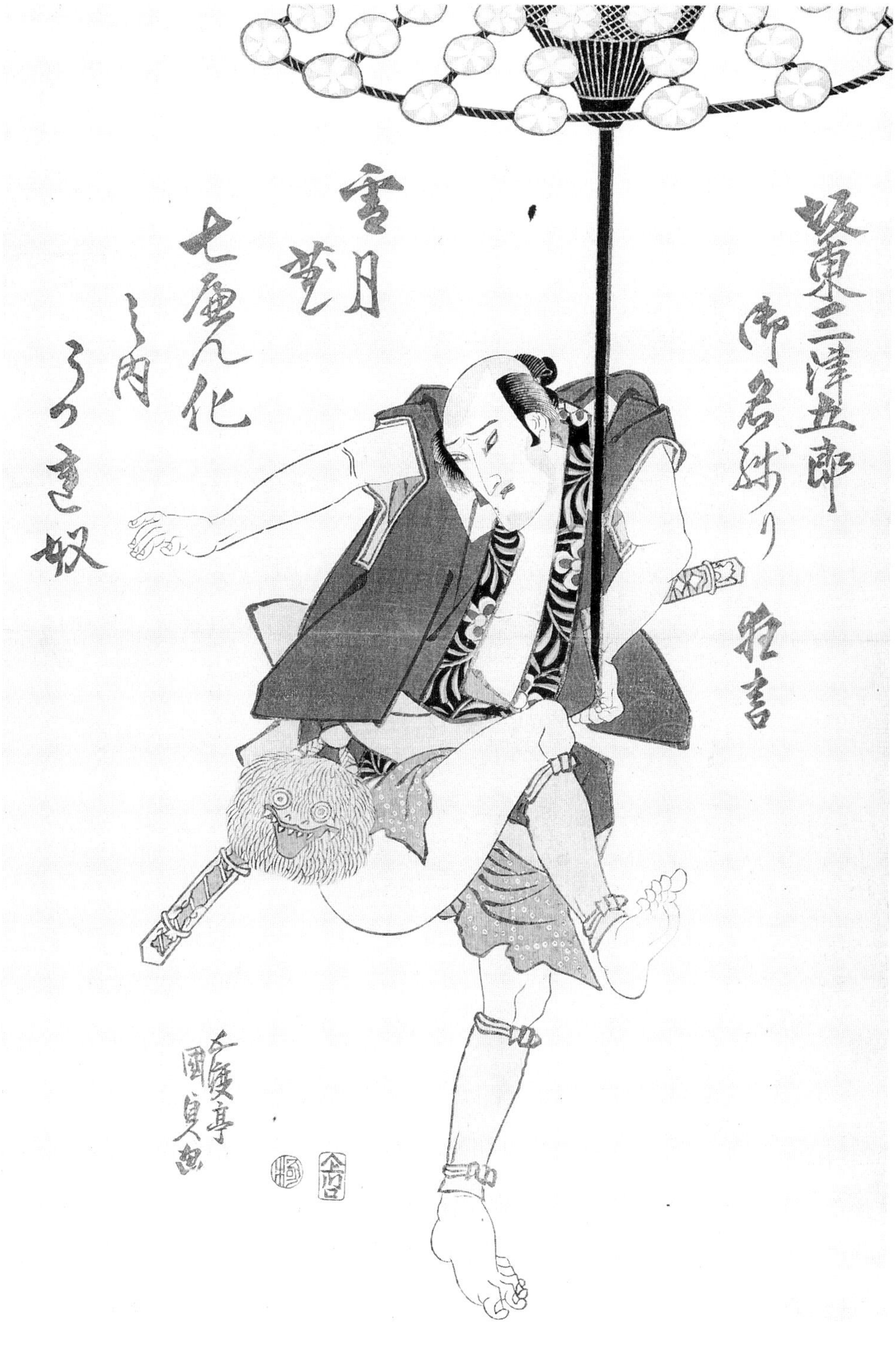

Tarô Kaja, the stupid servant in *Suehirogari* (see no. 80), is here shown performing his dance armed with the umbrella he has bought by mistake.

82. Utagawa Kunisada (1786-1864)
The Actor Bandô Mitsugorô III in a Farewell Performance
Edo period, 1820
Signed: Gotôtei Kunisada ga
Publisher: Kawaguchiya Uhei
Color woodblock print: vertical *ôban*
15 x 10 1/4 in. (38.1 x 26 cm.)
Collection of William Green, promised gift to Mead Art Museum, Amherst College

Mitsugorô III (1775-1831) executed a Kabuki dance at the Nakamura theater in September 1820 as a farewell performance (*onagori kyôgen*) before leaving Edo for a tour of Osaka. The seven costume changes (*shichi henge*) included one in which he danced with a flower umbrella (*hanagasa*), a stage umbrella decorated with paper blossoms in place of the usual cover (see no. 83).[1]

Kunisada has correctly observed the way in which a Kabuki actor must hold the umbrella—at the bottom of the handle—in order to manipulate it easily during complicated dance routines.

1. Ihara (1973), Vol. 6, 72. A *surimono* by Hokusai in the Brooklyn Museum commemorates the same performance with the accoutrements of the seven costume changes, including the umbrella. See Forrer (1991), no. 95.

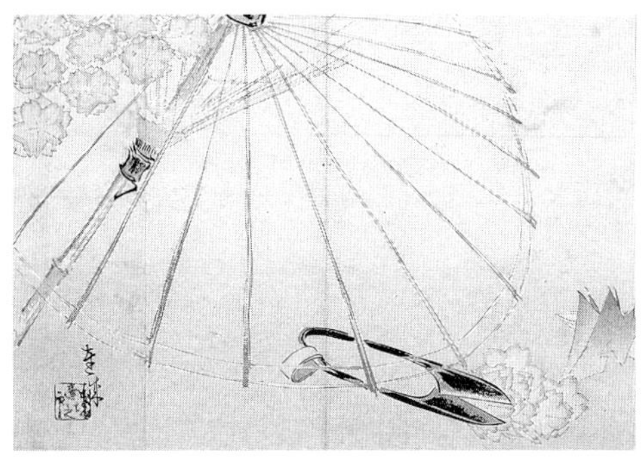

83. *Dance Umbrella*
From *Bijutsukai* (Ocean of art), edited by Yamada Naosaburô, Vol. 26
Meiji period, 1898
Signed: Renjô; sealed: Renjô no in
Publisher: Unsôdô, Kyoto
Color woodblock-printed illustrated book
Fold-out page: 9 1/2 x 13 in. (24 x 33 cm.)
Ravicz Collection

Paper cherry blossoms are attached to the ribs of a dance umbrella (see no. 82). To the lower left are some unattached flowers, with the scissors and pink paper used to make them.

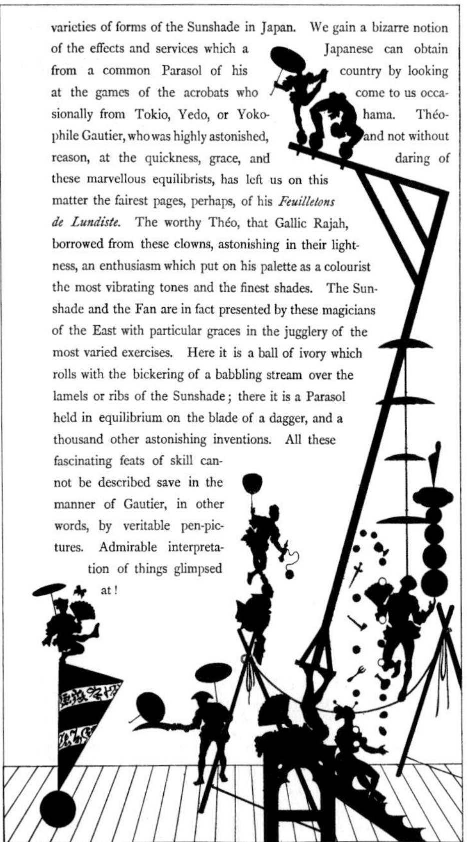

varieties of forms of the Sunshade in Japan. We gain a bizarre notion of the effects and services which a Japanese can obtain from a common Parasol of his country by looking at the games of the acrobats who come to us occasionally from Tokio, Yedo, or Yokohama. Théophile Gautier, who was highly astonished, and not without reason, at the quickness, grace, and daring of these marvellous equilibrists, has left us on this matter the fairest pages, perhaps, of his *Feuilletons de Lundiste.* The worthy Théo, that Gallic Rajah, borrowed from these clowns, astonishing in their lightness, an enthusiasm which put on his palette as a colourist the most vibrating tones and the finest shades. The Sunshade and the Fan are in fact presented by these magicians of the East with particular graces in the jugglery of the most varied exercises. Here it is a ball of ivory which rolls with the bickering of a babbling stream over the lamels or ribs of the Sunshade; there it is a Parasol held in equilibrium on the blade of a dagger, and a thousand other astonishing inventions. All these fascinating feats of skill cannot be described save in the manner of Gautier, in other words, by veritable pen-pictures. Admirable interpretation of things glimpsed at!

84. Paul Avril (1843-1904)
Japanese Acrobats
From Octave Uzanne, *The Sunshade, The Glove–The Muff*
Publisher: J. C. Nimmo and Bain, London, 1884
Page: 10 3/4 x 7 1/4 in. (27.3 x 18.4 cm.)
The Fine Print Collection: The Newark Public Library, R741.2.Z11

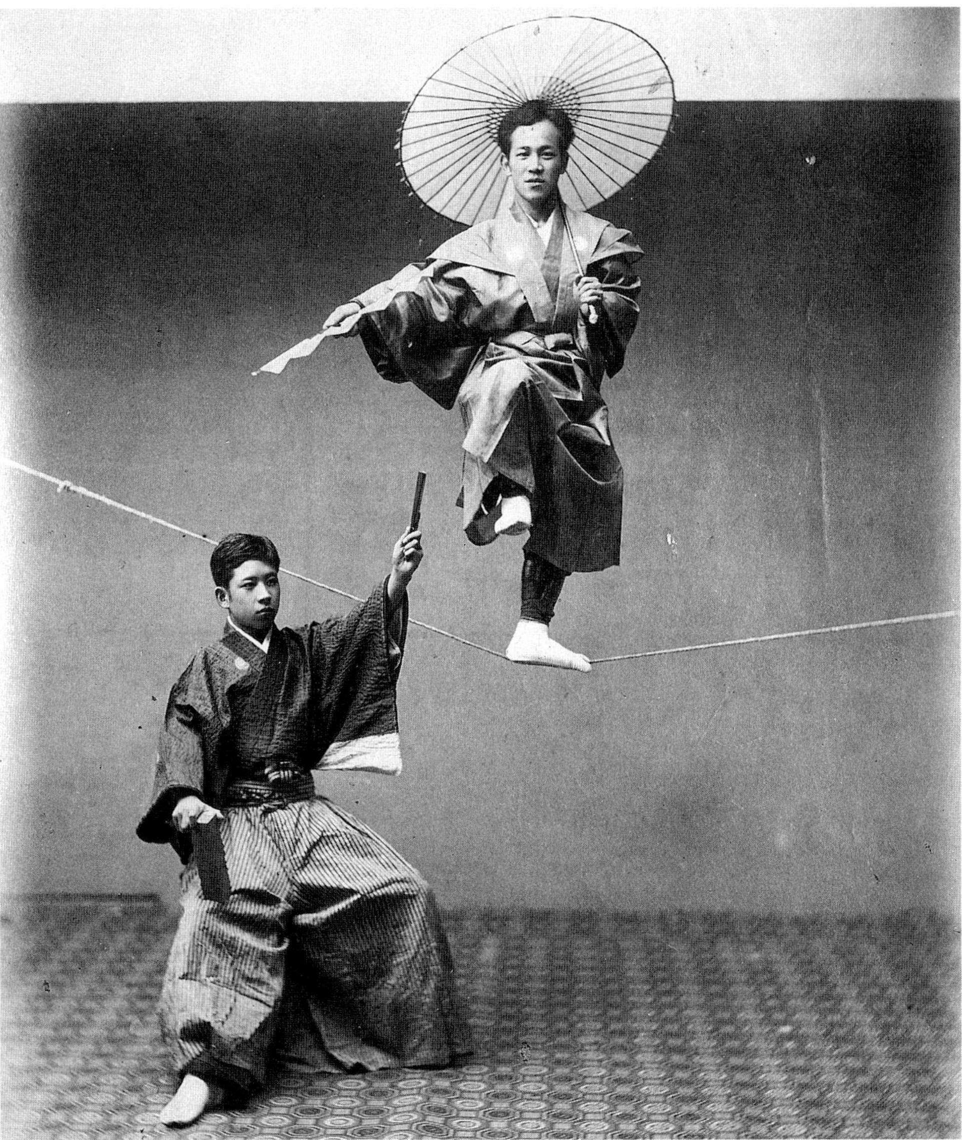

The French writer and bibliophile Louis-Octave Uzanne (1852-1931) here comments on the troupes of Japanese acrobats performing with parasols and fans who visited Europe in the late 19th century. The book is a translation of the second volume of Uzanne's *Les Ornements de la femme*, originally published in Paris in 1882. Avril's illustrations enliven nearly every page of this early history of the umbrella.

85. Kusakabe Kimbei (1841-1934)
Tightrope Walker
Meiji period, 1890s
Hand-colored albumen print
10 1/4 x 7 3/4 in. (26 x 19.7 cm.)
Horesh Collection, London

A street tightrope walker and his assistant are posed in the photographer's studio. As in Avril's rendering (no. 84), Japanese acrobats often balanced themselves with a parasol and a fan.

A vivid depiction of acrobats in action is given in a mid-19th-century handscroll, where their feats are accompanied by inspirational, didactic messages that may have been sung by the performers (no. 85a). The tightrope walker's text reads: "The spider takes a thin thread to catch a dragonfly; the merchant who starts with only a little money is able to make it grow into a large amount; water originating from a mountain stream eventually becomes warm. If you work hard you won't be poor."

85a. Artist unknown, *Osaka Acrobats* (detail), late Edo period, ca.1850. Handscroll; ink and color on paper. The Metropolitan Museum of Art, Gift of Mrs. Henry J. Bernheim, 1945

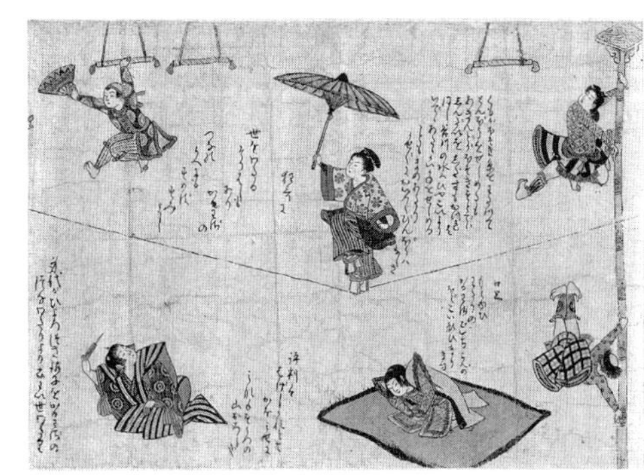

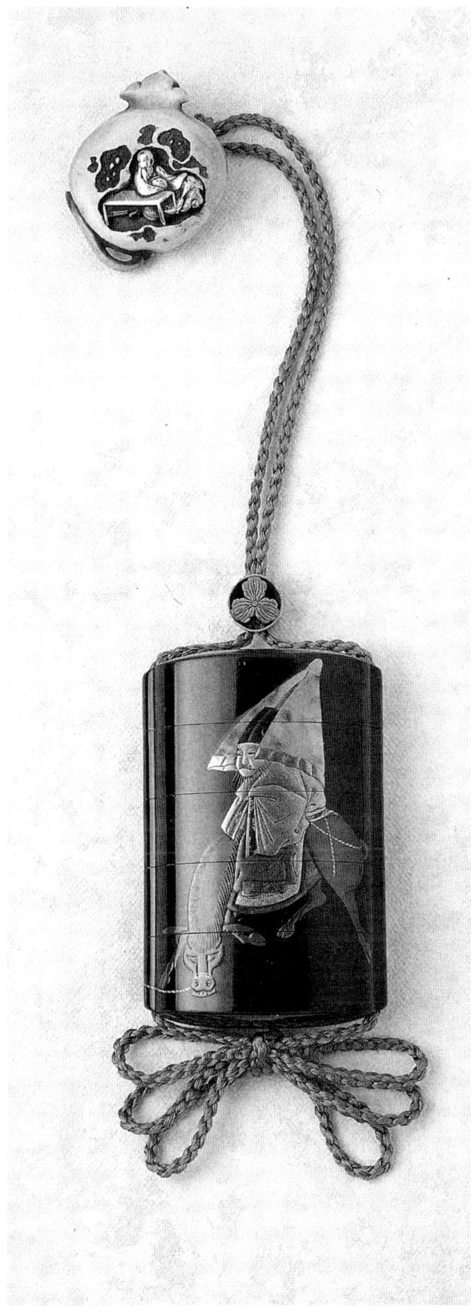

86. *Inrô*: Poet riding a donkey
Edo period, 18th-early 19th century
Signed: Jôsetsu
Black lacquer ground with colored raised lacquer and mother-of-pearl inlay
Netsuke: the Japanese poet Hitomaro; ivory inlaid with silver
Ojime: oak-leaf crest; silver
3 1/16 x 2 x 15/16 in. (7.8 x 5.1 x 2.4 cm.)
The Weston Collection

The venerable man of letters, relaxed or even inebriated, riding a donkey or horse, is an archetypal theme in Japanese ink painting. The celebrated Chinese poets Du Fu (712-770), Li Bai (701-762) and Su Shi (1037-1101) are often shown in this way, and it is not always possible to tell which of them was intended as the subject. Du Fu wrote of falling off a horse while drunk, and of spending "more than three years on a donkey's back" traveling in service to the state: "Mornings, I knock on the doors of rich youth, Evenings, I follow in the dust of the fast horses. Left-over wine and the roast that is cold I swallow together with my pride and my tears."[1] Su Shi wrote that his horse had died and he arrived at his destination, Mian Pond, riding a mule: "The road was long, the people in difficulties, and the lame mule brayed."[2] There is no mention of umbrellas, however.

Whoever the poet may be on this *inrô*, or medicine container, his torn umbrella hints at the hardships he must endure in the line of duty. The mother-of-pearl inlay may represent snow that has settled on the cover; the design on the reverse shows snow on bamboo.

1. Hung (1952), 56. For the poem titled "Drunk, I Fell from Horseback," see ibid., 250.
2. This is the last line of Su Shi's poem "Matching Ziyou, at Mian Pond, Thinking of the Past"; Fuller (1990), 99. The author is indebted to Professor Maggie Bickford, Brown University, for this citation.

87. *Knife Handle* (*kozuka*): Rats eating an umbrella
Hamano school, Edo period, 18th century
Gold and copper on *shibuichi* ground
3 3/4 x 1/2 in. (9.5 x 1.3 cm.)
Collection of Mr. and Mrs. Joel H. Frankel

Three rats, elegantly carved in two tones of gold with copper spots, are nibbling at a *janome*, while a fourth, betrayed by its protruding curly tail, is hidden inside. The umbrella is gold with a center band (the *nakabari* paper) of copper. The damage already inflicted by the rats is suggested by two thin golden lines jutting out from the side of the umbrella–loose ribs from which the paper has been shredded.

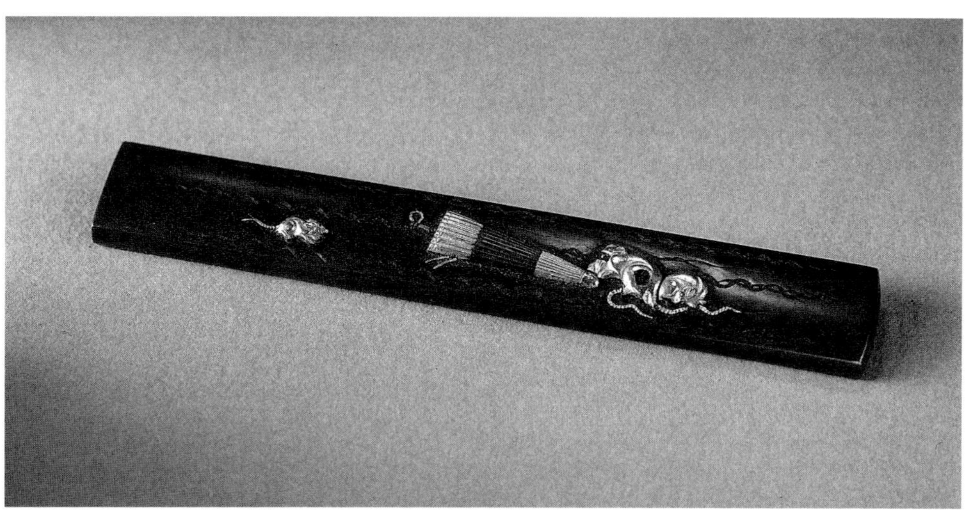

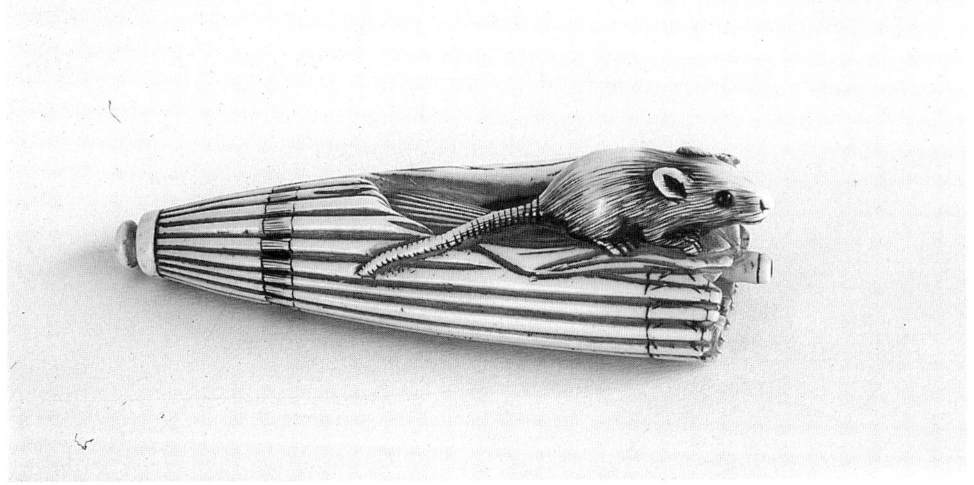

88. *Netsuke*: Rat eating an umbrella
Late Edo period, mid-19th century
Ivory and black coral
1 1/2 in. x 3 3/8 in. (3.8 x 8.6 cm.)
Floyd Segel Collection

Why is a rat chewing on an umbrella? Because the paste that fastens the paper to the ribs is made of a very tasty cassava-root starch (see fig. 8). Umbrella makers in Gifu have been heard to complain that rats will slip into their workshops at night and gnaw away the bristles of their paste brushes. The umbrella stick here is too stumpy to be realistic, but a longer one would have been inappropriate for a netsuke, which must of necessity be compact in shape. The umbrella cover is quite realistically detailed, however, with a double line of threads and a cross-hatching design incised around the bottom. The dark band incised around the top suggests that this may be a *janome*; the lively-looking rat, its eyes inlaid with black coral, is feasting on an umbrella of good quality.

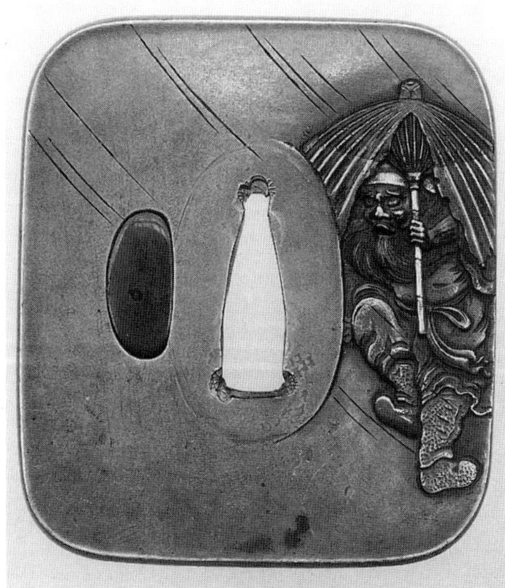

89. *Sword Guard* (*tsuba*): Shôki the Demon Queller
Attributed to Tsuneshige, Nara school, Edo period, 18th century
Inlay of *shakudô*, *shibuichi*, gold, and copper on brass plate, incised
2 7/8 x 2 5/8 in. (7.3 x 6.7 cm.)
The Metropolitan Museum of Art, Bequest of Edward G. Kennedy, 1932, 33.40.11

Shôki, or Zhong Kui, as he is known in Chinese legend, was a failed examination candidate of the Tang dynasty (618-906). He committed suicide in frustration and shame, but his spirit returned to the court of the emperor, Minghuang (712-56), where he served as the official queller of demons. On this sword guard he hides behind his ominously tattered umbrella as he searches for the demon (*oni*), shown clinging to a pine tree on the reverse of the guard.

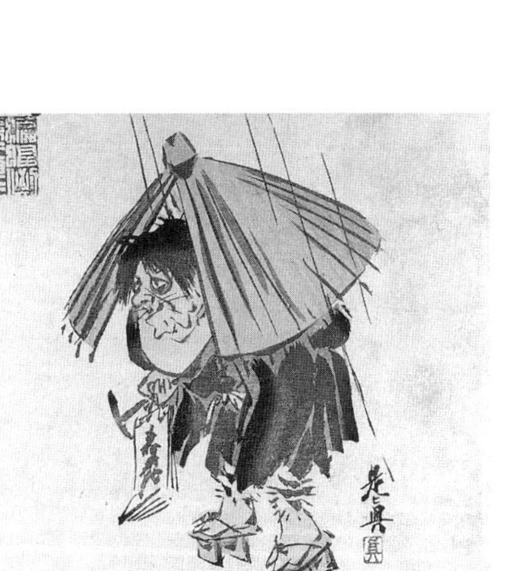

90a. Shibata Zeshin (1807-1891), *Praying Demon*, Meiji period, late 19th century. Color woodblock print. Collection of Robert O. Muller

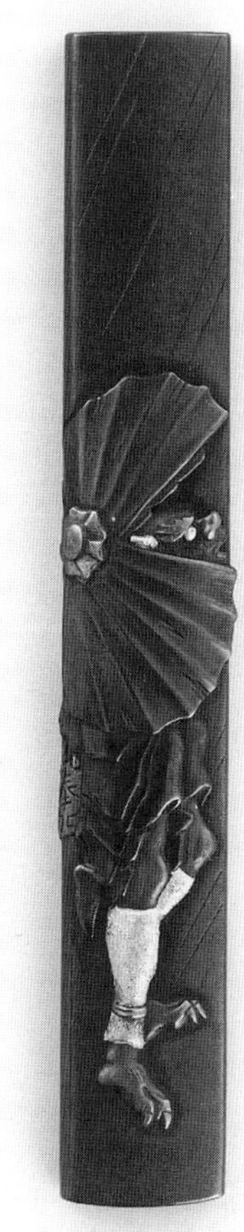

90. *Knife Handle* (*kozuka*): Praying demon
Late Edo period, ca. 1850
Signed: Oishi Akichika, with *kaô*
Carved in relief and incised, with inlay of silver, *shakudô*, gold, and copper on *shibuichi* plate
L. 3 3/4 in. (9.5 cm.)
The Metropolitan Museum of Art, Purchase, Rogers Fund, 1912, 12.37.143

Demons (*oni*) in Japanese art are typically conceived as mischievous and grotesque, with two short horns, prominent sharp incisors, bulging eyes, and hands and feet with three clawed digits. In the Edo period the praying demon (*oni no nembutsu*) is shown in the guise of an itinerant priest in clerical garb, holding both a mallet to strike the gong that hangs around his neck and a temple registry book (*sankachô*); the characters for *sanka* appear on the registry book in this example. The demon's significance is unclear; perhaps he implies that salvation is possible even for the most degraded. Sometimes an umbrella is shown strapped to his back, but often, as here and in a later woodblock print (no. 90a), a humble *bangasa* protects him in a rainstorm, indicated on the knife handle by incised lines. In a humorous touch, emphasizing the poverty of the wandering "monk," his head is shown poking through a large tear in his umbrella.

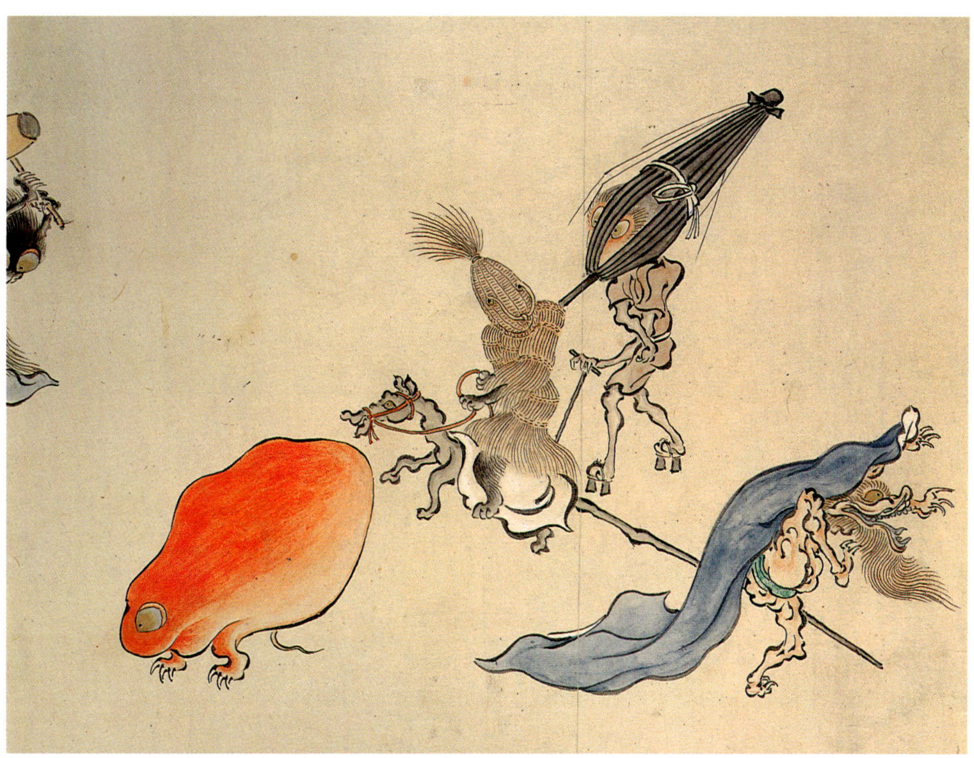

91. Attributed to Okada Tamechika (1823-1864)
Night Parade of One Hundred Demons: Umbrella Monster (detail)
Late Edo period, mid-19th century
Handscroll; ink, color and gold on paper
13 3/4 x 488 in. (35 x 1239.9 cm.)
Spencer Collection, The New York Public Library, Astor, Lenox and Tilden Foundations

The handscroll "Night Parade of One Hundred Demons" tells the tale of a haunted house in Kyoto during the troubled years of the late 12th century. A young man spends the night with an old retainer, left alone in charge of a once-elegant mansion in the capital, and is horrified by the apparition of demons who create a frightening racket until dawn. Some are the spirits of musical instruments; others take the form of common household objects such as cooking pots, trivets, kettles, straw sandals and an old umbrella. Miyeko Murase has written that "mixed with the ancient fear of darkness is another old Japanese belief that used, worn household utensils can turn into evil spirits and lead humans astray."[1] Perhaps this accounts for the fascination that broken umbrellas seem to have for Japanese artists.

In this detail a horseman, mounted on a broken-down nag and accompanied by an umbrella monster, looks back over his shoulder at a blue-robed demon with a dragon's head. The rider is a straw-sandal (*waraji*) monster: the end of the sandal looks like the tuft of hair on the head of a medieval samurai, and sandal straps have become his eyes and mouth. He wears a straw garment like that used to wrap a bale of rice, tied off in sections to resemble the lamellar construction of Japanese armor. The decrepit umbrella behind him, with loose ribs flying out on either side, is the headdress of an emaciated figure with a red face, pointy snout, and bulging eyes—the head of a rat? It is tied around the center with a white ribbon in the manner of a formal long-stick umbrella (*nagaegasa*). High-class umbrellas have curved ribs that nearly touch at the bottom when closed, as seen here. The two monsters evoke the familiar sight of an attendant carrying a furled umbrella for his master in a daimyo procession. In a later version of the theme by another artist (no. 91a), the umbrella monster has a cloth bag of the sort used to protect *tsumaoregasa* when closed, worn as though it were a cap, and the stick is shortened to resemble a pointed red beak.

This scroll, a cornucopia of bizarre and macabre products of the Japanese imagination, is a fairly close copy of the earliest extant version of the theme, a fragmentary 16th-century scroll in the Shinjuan at Daitoku-ji temple, Kyoto.[2] The so-called Hundred Demons entered the repertoire of Japanese folklore in the late Heian period. Fujiwara no Yorinaga (1120-1156) mentions a sighting of one hundred demons in 1141 in his diary, the *Taiki*.[3]

1. Murase (1986), 135.
2. Komatsu (1979), 78.
3. Ibid., 126; and Takeuchi (1987), 8.

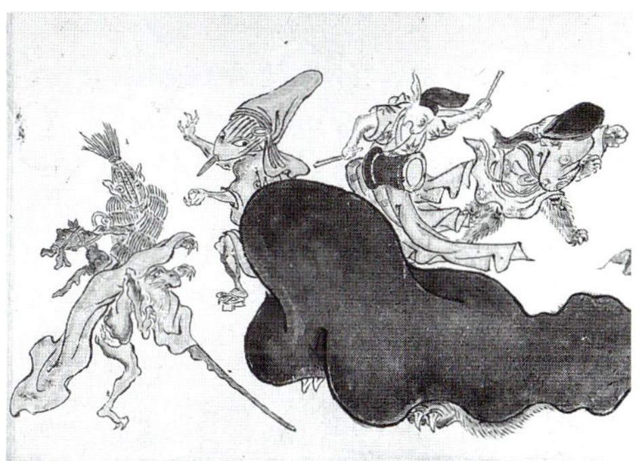

91a. Artist unknown, *Night Parade of One Hundred Demons* (detail), late Edo-early Meiji period, late 19th century. Handscroll. The Mary and Jackson Burke Collection

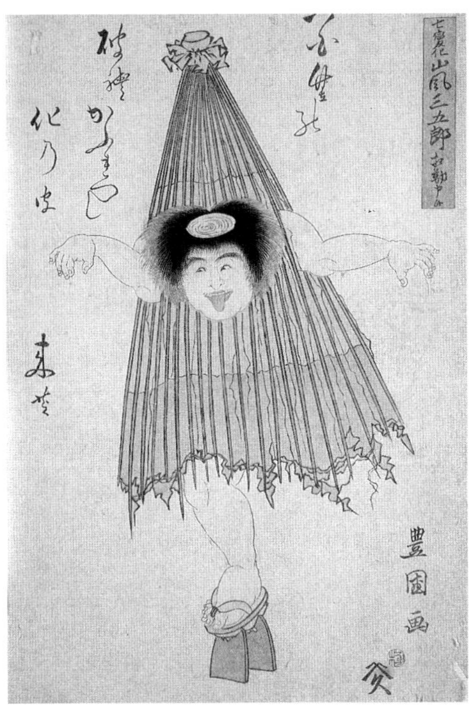

Color plate, p. 46

92. Utagawa Toyokuni (1769-1825)
The Actor Arashi Sangorô III Performing as an Umbrella Monster
Edo period, ca. 1810
Signed: Toyokuni ga
Publisher: Yamamoto Kyûbei
Color woodblock print; vertical *ôban*
13 7/8 x 9 11/16 in. (35.2 x 24.6 cm.)
Kupferstich-Kabinett, Staatliche Kunstsammlungen Dresden

The humorous seventeen-syllable poem (*senryû*) inscribed on this print is signed by Raishi, the poetry name of the actor Arashi Sangorô III (d. 1833). He inherited the poetry and stage name Raishi from his father and was known at the end of his career as Arashi Raishi II. The poem reads:

Hanagasa no	My flower umbrella
yabure-kabure ya	tattered and worn–
bake no kawa	in the guise of a monster![1]

A one-legged umbrella monster with a long tongue appeared on the scene with the surge of ghost plays in the early 19th century. This print documents a performance in which Sangorô came onstage as a tattered *bangasa* in the course of a Kabuki dance comprising seven costume changes (*shichi henge*). The knee of Sangorô's retracted left leg is just visible under the rim of the umbrella. One of the properties in a seven-costume performance was either a hat or an umbrella covered with flowers (see no. 82); the word *hanagasa* describes both.

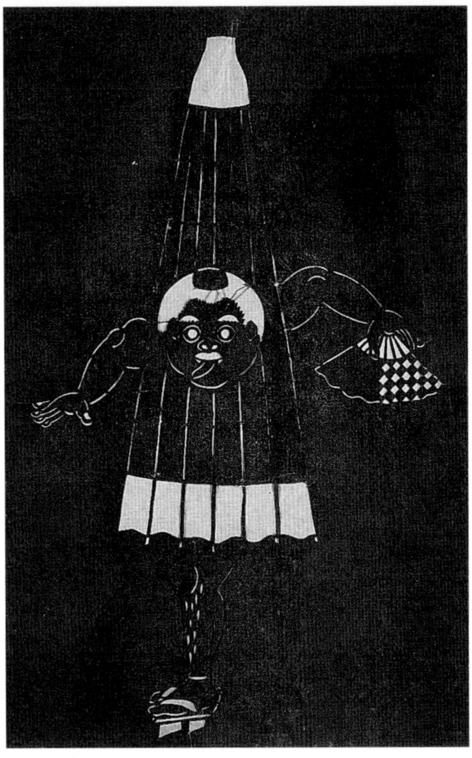

This umbrella demon has a depression on his head, suggesting that he is doubling as a *kappa*, another nasty goblin from Japanese folklore (a green *kappa* is shown beside the umbrella monster pictured in no. 94). *Kappa* need the depression to hold water, which is essential to their survival. One of their unpleasant habits is sucking the liver of a victim out through his or her anus.

1. Translation by John Carpenter. In this poem the character for *kasa* in *hanagasa* means "hat" in modern Japanese, but traditionally it also had the meaning of "umbrella."

93. *Dyer's Stencil*: Umbrella monster
Late Edo-early Meiji period, 19th century
Paper, with silk threads
15 1/2 x 10 1/8 in. (39.4 x 25.8 cm.)
Kupferstich-Kabinett, Staatliche Kunstsammlungen Dresden

This umbrella monster, an echo of Toyokuni's actor print (no. 92), was designed for the repeat decoration of a kimono.

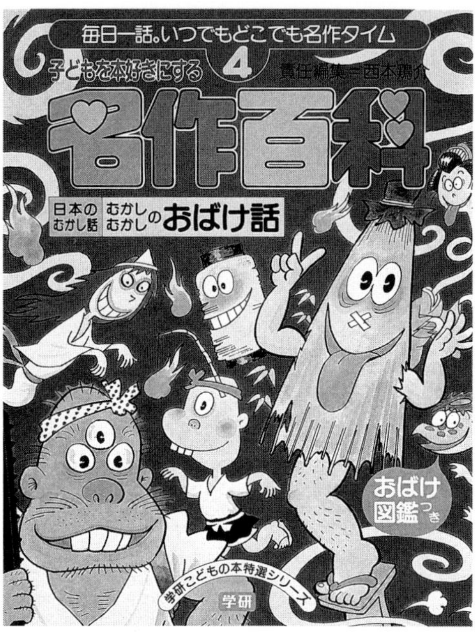

94. *Cover of a Children's Book*
Japanese Fairy Tales: Very Very Old Monster Tales
Volume 4 of *Meisaku hyakka* (Encyclopedia of masterpieces), 1st ed. 1986
Shôwa-Heisei periods, 1990
Publisher: Gakken, Tokyo
10 1/8 x 8 1/4 in. (25.7 x 21 cm.)
Collection of Lisa and Ken Normand, Sugamo, Tokyo

The umbrella goblin is still popular in Japanese comics and television serials, especially in the summer, when ghosts are intended to send refreshing chills down the spine. This is a story book for children ages three to seven. The one-legged, long-tongued *bangasa* monster on the cover reappears on page 68 with the short description: "The umbrella demon startles people with its laughing sound, 'ke, ke, ke!'"

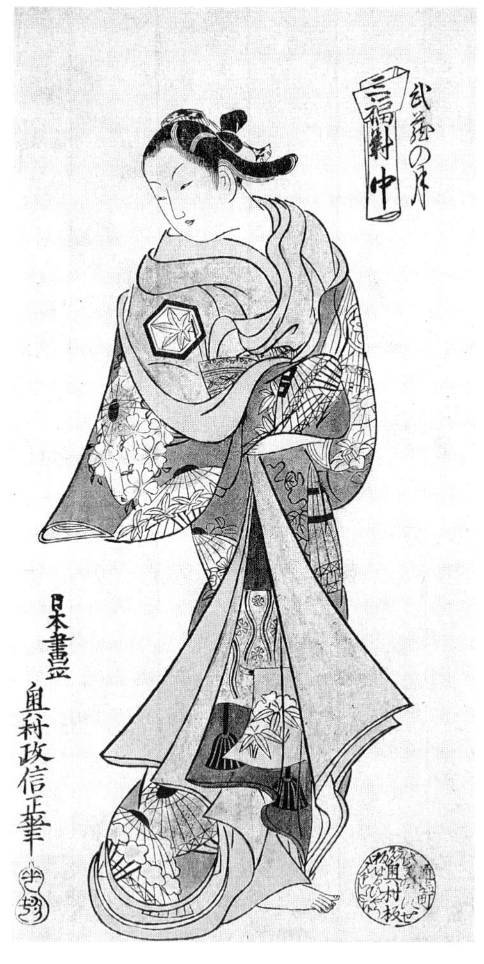

95. Okumura Masanobu (1691-1768)
The Moon of Musashi Province
Edo period, 1730s
Signed: Nihon gakô Okumura Masanobu shôhitsu; sealed: Okumura
Publisher: Okumura Masanobu
Woodblock print with hand-painted pigments, *urushi-e*; center panel of *hosoban* triptych
12 7/16 x 6 1/16 in. (31.8 x 15 cm.)
The Metropolitan Museum of Art, The Howard Mansfield Collection, Purchase, Rogers Fund, 1936, JP2640

Among the different types of umbrella decorating the coat of this barefoot courtesan are dance umbrellas covered with artificial paper flowers (see nos. 82, 83). The gray undergarment has a design of two "curtains of state" (*kichô*) suspended from black lacquer stands. This is the central sheet of an untitled "snow, moon and flower" (*setsu-gekka*) triptych, a grouping that was popular in the Edo period. The courtesan here representing the moon may be Takao of the Miuraya, one of the houses in the Yoshiwara pleasure district.

96. *Crests*
From *Irohabiki monchô* (Book of crests in the order of the *iroha* alphabet), edited by Tanaka Kikuo
Meiji period, 1881
Publisher: Matsuzaki Hanzô, Tokyo
Copperplate-printed illustrated book
Page: 2 3/4 x 6 3/8 in. (7 x 16.2 cm.)
The Fine Print Collection: The Newark Public Library, T.161 44

These crests are arranged in the order of the Japanese *kana* syllabary, or alphabet, known as the "*iroha.*" Crests (*mon*) are designs adopted as insignia by Japanese families, individuals or groups for ornament on formal costumes and personal possessions. The designs were originally used as favorite patterns by courtiers and as heraldic emblems by samurai. By the Edo period, however, even commoners, although they had no surnames, adopted emblems for their fancy clothing. Tradesmen took crests for trademarks and used them to decorate everything from toys to umbrellas. Kabuki actors and courtesans also aped the elite and often took more than one crest. The designs became small and symmetrical, and it was popular to enclose them in a circle. There are between 4,000 and 5,000 design variations. During the the Edo and Meiji periods they were published in designers' catalogues known as *monchô*, usually in black and white. The two umbrella crests in this book also appear in no. 97.

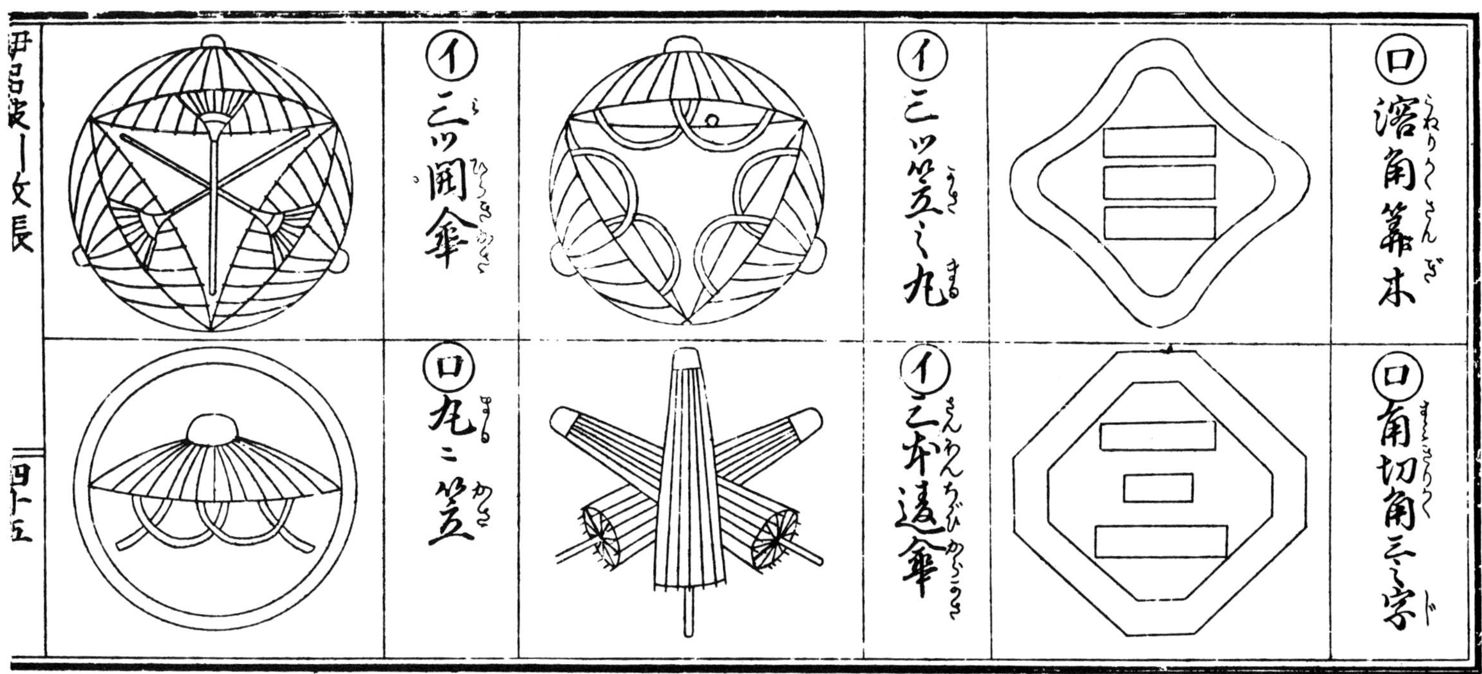

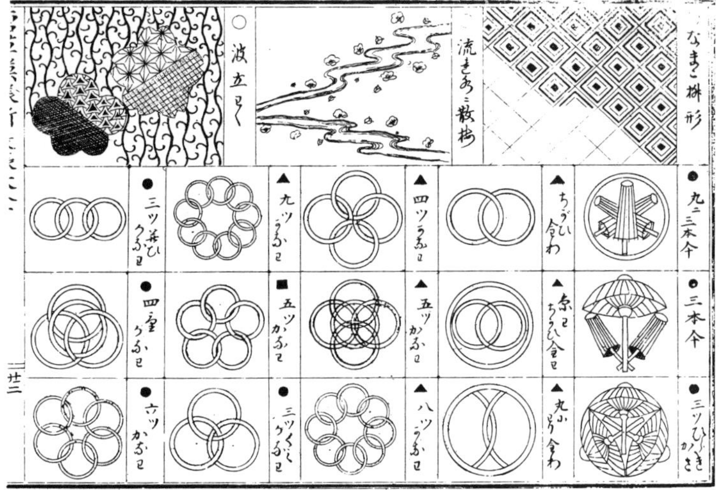

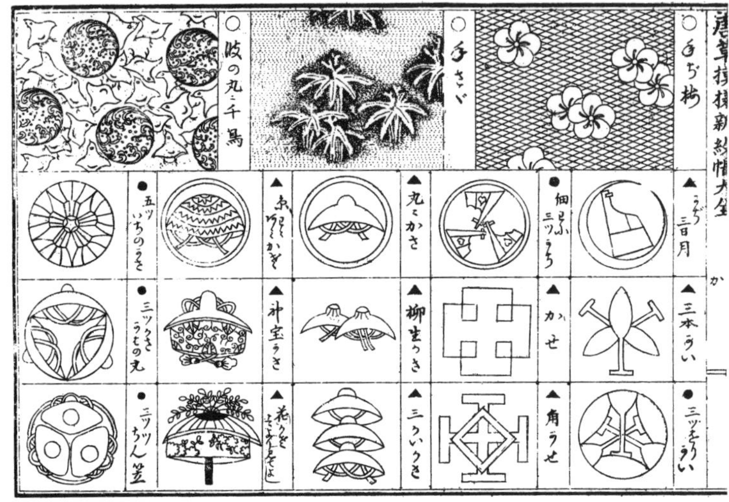

97. *Crests*
From *Karakusa moyô: Musô kôeki monchô* (Arabesque patterns: Peerless and extensively useful book of crests), edited by Murakami Masataka
Meiji period, 1885
Publisher: Maekawa Zembei, Osaka
Woodblock-printed illustrated book
Page: 4 3/8 x 6 1/4 in. (11.2 x 16 cm.)
The Fine Print Collection: The Newark Public Library, M 972 44

Like the preceding book, this catalogue for designers is arranged in the order of the Japanese *iroha* alphabet. The three umbrella crests follow nine hat crests (both pronounced *kasa*) in the *ka* section of the book. By the Meiji period there were three standard umbrella crests in use, each with three crossed umbrellas. The umbrellas are shown open and closed and in a combination of the two.

98. *Dyer's Stencil*: Umbrellas, water and duckweed
Meiji period, late 19th century
Paper, silk thread
12 5/8 x 16 3/4 in. (32.1 x 42.5 cm.)
Cooper-Hewitt National Museum of Design, Smithsonian Institution, Gift of Miss Helen Snyder, 1976-103-103

In this stencil, open *janome* umbrellas, viewed from above, are linked to create a beautifully rhythmic design. The Japanese use stencils (*katagami*) as one method of dyeing textiles. *Katagami* are made from tough, handmade paper pasted together in several layers, treated with astringent persimmon juice or tannin for strengthening, and waterproofed with an application of hard-drying oil. At the cutting stage, eight or nine sheets are stacked, with the artist's drawing on top as a guide, and the cutter's blade is pressed deeply to cut through the stack. In order to strengthen the patterns, some of which are minute and fragile, a network of vertical and horizontal silk threads is then placed between every two cut sheets of paper. With persimmon juice used as an adhesive, the papers enclosing the silk are refitted with precision.

In dyeing, a single stencil is moved gradually across a piece of material to produce the design. Rice paste is applied to the fabric through the stencil and the fabric is then dipped in dye. (When the paste is applied, the hardly visible silk threads in the cutout sections roll just enough not to register on the fabric.) After rinsing, the areas corresponding to the cutout sections of the stencil remain as the resist pattern.

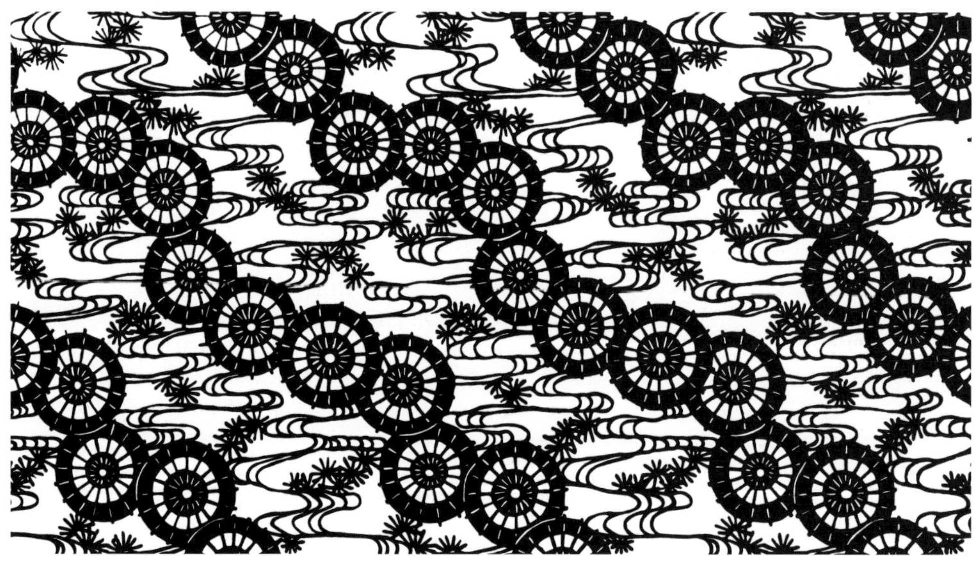

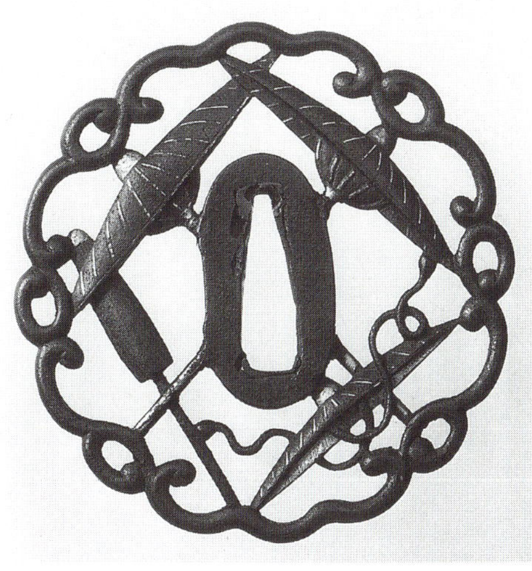

99. *Sword Guard* (*tsuba*): Hat and three umbrellas
Kyô-Shôami type; Edo period, Genroku era (1688-1703)
Sand iron and hammered sheet gold; a few iron bones on the edge
Diam. 3 1/4 in. (8.3 cm.)
The Metropolitan Museum of Art, Bequest of Edward G. Kennedy, 1932, 33.40.34

The openwork design of this sword guard incorporates a rain hat at lower right and three umbrellas, two open and one closed. Tendril-like forms describe the rim.

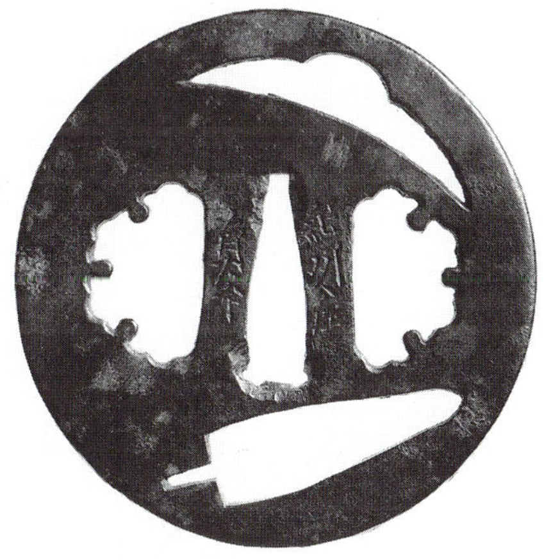

100. *Sword Guard* (*tsuba*): Hat, umbrella and snowflakes
Signed: Kishû jû Teimei [Teimei, a resident of Kii province, active ca.1700]
Mid-Edo period
Iron
3/16 x 3 1/8 in. (0.5 x 7.9 cm.)
Vancouver Museum Collection, DB531

Openings to either side of the tang hole accommodated the auxiliary knife, known as a *kozuka* (small handle), and the *kôgai*, an all-purpose skewer that served as a hair arranger. The outer side of each opening takes the form of a stylized snowflake—a seasonal reference for the openwork shapes of sedge hat and closed umbrella.

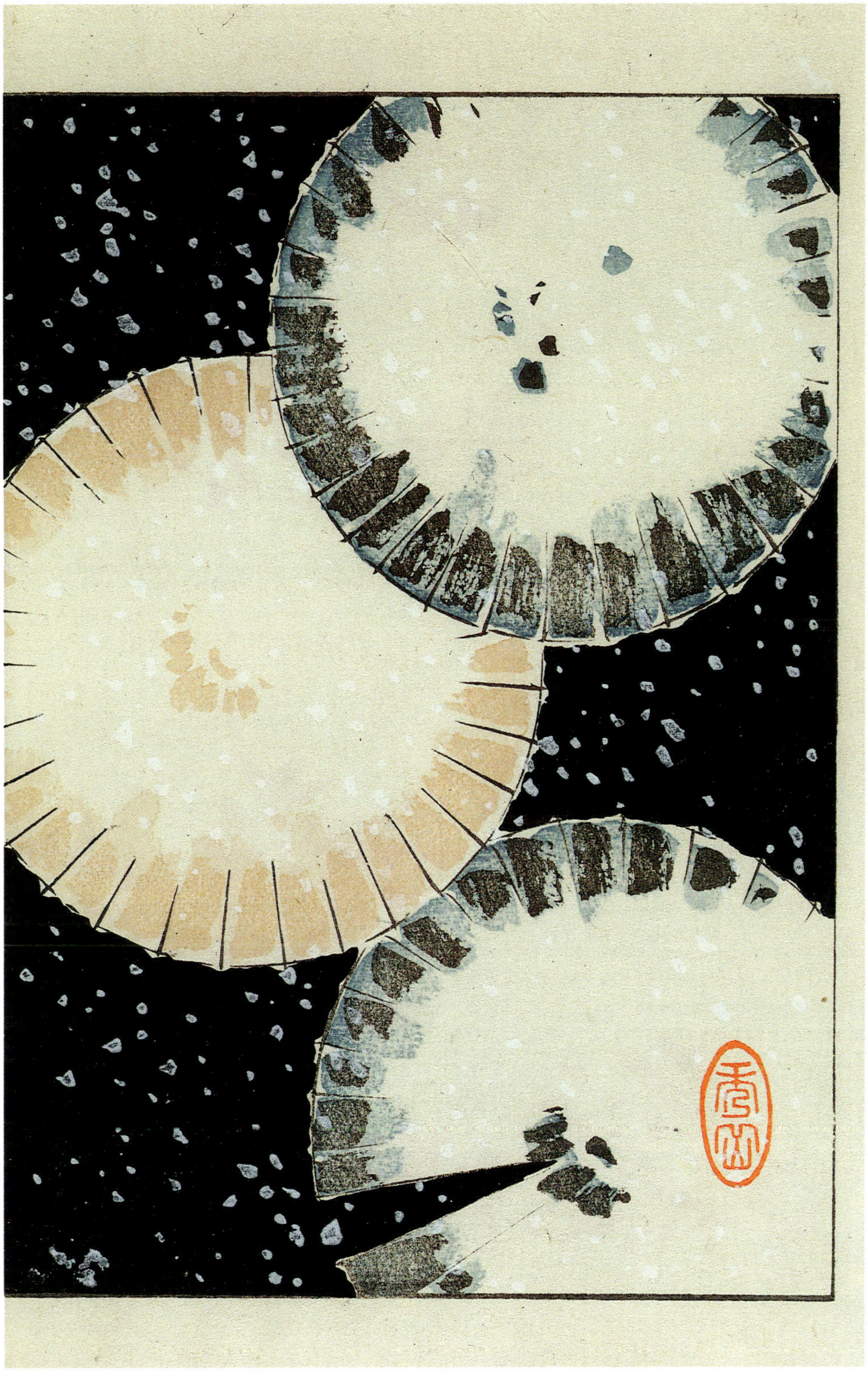

101. Artist unknown
Umbrellas in Snow
From: *Bijutsukai* (Ocean of art), Vol. 1
Meiji period, 1904
Color woodblock-printed illustrated book
Publisher: Unsôdô, Kyoto
9 1/2 x 6 3/8 in. (24.1 x 16.2 cm.)
The Fine Print Collection: The Newark Public Library, A61.132.44

This illustration is from a compendium of stunning, stylized patterns, probably intended for use by textile designers. The publisher, Yamada Naosaburô, was himself a designer and his firm, Unsôdô, in Kyoto at the intersection of Teramachi and Nijô, produced many such design books around the turn of the century. (For another of his publications, see no. 83.)

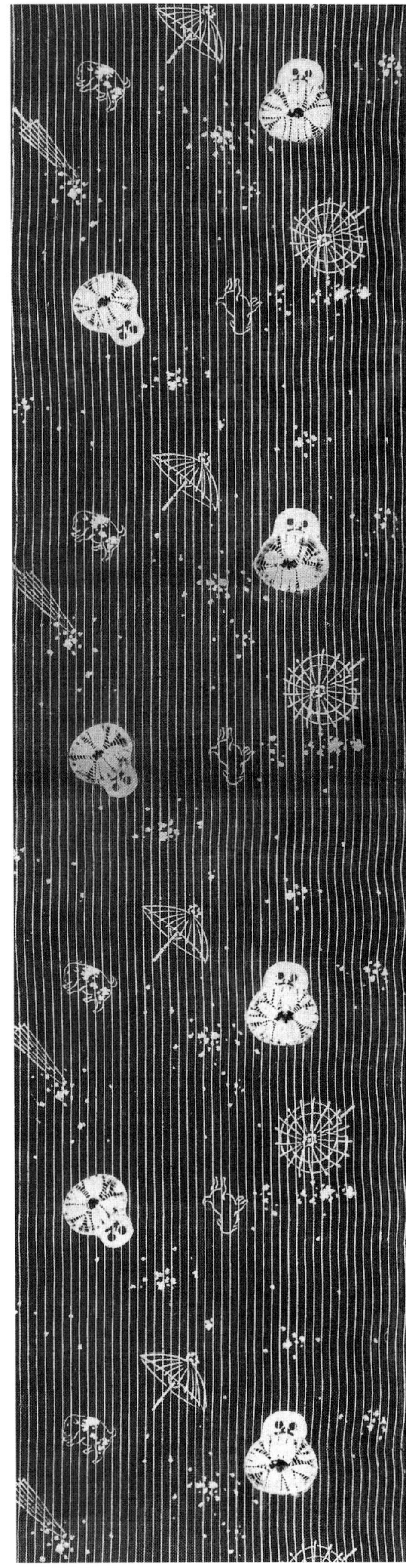

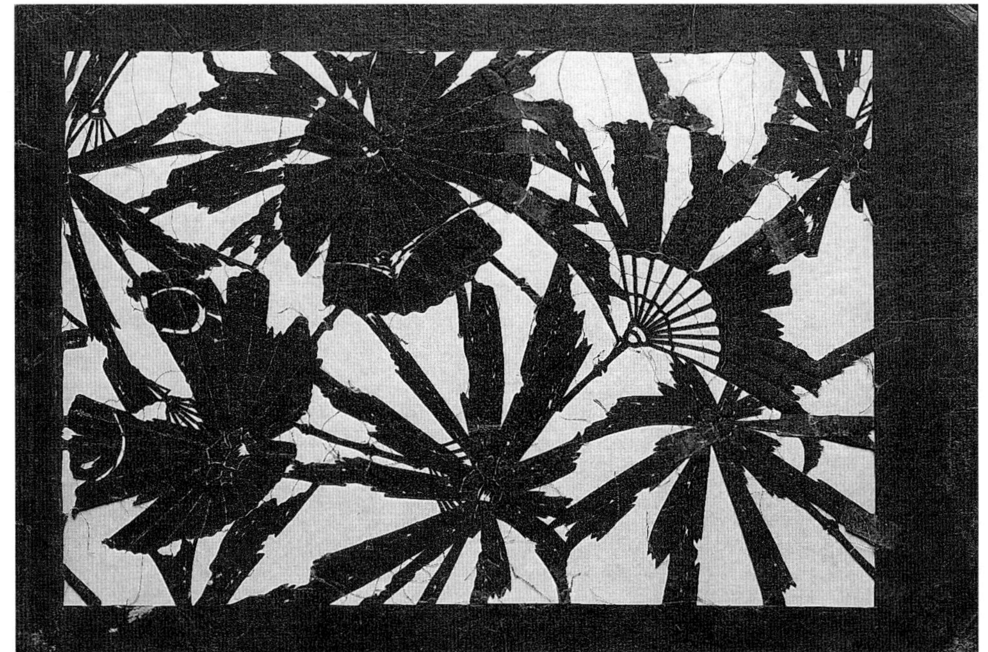

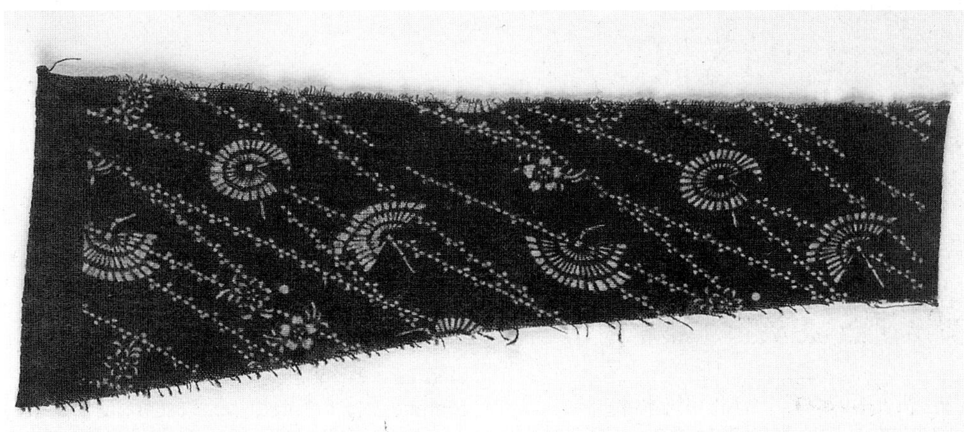

102. *Fabric for a Kimono*
Meiji period, late 19th century
Stencil-dyed cotton
52 3/8 x 13 1/2 in. (133 x 34.3 cm.)
Christensen Fund Collection of Japanese Textiles, on long-term loan to the Seattle Art Museum, L89.6.285

Floating on a striped ground scattered with snowflakes are open and closed umbrellas, interspersed with snowmen and puppies.

103. *Dyer's Stencil*: Broken umbrellas
Meiji period, late 19th century
Paper, silk thread
16 3/8 x 25 1/4 in. (41.6 x 64.1 cm.)
The Cleveland Museum of Art, CMA 25.213

The tattered remnants of at least seven *bangasa* form an unusual design: one umbrella has been blown inside out; others have their covers ripped open, allowing a glimpse of the stretchers. The two better-preserved *bangasa* on the left have crests cut into their covers. The stencil, used in dyeing cotton, has suffered somewhat from wear and tear—the umbrellas now show rather more damage than their designer intended.

104. *Stencil-dyed Cotton*: Broken umbrellas, cherry blossoms and willow branches
Meiji period, late 19th century
5 x 13 1/2 in. (12.7 x 34.3 cm.)
Jitsugetsukan, Tokyo

The pattern shows umbrellas torn and blown inside out by a brisk spring wind.

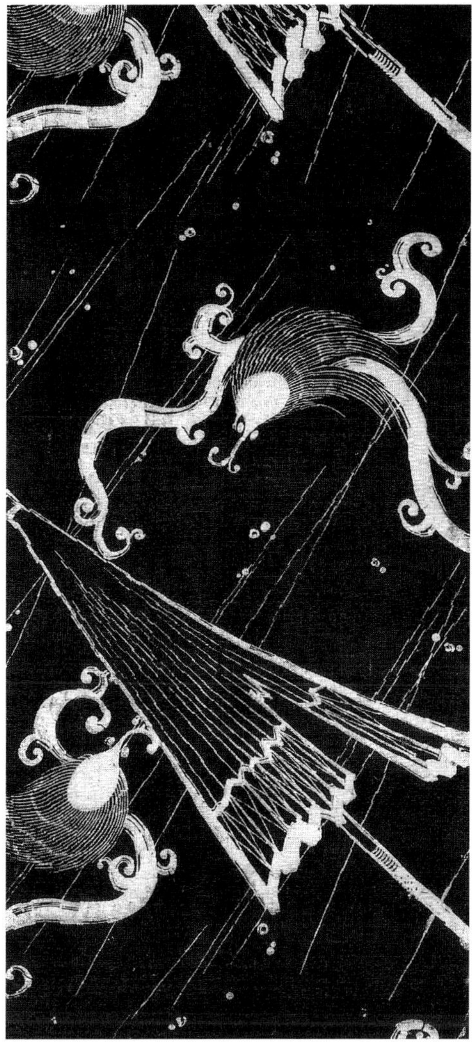

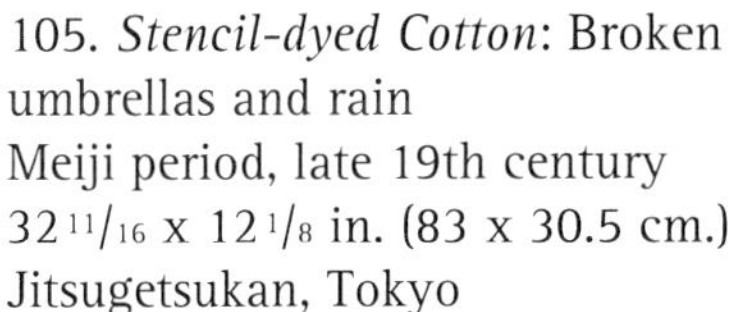

105. *Stencil-dyed Cotton*: Broken umbrellas and rain
Meiji period, late 19th century
32 11/16 x 12 1/8 in. (83 x 30.5 cm.)
Jitsugetsukan, Tokyo

Interspersed with the umbrellas is a mysterious form that may be a straw raincoat but that has also been identified as the god of rain.

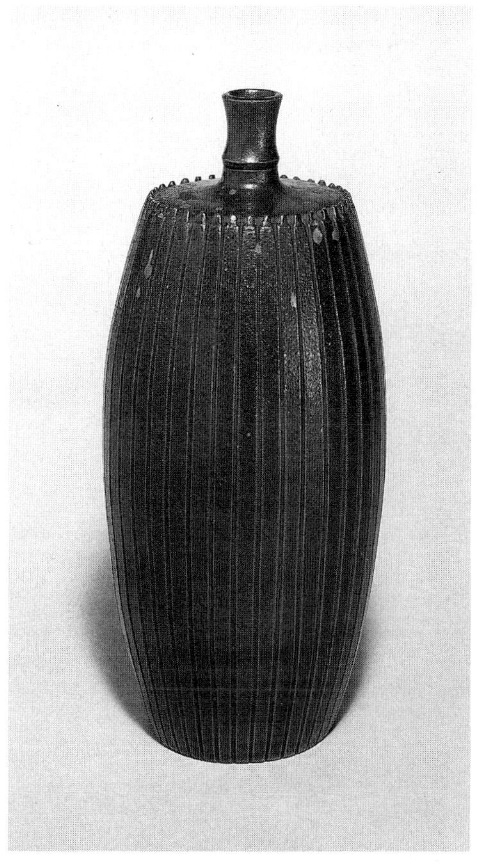

106. *Sake Bottle*
Edo period, early 19th century
Imbe-de, Bizen ware; stoneware with iron slip
9 3/4 x 3 3/4 in. (24.7 x 9.5 cm.)
The Brooklyn Museum, Gift of Mrs. John Lyden, 1992.148.2

Although umbrella-shaped sake bottles (*kasa dokkuri*) were a specialty of Tamba potters in the Edo period, this example is from Bizen province, where potters were also striving to make their mark with inventive, novel designs.[1] The sophisticated sake bottles from the town of Imbe, whose ceramics are known as *Imbe-de*, were highly valued for special ceremonial occasions. Thinly potted, they are made of a very smooth, fine-grained, dark brown clay that is coated with iron slip and commonly flecked with little dots of yellowish wood ash, here creating the happy effect of snowflakes. The elegant shape and precision of this example—the neck is modeled as a bamboo stick and the ribs are realistically defined—suggest a date in the 19th rather than the 18th century. The bottle bulges at the center in imitation of a closed umbrella. The potter mistakenly made the rib tips narrower than the ribs, a decorative affectation that would have been quite impractical; such pencil-thin tips on an actual umbrella would break off easily or poke someone with painful results.

1. For a related example, see Aichi-ken tôji shiryôkan (1986), fig. 36.

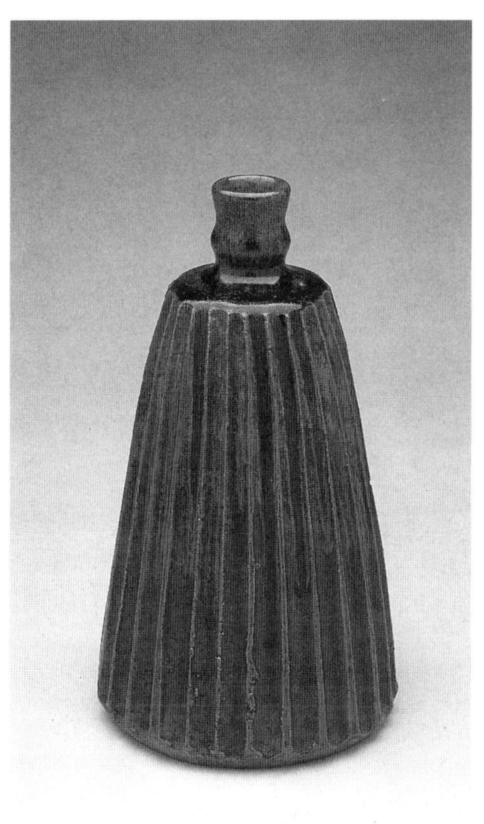

107. *Sake Bottle*
Edo period, late 18th-19th century
Unknown workshop, possibly Satsuma ware; stoneware with iron glaze
7 1/2 x 4 1/2 in. (19.1 x 11.4 cm.)
Collection of Mr. and Mrs. Leighton R. Longhi

The shape is that of a closed umbrella truncated at the center at its widest point, which gives the bottle a stable bottom. The glaze resembles that found on Satsuma pieces in the late Edo period, but there were hundreds of small kilns at this time and it is not always easy to identify their wares.

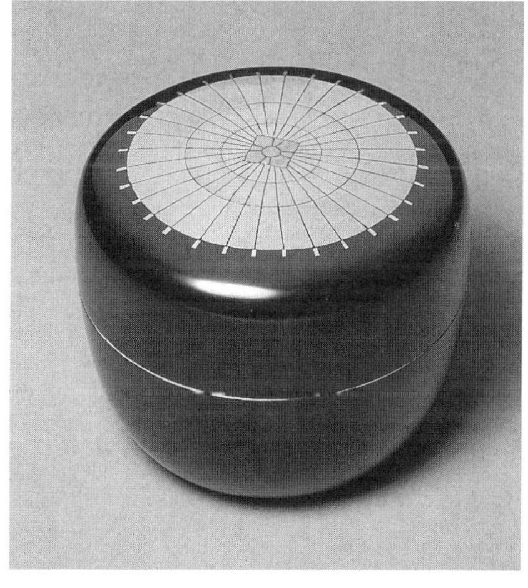

108. Suzuki Hyôsaku II (1905-1991)
Tea Caddy (*hira-natsume*)
Shôwa period, mid-20th century
Black lacquer, lid sprinkled with gold, silver and blue-gold powders
2 1/2 x 3 3/8 in. (6.3 x 8.5 cm.)
Collection of Mutsumi and Misako Suzuki, Kyoto

The inner band of the gold *janome*-type umbrella cover on the circular lid is silver and the protective cap (*kappa*) at the center blue-gold.

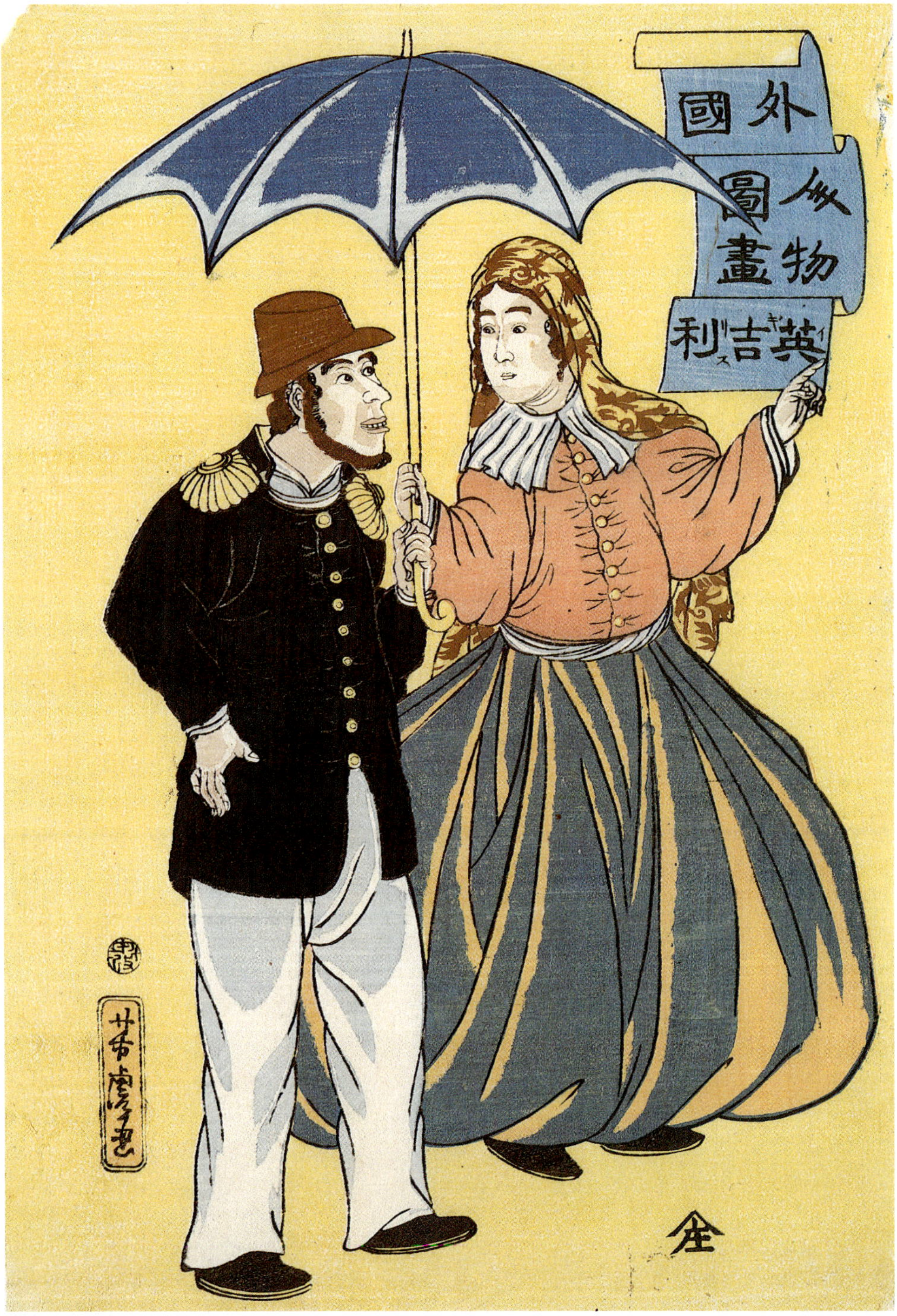

109. Utagawa Yoshitora (active 1830s-70s)
The English
Series: Pictures of Foreigners
Edo period, 1860
Signed: Yoshitora ga
Publisher: Yamada Shôjirô
Color woodblock print; vertical *ôban*
14 3/4 x 10 in. (37.5 x 25.4 cm.)
The Metropolitan Museum of Art, Gift of Lincoln Kirstein, 1959, JP3182

An English couple in Yokohama, which had opened to Western traders in 1859, shares an umbrella in the manner of the traditional lovers' *aiaigasa* (see no. 67).

Simply drawn, with a small hook handle of a type popular during the 1860s and 1870s,[1] the umbrella is just one of many exotic elements pictured by the artist. He is equally fascinated by the gentleman's epaulets and beard, and by the woman's bizarre pantaloons and shawl. Yoshitora even attempts rudimentary Western-style shading, which is rather effective in modeling the umbrella.

1. See Farrell (1985), 49, pl. 5.

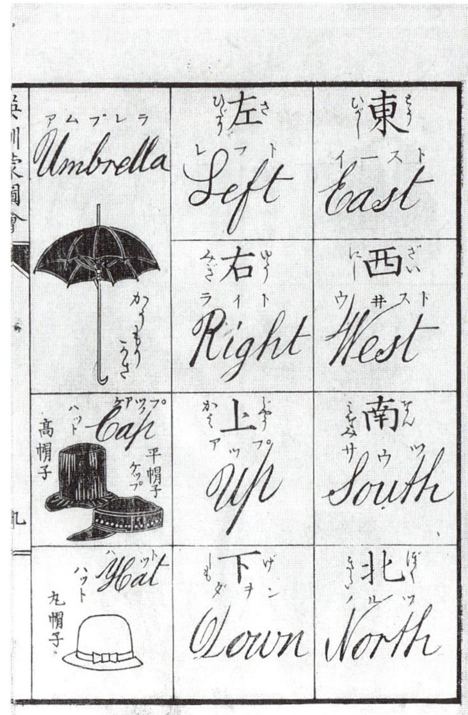

110. Artist unknown
Umbrella, Cap, Hat . . .
From *Eiji kunmô zukai* (Illustrated manual of English instruction)
Meiji period, 1871
Publisher: Kimura Sôsuke and Ogawa Kinsuke, Kyoto
Woodblock-printed illustrated book
Page: 8 3/4 x 5 1/2 in. (22.2 x 14 cm.)
The Metropolitan Museum of Art, Gift of Mrs. Harold G. Henderson, 1986, JIB206

This page is taken from a booklet that is at once a primer for English vocabulary and a guide for the bewildered samurai unfamiliar with Western apparel.

The umbrella is probably an *en-tout-cas* (a combined umbrella and parasol, usually with a colored rather than a black cover and always plain without trimming.) The small hook handle, like that in no. 109, is typical of the 1860s and 1870s. Some artistic license has been taken in the depiction of the runner and stretchers, which would not be so visible in an actual open umbrella.

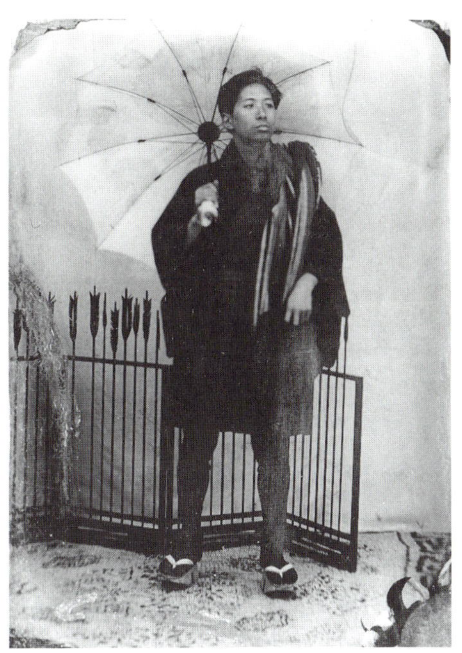

111. Photographer unknown
Young Man with Western Umbrella
Meiji period, early 1870s
Ambrotype
3 3/4 x 2 3/4 in. (9.5 x 7 cm.)
Courtesy of Charles Schwartz Early Photography, New York

The Western umbrella replaced the samurai sword as a badge of status at the beginning of the Meiji period. This young man, posing in front of an arrow stand, sports a fashionable Western-style haircut.

The ambrotype process in photography was replaced by albumen prints in the 1870s.

112. Utagawa Hiroshige III (1843-1894)
Additional Famous Places in Tokyo: View of Benten on Nakanoshima in Shinobazu Pond, Ueno Park
Meiji period, 1881
Signed: Ôju Hiroshige
Publisher: [illegible]
Color woodblock prints; triptych, vertical *ôban*
Together: 14 3/4 x 29 1/8 in. (37.5 x 74 cm.)
The Metropolitan Museum of Art, Gift of Lincoln Kirstein, 1959, JP3259

This triptych shows the imperial family out for a stroll under the cherry blossoms in Ueno Park (see p. 57 and fig. 62), in the suburbs of Tokyo. In accordance with protocol at the time, the family was not identified in the title of the print, which records a purely imaginary incident. The emperor and empress (she is at the center of the left panel, a discreet distance behind her husband) are accompanied by seven ladies-in-waiting, one of whom holds a small child, the future crown prince, who would have been nearly two at this time. Only the men, including the police in the background, are in Western clothing. Emperor Meiji (1852-1912) adopted his Western uniform as early as 1872, but Empress Haruko (later known as Dowager Empress Shôken, 1850-1914) and her ladies wear brocade outer coats (*uchikake*) over loose divided trousers (*hakama*) of heavy red silk and multiple layers of snowy-white silk under-kimono. Their hair is stiffened into thin haloes behind their faces, falling to the waist, but tied here and there with bits of white paper. The empress, impressively calm and dignified, carries a folding fan of painted wooden slats. This was the traditional aristocratic look fashionable at the time, and the favorite—if incongruous—accessory was a fancy French silk umbrella.

The umbrellas in Hiroshige's print, held in the manner of the traditional umbrella of status, may represent *en-tout-cas* (meaning that the silk is waterproofed). The dark covers with contrasting bands near the edges are typical of the 1820s to the 1840s; by 1881 it would have been unusual for an umbrella cover in Europe to be anything other than black. (Emperor Meiji's black silk umbrella with an ivory handle and a button for "one-touch" opening can be found today in the Bunka Gakuen Costume Museum in Tokyo.)[1] The contrasting bands may have been an imaginative evocation of the *yakko* umbrella. The artist definitely used his imagination: it is quite impossible for the cover of a parasol or umbrella to form arches between the ribs, as here. Parasols of the period, although large, were lavishly trimmed, and these have colorful silk tassels hanging from a hole in the handle, a French feature introduced in the 1880s.[2] The white ceramic spheres at the rib tips are clearly indicated.

1. Bunka gakuen fukushoku hakubutsukan (1983), pl. 5. The author is indebted to Sato Yasuko, Bunka Joshi University, Tokyo, for this reference.
2. Letter to the author from Jeremy Farrell, Nottingham, April 29, 1992.

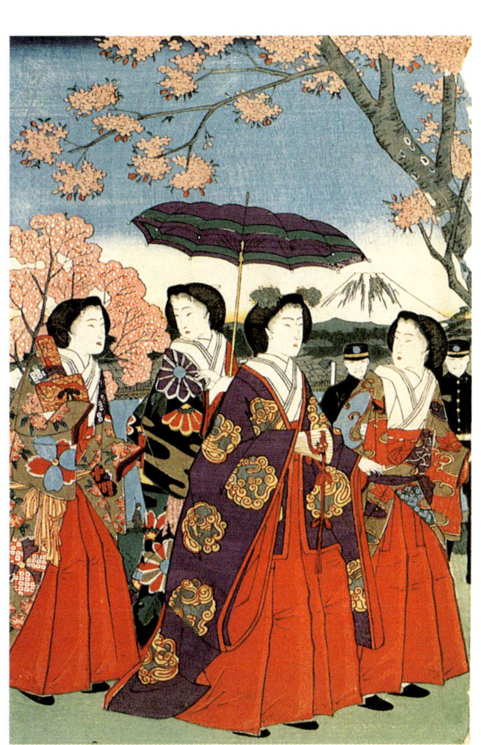

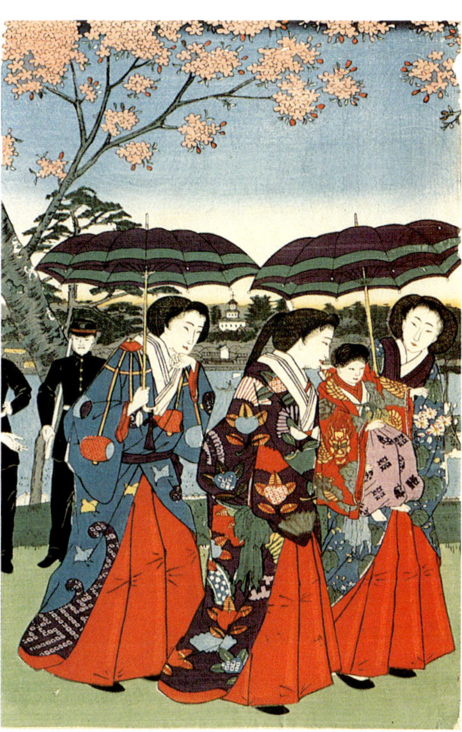

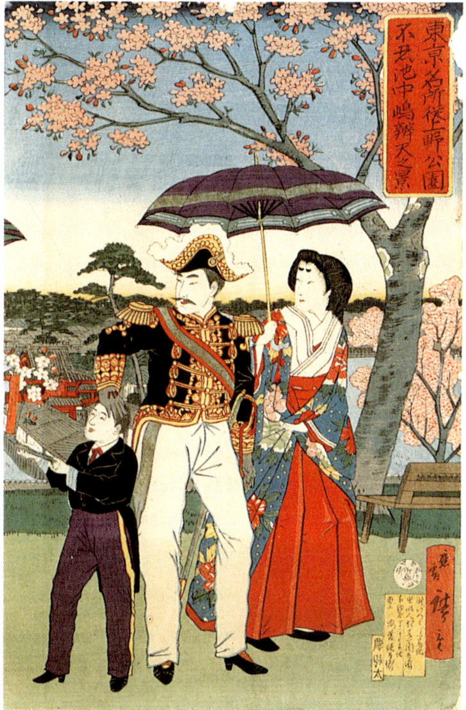

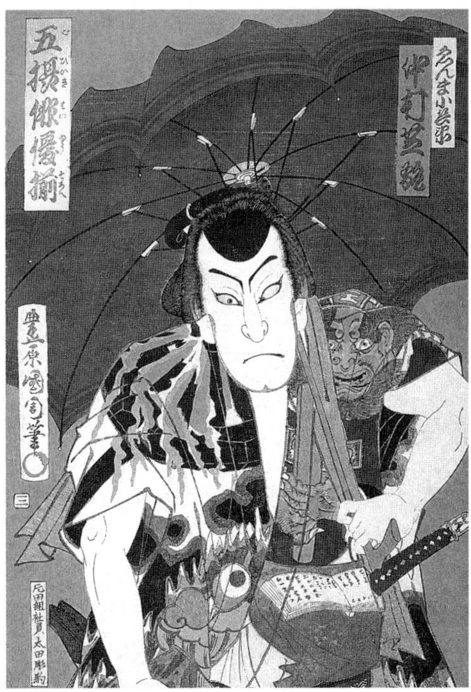

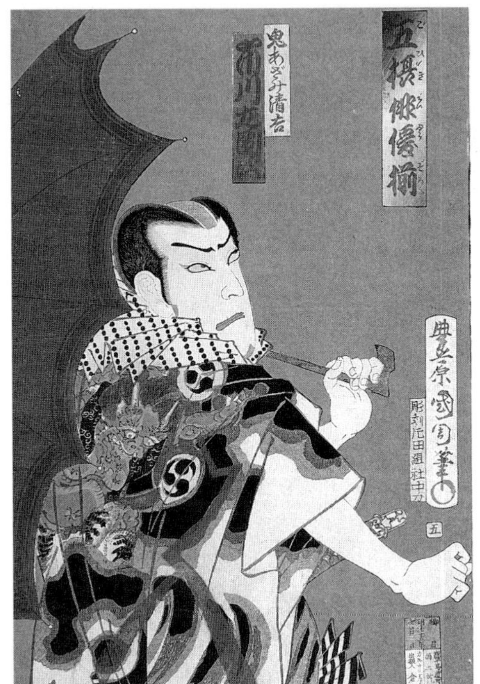

113. Toyohara Kunichika (1835-1900)
113/1. *Nakamura Shikan IV in the role of Emma Kobei*
113/2. *Ichikawa Sadanji I in the role of Oni Azami Seikichi*
Series: Parade of Five Great Stars
Meiji period, 1882
Signed: Toyohara Kunichika *hitsu*; sealed by the artist
Publisher: Kurata Daisuke
Color woodblock prints; vertical *ôban*
Each: 13 7/8 x 9 1/8 in. (35.2 x 23.2 cm.)
Collection of Ayako Abe

In no. 113/1 Kunichika has given a faithful depiction of an umbrella of about 1860-70. It appears to have a ten-rib all-metal frame; the artist has even shown the small pieces of fabric around the middle bits, the joints between the stretchers and ribs, which protect the cover from wear. The small white spheres at the rib tips, made of ceramic or vitreous-enameled metal, are also clearly visible in both prints. Handles of the period, however, were usually more ornate than these examples.[1]

The pale blue disc between the ribs and the cover at the top center of the umbrella in no. 113/1 is called an inside cap and is also protection against wear. European inside caps were normally black, or matched the color of the cover in an *en-tout-cas*. The example here is probably a case of artistic license; Japanese artists liked to emphasize minor details, the purpose of which they might not understand (and sometimes misinterpreted) when depicting a European object.

These two prints are from a set of portraits of five famous actors in five different plays by Kawatake Mokuami, the foremost Kabuki dramatist. Each holds a Western umbrella and wears an appropriate but fantastic costume. The umbrellas are not integral to their roles (both plays are, in fact, pre-Meiji and thus predate the use of Western umbrellas), but are mere fashionable attributes supplied by the artist, an allusion, probably, to Mokuami's famous play *Shiranami gonin otoko* (The five bandits), also known as *Benten Kozô*, first performed in 1862. In the well-known Mustering scene five thieves line up on the *hanamichi* with open umbrellas held aloft; the word *shiranami* (bandit) is written in bold black characters on each of the otherwise plain *bangasa*.[2] Kunichika first used a Western umbrella in another portrait of Nakamura Shikan IV in his 1873 series *Haiyû rokkasen* (Actors as six immortal poets).[3]

In no. 113/1, the popular Nakamura Shikan IV (1830-1899) is shown with the figure of Emma, king of hell, depicted on the robe over his left shoulder, a reference to his role as Emma Kobei in the play of that name (also called *Noborigoi taki no shirahata*), first performed in 1851. Kobei, a carver of Buddhist images and a petty criminal, commits suicide after learning that he has unwittingly abetted an incestuous love affair.

In no. 113/2, Ichikawa Sadanji I (1842-1904) is wearing a garment decorated with the god of thunder, shown as a horned demon (*oni*) with a circle of thunder-making drums. This alludes to the actor's role as Oni Azami Seikichi (Demon Thistle Seikichi) in *Kosode Soga azami no ironui*, popularly known as *Izayoi Seishin* (Sixteenth Night and Seishin), a play first performed in Edo in 1859. Seishin is a young monk who, after a failed suicide attempt with his lover, the prostitute Izayoi (the "Sixteenth Night," when the moon begins to wane), embarks on a life of crime under the name of Oni Azami Seikichi.

Kunichika portrays both actors frozen in a climactic pose known as a *mie*. While contorting his limbs, the actor may also open his eyes wide and at the critical moment slowly cross one pupil in the direction to which he wishes to call attention, sometimes turning down the corners of his mouth in an exaggerated manner at the same time.

1. Letter to the author from Jeremy Farrell, Nottingham, April 29, 1992.
2. For the interpretation of these Kabuki subjects, the author is indebted to Mark Oshima. The Mustering scene from *Benten Kozô* is translated in Leiter (1979b), 37ff.
3. Musée de la Mode et du Costume (1989), fig. 94.

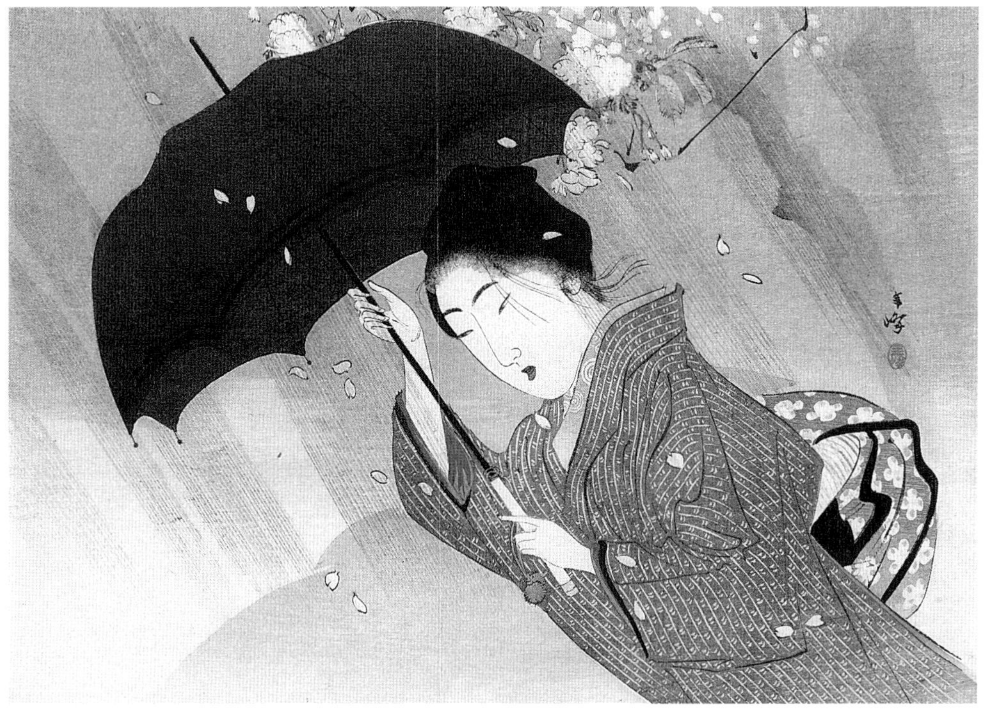

114. Kobayashi (Tsutsui) Toshimine (active early 20th century)
Shower Under Cherry Trees
From the journal *Bungei kurabu* (Literary club)
Meiji period, ca. 1910
Signed: Toshimine; sealed: Toshimine
Color woodblock print
8 13/16 x 11 5/8 in. (22.2 x 29.5 cm.)
The Metropolitan Museum of Art, Gift of Lincoln Kirstein, 1959, JP3291

The umbrella, presumably an *en-tout-cas*, is somewhat stylized: the ball rib tips are too long and the ivory handle is quite plain. The latter may well be Japanese, since many ivory handles for umbrellas and parasols were exported to the West from the 1880s onward (see no. 116). The deep, domed cover is typical of the early 20th century, and was much appreciated by Japanese women. The black stick was burnished by the printer to resemble lacquer.

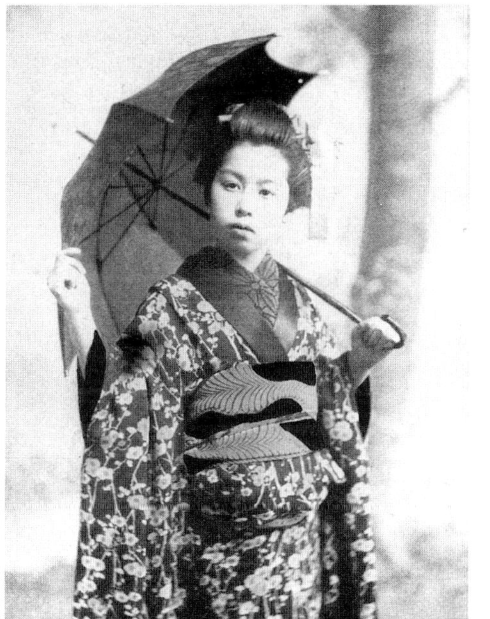

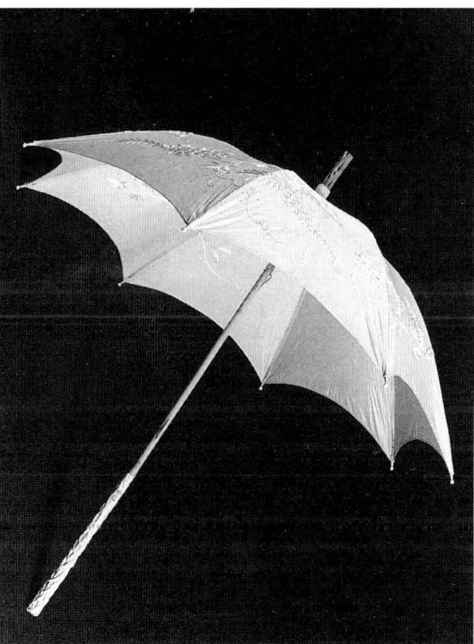

115. Photographer unknown
The Modern Geisha
Meiji period, ca.1900-10
Real photo postcard; hand-colored gelatin silver print
5 1/2 x 3 1/2 in. (14 x 8.9 cm.)
Horesh Collection, London

Posed against a painted backdrop, the geisha handles her *en-tout-cas* with haughty self-confidence.

116. *Parasol*
Meiji period, late 19th century
Japanese: silk cover; carved ivory handle signed: Yoshitsugu; and sealed: Tsugu
Frame and stick (stamped: B. Altman and Co., New York) assembled in the U.S.
L. 31 in. (78.7 cm.); Diam. 33 in. (83.8 cm.), when opened
Collection of Orientations Gallery, New York

The cream-colored silk cover embroidered with a wisteria design and the ivory handle carved with iris were made to order in Japan for the B. Altman department store in New York City. The metal frame, ivory rib tips, and wood stick are of local manufacture. Benjamin Altman (1840-1913), founder of the store that bore his name, was himself a serious collector of Japanese lacquer and sword fittings and of Chinese porcelain, cloisonné and jade, as well as of European paintings, tapestries and furniture, all of which he left to the Metropolitan Museum of Art.

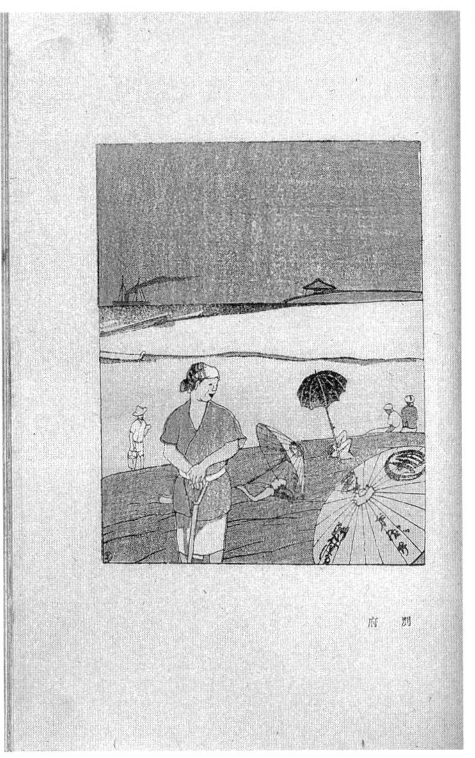

117. Mizushima Nihou (or Nihofu) (1884-1958)
Beppu
From *Tôkaidô gojûsantsugi fu setonaikai* (Fifty-three stages of the Tôkaidô. Supplement: The Inland Sea)
Taishô period, 1920
Publisher: Bunendô
Color woodblock print in a typeset hardcover book
Page: $7\frac{3}{16}$ x $4\frac{13}{16}$ in. (18.3 x 12.2 cm.); image: $3\frac{9}{16}$ x $3\frac{1}{16}$ in. (9.1 x 8 cm.)
Ravicz Collection

Nihou's travel journal includes a stopover at Beppu, a famous hot-spring resort on the eastern coast of Kyûshû, on the Inland Sea.[1] A special feature of the spa are hot sand baths on the beach, where people half bury themselves in the black sand, as shown in this illustration. The artist, who embellished his text with twenty-nine color woodcuts and forty-nine line drawings, was a professional cartoonist, known for his baseball cartoons in the Osaka *Asahi News*. In this miniature, a uniformed attendant in the foreground holds a shovel used to bury people in the healing sands. A steamship in the distance provides daily service between Beppu and Osaka. Acting as sunshades are two *bangasa* of the sort provided by local inns, and one Western umbrella, its stick elongated by tying it to a pole.

Nihou's account of this scene is both humorous and frightening, calling to mind the fact that there are numerous *jigoku* (hells, i.e., boiling ponds) at Beppu. The author was unhappy and uncomfortable. He found the people unfriendly, had trouble locating lodging, and was disturbed by the oppressive dampness and humidity that engulf the area and by the smell of sulfur emanating from the ground. When he saw the sand baths that he had heard so much about, the bathers were not the beauties depicted on postcards advertising the spot, but dusty, unattractive old men and women, moaning and groaning in the hot sand. They had propped up Western umbrellas to keep the direct rays of the sun from burning their exposed, upturned faces. Disgusted by their grotesque appearance, Nihou found himself observing the scene with mixed feelings of both derision and sympathy.

1. The genre of travel sketch-books, many published by Kanao Tanejirô (1879-1947) under his Bunendô imprint, flourished between 1905 and 1920. The subject is discussed by Johnson (1990).

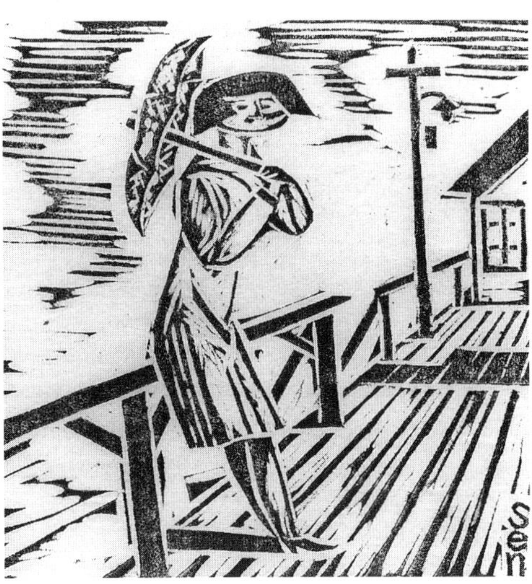

118. Maekawa Sempan (1889-1960)
Parasol
From the portfolio *Yagai shôhin* (Small outdoor works), Vol. 1, Set no. 2
Shôwa period, 1929
Signed: Sen
Woodblock print
Image: $5\frac{1}{2}$ x $5\frac{1}{2}$ in. (14 x 14 cm.)
Ravicz Collection

Sempan was a leading artist of the creative-print (*sôsaku hanga*) movement, which arose in the early 20th century in opposition to the traditional reliance on professional artisans. A caricaturist and magazine illustrator, he spent seven years laboriously teaching himself to make woodcuts. He carved and printed the miniatures in this portfolio himself. His *moga*, or modern girl, holds a six-rib Western parasol.

"When I realized I could turn back into a tiger again I felt a little better and calmed down. Now I think I should leave behind my skin, after all."

Takei, who was an illustrator for a children's magazine, began to express himself as a creative artist in the early 1930s and designed at least 266 limited-edition miniature books drawn from the world of children and toys. He was inspired by his own collection of folk toys and by Paul Klee.[1] At first he called his miniatures *Takei mamebon* (Takei's bean books), but later switched to *Takei kanpon* (Takei's printed books). "Tiger of the 20th Century" was his sixty-fourth miniature book, with woodblocks carved and printed in Tokyo by the artist himself.

1. Merritt (1990), 269-270.

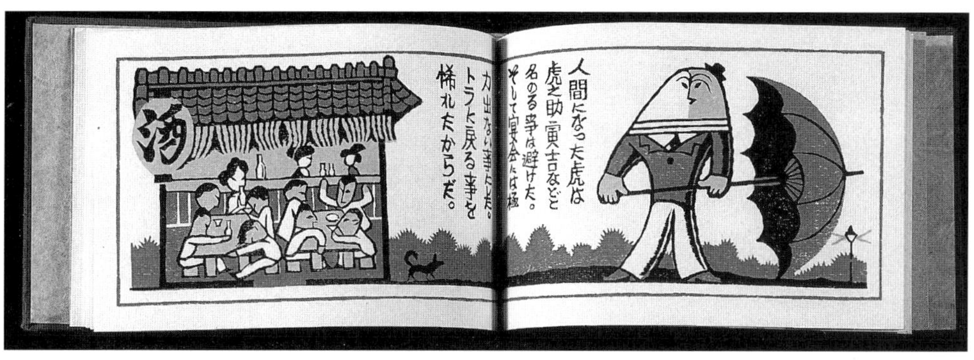

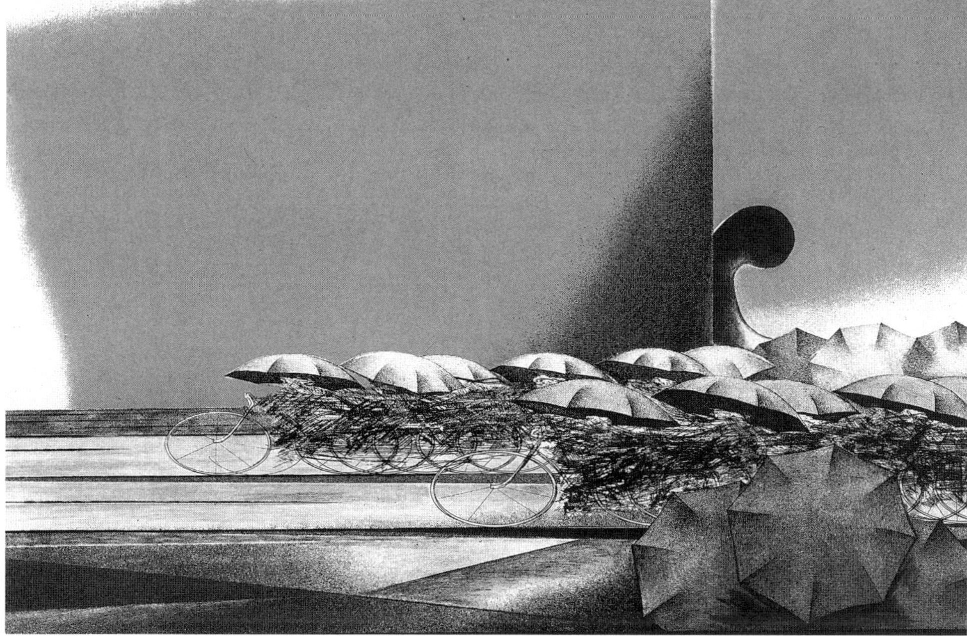

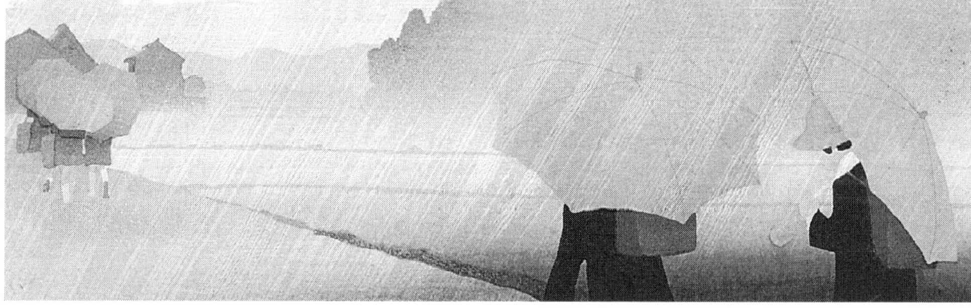

119. Takei Takeo (1894-1983)
Mr. Tiger
From *Nijusseiki no tora* (Tiger of the 20th century)
Shôwa period, 1966
Color woodblock-printed illustrated book; numbered 172/300
Page: 3 3/16 x 4 3/4 in. (8.1 x 12 cm.)
Lawrence and Bessie Weinberg Collection, Chicago

The story is about a tiger (*tora*) who turns into a man. Roughly paraphrased, it begins: "I am a tiger of the 20th century, but tigers are not fashionable. Should I be a truck, a trunk or a radio? I don't want to be something small. Perhaps it would be appropriate to be a man. Instead of leaving my tiger skin for posterity, it would be better to leave behind my good name."

In the illustration shown here the hero holds a large, Western-style umbrella, part of his natty costume as a well-dressed Japanese man and a symbol of his having become a human being. He keeps a safe distance from the bar on the left, with its customers in various stages of inebriation, for, as the text explains: "The tiger that became a human didn't name himself Toranosuke or Torakichi. He didn't go to parties because he was afraid of turning back into a tiger." In Japan the saying is that a person who is drunk and boisterous has turned into a big tiger. Even taking a name with the word *tora* in it might bring out his tiger nature.

The hero is eventually disillusioned with life as a human. He resigns from his job in an office and begins drinking heavily.

120. Kuroda Shigeki (b. 1953)
Infinite Red
Shôwa period, 1984
Signed and numbered: Shigeki Kuroda, 35/50
Etching, aquatint and drypoint
19 1/2 x 25 3/4 in. (49.5 x 65.4 cm.)
The Fine Print Collection: The Newark Public Library

Kuroda has made his reputation on permutations of the single bizarre theme of speeding bicyclists with Western umbrellas.

121. Daniel Kelly (b. 1947), American
Buttercups
1983
Signed and numbered: Daniel Kelly, 237/250
Color woodblock print on French paper
9 9/16 x 30 in. (24.2 x 76.2 cm.)
The Metropolitan Museum of Art, Anonymous Gift, 1986, JP3698

Daniel Kelly, originally from Idaho, has lived in Kyoto on and off since 1977. He observed these Japanese girls with book bags, rubber boots and yellow vinyl umbrellas walking to school on a country road on a misty, rainy day.

122. *Covered Jar*
Arita ware; porcelain painted in Kakiemon-style enamels
Edo period, late 17th century
Cover: Delftware, 1701-22
H. 21 5/8 in. (55 cm.)
Porzellansammlung, Staatliche Kunstsammlungen Dresden

This jar was made in a small porcelain factory in the town of Arita, near Nagasaki, for export to Europe. It was probably commissioned by the Dutch East India Company at a time when, owing to unsettled conditions caused by the fall of the Ming dynasty in 1644, Chinese wares were temporarily difficult to obtain. Porcelain exports from Japan peaked in the 1680s.

The shape is Chinese and the panel design shows two Chinese figures of indeterminate sex, one holding a Chinese-style fan, the other a domed parasol. The parasol is depicted without ribs, as if the painter was following a model that left him slightly confused. The inspiration for the composition of plum, crysanthemum and bamboo with oversize bird and blossoms comes from Chinese enamels of the late Kangxi period (1662-1722), and the figure types can be found in 17th-century Chinese blue and white export wares of the Transitional period (1620-83).[1]

Massive jars such as this were destined for display in European palaces, in this case either the building called the Dutch Palace or its successor, the uncompleted Japanese Palace of Frederick Augustus I (1670-1733), elector of Saxony and king of Poland, better known as Augustus the Strong, who began forming his important collection of Oriental porcelain in Dresden around 1715.[2]

1. Kilburn (1981), no. 106; and Little (1983), no. 20.
2. Reichel (1981), 119-122, no. 18.

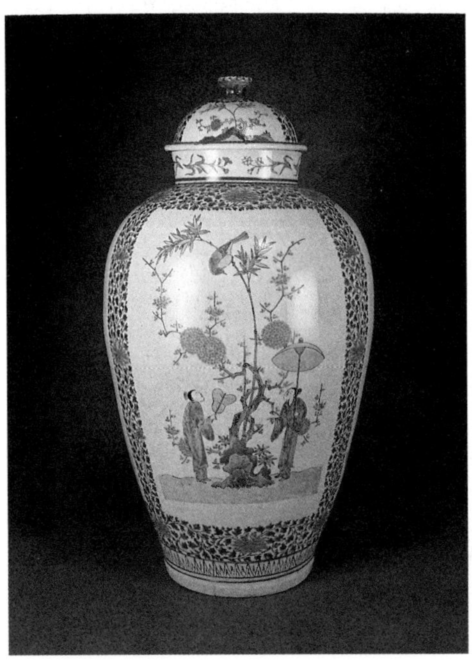

Color plate, p. 55

123. *Imari Plate: Parasol Ladies*
Edo period, ca. 1740
Arita ware; porcelain with underglaze blue and overglaze enamels
Diam. 9 5/16 in. (24 cm.)
The Mary and Jackson Burke Collection

The design on this Western-style dinner plate was derived from a watercolor drawing by the Dutch artist Cornelis Pronk (1691-1759). Pronk's chinoiserie design (no. 123a), one of three ordered by the Dutch East India Company in 1734 for manufacture in China and Japan, has been interpreted by the Japanese artist in his own terms.

Pronk's drawing shows a Chinese noblewoman standing at the edge of a pond and making a gesture toward three wading birds on the ground in front of her; a maidservant holds a fringed silk parasol overhead. A duck is just diving into the pond and there are reeds and grasses in the background. Birds, maid and mistress are repeated in medallions around the rim. The design was copied quite faithfully by Chinese potters at the Jingdezhen kilns in Jiangxi province.

The freely drawn Japanese version strays rather far from the model, however. The proper noblewoman has been transformed into the more familiar ukiyo-e courtesan, a lovely denizen of the pleasure quarters. With her hands hidden in the folds of her kimono, she stands demurely beneath a pink paper parasol that is delineated with considerable detail, including bands of red embroidery on the stretchers. The duck was apparently misunderstood by the Japanese copyist, and now resembles a flower bud. The maid has her head turned backward in an awkward manner that makes little sense. In the licensed quarters it would be quite inappropriate, of course, for the parasol to be carried by a woman. Cumbersome and heavy, the long-stick umbrellas of status were of necessity and by regulation carried over courtesans by strong footmen (see nos. 49, 51).

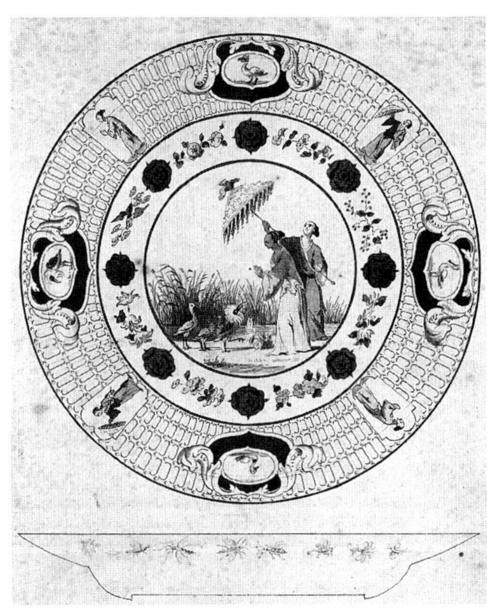

123a. Cornelis Pronk (1691-1759), *Design for Porcelain: Parasol Ladies*, 1734-38. Watercolor. Rijksmuseum, Amsterdam

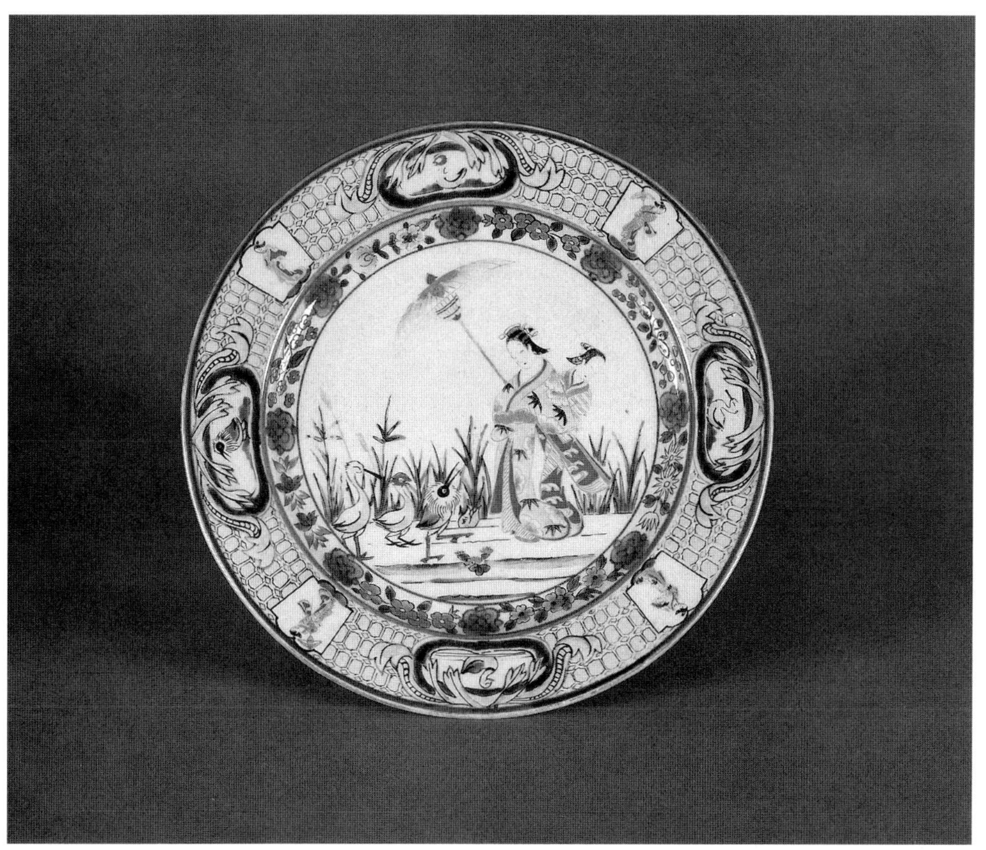

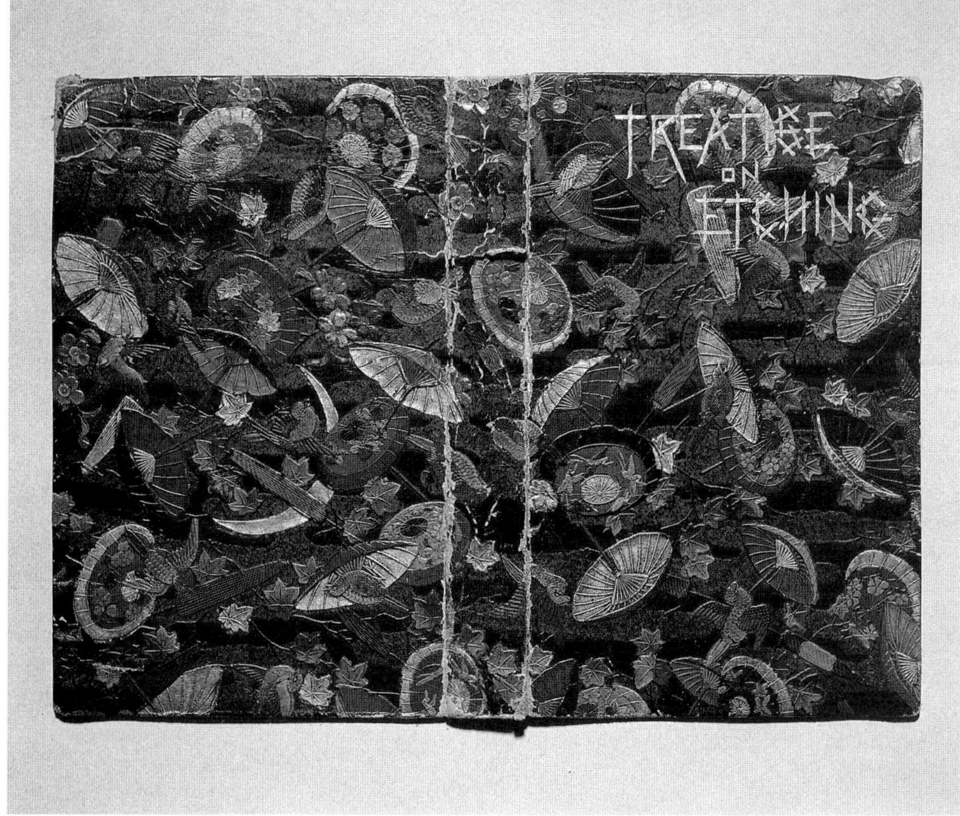

124. *Folder*
Meiji period, ca.1870-85
Japanese: embossed and painted leather, with gold leaf; title applied in France
Overall: 9 1/2 x 13 5/16 in. (24.2 x 33.9 cm.)
The Cleveland Museum of Art, Ingalls Library, Gift of George A. Goddard

This folder was made as a cover for the deluxe edition of Maxime Lalanne's *Treatise on Etching*, translated from the French by J. A. Delaborde, Paris. The first French edition was published in 1866 and the latest American edition in 1885. This volume, undated, is printed in both French and English. The folder was probably chosen by an early owner, not by the publisher. It was the custom of French publishers to leave books unbound so that the collector could commission the binding or cover.

The design is a mélange of typically Japanese motifs selected to delight a Western audience. Open and closed umbrellas (including the *janome* type, painted parasols [*e-higasa*] and *bangasa*) are decoratively intermingled with birds, maple leaves and cherry blossoms drifting against horizontal bands of cloud on a dark-brown granulated ground. The Japanese craftsman paid careful attention to an accurate rendering of the most minute details of the design.

The craft of so-called gilt leather, Moorish in origin, was developed in Europe in the early Middle Ages. Tanned hides were cut into standard sizes, covered with silver foil and varnished to give a golden gloss (the yellow varnish caused the silver to appear gold). It was a Dutchman who invented the technique of embossing thin sheets of gilt leather on wood press-molds in the early 17th century. Long vertical pieces of gilt leather (*goudleer*) were in vogue as wall hangings in the 17th and 18th centuries, second only to tapestry as the most sumptuous (and expensive) mural decoration. The Dutch East India Company brought some samples to Japan, at first as gifts for the shogun and other dignitaries and then for private trade. The Japanese had no use for wall covering, of course, but they cut up pieces to make exotic-looking tobacco pouches, draw-string purses, and small boxes and screens, among other things. As demand increased in the 18th century, the imports, called *kinkarakawa* (gold Chinese leather), were imitated by the leather craftsmen of Himeji, a city famous for the production of white leather.

In general, Japanese gilt leather seems to have been relatively flat (unlike the highly embossed European versions) and to emphasize clearly etched linear design; gold leaf was applied only selectively, not all over. Today one Japanese craftsman has revived the technique, using it to produce shoes and handbags, and even versions of Old Masters.[1]

Small panels of embossed and painted leather with traditional Japanese motifs were made for export in the Meiji period. As late as 1903, the influential Boston-based Japanese art dealer Bunkio Matsuki (1867-1934) was selling such panels at auction at the American Art Association in New York. Some are identified in his catalogue as 18th-century Himeji leather, others as modern. Meiji leather panels were apparently purchased at the Matsuki sale by New York collectors Mr. and Mrs. Henry O. Havemeyer and are now in the Metropolitan Museum of Art. The dimensions (approximately 10 1/2 x 6 1/2 inches) are ideally suited for book covers.[2]

The Cleveland folder corresponds exactly with one section of a larger embossed and painted leather panel, 24 1/8 x 24 1/8 inches square, in the George Walter Vincent Smith Museum, Springfield, Massachusetts.[3] Presumably both pieces were made on the same mold. There are three quite similar pieces of Japanese leather, each about 20 inches (50 cm.) square, with Japanese motifs (butterflies and fans) in the Rijksdienst beeldende Kunst, Veere, The Netherlands.[4]

1. Nihonten kikaku renrakukai, eds. (1989), 130-131; Tanaka-van Daalen (1988); and Morishita et al. (1990).
2. Acc. nos. 29.100.482-487. See American Art Association (1903), 20; Matsuki offered Dutch gilt-leather fragments at the same auction.
3. This panel has been erroneously described as a wallpaper sample (Hosley [1990], 74, 180), a confusion with *kinkarakawagami*, imitation gilt leather made from handmade paper treated to capture the look of embossed leather. Wallpaper of this kind, usually based on contemporary European designs (unlike the conventional native motifs favored by Meiji leather workers), was in production by 1870 and was actively exported to the West as a luxury item between the mid-1880s and 1915, when unadorned walls became the popular preference.
4. Letter to the author from Dr. Eloy F. Koldeweij, University of Leiden, August 11, 1992. The author is also grateful for assistance from Ann B. Abid, Head Librarian, The Cleveland Museum of Art; Niikura-Matsumura Eri, The National Museum of Modern Art, Tokyo; Emil G. Schnorr, Conservator, George Walter Vincent Smith Museum; and Joanne Warner, Cooper-Hewitt Museum, New York. See Nylander, Redmond and Sander (1986), 243; Leung (1988); and Lynn (1980), 441.

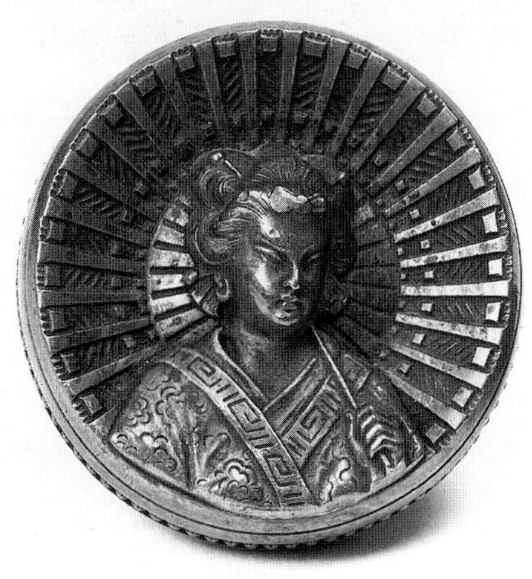

125. *Doorknob*: Japanese woman with parasol
Patent dated June 3, 1879
Bronze: stamped on reverse: Russell and Erwin Manufacturing Company, New Britain, Connecticut
Diam. 2 5/8 in. (6.7 cm.)
Collection of Michael and Claire Higgins

Less than three years after the success of the Japanese Pavilion at the Philadelphia Centennial, Connecticut hardware manufacturers responded to the demand for things Japanese. This doorknob was compression-cast in a clay mold, a new technique patented by Russell and Erwin for the purpose of reproducing fine details.

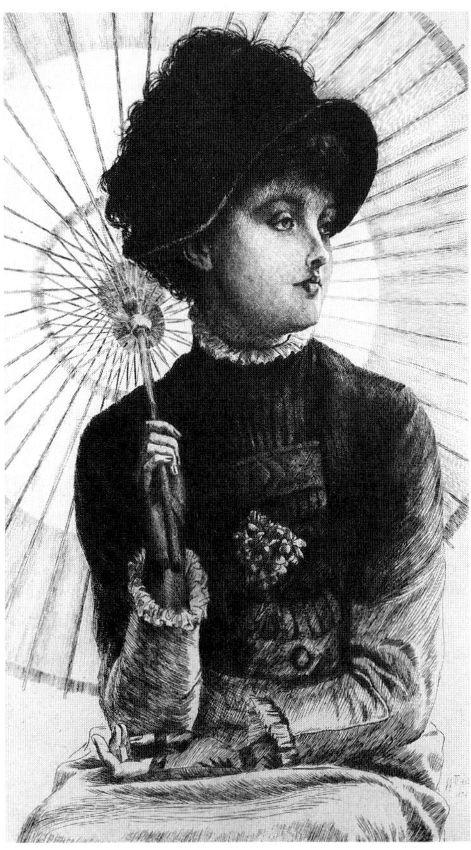

126. James Jacques Joseph Tissot (1836-1902), French
Summer
1878
Etching and drypoint
17 1/4 x 12 1/8 in. (43.8 x 31 cm.)
The Metropolitan Museum of Art, Harris Brisbane Dick Fund, 1924, 24.13.6

The French painter and etcher James Tissot met Kathleen Newton in London in 1876, and she lived with him there until her death from tuberculosis in 1882. She became the subject of a series of prints that looked to Japanese *bijin-ga* (pictures of beautiful women) for their inspiration. *Summer* recalls the tightly cropped, idealized portraits of Utamaro (see no. 14), but remains bound by Western conventions of three-dimensional modeling.

The Japanese parasol in nos. 126 and 127 is an inexpensive sunshade (see p. 59 and fig. 63); the paper was probably not oiled and there is no decorative embroidery on the stretchers. It may well have come from Gifu. Gifu umbrellas were being exported to Europe by the local wholesalers as early as 1878, the year of the Paris Exposition, when Japonisme was at its peak.

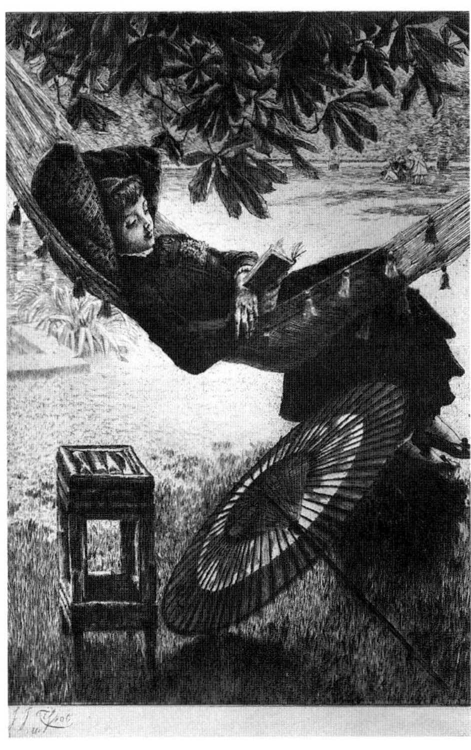

127. James Jacques Joseph Tissot
The Hammock
1880
Etching and drypoint
14 11/16 x 10 7/8 in. (37.3 x 27.6 cm.)
The Metropolitan Museum of Art, Gift of Marilyn Walter Grounds, 1982, 1982.1181.24

See no. 126.

128. Félix Vallotton (1865-1925), French (born Switzerland)
The Shower (L'Averse)
From *Paris Intense*
1894
Signed: FV.94
Zincograph
13 x 19 7/8 in. (33 x 50.5 cm.)
Print Collection, Miriam and Ira D. Wallach Division of Art, Prints and Photographs, The New York Public Library, Astor, Lenox and Tilden Foundations

Vallotton, swept up in the turn-of-the-century print revival, had an immediate affinity with the Japanese woodcut. Here he uses its steep diagonal perspective to add both drama and ironic detachment to a scene of Parisians scattering to escape a downpour. The umbrellas are European, but the artist seems to have been inspired by Japanese depictions of similar incidents, such as those by Hokusai and Hiroshige (nos. 17, 20). Vallotton moved to Paris from Switzerland in 1882 and became a French citizen in 1900. This is one of the artist's series of seven views of life in the city streets published by L. Joly in 1894.

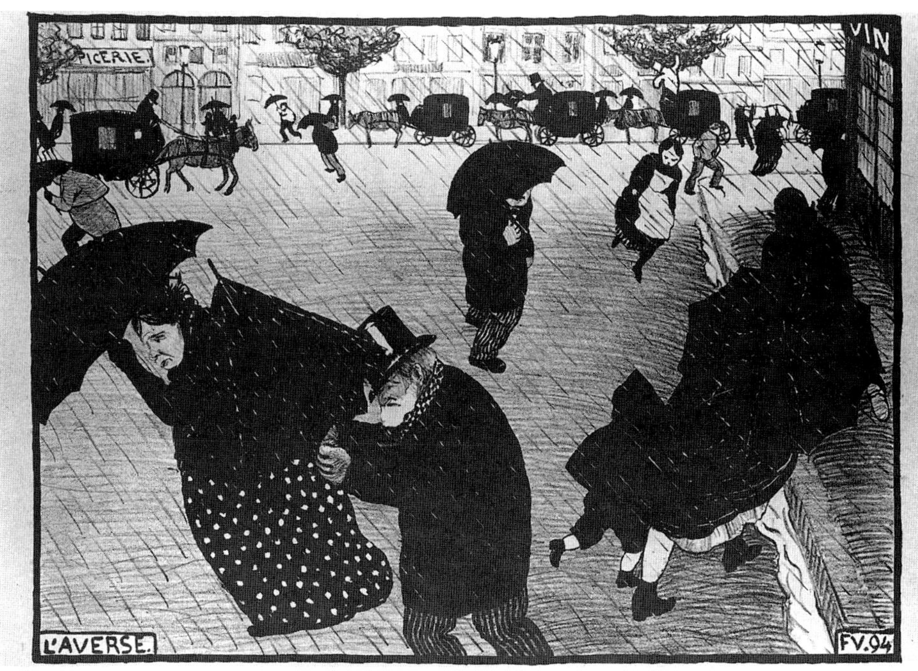

129. Bertha Lum (1869-1954), American
A Rainy Twilight
1905
Signed: Bertha Lum
Color woodblock print on Japanese paper
6 15/16 x 9 13/16 in. (17.6 x 24.9 cm.)
Collection of Robert O. Muller

The artist went to Japan on her honeymoon in 1903, and after returning to Minneapolis she began to make color woodblock prints in the Japanese manner. Lum later spent many years working in Japan and China.

Here figures walking in the rain past an inn or restaurant carry lanterns and shield themselves with *bangasa*. The "Japanese" writing and trademark (*yagô*) on the nearest umbrella are approximations of the real thing.

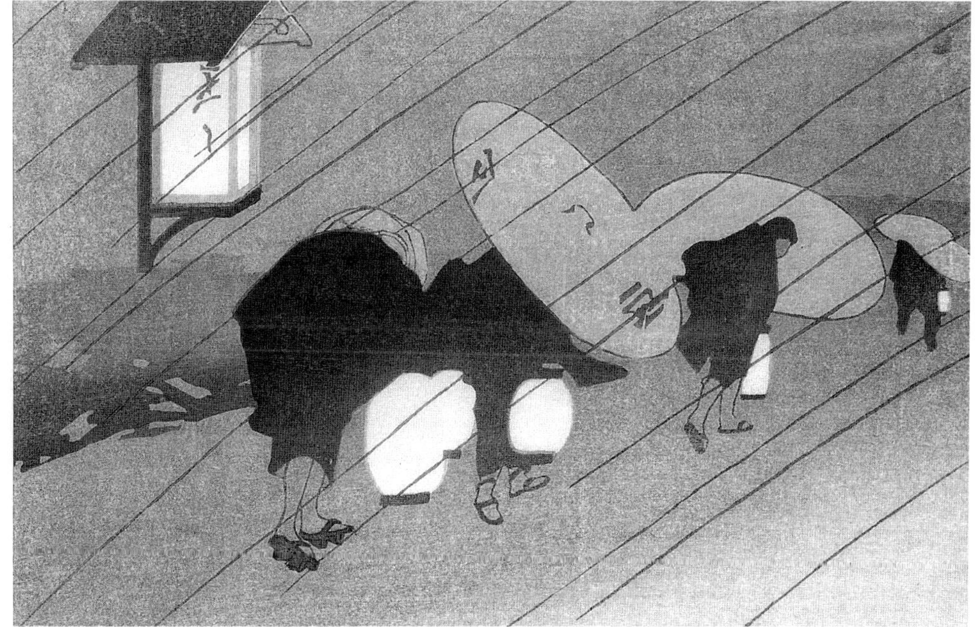

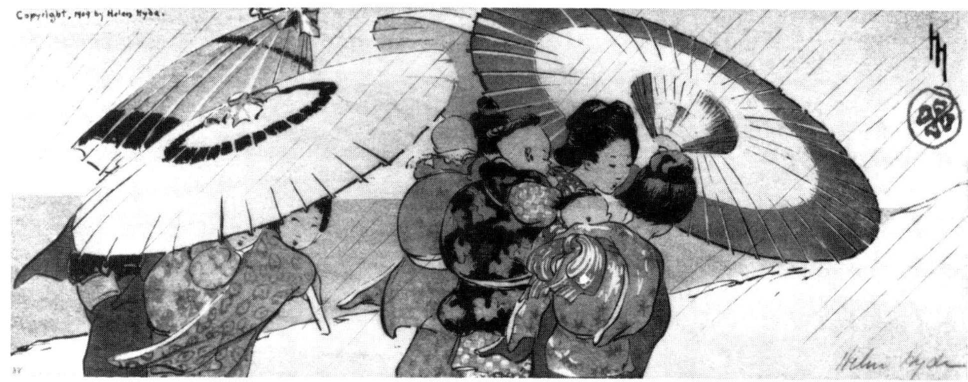

130. Helen Hyde (1868-1919), American
Summer Shower
1909
Signed: Helen Hyde, with the artist's initials and clover seal
Color woodblock print on Japanese paper
8 15/16 x 16 9/16 in. (22.7 x 42 cm.)
Collection of Andrew Terry Keats

Helen Hyde moved to Japan in 1899 and for fifteen years specialized in picturesque Japanese themes. In this print she has accurately observed a variety of umbrellas (two *bangasa* on the left and a *yakko* umbrella on the right), shown from every possible angle.

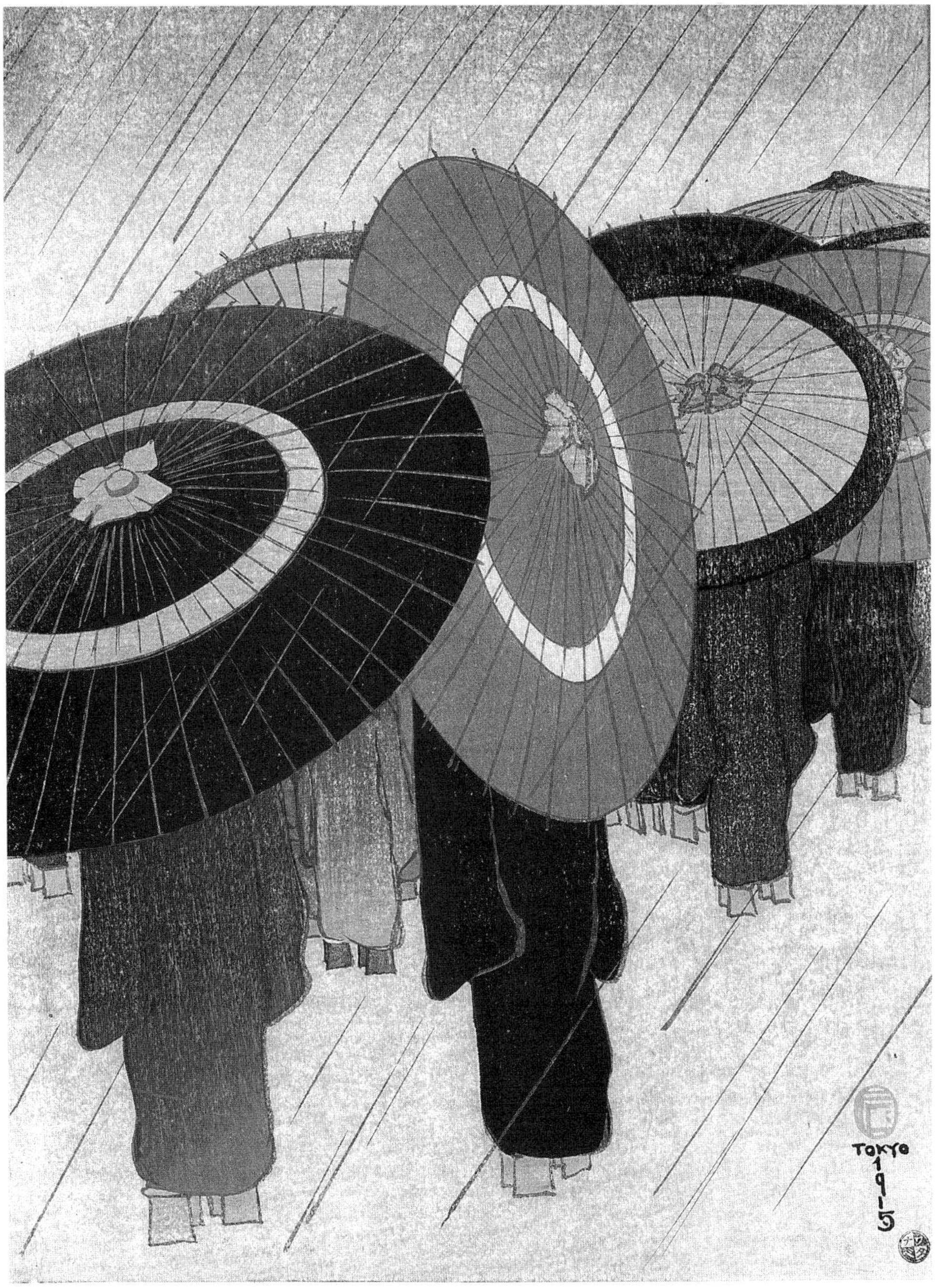

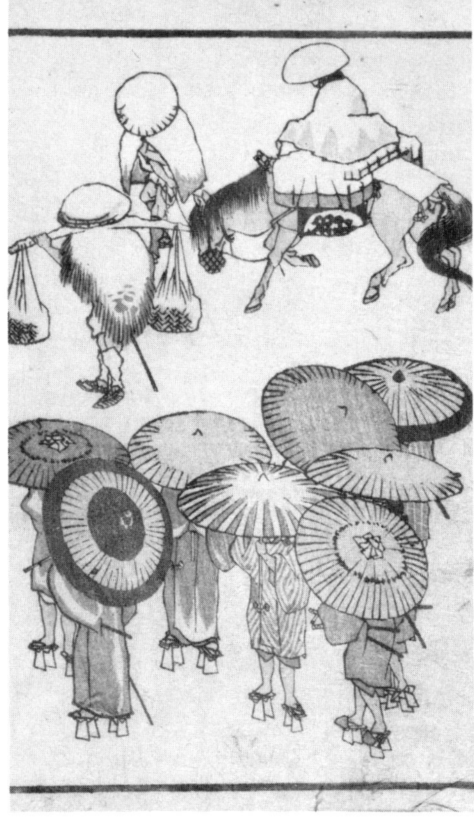

131a. Katsushika Hokusai (1760-1849), *Figures in Snow and Rain*. From *Manga* (Book of humorous sketches), Vol. 1, 2nd ed., Edo period, 1828 or later. Color woodblock-printed illustrated book. The Metropolitan Museum of Art, Rogers Fund, 1931

131. Friedrich (Fritz) Capelari (1884-1915), Austrian
Umbrellas
Taishô period, 1915
Signed: FC
Publisher: Watanabe Shôzaburô, Tokyo
Color woodblock print
$11^1/_4$ x $8^1/_4$ in. (28.6 x 21 cm.)
Collection of Robert O. Muller

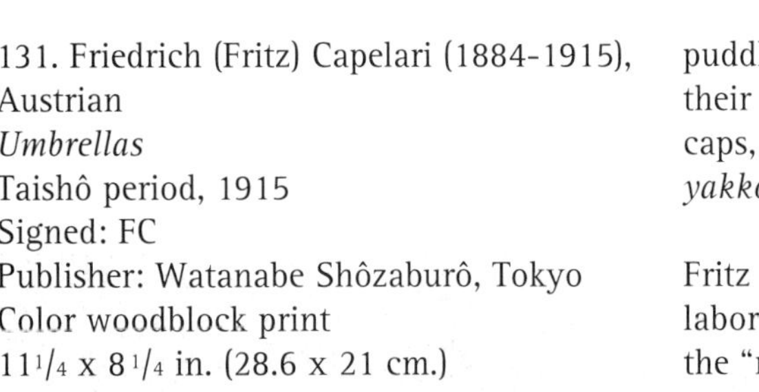

On the left in this print of girls returning from school in the rain are two *janome* umbrellas with the narrow white band that characterizes 20th-century examples. There is a *yakko* umbrella with a single band of color on the right. Capelari gives all of his umbrellas decorative paper caps.

The composition echoes a group of figures in the rain in Hokusai's *Manga* (no. 131a), standing on tall geta to prevent the hem of the long kimono from dragging in puddles of water. Hokusai includes among their umbrellas two *bangasa* with paper caps, a *janome* at the lower left, and a *yakko*-type umbrella at the upper right.

Fritz Capelari was the first artist to collaborate with the publisher Watanabe in the "new-print"(*shin hanga*) movement, intended to revitalize the printmaking tradition in Japan.

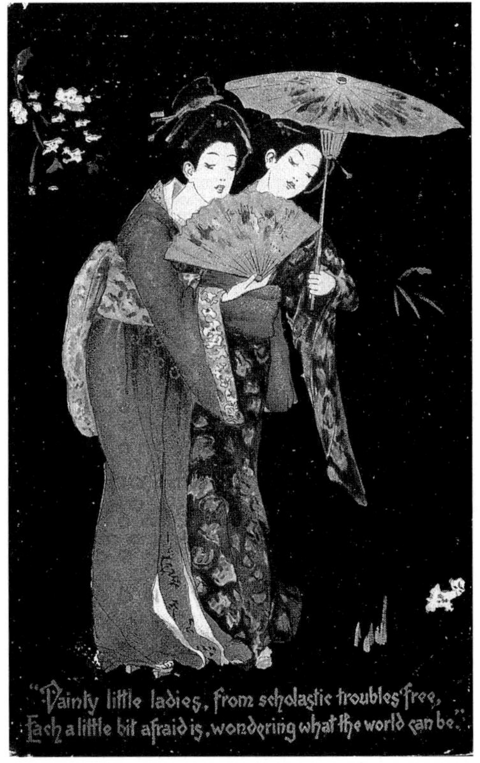

132. Artist unknown
Dainty Little Ladies
English, postmarked 1907
Postcard; chromolithograph
$5^1/_2$ x $3^1/_2$ in. (14 x 8.9 cm.)
Horesh Collection, London

Cherry blossoms, kimono, fan, parasol—all the Edwardian stereotypes of exotic Japan are present in this coy allusion to Gilbert and Sullivan's *Mikado*, which was performed 1,000 times between 1885 and 1896. The caption—"Dainty little ladies, from scholastic troubles free / Each a little bit afraid is, wondering what the world can be"—slightly misquotes the chorus in Act 1 heralding the arrival of the "three little girls from school," Yum-Yum, Peep-Bo, and Pitti-Sing.[1]

The Anglo-Japanese Alliance of 1902, renewed in 1905, contributed to the production of huge numbers of postcards with Japanese themes. The artist here failed to observe the parasol closely, however, since the stretchers are not fully extended.

1. See Gilbert (1910), 65; and Baily (1952), references provided by David Waterhouse, University of Toronto.

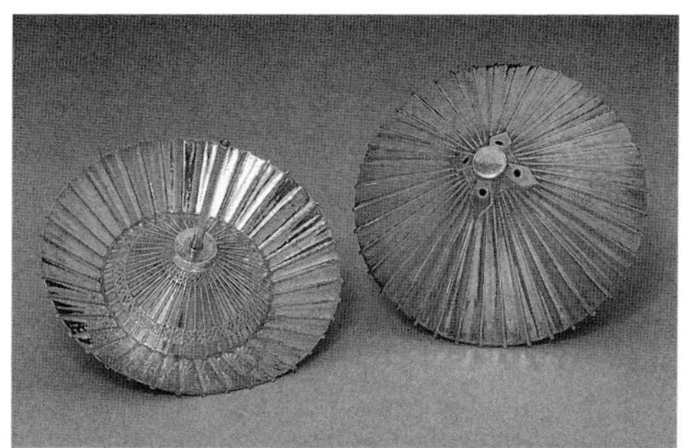

133. *Pair of Salt and Pepper Shakers*: Open umbrellas
Meiji-Taishô periods, early 20th century
Silver; each stamped STERLING and 950
$2^1/_4$ x $2^3/_4$ x $2^3/_4$ in. (5.7 x 7 x 7 cm.)
Private Collection, New York

Silver salt and pepper shakers were made for export in a wide variety of Japanese forms, from straw sandals to shamisen and arched bridges, no doubt providing conversation pieces for dinner parties in the West. Little is known of the history of their manufacture, but they were probably produced in Yokohama, the main point of export to the West. Japanese export silver is often signed with the names of Japanese craftsmen or firms (Musashiya Yokohama, for example) and marked *jungin* (pure silver). Salts dated to around 1900 are also known with the mark "Arthur Bond, Yokohama Sterling"—presumably a British or American firm. The "Sterling" stamp is used only in the American market. Britain and Europe would have required an official hallmark or an import mark added at customs. The number 950 refers to the purity of the silver content out of a possible 1,000; the U.S. standard is 925.

The pair of umbrellas shown here is structurally correct. The craftsman was careful to replicate the rattan wrapping on the handles, the fluting on the runners (*temoto rokuro*), the bands of embroidery, and forty ribs. The sticks unscrew, and the cavity beneath the open stretchers holds the salt and pepper. The pepper shaker has four holes in the cap covering the top notch, the salt eight.

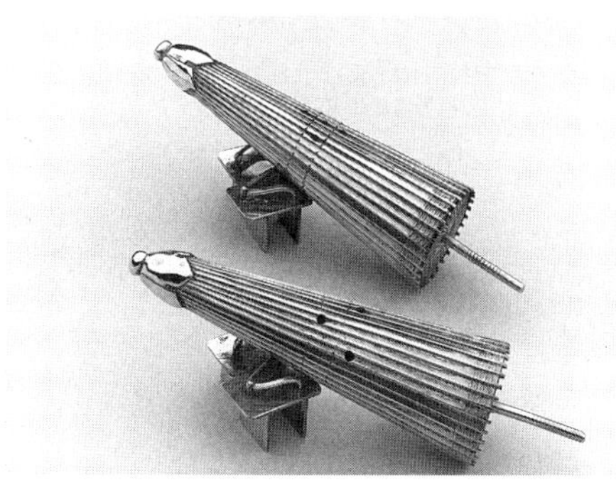

134. *Pair of Salt and Pepper Shakers*: Closed umbrellas
Japanese, 20th century
Silver; each stamped STERLING and 950
$1^3/_{16}$ x 1 x $3^9/_{16}$ in. (3 x 2.5 x 9 cm.)
Collection of Geoffrey Oliver

These umbrella-shaped shakers rest on geta, another reference to rain. The sticks unscrew, revealing a cavity inside to hold the salt and pepper. Shaker holes have been pierced halfway along the ribs.

135. Stephan Köhler (b. 1959), German
Rain Is Heaven on Earth
Tokyo, October 7, 1991
Photograph by Haneda Hisatsugu (b. 1946), Japanese; Ciba print
Courtesy of Haneda Hisatsugu

One thousand and one traditional Gifu umbrellas made a rainbow pattern when they were set afloat in the rain on the Akasaka Mitsuke waterway in downtown Tokyo at noon on October 7, 1991. The event was conceived and choreographed by German artist Stephan Köhler, who has lived in Gifu prefecture since 1987, and who intended it to honor the skills and contribution of Gifu craftsmen. He timed it to coincide with the Christo event (no. 136), which, however, was postponed for two days owing to the heavy rains in Japan.

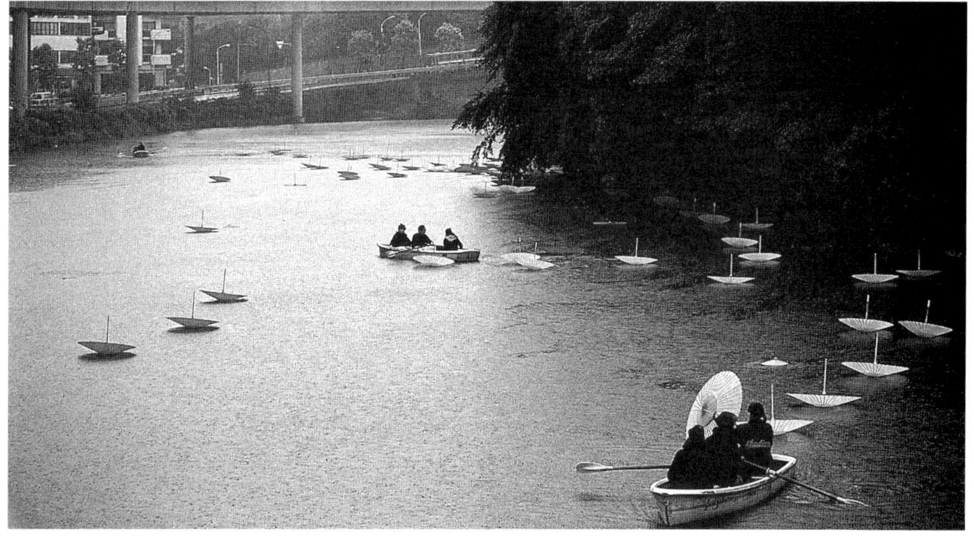

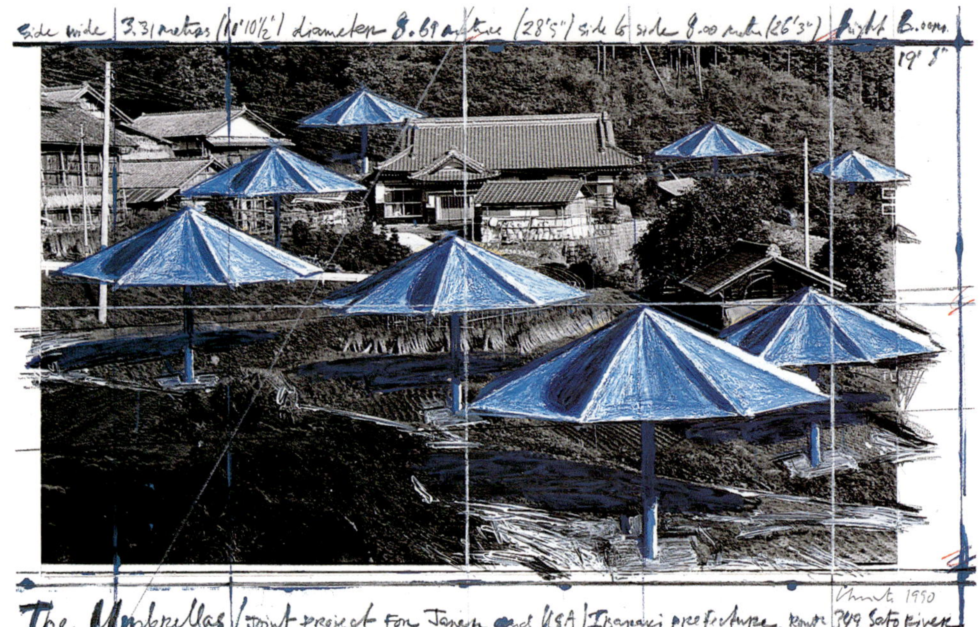

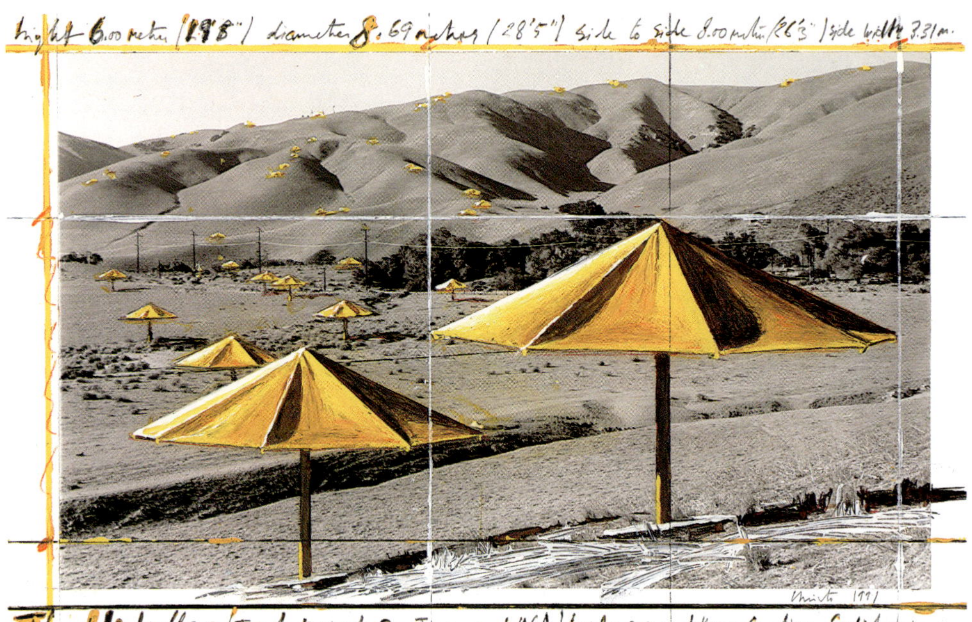

136. Christo (b. 1935), American (born Bulgaria)
The Umbrellas, Joint Project for Japan and USA
136/1. Japan site: Jinba, Satomi, Ibaraki prefecture, 1990; copyright Christo 1990
136/2. California site: Los Angeles County, 1991; copyright Christo 1991
Collages with pencil, crayon, photographs by Wolfgang Volz, enamel paint and charcoal
Each: 14 x 22 in. (35.5 x 56 cm.)
Collection of Jeanne-Claude Christo

On October 9, 1991, Christo ordered the simultaneous opening of 3,100 gigantic umbrellas in order to dramatize the differences and similarities between two inland valleys, one 75 miles north of Tokyo, the other 60 miles north of Los Angeles—a project financed entirely by the artist. The umbrellas were removed on October 27. Christo, who has lived in New York City since 1964, made his first trip to Japan in 1969. Excited by the energy of the people and the material wealth of the country, yet struck by the great cultural differences between Japan and the West, he conceived the idea of a temporary work of art in two parts that would serve as a "diptych," a comparison between East and West. In 1984, to illustrate the theme in terms of space, he chose the umbrella, a universal symbol of shelter. Cloth, Christo's chosen medium of expression, was used to create structures the height of a two-story house (19 ft. 8 in.) with a translucent "roof" extending 28 feet in diameter. Each was cranked open in only 45 seconds.

The intimacy of a narrow valley in Ibaraki prefecture was selected as typifying the tight living conditions in Japan (the entire country is roughly the size of California but only eight percent is usable for building). There the artist planted closely spaced blue umbrellas, their color evoking both serenity and the humid climate of Japan; ninety umbrellas were actually placed in the Sato River. The topography and climate of southern California represent the opposite extreme. Cheerful yellow umbrellas were spread in whimsical configurations over the vast expanse of dry, uncultivated grazing land.

The geometry of the octagonal shape and the movement of the cloth in the triangular spaces between the straight ribs were important to the visual effect sought by the artist. Above all, it was the moment of "blooming," the rapid, simultaneous opening of thousands of umbrellas at sunrise that was the emotional high point for Christo's audience.

Bibliography

Aichi-ken tôji shiryôkan
1986 *Tokubetsuten: Kinsei no Imbe-yaki* (Special exhibition: Modern Imbe ceramics), exh. cat. (Seto, 1986).

Akiyama Terukazu and Matsubara Saburo
1969 *Arts of China: Buddhist Cave Temples, New Researches*, trans. Alexander Soper (Tokyo and Palo Alto, 1969)

American Art Association
1903 *Catalogue of Rare Objects in Brass, Leather, and Wood Illustrating the Art of Old Japan Sold by Bunkio Matsuki*, February 12-14 (New York, 1903).

Avitabile, Gunhild
1991 *Early Masters: Ukiyo-e Prints and Paintings from 1680 to 1750*, exh. cat. (New York, 1991).

Baekeland, Frederick
1980 *Imperial Japan: The Art of the Meiji Era (1868-1912)*, exh. cat. (Ithaca, 1980).

Baily, Leslie
1952 *The Gilbert and Sullivan Book* (London, 1952).

Biot, Edouard C., trans.
1851 *Le Tcheou-li* (Paris, 1851).

Blakemore, Frances
1979 *Japanese Design Through Textile Patterns* (New York and Tokyo, 1979).

Blyth, H. R.
1952 *Haiku*, Vol. 4 (Tokyo, 1952).

Bock, Felicia, trans.
1972 *Engi-Shiki: Procedures of the Engi Era* (Tokyo, 1972), 2 vols.

Bowers, Faubion
1952 *Japanese Theater* (New York, 1952).

Bunka gakuen fukushoku hakubutsukan (Bunka Gakuen Costume Museum)
1983 *Kindai no yôsô* (Modern Western-style dress), exh. cat. (Tokyo, 1983).

Carswell, John
1985 *Blue and White: Chinese Porcelain and Its Impact on the Western World*, exh. cat. (Chicago, 1985).

Coomaraswamy, Ananda K.
1935 *La Sculpture de Bodhgayâ* (Paris, 1935).

Cooper, Michael, S. J., ed. and trans.
1973 *This Island of Japon: João Rodrigues' Account of 16th-Century Japan* (Tokyo and New York, 1973).

Crawford, T. S.
1970 *A History of the Umbrella* (New York, 1970).

Dam, Peter van
1987 "The Royal Bazar of Dirk Boer: Early Japonism in The Hague Around 1840," *Andon*, Vol. 7, no. 25 (1987), 16-19.

De Becker, J. E.
1971 *The Nightless City*, first published in Tokyo, 1899 (Rutland, Vt., and Tokyo, 1971).

Edo meisho zue (Famous sites in and about Edo)
1919-20 Saitô Yukio, Saitô Yukitaka, and Saitô Gesshin, with illustrations by Hasegawa Settan (Tokyo, 1834-36), 4 vols., reissued in Dai Nihon meisho zue (Famous views of Japan), ed. Harada Kan, Vols. 3-6 (Tokyo, 1919-20).

Ema Tsutomu, Nishioka Toranosuke, and Hamada Giichirô, eds.
1967 *Kinsei fûzoku jiten* (Dictionary of modern customs) (Tokyo, 1967).

Farrell, Jeremy
1985 *Umbrellas and Parasols* (London, 1985).

Forrer, Matthi
1991 *Hokusai: Prints and Drawings*, exh. cat. (Munich and London, 1991).
1985 *Eirakuya Tôshirô, Publisher at Nagoya* (Amsterdam, 1985).

Forrer, Matthi, and Roger Keyes
1979 "Very like a Whale?–Hokusai's Illustrations for the Genroku Poem Shells," in *A Sheaf of Japanese Papers: In Tribute to Heinz Kaempfer on his 75th Birthday*, ed. Matthi Forrer, Willem R. van Gulik, and Jack Hillier (The Hague, 1979), 35-57.

Fukuzawa Yukichi
1966 *The Autobiography of Fukuzawa Yukichi*, rev. trans. Eiichi Kiyooka; first published in Tokyo, 1948 (New York and London, 1966).

Fuller, Michael
1990 *The Road to East Slope: The Development of Su Shi's Poetic Voice* (Stanford, 1990).

Genshoku ukiyo-e daihyakka-jiten henshû-iinkai, ed.
1980-82 *Genshoku ukiyo-e daihyakka-jiten* (Encyclopedia of ukiyo-e in full color) (Tokyo, 1980-82), 11 vols.

Gernet, Jacques
1962 *Daily Life in China on the Eve of the Mongol Invasion, 1250-1276*, trans. H. M. Wright (New York, 1962).

Gilbert, W. S.
1910 *Iolanthe and Other Operas* (London, 1910).

Goodwin, Shauna
1988 "The Realm of Pleasure: *A Cherry Blossom Viewing Picnic* in the Brooklyn Museum," *Orientations*, Vol. 19, no. 6 (June 1988), 40-49.

Gravalos, Mary Evans O'Keefe, and Carol Pulin
1990 *Bertha Lum* (Washington, D.C., and London, 1990).

Gugong bowuyuan (Palace Museum) Editorial Committee
1981 *Zhongguo lidai huihua: Gugong bowuyuan cang hua ji* (Chinese painting of the various dynasties: Collected paintings stored in the Palace Museum), Vol. 2 (Beijing, 1981).

Halén, Widar
1987 "Japan Mania: Collecting of Japanese Art Around the Meiji Restoration," *Andon*, Vol. 7, nos. 27/28 (1987), 112-123.

Hara Shinkichi
1931 *Die Meister der Japanischen Schwertzierarten* (Masters of Japanese sword furniture) (Hamburg, 1931).

Harada Yoshito and Komai Kazuchika, eds.
1937 *Shina koki zukô* (Chinese antiquities), Vol. 2 (Tokyo, 1937).

Hillier, Jack
1991 *The Japanese Picture Book: A Selection from the Ravicz Collection* (New York, 1991).
1987 *The Art of the Japanese Book* (London, 1987), 2 vols.

Hosley, William
1990 *The Japan Idea: Art and Life in Victorian America*, exh. cat. (Hartford, 1990).

Hung, William
1952 *Tu Fu: China's Greatest Poet* (New York, 1952).

Huntington, Susan
1985 *The Art of Ancient India* (New York and Tokyo, 1985).

ICU Hachirô Yuasa Memorial Museum
1985 *Japanese Paper Stencil Designs*, exh. cat. (Tokyo, 1985).

Ihara Saikaku
1981 *Tales of Samurai Honor*, trans. Caryl Ann Callahan (Tokyo, 1981).

Ihara Toshirô
1973 *Kabuki nempyô* (Chronological table of Kabuki), ed. Kawatake Shigeyoshi and Yoshida Teruji (Tokyo, 1973), 8 vols.

Illustrated Catalogue of A. A. Vantine and Co. Importers . . .
[1880] (New York, [1880]).

Ing, Eric van den, and Robert Schaap
1992 *Beauty and Violence: Japanese Prints by Yoshitoshi (1839-1892)*, introduction by John Stevenson, exh. cat. (Bergeyk, 1992).

Jenkins, Donald
1973 *The Ledoux Heritage; The Collecting of Ukiyo-e Master Prints*, exh. cat. (New York, 1973).
1971 *Ukiyo-e Prints and Paintings: The Primitive Period, 1680-1745*, exh. cat. (Chicago, 1971).

Johnson, Scott
1990 "Sketch-tour Books and Prints of the Early Twentieth Century," *Andon*, Vol. 10, no. 37 (1990), 3-33.

Jorg, C. J. A.
1980 *Pronk Porcelain: Porcelain After Designs by Cornelis Pronk*, exh. cat. (Groningen, 1980).

Katagiri Yoshikazu
1985 *Kanô no wagasa* (Umbrellas of Kanô), exh. cat. (Gifu City, 1985).

Kaufman, Laura S.
1980 *"Ippen Hijiri-e:* Artistic and Literary Sources in a Buddhist Handscroll Painting of Thirteenth-century Japan," Ph.D. diss. (New York University, 1980).

Keene, Donald
1971 *Landscapes and Portraits: Appreciations of Japanese Culture* (Tokyo and Palo Alto, 1971).
1961 *Major Plays of Chikamatsu* (New York and London, 1961).

Keene, Donald, ed.
1955 *Anthology of Japanese Literature from the Earliest Era to the Mid-Nineteenth Century* (New York, 1955).

Kenney, Don
1968 *A Guide to Kyogen* (Tokyo, 1968).

Kilburn, Richard S.
1981 *Transitional Wares and Their Forerunners*, exh. cat. (Hong Kong, 1981).

Kitagawa Morisada
1989 *Ruijû kinsei fûzoku shi* (Compilation of records of modern customs), also known as *Morisada mankô* (Observations by [Kitagawa] Morisada). Revision by Muromatsu Iwao of the 30-volume manuscript version of 1853, first printed in 1928 (Tokyo, 1989).

Kitagawa Tadahiko and Yasuda Akira, eds.
1972 *Kyôgen-shû* (Anthology of Kyôgen), in Nihon koten bungaku zenshû (Anthology of classical Japanese literature), Vol. 35 (Tokyo, 1972).

Kobayashi Tadashi
1992 *Utamaro*, Vol. 2 in Meihin senbutsu ukiyo-e (Masterpieces of ukiyo-e), Vol. 4 (Tokyo, 1992).
1991 *Harunobu*, in Meihin senbutsu ukiyo-e (Masterpieces of ukiyo-e), Vol. 1 (Tokyo, 1991).
1988 *Hanabusa Itchô*, in Nihon no bijutsu (Arts of Japan), no. 260 (Tokyo, 1988).
1987 "Shinshutsu no shoki rakuchû rakugai-zu byôbu ni tsuite" (Recently discovered early screens of sights in and around the capital), *Kokka*, no. 1105 (1987), 19-24.

Kobayashi Tadashi and Sakakibara Satoru
1978 *Morikage/Itchô*, in Nihon bijutsu kaiga zenshû (Japanese painting), Vol. 16 (Tokyo, 1978).

Kodansha Encyclopedia of Japan
1983 (Tokyo and New York, 1983), 9 vols.

Koji ruien (Classified references from the past)
1984 "Kiyôbu" (Utensils), Vol. 54, part 2, ed. Hosokawa Junjirô et al., first published 1912 (Tokyo, 1984).

Koike Tomio and Chikamatsu Machiko
1991 *Trousseau Heirlooms of Daimyo Ladies: Treasures from the Tokugawa Art Museum*, no. 7, exh. cat. (Nagoya, 1991).

Komatsu Shigemi et al.
1979 *Nôe hôshi ekotoba, Fukutomi sôshi, Hyakki yagyô emaki* (Story of the priest Nôe, Story of old man Fukutomi, Story of the night parade of one hundred demons), in Nihon emaki taisei (Compilation of Japanese illustrated handscrolls), ed. Komatsu Shigemi, Vol. 25 (Tokyo, 1979).

Lane, Richard
1989 *Hokusai: Life and Work* (New York, 1989).

Lawton, Thomas
1973 *Chinese Figure Painting*, exh. cat. (Washington, D.C., 1973).

Leiter, Samuel L.
1979a *Kabuki Encyclopedia: An English-Language Adaptation of KABUKI JITEN* (Westport, Conn., and London, 1979).

Leiter, Samuel L., trans.
1979b *The Art of Kabuki* (Berkeley, 1979).

Leung, Felicity L.
1988 "Japanese Wallpaper in Canada," *Material History Bulletin* (Fall, 1988), 35-42.

Levy, Dana (photographs), and Lea Sneider and Frank B. Gibney (text)
1983 *Kanban: Shop Signs of Japan*, exh. cat. (New York and Tokyo, 1983).

Li Xueqin
1985 *Eastern Zhou and Qin Civilizations*, trans. K. C. Chang (New Haven and London, 1985).

Lim, Lucy
1987 *Stories from China's Past: Han Dynasty Pictorial Tomb Reliefs and Archaeological Objects from Sichuan Province, People's Republic of China* (San Francisco, 1987).

Link, Howard
1980 *Primitive Ukiyo-e from the James A. Michener Collection in the Honolulu Academy of Arts* (Honolulu, 1980).

Linschoten, Jan Huygen van
1596 *Itinerario, voyage ofte schipvaert van Jan Huygen van Linschoten naer Oost ofte Portugaels Indien . . .* with engravings after van Linschoten by Joannes and Baptista à Doetechum (Amsterdam, 1596).

Little, Stephen
1983 *Chinese Ceramics of the Transitional Period: 1620-1683*, exh. cat. (New York, 1983).

Loehr, Max
1980 *The Great Painters of China* (New York, 1980).

Lynn, Catherine
1980 *Wallpaper in America* (New York, 1980).

Manyôshû: The Nippon Gakujutsu Shinkôkai Translation of One Thousand Poems
1965 Foreword by Donald Keene (New York and London, 1965).

Mason, Penelope
1990 "Jigoku Tayu: A Macabre Theme in Meiji Art," *Orientations*, Vol. 21, no. 1 (January 1990), 58-63.

McCullough, Helen
1985 *Kokin Wakashû: The First Imperial Anthology of Japanese Poetry* (Stanford, 1985).

Meech, Julia
1993 "For the Good of the Nation," *Asian Art*, Vol. 6, no. 1 (Winter 1993), 2-6.

Meech, Julia, and Gabriel Weisberg
1990 *Japonisme Comes to America: The Japanese Impact on Graphic Arts, 1876-1925* (New York, 1990).

Meech-Pekarik, Julia
1986 *The World of the Meiji Print: Impressions of a New Civilization* (New York and Tokyo, 1986).
1977 "Disguised Scripts and Hidden Poems in an Illustrated Heian Sutra: Ashide and Uta-e in the Heike Nôgyô," *Archives of Asian Art*, Vol. 31 (1977), 52-75.

Meech-Pekarik, Julia et al.
1979 *Metoroporitan bijutsukan, Nyûyôku kôritsu toshokan* (The Metropolitan Museum of Art, The New York Public Library), in Ukiyo-e shûka (Collections of ukiyo-e), Vol. 7 (Tokyo, 1979).

Merritt, Helen
1990 *Modern Japanese Woodblock Prints: The Early Years* (Honolulu, 1990).

Miki Fumio
1967 *Haniwa*, in Nihon no bijutsu (Arts of Japan), no. 19 (Tokyo, 1967).

Miya Tsugio
1971 *Ippen Hijiri-e* (Pictorial biography of Saint Ippen), in Nihon emakimono zenshû (Japanese scroll painting), Vol. 11 (Tokyo, 1971).

Miyamoto Keitarô
1968 *Kaburimono, kimono, hakimono* (Headgear, kimono, footwear) (Tokyo, 1968).

Montanus, Arnoldus
1670 *Atlas Japannensis: Being Remarkable Addresses . . . from the East-India Company of the United Provinces, to the Emperor of Japan . . .*, trans. John Ogilby (London, 1670).

Morishita Masayo, Kôno Minoru, Kume Yasuo and Yamamoto Masaji
1990 *Kinkarakawa* (Gilt leather), ed. Fukuzumi Haruo, INA BOOKLET, Vol. 3, no. 4, first published 1984 (Tokyo, 1990).

Morohashi Tetsuji
1974 *Dai kanwa jiten* (Dictionary of Chinese characters), Vol. 9, first published 1959 (Tokyo, 1974).

Morris, Ivan, trans. and ed.
1967 *The Pillow Book of Sei Shônagon* (London, 1967), 2 vols.
Murasaki Shikibu
1979 *Genji monogatari* (The Tale of Genji), Vol. 2, in Nihon koten zenshû (Complete Japanese classics), ed. Ikeda Kikan, 3rd ed. (Tokyo, 1979).
1976 *The Tale of Genji*, trans. and introduction Edward G. Seidensticker (New York, 1976), 2 vols.
1959 *Genji monogatari*, Vol. 2, in Nihon koten bungaku taikei (Outline of classical Japanese literature), Vol. 15, ed. Yamagishi Tokuhei (Tokyo, 1959).
Murase, Miyeko
1986 *Tales of Japan*, exh. cat. (New York and Oxford, 1986).
1990 *Masterpieces of Japanese Screen Painting* (New York, 1990).
Musée de la Mode et du Costume
1989 *Les Accessoires du temps: Ombrelles, parapluies*, exh. cat. (Paris, 1989).
Narazaki Muneshige et al., eds.
1978 *The National Museum of Ethnology, Leiden: Philipp Franz von Siebold's Ukiyo-e Collection*, with text by W. R. van Gulik (Tokyo, 1978), 3 vols.
Needham, Joseph
1965 *Science and Civilization in China*, Vol. 3, Vol. 4, part 2 (Cambridge, 1965).
Newman, Sasha M.
1991 *Félix Vallotton*, exh. cat. (New Haven, 1991).
Nihon shoki (Chronicles of Japan)
1952 Kuroita Katsumi, ed., in Kokushi taikei (Standard works of Japanese history), Vol. 1 (Tokyo, 1952).
Nihongi: Chronicle of Japan from the Earliest Times to A.D. 697
1956 Trans. W. G. Aston. Reprint of the 1896 publication (London, 1956).
Nihonten kikaku renrakukai, eds.
1989 *Kinkarakawa no sekai* (The world of gilt leather), exh. cat. (Tokyo, 1989).
Nylander, Richard C., E. Redmond and P. Sander
1986 *Wallpaper in New England* (Boston, 1986).
Ogawa Morihiro
1987 *Japanese Swords and Sword Furniture in the Museum of Fine Arts, Boston* (Boston, 1987).
Okada Rokuo
1955 *Japanese Proverbs and Proverbial Phrases* (Tokyo, 1955).
Pantzer, Peter
1990 "Japonisme in Austria, or: Art knows no Boundaries," in Peter Pantzer and Johannes Wieninger, *Verborgene Impressionen / Hidden Impressions*, exh. cat. (Vienna, 1990), 23-36.
Pearson, Richard
1992 *Ancient Japan*, exh. cat. (Washington, D.C., 1992).
Pomeroy, Charles A.
1968 *Traditional Crafts of Japan: Illustrated with the Eighteenth-Century Artisan Prints of Tachibana Minkô* (New York and Tokyo, 1968).
Pratt, Peter
1931 *History of Japan*, ed. M. Paske-Smith, Vol. 1 (Kobe, 1931).
Reichel, Friedrich
1981 *Early Japanese Porcelain: Arita Porcelain in the Dresden Collection*, trans. Barbara Beedham (London, 1981).
Rosenfield, John, and Shûjirô Shimada
1970 *Traditions of Japanese Art: Selections from the Kimiko and John Powers Collection*, exh. cat. (Cambridge, Mass., 1970).
Ryder, J. H.
1889 "A Chapter on Umbrellas," *Peterson's Magazine* (July 1889), 33-36.
Sakamoto Mitsuru and Ide Yoichirô
1982 *Fûzokuga—Namban fûzoku* (Genre painting—customs of Southern Barbarians), in Nihon byobu-e shûsei (Japanese screen painting), Vol. 15 (Tokyo, 1982).
Sato, Tomoko, and Toshio Watanabe
1991 *Japan and Britain: An Aesthetic Dialogue*, exh. cat. (London, 1991).
Shibui Kiyoshi
1932-33 *Ukiyo-e Naishi: Old Documents Concerning Human Life, Instincts and Emotions as Interpreted by Japanese Artists, in the 18th and Earlier Parts of the 19th Centuries*, Vol. 2 (Tokyo, 1932-33).
Shimonaka Hiroshi, ed.
1991 *Kabuki jiten* (Kabuki dictionary) (Tokyo, 1991).
Smith, Henry
1988 *Hokusai: One Hundred Views of Fuji* (New York, 1988).
Smith, Lawrence, ed.
1988 *Ukiyoe: Images of Unknown Japan* (London, 1988).
Stephens, Amy Reigle, ed.
1993 *The New Wave: Twentieth-Century Japanese Prints from the Robert O. Muller Collection* (London, 1993)
Stern, Harold P.
1969 *Master Prints of Japan* (New York, 1969)
Strommenger, Eva
1962 *Fünf Jahrtausende Mesopotamien, die Kunst von den Anfängen um 5000 v. Chr. bis zu Alexander dem Grossen* (Munich, 1962).
Sugimoto Masayoshi and David L. Swain
1978 *Science and Culture in Traditional Japan, A.D. 600-1854* (Cambridge, Mass., and London, 1978).
Suzuki Jûzô
1992 *Kuniyoshi* (Tokyo, 1992).
1970 *Hiroshige* (Tokyo, 1970).
Takahashi Seiichirô and Yoshida Sô
1974 *Kiyochika*, in Ukiyo-e taikei (Outline of ukiyo-e), Vol. 12 (Tokyo, 1974).
Takazu Daisaburô
1930 *Nihon wagasa hôkan* (Handbook of Japanese umbrellas) (Osaka, 1930).
Takeda Tsuneo et al.
1978 *Sairei—Kabuki* (Festivals—Kabuki), in Nihon byôbu-e shûsei (Japanese screen painting), Vol. 13 (Tokyo, 1978).
Takeuchi, Melinda
1992 *Taiga's True Views: The Language of Landscape Painting in Eighteenth-Century Japan* (Stanford, 1992).
1987 "Kuniyoshi's Minamoto Raikô and the Earth Spider: Demons and Protest in Late Tokugawa Japan," *Ars Orientalis*, Vol. 17 (1987), 5-38.
Tanaka-van Daalen, Isabel
1988 "Some Remarks on an Exhibition of Contemporary Japanese Goldleather," *Andon*, Vol. 8, no. 29 (1988), 79-82.
Terashima Ryôan
1983 *Wakan sansai zue* (Japanese-Chinese illustrated assemblage of the three components of the universe), ed. Wakan sansai zue kankô iinkai, 11th rev. ed. in 2 vols.; first published as a woodblock-printed book in Osaka, 1712 (Tokyo, 1983).
Tokyo National Museum
1973 *Tokubetsu tenkan: Haniwa* (Special exhibition: *Haniwa*), exh. cat. (Tokyo, 1973).
Uehara Kazu et al.,
1982 *Asuka, Hakuhô no bijutsu—Takamatsuzuka to Fujiwarakyô* (The art of the Asuka and Hakuhô periods—the Takamatsuzuka tomb and the capital at Fujiwara), in Nihon bijutsu zenshû (Compendium of Japanese art), ed. Tanaka Ichimatsu and Fukuyama Toshio, Vol. 3 (Tokyo, 1980).
Uzanne, Octave
1884 *The Sunshade, The Glove—The Muff* (London, 1884).
Valenstein, Suzanne G.
1989 *A Handbook of Chinese Ceramics*, rev. ed. (New York, 1989).
Vos, Ken
1987 "Early Methods of Collecting Japanese Objects for Museums," in Matthi Forrer and Ken Vos, *Kawahara Keiga: Photographer Without a Camera*, exh. cat. (Leiden, 1987), 21-23.
Waley, Paul
1984 *Tokyo Now and Then: An Explorer's Guide* (New York and Tokyo, 1984).

Watanabe Shôzaburô
1936 *Catalogue of Wood-cut Colour Prints of S. Watanabe* (Tokyo, 1936).
Watanabe Tadasu, ed.
1974 *Watanabe Shôzaburô* (Tokyo, 1974).
Waterhouse, David
1982 *Bosuton bijutsukan* (Museum of Fine Arts, Boston): *Harunobu*, 2 vols., in Ukiyo-e shûka (Collections of ukiyo-e), 2 supplemental vols. (Tokyo, 1982).
1964 *Harunobu and His Age* (London, 1964).
Weinstein, Lucie Ruth
1978 "The Hôryûji Canopies and Their Continental Antecedents," Ph.D. diss. (Yale University, 1978).
Wentworth, Michael Justin
1984 *James Tissot* (Oxford, 1984).
1980 "Tissot and Japonisme," in *Japonisme in Art: An International Symposium*, ed. Society for the Study of Japonisme (Tokyo, 1980), 127-146.
Wheelwright, Carolyn
1986 *"Taking Shelter from the Rain*: A Genroku Period Genre Painting by Hanabusa Itchô," *Orientations*, Vol. 17, no. 9 (September 1986), 18-25.
Whitney, Clara A. N.
1979 *Clara's Diary: An American Girl in Meiji Japan*, ed. M. William Steele and Tamiko Ichimata (Tokyo, 1979).
Winkel, Margarita
1991 *Souvenirs from Japan: Japanese Photography at the Turn of the Century* (London, 1991).
Worswick, Clark, ed.
1979 *Japan: Photographs, 1854-1905*, exh. cat. (New York, 1979).
Yabushita Hiroshi
1987 "Kanô no wagasa—sono rekishi to shikumi" (Kanô umbrellas—their history and construction), *Gifu-shi rekishi hakubutsukan kenkyû kiyô* (Gifu City Museum of History Research Bulletin), Vol. 1 (March 1987), 30-44.
Yamaguchi Keizaburô
1983 *Kiyonaga, Shunchô*, in Nikuhitsu ukiyo-e (Ukiyo-e brocade prints), Vol. 5 (Tokyo, 1983).
Yokohama kaikô shiryôkan, ed.
1990 *Meiji no Nihon: "Yokohama shashin" no sekai* (Meiji Japan: The world of "Yokohama photographs") (Yokohama, 1990).
Young, Rodney S.
1981 *The Gordion Excavations—Final Reports*: Vol. 1. *Three Great Early Tumuli* (Philadelphia, 1981).
Zimmer, Heinrich
1968 *The Art of Indian Asia: Its Mythology and Transformations*, ed. Joseph Campbell, 2nd ed. rev. (Princeton, N.J., 1968), 2 vols.

Reproduction Credits

All photographs have been supplied by the owners of the works of art unless noted below. The names of photographers whose work is displayed in the exhibition are cited in the catalogue entries.

Argentum Photographic Services, Seattle: no. 6
Shamlian Armen: nos. 84, 96, 97, 101, 120
Pat Bazelon, The Brooklyn Museum: nos. 67, 106
Herbert Boswank: nos. 92, 93
Buschauer Designer Photography, Barrington, Illinois: no. 86
Sheldan Comfert Collins: nos. 15, 91a
John Dessarzin: no. 116
Tibor Franyo: nos. 30, 61, 62
Courtesy of Fujisawa shôten, Gifu City: diag. 2; redrawn by Stefanie Krieg-Elliott
Ben Grishaaver: nos. 16, 16a, 48
Scott Hyde, courtesy of Art Resource, New York: no. 98
Images 4: nos. 4, 5, 7, 17, 18, 57, 75, 85, 94, 104, 105, 107, 111, 115, 125, 132, 134
Justin Kerr, The Brooklyn Museum: no. 47
After Kobayashi (1988), fig. 12: no. 77a
Kodansha, Ltd.: nos. 27, 43, 73
Stephan Köhler: figs. 1, 3-10; no. 76
Adapted from Kokufuda Hanzô, *Kôgei hyakka daizukan* (Illustrated encyclopedia of crafts), 2nd ed. (Tokyo, 1977): diag. 4
Steven A. Lonsdale: nos. 41, 87
Paul Macapia: no. 102
After Miki (1967), fig. 2: fig. 50
Carl Nardiello: no. 123; figs. 12, 56
Otto E. Nelson: no. 112
Daniel Sedano: nos. 51, 108, 133
Joseph Szaszfai: no. 24, 44, 53, 90a, 129, 131
Richard Todd: nos. 2, 3, 10, 40, 49, 50, 54, 80, 83, 117, 118
Courtesy of the Tokyo National Research Institute of Cultural Properties: fig. 53
Michael Tropea: nos. 45, 119
After Worswick (1979), 60: fig. 66
Hiroshi Yabushita: figs. 11-44
Courtesy of Hiroshi Yabushita: fig. 51, diags. 1, 3; diag. 3 redrawn by Stefanie Krieg-Elliott
After Zimmer (1968), Vol. 2, pl. 89: fig. 47